Textual Entanglements

signale
modern german letters, cultures, and thought

Series Editor: Paul Fleming, Cornell University
Peter Uwe Hohendahl, Founding Editor

Signale: Modern German Letters, Cultures, and Thought publishes new English-language books in literary studies, criticism, cultural studies, and intellectual history pertaining to the German-speaking world, as well as translations of important German-language works. Signale construes "modern" in the broadest terms: the series covers topics ranging from the early modern period to the present. Signale books are published under a joint imprint of Cornell University Press and Cornell University Library. Please see http://signale.cornell.edu/.

Textual Entanglements

Handke, Bernhard, Rilke, and the Materiality of Literature

Jacob Haubenreich

A Signale Book

Cornell University Press and Cornell University Library
Ithaca and London

Cornell University Press and Cornell University Library gratefully acknowledge the College of Arts & Sciences, Cornell University, for support of the Signale series.

Copyright © 2025 by Jacob Haubenreich

All rights reserved. Except for brief quotations in a review, this book, or parts thereof, must not be reproduced in any form without permission in writing from the publisher. For information, address Cornell University Press, Sage House, 512 East State Street, Ithaca, New York 14850.

First published 2025 by Cornell University Press and Cornell University Library

Library of Congress Cataloging-in-Publication Data

Names: Haubenreich, Jacob, author.
Title: Textual entanglements : Handke, Bernhard, Rilke, and the materiality of literature / Jacob Haubenreich.
Description: Ithaca : Cornell University Press, 2025. | Series: Signale : modern German letters, cultures, and thought | Includes bibliographical references and index.
Identifiers: LCCN 2024033614 (print) | LCCN 2024033615 (ebook) | ISBN 9781501781162 (hardcover) | ISBN 9781501781155 (paperback) | ISBN 9781501781179 (epub) | ISBN 9781501781148 (pdf)
Subjects: LCSH: Austrian literature—20th century—History and criticism. | Authorship. | Manuscript preparation (Authorship) | Books and reading. | Handke, Peter—Criticism and interpretation. | Bernhard, Thomas—Criticism and interpretation. | Rilke, Rainer Maria, 1875–1926—Criticism and interpretation. | LCGFT: Literary criticism.
Classification: LCC PT3818 .H37 2025 (print) | LCC PT3818 (ebook) | DDC 833/.909—dc23/eng/20241031
LC record available at https://lccn.loc.gov/2024033614
LC ebook record available at https://lccn.loc.gov/2024033615

Contents

Acknowledgments — vii

Abbreviations — xi

Introduction: Expanding the Field of Interpretation — 1

1. Handke's Slow Making — 23
   - Dance — 30
   - Thing-Picture — 46
   - Stroke — 61
   - Script — 84

2. Bernhard's Productive Destruction — 120
   - Correction — 127
   - Madness — 144
   - Rhythm — 161
   - Destruction — 175

3. Rilke's Embodied Figuration   211
   Narrating   222
   Striking   249
   Seeing   277

Epilogue: "The Whole" in the Digital Age   298

Index   305

Acknowledgments

In reflecting upon the entanglement of various kinds of participants across the whole process of textual production, I am reminded of the numerous people, experiences, and institutions that have shaped this book's production and enabled me to write it. These acknowledgments at once express my thanks and represent a kind of *Entstehungsgeschichte* of this book. I owe an enormous debt of gratitude to Winfried Kudszus, who first introduced me to Rilke's *Notebooks of Malte Laurids Brigge*, and who encouraged me to allow my work to evolve in unexpected ways that first led me to the archives. I simply would not have made it through the early stages of my career without Winfried as a mentor. I am thankful to the faculty at UC Berkeley and the numerous friends, interlocutors, and colleagues there who were involved in my intellectual formation—Kurt Beals, Paul Dobryden, Robin Ellis, Melissa Etzler, Karen Feldman, Deniz Gökturk, Jenna Ingalls, Regina Karl, Anne Kolb, Claire Kramsch, Niklaus Largier, Priscilla Layne, Ashwin Manthripragada, Emina

Mušanović, Elaine Tennant, Dagmar Theison, and Azadeh Yamini-Hamedani. A particular thanks goes to Dorothy Hale, who, as a teacher and mentor, modeled many traits to which I aspire. The roots of my career and thus of this book also extend deeper: from my time as an undergraduate at Washington University, I am thankful to Matt Erlin, Jennifer Kapczynski, Lutz Koepnick, and above all Erin McGlothlin. I wish to thank the numerous friends and colleagues at the College of the Holy Cross, Southern Illinois University at Carbondale, and Johns Hopkins University who have offered me mentorship, friendship, intellectual community, and emotional support: Shane Butler, Carola Daffner, Alison Erazmus, Laurel Frederickson, Christiane Frey, Jennifer Gosetti-Ferencei, David Johnson, Min Kyung Lee, Patrick McGrath, Ryan Netzley, Katrin Pahl, Leo Proietti, Erin Rowe, Caroline Schopp, Sylvia Schmitz-Burgard, Joe Shapiro, Jennifer Smith, Yasuko Taoka, Rochelle Tobias, Jonathan Wiesen, and Natasha Zaretsky.

I am thankful to the staffs and researchers at the various institutions where I conducted research for this book: the Deutsches Literaturarchiv, the Literaturarchiv der Österreichischen Nationalbibliothek, the Österreichische Akademie der Wissenschaften, and the Schweizerisches Literaturarchiv. Particular thanks are due to Hanno Biber, Evelyn Breiteneder, Ulrich von Bülow, Bernhard Fetz, and Thomas Richter, for their support. Numerous other colleagues have been collaborators and thoughtful and engaged interlocutors, and have invited me to present portions of my research: Stefano Apostolo, Gizem Arslan, Hannes Bajohr, Urs Büttner, Thorsten Carstensen, Carol Anne Costabile Heming, Ilinca Iuraşcu, Claudia Keller, Mike Lützeler, Catherine Marten, Katharina Pektor, and Oliver Ruf, among many others. A special thanks to Catriona MacLeod, who has generously supported me time and time again throughout the development of my career.

The research for this book was generously funded by the Deutscher Akademischer Austauschdienst, the Deutsches Literaturarchiv Marbach, the Fulbright Program, the Österreichischer Austauschdienst, and the Rare Book School. I am thankful to Paul Fleming, the editorial staff at Cornell University Press, and the editorial board of the Signale series for their assistance, feedback, and support for this book, as well as to the anonymous reviewers of my manuscript, who provided particularly astute, constructive feedback.

I am fortunate to have many dear, reliable friends who have supported me personally and intellectually along this entire journey. Adam Fazio, Elizabeth Ferrell, Edwin Harvey, Jenny Sakai, and Karl Whittington I have known since my early years of graduate school; Carola Daffner, Alison Erazmus, Haley Farthing, Laurel Frederickson, Patrick McGrath, Ryan Netzley, and Joe Shapiro I met in Carbondale. Elizabeth Ferrell, Laurel Frederickson, and Joe Shapiro in particular read drafts and engaged in countless conversations that shaped the development of this book and fueled my confidence in it.

I owe a particular debt of gratitude to my friend and developmental editor Lisa Regan of TextFormations, without whom this book would not exist. Lisa is one of the most diligent, insightful, engaged readers and interlocutors that I have ever had, and has also supported me at some of the most difficult moments during the process of writing this book.

I am grateful to my parents and my sister for their unconditional love and support throughout my life, education, and career; and to my grandparents, who played a very influential role in my development, fostering my interest in travel, in discovering new places and cultures, and in the arts.

I finally wish to thank Aaron Hyman, without whose love, support, and friendship I would not be where I am today, both as a person and as a scholar. Through discussion of ideas, arguments, and materials, through his belief in me and this book, and by reading and editing innumerable drafts of articles, chapters, and conference presentations, Aaron has also been the single most important intellectual influence throughout my development and the generation of this book.

Abbreviations

Handke

LMSV   Peter Handke, "The Lesson of Mont Sainte-Victoire," in *Slow Homecoming*, trans. Ralph Manheim (New York: New York Review of Books, 2009), 139–211.

LSV   Peter Handke, *Die Lehre der Sainte-Victoire* (Frankfurt am Main: Suhrkamp, 1980).

Bernhard

C   Thomas Bernhard, *Correction*, trans. Sophie Wilkins (New York: Vintage International, 1979).

W   Thomas Bernhard, *Werke*, 22 vols., ed. Martin Huber and Wendelin Schmidt-Dengler (Frankfurt am Main: Suhrkamp, 2003–2015).

WN   Thomas Bernhard, *Wittgenstein's Nephew*, trans. Ewald Osers (London: Quartet, 1986).

Rilke

BT   Rainer Maria Rilke, *Die Aufzeichnungen des Malte Laurids Brigge: Das Manuskript des "Berner Taschenbuchs"— Faksimile und textgenetische Edition*, ed. Thomas Richter and Franziska Kolp (Göttingen: Wallstein, 2012).

KA   Rainer Maria Rilke, *Werke: Kommentierte Ausgabe in vier Bänden*, ed. Manfred Engel, Ulrich Fülleborn, Horst Nalewski, and August Stahl (Frankfurt am Main: Insel, 1996).

MLB   Rainer Maria Rilke, *The Notebooks of Malte Laurids Brigge*, trans. Robert Vilain (Oxford: Oxford University Press, 2016).

Introduction

Expanding the Field of Interpretation

"How shall I begin? It's the simplest thing in the world, I told myself, and I can't understand why this simplest thing in the world eludes me. Perhaps I've made too many notes, written down too much about Mendelssohn Bartholdy on these hundreds and thousands of bits of paper that are piled up on my desk?"[1] Thomas Bernhard's novella *Beton* (*Concrete*, 1982) is the story of a writer who cannot begin to write.[2] Or rather, who cannot write what he wants to write. Instead, Rudolf, an amateur musicologist, generates a meandering, quasi stream-of-consciousness text that proceeds for nearly 150 pages without pause. Typical for Bernhard's prose, there are no paragraph, section, or chapter breaks in the entire text, which

---

All translations are mine unless otherwise noted. The gendering of translations reflects the original texts.

1. Thomas Bernhard, *Concrete*, trans. David McLintock (New York: Vintage, 1984), 31.
2. Thomas Bernhard, *Beton* (Frankfurt am Main: Suhrkamp, 1982).

thematizes Rudolf's inability to begin writing a study of the composer Felix Mendelssohn. The passage cited above is but one of many throughout the text in which Rudolf perpetually returns to the question of beginning, with varying hypotheses on why he cannot begin.

As evidenced by his published oeuvre, Bernhard himself did not have this trouble. But his process of writing differed from that of his prototypical writer-narrators, many of whom are similarly unable to begin, constructing entire studies in their minds that they are unable to materialize on paper. Bernhard's process of textual generation involved many starts: in episodic fits of writing, Bernhard would sit at the typewriter with a blank sheet and begin to type furiously, completely filling it with text by elaborating on a theme or motif in a quasi-improvisational manner until he reached the bottom of the page. This procedure enabled him to shuffle and reorder the resulting "page-episodes" into a draft text version, and even to move pieces of writing between work projects. Whereas Bernhard's protagonists prepare and build up to a monumental beginning moment, at which point they fail, Bernhard was always just writing, piecing his texts together along the way.

In writing about people who are unable to write, Bernhard thus generated a massive amount of writing. Yet it is not simply that Bernhard succeeds whereas his protagonists fail; *how* Bernhard goes about writing his texts remains woven into their formal, stylistic, structural, and thematic dimensions. In the published version of *Concrete*, the passage cited above falls somewhere within the 150-page, typographically undifferentiated deluge of writing. In the typescript version of *Concrete*, by contrast, this passage is found at the very top of a sheet (figure 0.1). That is to say, at some point in composing the text—likely not the beginning of the process, but a beginning, indeed one of many—Bernhard inserted a blank sheet into the typewriter and began by typing, "How shall I begin?" The narration of beginning, the question of how to begin, is itself in fact a beginning, corresponding to a material "beginning" in Bernhard's writing process. The question "How shall I begin?" refers not only to Rudolf's fictional quandary, but to the actual scene of the text's production.

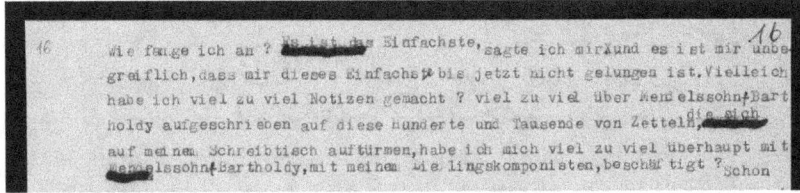

Figure 0.1. Thomas Bernhard, Beton, ÖLA 563/W5/1, 16. Literaturarchiv der Österreichischen Nationalbibliothek, Vienna.

Bernhard's texts do not merely *thematize* writing and other creative processes; they are, in very concrete ways, directly shaped by Bernhard's idiosyncratic methods and practice of writing. In this and many other ways, something of the physical activity of writing, what happens visually and materially on the typescript page, spills into the textual representation, remaining entangled within it. Bernhard's process of composing his texts, I argue, is not incidental to his literary work; rather, it is a crucial component of his broader *project* of writing.

For much of modern literary history, so-called *Vorstufen, avanttexte*, or prepublication materials—notes, manuscripts, text drafts, editorial correspondence, and other materials left behind in the process of generating text—have been considered secondary to published texts, paratextual with respect to the primary object of literary investigation: the Text. In this book I focus on three writers who all left behind material traces of their writing process, but to varying degrees: from numerous notebooks and carefully constructed text versions, to piles of disorganized typewritten sheets, to a single manuscript fragment. This is the literal stuff of literature. Housed in archives where scholars can consult them, and increasingly accessible in print and digital editions, these materials are beginning to receive more attention. My purpose in this book, however, is not simply to rectify oversights or fill lacunae, leaving the published texts untouched. Instead I suggest that centering these materials as part of a more capacious understanding of what constitutes the text both enables us to more fully comprehend these writers' projects of writing and also expands our view of the material-semiotic complexity of literature as an art form.

Process, Product, Project

In what follows I examine the work of three of the most significant German-language writers of the long twentieth century: Peter Handke (1942–), Thomas Bernhard (1931–89), and Rainer Maria Rilke (1875–1926). Although all three are from Austria, they differ notably: Rilke might be seen to have inaugurated modernist literature; Bernhard and Handke were contemporaries whose careers began in the 1960s; Rilke influenced Handke; Bernhard detested Rilke; and Bernhard and Handke mutually despised each other's work. Various kinds of relationships between these writers can be and have been charted. Rilke might be considered a forefather, embraced or rejected, of the later writers. Triangulated, Handke and Bernhard can be seen to represent two trajectories of twentieth-century literature indebted to Rilke, particularly to his middle period (1902–10): Handke and Rilke were both powerfully influenced by the paintings of Paul Cézanne;[3] and Rilke's novel *Die Aufzeichnungen des Malte Laurids Brigge* (*The Notebooks of Malte Laurids Brigge*, 1910) is an important predecessor for the radical linguistic skepticism of Bernhard's writing.[4] The story I tell in this book, however, is not one of heredity. Despite overlaps between Rilke's and Handke's receptions of Cézanne—both writers undergo a process of "learning to see" and learning to write anew, and Handke's *Die Lehre der Sainte-Victoire* (*The Lesson of Mont Sainte-Victoire*, 1980) has even been described as the "completion" or a "re-edition" of Rilke's *Briefe über Cézanne* (*Letters on Cézanne*, 1952)—there is no evidence that Handke ever read Rilke's *Letters*.[5]

---

3. For studies that treat both writers, see Martina Kurz, *Bild-Verdichtungen: Cézannes Realisation als poetisches Prinzip bei Rilke und Handke* (Göttingen: Vandenhoeck und Ruprecht, 2003); Jutta Heinz, "Cézanne-Erlebnisse bei Rainer Maria Rilke und Peter Handke: Ansätze zu einer literarischen Phänomenologie," *Hofmannsthal-Jahrbuch* 21 (2013): 367–89.

4. Rainer Maria Rilke, *Die Aufzeichnungen des Malte Laurids Brigge*, 2 vols. (Leipzig: Insel, 1910); Rainer Maria Rilke, *The Notebooks of Malte Laurids Brigge*, trans. Robert Vilain (Oxford: Oxford University Press, 2016).

5. Peter Handke, *Die Lehre der Sainte-Victoire* (Frankfurt am Main: Suhrkamp, 1980); Rainer Maria Rilke, *Briefe über Cézanne* (Leipzig: Insel, 1952); Waltraud

What unites these writers in this study is less their literary historical affinities and tensions than the fact that for all three, the material, media-specific dimensions of textual production were a crucial, constitutive component of their broader projects of writing. One of my central contentions is that we can consider all the various stages of a text's production—from earliest draft material to final proofs—as part of a broader "whole," not "prior to" or "outside of" the text, but instead as part of the literary work.[6] The nature and scope of the materials to be included, however, will differ for different writers in different historical contexts and media configurations. Handke wrote slowly and methodically, recording continuously in his notebooks and gathering notes into text drafts that he meticulously revised across numerous versions. Bernhard wrote rapidly and explosively, hammering into the typewriter to fill numerous pages with text to be shuffled through in piecing text versions together. Both writers left behind robust archives of materials that enable us to trace the entire process of textual production, from the scenes of writing and editing to publishing and reading. We know much less about how Rilke wrote. In the case of *The Notebooks*, only a small portion of the work's material production survives. Each case study in this book employs a different methodological approach, but they all share a common starting point: a combination of what we *know* and what we *have*. What do we know about a given author's process/project of writing, and how much material evidence of this process remains extant and accessible for examination?

Wiethölter, "Auge in Auge mit Cézanne: Handkes 'Lehre der Sainte-Victoire,'" *Germanisch-romanische Monatsschrift* 71 (1990): 422.
 6. Contemporary editorial theory conceives of the "work" similarly. Peter L. Schillingsburg, for example, defines the work as "that which is manifested in and implied by the material and linguistic forms of texts thought to be variant forms of a single literary entity." Schillingsburg, *Resisting Texts* (Ann Arbor: University of Michigan Press, 1997), 101. Rüdiger Nutt-Kofoth similarly writes that "all texts that were generated in the production of the work are a component of this work." Nutt-Kofoth, "Schreiben und Lesen: Für eine produktions- und rezeptionsorientierte Präsentation des Werktextes in der Edition," in *Text und Edition: Positionen und Perspektiven*, ed. Rüdiger Nutt-Kofoth (Berlin: Erich Schmidt, 2000), 169–70.

My investigation of Handke's production of *The Lesson of Mont Sainte-Victoire* begins with Handke's notebooks: filled with reflections, landscape descriptions, notes on artworks viewed in museums, and quotes from texts read, more than 230 of these notebooks are housed at the German Literature Archive in Marbach. Handke's note-taking process, as part of his broader project of slowness and close looking, is well-known and well-studied; it also features prominently, for example, in the 2017 documentary film on the writer.[7] Less understood, however, are the slow and meticulous processes by which Handke transformed these notes into printed works: Handke gathered notes in constructing a first version of *The Lesson*, which was heavily revised and followed by two text versions and no fewer than three sets of hand-edited page proofs. These materials are dispersed between the Austrian National Library (which houses Handke's *Teilvorlass*) and the German Literature Archive, which houses the archives of Suhrkamp Verlag editor Siegfried Unseld, Handke's editor for the first several decades of his career. Examining the "whole" process of Handke's textual production enables us to see how significant his material process is for understanding his published text. Indeed, in *The Lesson*, I argue, Handke *enacts* a theory of writing that is never fully articulated but graspable only through examining his process of writing itself.

Bernhard left behind a similarly vast trove of materials—text versions and page proofs, but also piles of pages whose connections to any particular published work are sometimes more obvious, sometimes less. These are similarly dispersed between Austria and Germany: Bernhard's *Nachlass* (literary estate) was acquired by the Austrian National Library in December 2022, and numerous materials are also found in the Siegfried Unseld Archive in Marbach (Suhrkamp was also Bernhard's primary publisher). Whereas Handke's process was highly meticulous, Bernhard's was much more chaotic.[8] In order to grasp Handke's project, I carefully reconstruct

---

7. *Peter Handke: Bin im Wald: Kann sein, dass ich mich verspäte*, directed by Corinna Belz (Piffl Medien, 2017).

8. On the "chaos" of Bernhard's writing and the state of his Nachlass upon his death, compare Stefano Apostolo, *Thomas Bernhards unveröffentlichtes Ro-*

the complex process of patching notes together and repetitively finetuning the text across multiple stages; my examination of Bernhard's writing, by contrast, works largely in the opposite direction, re-reading numerous passages from published texts through the lens of Bernhard's material production to show how key thematic and stylistic dimensions of his writing—such as its plot-destroying rhythms, repetitiveness, and digressiveness—emerged directly out of his idiosyncratic process.

Rilke's writing process is a different matter. The largest and virtually only surviving document of Rilke's generation of *The Notebooks* is the so-called *Berner Taschenbuch* (the Bernese Notebook), a manuscript fragment corresponding roughly to the second half of the novel.[9] In chapter 3, I examine how and to what degree we can consider the entanglements of material process within textual product when few traces of that process remain. Examining Rilke's writing in the Bernese Notebook, I show, nonetheless enables us to sense how powerfully the materiality and visuality of Rilke's manuscript production became incorporated into the novel's figuration, haunting it like a phantom limb, even when we cannot return to examine its material origins.

In investigating these diverse writerly projects, I examine texts that were produced at particular moments of crisis, transition, or crystallization in these writers' careers. Handke's *The Lesson of Mont Sainte-Victoire* represents the overcoming of a crisis of writing that resulted in a dramatic poetological shift—a "turn to nature" involving the cultivation of a new mode seeing, what Alexander Honold has recently described as "the geological gaze."[10] A continuation of

---

manprojekt Schwarzach St. Veit: Das Konvolut, die Fassungen und ihre Deutung (Mattighofen: Korrektur, 2019), 21–23.

9. The original is housed at the Swiss Literature Archive in Bern. A facsimile has been published: Rainer Maria Rilke, *Die Aufzeichnungen des Malte Laurids Brigge: Das Manuskript des "Berner Taschenbuchs"—Faksimile und textgenetische Edition*, ed. Thomas Richter and Franziska Kolp (Göttingen: Wallstein, 2012). Two earlier versions of the beginning, the content of which relates to the fifteenth entry, have been published; these manuscripts are clean copies (the working manuscripts are not extant). On these materials and their publication history, see W 3:866–68.

10. Alexander Honold, *Der Erd-Erzähler: Peter Handkes Prosa der Orte, Räume und Landschaften* (Stuttgart: Metzler, 2017), 138–49.

Handke's groundbreaking work *Langsame Heimkehr* (*Slow Homecoming*, 1979) and, in part, a reflection on that work's generation, *The Lesson* both articulates and puts into practice a new poetological paradigm based largely on Handke's engagement of Cézanne—an engagement that began prior to and developed during and after Handke's writing of *Slow Homecoming*. In *The Lesson*—a generic hybrid of travel narrative, art historical treatise, and poetic manifesto—Handke not only narrates how the painter Paul Cézanne became a teacher, but puts into practice the lesson he learned by attempting to translate the painter's process into a new writing method. Bernhard's novel *Korrektur* (*Correction*, 1975) marks a turning point in his career: a radicalization of the aesthetic program he had begun developing in his earlier prose works and a crystallization of many characteristic features of his later work.[11] *Correction* is the report of an unnamed narrator's overwhelming attempts to sort and sift the massive, disorganized Nachlass of his deceased friend Roithamer; Roithamer's process of revising and correcting his masterwork is so excessive—in ways that strikingly resemble Bernhard's own—that he nearly destroys it, challenging the narrator's later efforts to edit it for publication. Highly self-reflexive, a testament to Bernhard's intensive *Nachlassbewusstsein*, this manuscript fiction (a work about a fictional manuscript) is also a Nachlass fiction, one that at times uncannily anticipates the future state and scandalous circumstances of Bernhard's own Nachlass.[12] Often considered to be the first modernist

---

11. Thomas Bernhard, *Korrektur* (Frankfurt am Main: Suhrkamp, 1975); Martin Huber and Wendelin Schmidt-Dengler, commentary to Thomas Bernhard, *Korrektur*, ed. Martin Huber and Wendelin Schmidt-Dengler, vol. 4 of Thomas Bernhard, *Werke*, ed. Martin Huber and Wendelin Schmidt-Dengler, 22 vols. (Frankfurt am Main: Suhrkamp), 350, 357.

12. Kai Sina and Carlos Spoerhase, eds., *Nachlassbewusstsein: Literatur Archiv Philologie, 1750–2000* (Göttingen: Wallstein, 2017). On Bernhard's "Nachlassbewusstsein," compare Apostolo, *Thomas Bernhards unveröffentlichtes Romanprojekt*, 23–31. On the notion of the manuscript fiction or "editor fiction," see Uwe Wirth, *Die Geburt des Autors aus dem Geist der Herausgeberfiktion: Editorial Rahmung im Roman um 1800: Wieland, Goethe, Brentano, Jean Paul und E. T. A. Hoffmann* (Munich: Fink, 2008). In his testament, Bernhard famously forbade the publication and performance of his works within Austria after his death. This prohibition was later overridden by the executors of Bernhard's estate when it was found to be not legally binding.

novel in the German language, Rilke's *The Notebooks of Malte Laurids Brigge* consists of seventy-one *Aufzeichnungen* (written sketches, entries) of the young, struggling poet Malte, who, overwhelmed by his experience of the Parisian metropolis, begins a process of learning to see and to write in a radically new way. The process of writing the novel itself, Rilke's first and only attempt to write a longer prose work, was tormented; Rilke felt that he barely "survived" it, and he fell into a deep crisis of writing that prevented him from publishing again for twelve years.[13]

Composed at particularly charged moments of transition, these works are all highly self-reflexive with respect to the process of writing. This, in part, is what makes them such ideal case studies. Examining the material production of these works enables us to see how their semantic dimensions not only reflect, but also were generated out of, these production processes, which remain inscribed within the works' formal, stylistic, structural, and thematic dimensions. Teasing out the entanglements of materiality and meaning in these works, in turn, sheds light on dynamics that play out across these writers' oeuvres more broadly.

Sharing a language and, to some degree, a cultural context, the writers and writing projects examined in this book bring into view a set of issues at the intersection of materiality, authorship, and agency that have been considerations within literary studies for quite some time now—relationships between intentionality and contingency, fictionality and actuality, intertextual and extratextual referentiality, to name a few. All of the works treated in this book are semi-autobiographical; in various ways, these writers experiment with the transformation or incorporation of biographical experience and real-world people, places, and events into textual representation—with expanding life into writing. In this book I ask: How exactly do these writers go about undertaking these experiments? The question is not (primarily) one of representation/depiction, but instead (also) one of material process. To grasp the dynamics of the autofictional

---

13. Rilke to Lou Andreas-Salomé, December 28, 1911, in Rainer Maria Rilke and Lou Andreas-Salomé, *Briefwechsel*, ed. Ernst Pfeiffer (Zurich: Max Niehans, 1952), 245–51, at 246.

in these works, I suggest, we must consider the "whole" process—the mesh of texts and textual processes that together constitute the literary work. As I will argue, how these authors actually wrote relates to, and in some cases directly generates, the various textual effects (such as form, style, structure, thematics, and intertextuality) through which these questions have been approached. We cannot fully engage with material process, however, without returning to and confronting the question of authorship, a topic that frequently is met with hesitation and uncertainty in contemporary literary studies. A reconsideration of authorship is thus key: for it is in the material-cognitive phenomenon of authorship—the activity through which text and world, materiality and meaning, fiction and autobiography meet—that writing process, textual product, and writerly project coincide.

Authorship and Materiality

As I examine in these chapters the entanglements of materiality and meaning in the production of literary works, I reconfigure questions of authorship that, long since "the death of the Author"—and despite various "returns" and "resurrections"—remain largely unaddressed within literary studies.[14] Poststructuralism shifted attention away from authorship, intentionality, and the creative process toward the role of language, intertextuality, and the reader in the generation of textual meaning.[15] Since then, fields such as media

---

14. See Seán Burke, *The Death and Return of the Author: Criticism and Subjectivity in Barthes, Foucault and Derrida* (Edinburgh: University of Edinburgh Press, 1998); William Irwin, ed., *The Death and Resurrection of the Author?* (Westport, CT: Greenwood, 2002).

15. The most canonical works include Roland Barthes, "The Death of the Author," in *The Rustle of Language*, trans. Richard Howard (New York: Hill and Wang, 1986), 49–55; Michel Foucault, "What Is an Author?," in *The Foucault Reader*, ed. Paul Rainbow (New York: Pantheon, 1984), 101–20; Jacques Derrida, "Structure, Sign, and Play in the Discourse of the Human Sciences," in *Writing and Difference*, trans. Alan Bass (London: Routledge, 2001), 351–70. For summary, contextualization, and critique of these discourses and their reception, particularly useful are An-

studies and book history have highlighted the material conditions of meaning production, while new materialism, agential realism, and actor-network theory have (re)considered the material agency of things and the distribution of agency across an array of human and nonhuman actants. To a degree, interest in materiality and material agency within literary studies has enabled scholars to sidestep questions of authorship. But a long-held reticence about the figure of the author has led the majority of literary scholars, particularly in North America, to shy away from questions of material process, which would too easily (though wrongly) seem to center on the figure of the author and their intentions.

These theoretical concerns can be brought to bear upon the following, more practical question: What role can or could the Nachlass play in literary criticism today and moving forward, particularly in light of the increasing accessibility of archival materials through digital platforms and editions?[16] Formerly, authors' Nachlässe were primarily seen as sources of information about authors' lives, correspondence, and travels; what the authors were doing and thinking about while writing their texts; and the changes their works underwent during the creative process. These considerations informed efforts to elucidate authors' "intentions" and, by extension, the meanings of their works. Today some might deem authors' manuscripts irrelevant to interpretation-oriented literary criticism, like relics or fetish objects of a bygone Author-cult that has long been deconstructed. In this book, I approach manuscripts and other prepublication materials in a fundamentally different way: namely, as traces of material, media-specific processes, and as products of agential networks that include human agents (authors, editors, designers) as well as other kinds of agency (material, social, intertextual). In so doing, I offer literary scholars working in any period theoretical

---

drew Bennett, *The Author* (London: Routledge, 2005); Graham Allen, *Intertextuality* (London: Routledge, 2000); Burke, *The Death and Return*.

16. Theory and scholarship on the archive and the role of literary Nachlässe are expansive. For a recent comprehensive study, see Petra-Maria Dallinger, Georg Hofer, and Bernhard Judex, eds., *Archive für Literatur: Der Nachlass und seine Ordnungen* (Berlin: De Gruyter, 2018).

lenses and methodological models for approaching material textual production as a fundamental, constitutive dimension of literary works.

For decades now we have known that "materiality matters," and that different media fundamentally shape how we think, speak, and write. For many literature scholars, however, it is not clear how we can approach writers' manuscripts and other material textual artifacts without simply reinscribing conceptions of authorship and modes of interpretation that have long been invalidated. The majority of literary scholars today do not have significant experience working in archives, and the skills for working with manuscripts are rarely part of doctoral training, particularly in North America. Many see literature archives as rarefied spaces for biographical or positivist textual scholarship. But when they avoid writers' manuscripts and other traces of material textual production, scholars fail to see how these materials can be brought to bear on pressing theoretical questions of materiality, mediality, intertextuality, and agency within contemporary literary studies today. When approached through a materialist lens, there is a great deal about the material production of texts that can be observed in writers' Nachlässe, even without specific archival or paleographic training, from papers, writing tools, and techniques employed to correction methods and incidental mark-making—but only if we care to examine the lives of literary works before they arrived in printed form.

In this book I re-center authorship by focusing on relationships between authorship and materiality. Conceiving authorship in terms of the agency of textual production, I ask: How can we allow for intentionality and contingency to simultaneously coexist? How can we bring intentionality back into discourse, not as authoritative mastery over meaning, but in dynamic relationship with writing materials, which also have a kind of agency? Various theoretical and methodological approaches have been developed that deal with authorship and its materials. Genetic criticism, a branch of textual criticism focused the "genesis" of texts, examines writing processes through analysis of all extant material traces thereof—notebooks, marginalia, manuscripts, and so on.[17] Through the production of historical-critical editions, German *Editionswissenschaft* similarly aims to reconstruct and mediate the entirety of a work's production, extending from earliest notes to not only the first published version but also beyond—that is, the edition history of works.[18] Scholarship on the *Schreibszene* (writing scene) approaches the activity of writing through a media-technical lens—namely, as an interactive "ensemble" of language, instrumentality, and bodily gesture.[19] Informed by new materialism (Jane Bennett), agential realism (Karen Barad), actor-network theory (Bruno Latour), and object-oriented ontology (Graham Harman, Timothy Morton), recent materialist-oriented studies of literature have focused on questions of distributed agency and the agency of things within literary works; indeed, theorists such as Bennett and Morton have deeply engaged with literature in the development of their theories.[20] These various perspectives each bring into focus certain dimensions of literary works and/or their production. None, however, grapples with the full scope and range of intersections that constitute the subject of this book: intersections of writing practice, media theory, textual materiality, textual representation, and theories of material agency spanning the entire arc of textual production, from the earliest stages of note-taking and drafting through editing and publishing into the material scene of reading.

17. For a recent introduction to the discipline, see Dirk van Hulle, *Genetic Criticism* (Oxford: Oxford University Press, 2022).
18. Sally Bushell offers a good overview of German, French, and Anglo-American approaches to scholarly editing in *Text as Process* (Charlottesville: University of Virginia Press, 2009).
19. Rüdiger Campe, "Writing; The Scene of Writing," trans. Bryan Klausmeyer and Johannes Wankhammer, *MLN* 136, no. 5 (2021): 973.
20. This literature is far too vast to cite in its entirety. Foundational works include Jane Bennett, *Vibrant Matter: A Political Ecology of Things* (Durham, NC: Duke University Press, 2010); Karen Barad, *Meeting the Universe Halfway: Quantum Physics and the Entanglement of Matter and Meaning* (Durham, NC: Duke University Press, 2007); Bruno Latour, *Reassembling the Social: An Introduction to Actor-Network-Theory* (Oxford: Oxford University Press, 2005); Timothy Morton, *The Ecological Thought* (Cambridge, MA: Harvard University Press, 2012); Graham Harman, *Tool-Being: Heidegger and the Metaphysics of Objects* (New York: Open Court, 2002).

Each of the approaches mentioned above sheds light on particular aspects of materiality and material agency in and of literature, but also leaves other dimensions out of view. I make my interventions at the interstices of these theories and methodologies. Through the production of historical-critical editions, German *Editionswissenschaft* aims to present all the stages of a work's material production, but stops at the textual interpretation of these materials; through transcription and mediation (digital/print) of manuscripts and other prepublication materials, these endeavors can inadvertently suppress key dimensions of material textuality and their significance. While embracing the interpretation of the so-called *avant-texte*, genetic criticism can similarly tend toward the positivist in its construction of complex genetic maps and genetic dossiers. Approaching the act of writing as a "non-stable ensemble of language, instrumentality, and gesture," scholarship on the scene of writing is attentive to the relationships between materiality and semantics but has tended to focus somewhat narrowly on the media-technical dimensions of writing without taking into account later stages of textual production (such as editing, publishing).[21] And despite the abundance of literary theoretical studies of materiality and objects in literary texts, many fewer studies simultaneously turn this critical gaze onto the materiality/material production of those texts, and the ways in which these dimensions might inform the interpretation of literary works.

In published versions of a literary work, all traces of the material writing process would seem to have been effaced, rendered invisible in the translation of the work from the material scene of writing into print. But the scene of writing and the scene of reading are not divided by an uncrossable chasm. Nor are materiality and meaning. As Karen Barad writes in *Meeting the Universe Halfway: Quantum Physics and the Entanglement of Matter and Meaning* (2007), "Matter and meaning are not separate elements. They are inextricably fused together."[22] The case studies of this book examine several ways in which textual materiality and process become entangled within the formal and semantic dimensions of literary works across the entire

---

21. Campe, "Writing," 973.
22. Barad, *Meeting the Universe Halfway*, 3.

arc of production and reception. The object of study is thus not just the writing process, or the published product alone, but instead the entanglement of materiality and meaning in the production and reception of literature, throughout the entangled scenes of writing, editing, publishing, and reading. This framework not only opens up new interpretative inroads into well-known texts, but also enables us to grasp these writers' broader projects of writing as experiments in authorship, in which the material, visual, and process dimensions of writing played a decisive, indeed agential, role. By attending to these aspects, I offer avenues for thinking through how integrating the analysis of materiality and process into interpretation can expand our understanding of the material-semiotic complexity of literary works, and of literature as an art form more generally.

Agency and Entanglement

As has become clear, two key concepts in the theoretical apparatus I advance and put into practice in these chapters are agency and entanglement. These concepts have been much discussed and debated in recent years; indeed, initially a book on textual entanglements may even seem belated. Familiar though these concepts and theoretical discourses may be, however, they have not been widely used to rethink the materiality of literature more broadly. Having emerged largely out of political theory, sociology, and science and technology studies, these concepts have been discussed by literary scholars but have not fundamentally transformed or expanded how we approach literature as such, either as an art form or as an object of study.

My discussions of distributed agency in this book are informed most of all by Jane Bennett. Bennett defines agency in terms of efficacy—"the ability to make things happen, to produce effects."[23] Agency, then, derives not only from human minds; all actions are effects of the "heterogenous assemblage" of human and nonhuman "actants."[24] To suggest that things (like notebooks and typewriters)

---

23. Bennett, *Vibrant Matter*, 5.
24. Bennett, *Vibrant Matter*, 23, 9.

also have agency is not to imply that they have the "same" kind of agency as humans;[25] nor is it to disregard the fact that not all humans have the same amount of agency, political and otherwise. The concept of distributed agency acknowledges that all agential action—including the activity of textual production, writing, authorship—occurs through the participation of nonhuman actants. As I explore in these chapters, the participation and efficacy of writing tools and other actants/factors of the scene of writing remain, to varying degrees, both tangible and legible in the material-semantic fabric of the textual product.

Although the approach I propose to the study of literature is informed by such conceptions of agency, it also has something to say to studies of material agency more broadly. This may be surprising, given that the Author was an archetype for the autonomous individual/subject whose agency has become gradually dispersed through successive theoretical waves and turns. Literature has frequently been drawn upon as a source for thinking about the material agency of things and the intertwining of human and nonhuman forms of agency. But literature is not made (only) of thoughts and ideas; though literary texts commonly bear the name of an author, literature itself is produced through an ontologically heterogeneous host of agencies. The study of the agency of literary production sheds light on and raises awareness of processes by which all writing, all texts—all human creativity, all human thought/discourse—are produced.

The second concept is entanglement. I borrow the term most directly from Karen Barad in theorizing the entanglement of materiality and meaning in the production and reception of literary texts. The basic structure of entanglement—the interconnectivity, intertwining, inextricability of various factors—underlies many other concepts in circulation in recent decades (such as the agential assemblage, and the scene of writing as an "ensemble" of factors). Drawing on Charles Darwin's vision of the "entangled bank" of

---

25. See Bruno Latour, "Third Source of Uncertainty: Objects Too Have Agency," in *Reassembling the Social*, 65–86. On the "Eigensinn" of writing implements, see Martin Stingelin, "Schreiben," introduction to *"Mir ekelt vor diesem tintenklecksenden Säkulum": Schreibszenen im Zeitalter der Manuskripte*, ed. Martin Stingelin, Davide Giuriato, and Sandro Zanetti (Munich: Fink, 2004), 9.

interconnected life-forms, ecological and literary theorist Timothy Morton speaks of the "mesh," a "whole" that is a "flowing, shifting, entangled mess of ambiguous entities" and that "does away with the boundaries between living and nonliving forms."[26] But how can such conceptions of entanglement and enmeshment be brought to bear on the study of textual production and material-structural-stylistic-semiotic interconnectivities that, I argue, constitute the literary work? Here Morton offers several other useful concepts. In *Ecology without Nature* (2007), Morton describes a phenomenon, common in nature writing, of "ecomimesis"—the evocation of the environmental or atmospheric circumstances in which texts were written, their ecological situatedness or embeddedness (for instance, "As I write . . .").[27] He also coins the term "ambient poetics," defined as "a materialist way of reading texts with a view to how they encode the literal space of their inscription," meaning "the physical and social environment" or "the spaces between the words, the margins of the page." These latter are examples of the "medial," one of six main elements of ambient poetics.[28] My book could be seen as a study of a certain kind of ambient poetics: the ways in which the materiality of writing manifests, in all kinds of ways, in the published versions of literary texts. My primary question is *how* this happens. The notion of entanglement, as I use it, describes both a state and a process: the entanglement of textual materiality within the formal and semantic dimensions of texts, as well a process that unfolds across the interconnected "whole" of textual production and reception. Just as the scene of writing is constituted by a "non-stable ensemble" of language, instrumentality (writing tools and techniques), and bodily gestures, we can also conceive of "scenes" of editing, publishing, and reading, each of which is similarly constituted by a range of materials,

---

26. Timothy Morton, "The Mesh," in *Environmental Criticism for the Twenty-First Century*, ed. Stephanie LeMenager, Teresa Shewry, and Ken Hiltner (London: Routledge, 2011), 22.
27. Timothy Morton, *Ecology without Nature: Rethinking Environmental Aesthetics* (Cambridge, MA: Harvard University Press, 2007), 8, 29–32.
28. Morton, *Ecology without Nature*, 3, 34.

tools, and techniques.[29] At every moment in a text's generation, the semantic content of language inscribed on the page is inextricably entangled within material, bodily processes of inscription. As a text gradually emerges and becomes transformed and transferred, via a host of processes and participants (editors, typesetters, book designers, and so forth), aspects of the phenomenological scene of writing remain entangled within the text's semantic, material, visual, and/or affective dimensions.

When we allow the materiality of textual process and production to come into view, thereby expanding the boundaries of the work, new levels of interpretation become possible. Another narrative becomes visible: the story of the work's making (literal fabrication). This story, however, does not simply result in the published work as its product; rather, it remains interwoven within the text itself. New dimensions of (self-)referentiality and intratextuality between the published version and its earlier incarnations become perceptible; in this way, all texts are semi-autobiographical, not with respect to their Authors but with respect to the distributed agency of their making. These dimensions, and the potential new readings they offer, do not become accessible until we reconnect the published text to its material production history and consider them together—as parts of an entangled or enmeshed "whole."

Making, Destruction, Figuration

I have structured this book as three chapters, each focused on the writing project of a single writer. Through analysis of a range of materials and processes—notes, notebooks, drafts, hand-corrected proofs, papers, writing tools, and cutting-and-pasting techniques, among others—each chapter highlights a particular dimension or aspect of textual materiality/process and its potential for opening up interpretative avenues for literary studies in general. This transpires

---

29. On the notion of the scene of reading, see *Leseszenen: Poetologie—Geschichte—Medialität*, ed. Irina Hron, Jadwiga Kita-Huber, and Sanna Schulte (Heidelberg: Universitätsverlag Winter, 2020).

in part, as discussed above, by bridging theoretical and methodological approaches but also genres of scholarship. For example, article- and chapter-length studies typically allow for the analysis of particular textual features or parts of a given writer's work, but they can only gesture to broader implications; book-length surveys may enable a broad view of a writer's oeuvre, sometimes through a particular theoretical lens, but can sometimes tend toward the summative and the reification of biographical narratives. Genetic critical studies of the *Entstehungsgeschichte* of writers' works, on the other hand, often include detailed descriptions of textual materials and reconstructed chronologies of a work's production, but do not always draw new interpretative insights. By structuring my book as three larger case studies, I aim to bridge or unify these sometimes siloed approaches; detailed material analysis of the generation of specific works integrates analysis of a wide range of specific textual features and phenomena that have been discussed in various other contexts, without attempting the comprehensive breadth of compendia or surveys of these writers' entire oeuvres.

Chapter 1 focuses on Peter Handke's material construction of texts, on writing as making and assembling. Chapter 2 examines the bodily, affective dimensions of reading Thomas Bernhard's writing, and the ways in which the material writing process generated significant material effects. Chapter 3 integrates the methodological insights of the first two chapters in confronting the fundamental question of the relationship between textual materiality and textual representation by focusing on Rainer Maria Rilke's conception and process of figuration via analysis of a partial manuscript fragment. The chapters are organized around key terms that are generated from these writers' work and are essential for understanding their material processes, and as such constitute nodes of particularly charged material-semiotic entanglement: *dance, thing-picture, stroke, script* (Handke); *correction, madness, rhythm, destruction* (Bernhard); narrating, *striking, seeing* (Rilke).

Chapter 1 centers on Peter Handke's generation of *The Lesson of Mont Sainte-Victoire*. In the late 1970s Handke underwent a crisis of writing that led to a "turn to nature," a shift toward a poetics of slowness and close looking rooted in a practice of daily note-taking.

In *The Lesson*, Handke narrates this transformation, in which the painter Paul Cézanne played a guiding role. Examining Handke's process of constructing the text—adopting a kind of "geological view" of the genesis of the text—reveals how he put into practice this lesson, analogizing Cézanne's method of *réalisation* by developing a kind of patchwork method of textual construction. The first part of the chapter examines Handke's engagement with Cézanne through analysis of his manuscript notebooks over a period of approximately a year and a half, from notes taken in museums and along the *route Cézanne* in Provence, to quotes from art theory and drawings that imitate Cézanne's technique.[30] The second part examines Handke's patchwork method of constructing *The Lesson*, an extended process that stretched across the entirety of note-taking, writing, editing, and proofing the text. In the end, I show that Handke's intermedial translation of Cézanne's painterly techniques amounts to a theory of writing as *Schrift-stellen*—a theory enacted through the process of writing itself.

Chapter 2 turns to examine the material scene of reading. Thomas Bernhard is well known both for his radical critiques of Austrian society as well as the experimental prose style in which they are delivered: a deluge of highly repetitive, rhythmic, hyperbolic, at times self-contradictory clauses that proceeds for page after page without pause. This language produces an experience of reading that is disorienting both cognitively and affectively; the reader is alternatively swept into the rhythms of Bernhard's writing and viscerally bombarded by repetitive verbal tirades. Scholars have examined in detail the thematization of destruction in Bernhard's texts, particularly in relation to the author's self-characterization as *Geschichtenzerstörer* (destroyer of stories).[31] But the unusual features of his prose emerged out of a writing process that was extraordinarily generative: Bernhard would hammer away rapidly and ferociously on the typewriter in explosive episodes, producing massive amounts of

---

30. The most thorough accounting of Handke's note-taking during this period is provided by Marit Heuß, *Peter Handkes Bildpoetik: Notieren, Zeichnen, Erzählen* (Göttingen: Wallstein, 2022), 233–65.

31. Thomas Bernhard, "Drei Tage," in *Der Italiener* (Frankfurt am Main: Suhrkamp, 1989), 83–84.

typescript pages. At first glance the material generativity of Bernhard's process would seem antithetical to the thematics of destruction so prominent in his work. But as I explore, creation and destruction are inextricably, dialectically intertwined in Bernhard's material process, in ways that spill into the content of the texts here examined. In the first section, I focus on *Correction*, the most self-reflexive of Bernhard's works with respect to his writing process, to show how the typical features of Bernhard's prose can be rooted in his idiosyncratic use of the typewriter and method of filling pages with text. In the second section, I demonstrate how understanding Bernhard's material process of writing enables new readings of a work that is much less obviously self-reflexive: *Wittgensteins Neffe* (*Wittgenstein's Nephew*, 1982).[32]

The insights of the first two chapters, focused on material construction and material reception (reading), are brought together in chapter 3, which confronts the central issue at the meeting point of material text studies and literary interpretation—the relationship between materiality and representation—through investigation of Rainer Maria Rilke's notion of figuration, around which there has developed a rich interpretative tradition. A key concept of his middle and late periods, Rilkean *Figur*, I show, is imbricated in the materiality of Rilke's manuscript production. But whereas ample material records allow us to carefully reconstruct Handke's and Bernhard's writing processes, only a fragmentary manuscript remains of Rilke's generation of *The Notebooks of Malte Laurids Brigge*, widely considered to be the first modernist novel in German and Rilke's first and only experiment with the genre. Though it is only a fragment, the so-called Bernese Notebook reveals how powerfully the materiality and visuality of Rilke's manuscript production became incorporated into the figurative dimensions of the work—for instance, how textual representations of abject bodiliness are enmeshed and entangled in the material "body" of the manuscript. Methodologically, this chapter serves in part as a case study for considering how the approaches developed in the first two chapters

---

32. Thomas Bernhard, *Wittgensteins Neffe* (Frankfurt am Main: Suhrkamp, 1982).

can be applied to works for which only partial documentary history remains.

For all three writers, major digital projects and facsimile editions have been completed or are in process. Increasingly, such resources are enabling the methodologies I model in this book to be practiced in ways and on a scale previously impossible. My concluding epilogue thus addresses digitization—the new possibilities it affords for research and pedagogy, as well as its limitations.

1

Handke's Slow Making

In his introduction to *The Textual Condition*, published in 1991, Jerome McGann writes that "today, texts are largely imagined as scenes of reading rather than scenes of writing. This 'readerly' view of text has been most completely elaborated through the modern hermeneutical tradition in which text is not something we *make* but something we *interpret*."[1] In the same year, Rüdiger Campe published his groundbreaking essay on the scene of writing, theorizing this scene as a "non-stable ensemble of language, instrumentality, and gesture."[2] In other words, all writing—all acts of inscription,

---

1. Jerome McGann, *The Textual Condition* (Princeton, NJ: Princeton University Press, 1991), 4.
2. Rüdiger Campe, "Die Schreibszene: Schreiben," in *Paradoxien, Dissonanzen, Zusammenbrüche: Situationen offener Epistemologie*, ed. Hans Ulrich Gumbrecht and Karl Ludwig Pfeiffer (Frankfurt am Main: Suhrkamp, 1991), 760; Rüdiger Campe, "Writing; The Scene of Writing," trans. Bryan Klausmeyer and Johannes Wankhammer, *MLN* 136, no. 5 (2021): 973.

all meaning production through writing—can be understood to occur through dynamic interactions of (1) language (linguistic signs in all their dimensions, such as spoken, written, semantic/semiotic); (2) instrumentality (writing instruments, media, materials, and media, such as pen, paper, typewriter, computer keyboard); and (3) gesture (the bodily activities of handwriting, typing, striking, swiping, and so on). In this chapter I focus on the "scene of writing" as a scene of making. Poststructuralist theorists conceived of text in terms of *bricolage*, intertextuality, and infinite chains or networks of signification. Peter Handke developed a method of writing that bears resemblance to these concepts but is rooted in specific material practices: a quasi-patchwork method of textual construction that extended over the entire arc of the production process. Methodologically, I employ in this chapter an approach that in certain respects is similar to that of genetic criticism, in that it traces the gradual composition of the text from Handke's manuscript notebooks through multiple hand-edited typescript versions and sets of page proofs into the design of the printed book.[3] Beyond merely presenting these documents, I attend closely to media-specific material aspects of production at every stage in the process in order to show not only how they give rise to specific textual effects but also how, through the material process itself, Handke enacts a *theory* of writing as *Schrift-stellen* (text-making).

In the late 1970s Handke underwent a crisis of writing that led to a so-called classical turn or "turn to nature," a reorientation from his more overtly political and linguistically experimental earlier work toward a new mode of narration that was mythic, epic, and

---

3. Katharina Pektor offers an excellent such study of *Der Chinese des Schmerzes*, including summary, biographical contextualization, presentation, chronological reconstruction, and discussion of the extant documents of its generation. Katharina Pektor, "'Aber wie nähere ich mich L.'s Geschichte?' Zur Entstehung von Peter Handkes Erzählung *Der Chinese des Schmerzes*," in *Peter Handke: Freiheit des Schreibens—Ordnung der Schrift*, ed. Klaus Kastberger (Vienna: Zsolnay, 2009), 109–32, 157–63, 254. These archival materials from the generation of *The Lesson* have been documented and annotated in the Handke*online* platform. See "Die Lehre der Sainte-Victoire," Handke*online*, ed. Klaus Kastberger, Katharina Pektor and Christoph Kepplinger-Prinz, Österreichische Nationalbiblikothek, https://handkeonline.onb.ac.at/node/122.

oracular in tone.[4] Out of this was born a project of slowness and reauratization that continues to define Handke's work to the present. In *The Lesson of Mont Sainte-Victoire*—a generic hybrid of travel narrative, philosophical/art-historical treatise, and poetic manifesto, and the second volume of the *Slow Homecoming* tetralogy—Handke narrates this transformation, in which the painter Paul Cézanne played a guiding role.[5]

In *The Lesson*, Handke not only narrates his encounter with Cézanne's painting but also puts into practice the "lesson" he learned from the painter—in effect, transforming a "scene of painting" into a "scene of writing." At the center of this lesson was Cézanne's project and material method of "realization": the process by which Cézanne perceived the things of the world in their essence and interconnectedness, and captured this in art, generating "harmonies parallel to nature" (LMSV 178). Though it was a central principle of his practice, Cézanne never offered a clear definition of the notion of realization—and neither, in the end, does Handke.[6] Rather than explaining it in abstract theoretical terms, Handke *narrates* the process by which he gradually came to comprehend Cézanne's painting as a "great thing-image-script-brushstroke-dance [*Ding-Bild-Schrift-Strich-Tanz*]" (LMSV 179).

The route by which Handke arrived at this understanding was at once conceptual and material: an initial encounter with Cézanne's work at an exhibition of the painter's late work at the Grand Palais

---

4. Hans Höller, *Eine ungewöhnliche Klassik nach 1945: Das Werk Peter Handkes* (Frankfurt am Main: Suhrkamp, 2013), 9; Alexander Huber, *Versuch einer Ankunft: Peter Handkes Ästhetik der Differenz* (Würzburg: Königshausen und Neumann, 2005), 111.

5. Peter Handke, *Die Lehre der Sainte Victoire* (Frankfurt am Main: Suhrkamp, 1980). The other works of the *Langsame Heimkehr* tetralogy include the title work *Langsame Heimkehr* (Frankfurt am Main: Suhrkamp, 1979), *Kindergeschichte* (Frankfurt am Main: Suhrkamp, 1981), and *Über die Dörfer* (Frankfurt am Main: Suhrkamp, 1981). On the generic hybridity of *Die Lehre*, see Claudia Albes, *Erzählen—Argumenteiren—Beschreiben: Zur Theorie und Interpretation moderner Prosatexte am Beispiel von Peter Handkes* Lehre der Sainte-Victoire (Trier: Wissenschaftlicher Verlag Trier, 2013); Martina Kurz, *Bild-Verdichtungen: Cézannes Realisation als poetisches Prinzip bei Rilke und Handke* (Göttingen: Vandenhoeck und Ruprecht, 2003), 43–52.

6. Kurz, *Bild-Verdichtungen*, 75.

in Paris in the spring of 1978—which included, among other things, fifteen paintings of Mont Saint-Victoire—catalyzed a journey that led Handke to visit numerous museums across Europe, and ultimately, to travel himself the famous *route Cézanne* in Provence, not once but twice in 1979 (July 3–6 and December 10–14).[7] Handke's own personal "route Cézanne" took place not only in museums and on hikes, but also on the page. In this chapter I explore this route, what Handke came to understand of Cézanne's material method, and how Handke translated this method into a material process of writing in constructing *The Lesson*.

At the foundation of Handke's experiment was a project of note-taking. In the mid-1970s—on precisely March 5, 1976, according to Katharina Pektor's dating[8]—Handke began a practice of daily note-taking—recording observations and impressions, descriptions and drawings of nature from routine walks and hikes, quotes by writers from Heraclitus to Heidegger, notes on artworks viewed in museums, and formulations of passages that would later appear in his published works.[9] In describing the emergence of his note-taking process, Handke writes: "I now practiced reacting to everything that happened to me with language. . . . It is not a narration of a consciousness, but instead the immediate, simultaneously captured reportage thereof."[10] A space for "spontaneous recording [*Aufzeichnung*] of aimless perceptions,"[11] Handke's notebooks are heterogeneous both in their semantic content—montages of thoughts, impressions, landscape descriptions, and quotes—and in

---

7. Christoph Kepplinger-Prinz, "Entstehungskontext," Handke*online*, https://handkeonline.onb.ac.at/node/1356.

8. Katharina Pektor, "'Wartet nur—ich bin jemand, der sich organisiert': Peter Handkes Projekt des Notierens," in *"Gedanken reisen, Einfälle kommen an": Die Welt der Notiz*, ed. Marcel Atze and Volker Kaukoreit (Vienna: Praesens, 2016), 311.

9. An extensively annotated catalogue of notebooks from 1971 to 1990 is presented on the Handke*online* platform: "Notizbücher 1971–1990," handkeonline.onb.ac.at/node/90. On the drawings in Handke's notebooks, see Christoph Kepplinger-Prinz and Katharina Pektor, "Zeichnendes Notieren und erzählendes Zeichnen: Skizzen, Zeichnungen und Bilder in Peter Handkes Notizbüchern von 1972 bis 1990," (2012), handkeonline.onb.ac.at/forschung/pdf/kepplinger-pektor-2012.pdf.

10. Handke, *Das Gewicht der Welt* (Salzburg: Residenz, 1977), 6.

11. Handke, *Das Gewicht der Welt*, 5.

their material form: each small enough to fit into a jacket pocket, ranging in format, paper quality, and binding, and sometimes reinforced with tape or adhesive bandages, they were inscribed using a diverse array of writing implements in numerous colors and contain a range of ephemera, from receipts, clippings, and photographs, to dried flowers and plant leaves. Formulations of text passages that would later appear in print pepper less-formed reflections and quotidian scribblings. Handke's notebooks are neither diaries nor journals in the traditional sense, nor are they merely pre-text for to-be-published works. Rather, they constitute the basis of a distinct artistic-writerly project that has undergirded Handke's published work to the present.

The cultivation of a practice of note-taking played a crucial role in Handke's poetological project of slowing down and learning to see anew, a project proclaimed in the title of the *Slow Homecoming* tetralogy. For example, Handke noted in July 1980, not long after he had completed corrections to the final page proofs for *The Lesson*, "I have become a writer through and through because I slow down through writing (differently than most such writers)."[12] Since its inception, Handke has drawn his note-taking into the sphere of his published work in various ways.[13] Beginning with *Das Gewicht der Welt* (*The Weight of the World*, 1977), Handke has published eight so-called journal volumes that present selections of notes in roughly chronological order, translated into standard printed form. Notes from the years 1976–80, which include the period of Handke's intensive engagement with Cézanne and production of *The Lesson*, were published in the second journal volume *Die Geschichte des Bleistifts* (*The Story of the Pencil*, 1982).[14] Offering glimpses of the scene of note-taking, reminders of their manuscript origins, numerous published texts include facsimiles of drawings and/or of whole

---

12. "Ich bin aber durch und durch Schriftsteller, weil ich mich schreibend ver-langsame (anders als die meisten so Schreibenden)" (Notizbuch 25, July 4, 1980, 261).

13. See Jacob Haubenreich, "Packaging Process: Peter Handke's Writing for Sale," in *Consumerism and Prestige: The Materiality of Literature in the Modern Age*, ed. Anthony Enns and Bernhard Metz (London: Anthem, 2022), 43–61.

14. Peter Handke, *Die Geschichte des Bleistifts* (Salzburg: Residenz, 1982).

notebook pages, on the covers and interspersed among the printed leaves. In 2015 a color facsimile edition of an excerpt of a notebook from 1978, which contains notes and drawings Handke recorded while in Alaska, was released, its pages reproduced to scale with a transcription.[15] A 2017 publication titled *Zeichnungen* (*Drawings*) presents drawings from the years 2007–17 extracted from Handke's notebooks, which were also displayed at a gallery exhibition in Berlin; many of these drawings were also reproduced in the most recent journal volume *Vor der Baumschattenwand nachts* (*Before the Treeshadowwall at Night*, 2016), where they are interspersed among verbal notes culled from the same period. And in 2022 an edition of a complete single notebook, titled *Die Zeit und die Räume: Notizbuch 24. April—26. August 1978* (*Time and Spaces: Notebook April 24—August 26, 1978*) was published.[16] Such mediations of Handke's notebooks in printed form gesture to the way the scene of note-taking suffuses Handke's entire published *oeuvre*, such that the process of note-taking cannot be separated from his published texts. Handke's notes do not merely provide "source" material for his texts; it was vital, as I will explore, for Handke to preserve essential elements of those notes throughout the textual generation process; this involved a gradual transformation from the scene of note-taking, via numerous stages, into the printed medium. For this reason, understanding Handke's note-taking practice is crucial for understanding Handke's published work in general.[17]

In this context, *The Lesson of Mont Sainte-Victoire* is a pivotal work. Handke thematizes the challenges of cultivating a new mode of writing oriented toward Cézanne's method of realization, challenges that were largely intermedial in nature. As part of his

---

15. Peter Handke, *Notizbuch: 31. August 1978–18. Oktober 1978* (Frankfurt am Main: Insel, 2015).

16. Peter Handke, *Die Zeit und die Räume: Notizbuch 24. April—26. August 1978*, ed. Ulrich von Bülow, Bernhard Fetz, and Katharina Pektor (Frankfurt am Main: Suhrkamp, 2022).

17. For good overviews of Handke's project of note-taking, see Pektor "'Wartet nur'"; Ulrich von Bülow, "Die Tage, die Bücher, die Stifte: Peter Handkes Journale," in Kastberger, *Peter Handke*, 237–66; and more recently, Marit Heuß's comprehensive study *Peter Handkes Bildpoetik: Notieren, Zeichnen, Erzählen* (Göttingen: Wallstein, 2022).

underlying experiment in perception—an attempt to penetrate through the surfaces of reality and perceive the inner structure and essence of nature—Cézanne would return to his "motifs" over and over, drawing and painting them again and again, producing numerous realizations of his subject.[18] The media technology of the notebook enabled Handke to cultivate a similar habitus: to move through the world slowly, with pen or pencil in hand, observing and recording instantaneously. But whereas for Cézanne each individual painting or drawing constituted a realization of his motif, Handke would somehow have to transfer his process of note-taking by consolidating the numerous viewpoints and insights gathered over hundreds of pages, into a *single* printed book, in order to transmit the lesson he had learned from Cézanne, to preserve it in a way that enabled readers to experience it for themselves. This gave rise to an extended process that stretched across the entirety of note-taking, writing, editing, and proofing the text.

Ultimately Handke came to conceive of Cézanne's realization as a "Ding-Bild-Schrift-Strich-Tanz" (thing-picture-script-stroke-dance): the "things" of nature, interconnected and engaged in a vibrant "dance," were transformed and preserved through the dramatic "stroke" of the painter's hand into a kind of "picture writing" or "picture script."[19] The concept "thing-picture-script-stroke-dance"—which we might grasp as an articulation of Cézanne's "scene of painting"—embraces both the approach to art-making that Handke gleaned from Cézanne, as well as the methods Handke used to analogize it in writing. As I will show, this hyphenated linguistic construct itself evolved step-by-step across the entire production process in conjunction with Handke's own experimental methods; it thus serves as a metonym for the process as a whole. In the four sections of this chapter I consider four interrelated ways

---

18. For a recent discussion of Cézanne's phenomenological project, see Luke Fischer, *The Poet as Phenomenologist: Rilke and the* New Poems (New York: Bloomsbury, 2015). See also Jutta Heinz, "Cézanne-Erlebnisse bei Rainer Maria Rilke und Peter Handke: Ansätze zu einer literarischen Phänomenologie," *Hofmannsthal-Jahrbuch* 21 (2013): 367–89.

19. The German term *Schrift* can be translated as "text," "writing," and "script."

Handke came to approach Cézanne, and that materialized through Handke's note-taking and composition of *The Lesson*: the choreographic, the ontographic, the typographic, and the bibliographic. The first two sections unpack Handke's Cézanne reception as it took place in his notebooks, through extensive investigation of notes, many of which are unpublished. The third and fourth sections examine in detail Handke's method of generating *The Lesson*, which began in his notebooks and extended through multiple typescript versions and sets of galley proofs into the form of the printed book.

Handke's reception of Cézanne has received a tremendous amount of scholarly attention—so much so, in fact, that Marit Heuß explicitly deemphasizes it in her monumental study of Handke's image poetics.[20] Among Heuß's primary objects of study is the "'transformation' of graphic images into linguistic images" in Handke's work;[21] in part, this is also my focus in this chapter. But instead of attending primarily to the notebooks, or to correlations between the notebooks and the printed version of the text, I examine the material-textual processes through which Handke executed this "transformation" across the *longue durée* of the text's production. In the end, I show that Handke's intermedial translation of Cézanne's method of realization amounts to a theory of writing as *Schrift-stellen*, "text-making"—a theory that is not articulated explicitly but instead is *enacted through the process of writing itself*.[22] To grasp this theoretical method, and the ways it remains legible in the published form of *The Lesson*, we must examine Handke's material process as closely as Handke examined Cézanne's.

Dance

The sixth chapter of *The Lesson* is titled "Das Bild der Bilder" ("The Picture of Pictures"): it focuses in large part on Handke's experience

---

20. Heuß, *Handkes Bildpoetik*, 222.
21. Heuß, *Handkes Bildpoetik*, 17.
22. On Cézanne's view of his practice as a theory, see Rolf Günter Renner, *Peter Handke: Erzählwelten-Bilderordnungen* (Stuttgart: Metzler 2020), 131.

of a single painting by Cézanne, *Rochers près des grottes au-dessus du Château-Noir* (1904), which Handke ultimately comes to see as the "picture of pictures," the apotheosis of Cézanne's method of realization. Handke introduces the painting as follows: "It was painted in the last years of his life, after the turn of the century. Like many of his earlier pictures, it depicts rocks and pine trees. The site is named in the title: *Rocks Near the Grottoes Above the Château Noir*. (The Château Noir is an old manor house above the village of Le Tholonet.) It is hard to say exactly what I understood. My strongest feeling at the time was one of 'nearness'" (LMSV 177). Standing before this painting, Handke sensed that he was witnessing something monumental, something he could not yet grasp in words but that registered as a feeling of nearness or proximity. Ultimately, Handke framed the revelatory power of Cézanne's painting as follows: "Has everything really vanished? Didn't it come to me, in those days at the Jeu de Paume, that Cézanne's great thing-image-script-brushstroke-dance, that miracle unique in the history of mankind, will open the world to us mortals for all time? Didn't I recognize those pines and rocks as the picture of pictures . . . ?" (LMSV 179). Handke's understanding of Cézanne's painting as "thing-picture-script-stroke-dance" came together gradually, piece by piece, a process traced over the course of the chapter. Not only does Handke narrate a series of experiences and epiphanies that enabled him to grasp Cézanne's painting in this way; he also represents this process mimetically, allowing the reader to witness the formation of the composite, hyphenated term—and thereby his thought—as it is gradually pieced together through the progression of the narration.

Handke's engagement with Cézanne stretched back over a period of more than two years before the publication of *The Lesson* on September 9, 1980. What drew Handke so profoundly to Cézanne was, in part, the painter's own project of slowness and repetition. On this topic, Handke transcribed a quote from Swiss writer and fellow note-taker Ludwig Hohl: "'slow work, the reluctance to replace with momentum' (L. Hohl on Cézanne)."[23] From his cabin in

---

23. "'das langsame Arbeiten, der Wiederwille, durch Schwung ersetzen zu wollen' (L. Hohl zu Cézanne)" (Notizbuch 22, November 10, 1979, 5–6).

Provence, Cézanne would venture out into the countryside, returning over and over to the same "motifs" but always rendering them differently. As Handke noted in Basel shortly after his first journey along the *route Cézanne*, "Cézanne in the art museum: over the course of decades he hardly changes his motifs and attitudes, only the way of painting."[24] Underlying Cézanne's experiment in painting was an experiment in perception, a project of learning to see *through* the material activity of painting or sketching.[25] Cézanne placed sensory perception at the center of his artistic project in a letter to his son, which Handke noted as follows: "'Because sensory impressions are the foundation of my task, I believe I am impenetrable' (October 15, 1906, to his son; last letter to him)."[26]

By cultivating this mode of perception, Cézanne was able to access a "picture" of the world behind or beneath the superficial appearance of things—a "Bild der Bilder [picture of pictures]" (*LSV* 80) or "Bild *hinter* den Bildern [picture behind the pictures]"[27] —defined by the dynamic interaction and interconnectivity of all things. Handke sensed something of this during his first encounter with Cézanne at the 1978 exhibit, noting, of the painting *La Carriére de Bibémus*, that "the picture began to tremble."[28] In the published version of *Die Lehre*, Handke quoted directly from his notebook—as he does at numerous other points throughout the text—in narrating his fateful experience at the exhibition: "'The picture has begun to tremble,' I jotted down at the time. 'What freedom, to be able to sing someone's praises'" (LMSV 155).[29]

Handke would eventually come to grasp this "trembling" of Cézanne's painting as a kind of "dance." Although "dance" is the last

---

24. "Cézanne im Kunstmuseum: Er ändert im Lauf der Jahrzehnte kaum die Motive und Einstellungen, nur die Malweise" (Notizbuch 21, July 14, 1979, 22).
25. See, for example, Fischer, *Poet as Phenomenologist*, 147.
26. "'Da Sinneseindrücke die Grundlage meiner Sache sind, glaube ich undurchdringlich zu sein' (15. Oktober 1906, an seinen Sohn; letzter Brief an diesen)" (Notizbuch 24, January 1, 1980, 45).
27. Notizbuch 20, May 15, 1979, 59.
28. "Das Bild fängt zu zittern an" (Notizbuch 15, n.d., 24).
29. Interestingly, Heuß overlooks this, stating that there is no evidence of the museum visit in Handke's notebooks, which she characterizes as a "Cézanne-Leerstelle" (*Handkes Bildpoetik*, 208–9).

term of the formulation "thing-picture-script-stroke-dance," it is the first element that he addresses in the chapter. It is at once an element of the five and all-encompassing—the "dance" of all elements at once. As Handke narrates, he did not come to see the dancelike quality in Cézanne's painting directly; rather, this element crystallized for him through an analogous experience of another artwork: namely, a scene from John Ford's film *The Grapes of Wrath* (1940), in which the protagonist, played by Henry Fonda, dances with his own mother. "All those present are dancing to ward off a grave menace: driven from place to place by landlessness, they are defending the bit of soil on which they have finally found a home and refuge [*Bleibe*], from the enemies all around them. Although the dancing is purely a stratagem (while whirling each other about [*sich rundum drehend*], mother, son, and all the rest exchange wily, vigilant looks), it is nevertheless a dance like other dances (and as none before it), a dance of warmth and solidarity [*herzlicher Zusammenhalt*]" (LMSV 177). Driven westward by the Dust Bowl, the migrant farmers hold a dance in their encampment. Local citizens who have burned other squatters' camps hope to incite a riot so that the police can drive the migrants away. The farmers dance, Handke writes, in order ward off this existential threat, to protect their "Bleibe," their place of rest and refuge, transitory though it may be. Handke describes the movement of mother and son dancing together, rotating around each other. Enclosed on the dance floor, individual pairs in this dance move slowly and rhythmically in a circular formation, as if drawn by a centrifugal force around a patch of precious land. The dance, Handke emphasizes, is a communal activity: all those present dance together, cohering in warm solidarity.

In the next paragraph, Handke distills what struck him about his experience of Cézanne's painting while watching this film scene, what it enabled him to comprehend more clearly: "Danger, dance, solidarity, warmth [*Herzlichkeit*]—these were the components of my feeling of 'nearness' as I stood looking at the painting" (LMSV 177). The warmth and solidarity of the farmers, dancing together in celebration and to protect themselves from the danger that threatens them, reminds Handke of the trees and rocks in Cézanne's painting;

these appear to be, not static and isolated, but instead joined together in dynamic, interactive, unifying movement, which he grasped in the moment as a feeling of nearness. Handke goes on to write, "Yes, my feeling of nearness [*Nähegefühl*] was an insight. In the year 1904, when this picture was painted, something irrevocable happened, a cosmic event; and the cosmic event was this picture" (LMSV 178.). In ways to be explored, what transpired through Cézanne's "thing-picture-script-stroke-dance"—an entanglement of things on the canvas that opened the "richness of the world [*das Reich der Welt*]" to the viewer, at a time when humans were becoming increasingly alienated from nature—was for Handke a monumental moment in the history of the world. For this reason, Handke saw Cézanne as "a teacher of mankind"; indeed, as "*the* teacher of mankind in the here and now" (LMSV 176).

In various ways, Handke saw Cézanne's painting as dancelike: the dance of the hand across the surface of the canvas, realizing a dance of things in nature. Traveling the *route Cézanne*, Handke experienced his own movement through the landscape as a kind of dance: "My pace was deliberately slow, as I walked in the whiteness of the mountain. . . . My even gait [*das gleichmäßige Gehen*] became a dance" (LMSV 163–64). Just like Handke discerned a dancelike quality in Cézanne's painting, so too might we grasp Handke's experimental writing as a fundamentally *choreographic* experiment, an experiment in dance-writing: a mode of moving slowly and steadily through the world, engaging with and attuning to the dynamic energy of things, and capturing this, transforming it—through the "choreography" of writing—into text. To convey the "lesson" he learned from Cézanne, to make palpable the vitality and inner unity of the world, Handke would also need to *choreograph* the reading experience, to develop particular textual strategies that would enable the reader, in turn, to see the world anew.

In Cézanne's Footsteps

Prior to and while drafting *The Lesson*, Handke questioned how he might apply Cezanne's teachings: "To transmit the lesson by applying it."³⁰ To do so, he would have to learn to write in an entirely new way: "I must learn to write lightly, <u>fleetingly</u> [*obenhin*]."³¹ Transmitting Cézanne's teachings would require analogizing his method of realization in writing, and numerous notes highlight different facets of how Handke envisioned this project. For example, his aim was not to depict an object "precisely," but instead to capture the "feeling" of it: "While writing, it's not the memory of the object that needs to be precise but instead that of the feeling; the feeling will then amalgamate ~~with the~~ while writing with the object without this: that would no longer be 'precision,' but instead 'realization' (sup.)."³² We see this in the chapter "The Picture of Pictures"—namely, in Handke's attempt to grasp "the feeling 'nearness.'" The emphasis on affect over objective description informs Handke's goal for *The Lesson* in general: "Not an essay, not a treatise: my aim is not ~~to argue~~ᵃⁿ argument, rather the gentle effect [*Nachdruck*] of a narrative."³³ Transmitting the lesson could not be accomplished through explanation; "realizing" in writing would require *imprinting* on the reader, producing a "sanfte Nachdruck" (gentle after-print) through narration—and more specifically, through the medium of print (*Druck*).

In numerous notes Handke reflects on the need to achieve a slow, patient mode of observing and writing through which the underlying interconnectedness and animacy of things could be revealed. He writes, "Peace would come into my writing if I were able, slowly

---

30. "Die Lehre weitergeben, indem ich sie anwende" (Notizbuch 24, September 1, 1980, 60).

31. "Ich muß leichthin schreiben lernen, <u>obenhin</u>" (Notizbuch 24, January 29, 1980, 91). Throughout this book, underlines, strike-throughs, and interlinear additions in quotations and translations of manuscript and typescript texts are, to the degree possible, rendered typographically.

32. "Beim Schreiben muß also nicht die Erinnerung an den Gegenstand genau sein, sondern an das Gefühl; das Gefühl wird sich dann ~~mit dem~~ⁱᵐ Schreiben mit einem Gegenstand ohne dies verbinden: das wäre nicht mehr 'Genauigkeit', sondern 'Realisation' (s.o.)" (Notizbuch 24, February 14, 1980, 107).

33. "Kein Essay, keine Abhandlung: meine Sache ist es nicht ~~zu~~ᵈᵉʳ ~~Beweisen~~, sondern der sanfte Nachdruck einer Erzählung" (Notizbuch 25, March 31, 1980, 99–100).

and carefully, to discern the sub-elements (divisions) of life (everything I have written seems to me to be too hectic; it proceeds too quickly.)"[34] By moving patiently and attentively through the world, the drama of visual perception itself—here the colors of things—would become visible: "<u>Wait</u> until the colors become <u>dramatic</u>, the olive trees and the wood-grey grassy surfaces (walking while waiting, waiting while walking)."[35] As Cézanne "waited" for the forms of nature to reveal themselves, Handke similarly described waiting for *words*, the substrate of his writing, to come to life in a similar way: "wait until all the good words liven ^up."[36]

In attempting to comprehend Cézanne's method, Handke often drew comparisons to other painters.[37] During an early visit to the Jeu de Paume, Handke contrasted the effect of slowness and groundedness achieved by Cézanne to the "lightness" of Impressionist painting: "the lightness is nice, but the lack of earth-heaviness, -toil, -slowness still irritates."[38] Handke envisioned these painterly effects to be produced through a similarly slow, patient, attentive painterly process: "Cézanne could <u>hang</u> onto things ~~with~~ in the power of his doubt . . . others give expression to things <u>too soon</u>, he <u>waits</u> on the time of each thing."[39] By cultivating a practice of slow, patient looking, Cézanne could perceive and capture the vitality of nature and the interconnectedness of all things, which many humans had lost the ability to see. Handke describes this in the following notes taken at the Louvre in Paris, shortly after his first trip to travel the *route Cézanne*: "'La Mer à l'Estaque': the painter sets the world

---

34. "Ruhe käme in mein Schreiben, wenn ich, bedächtig, die Teileinheiten (Einteilungen) des Lebens herausfände (so scheint mir alles, was ich geschrieben habe, zu hektisch; es läuft zu schnell ab)" (Notizbuch 21, July 11, 1979, 37).

35. "<u>Warten</u>, bis die Farben <u>dramatisch</u> werden, der Olivenbäume und der holzgrauen Grasflächen (wartend gehen, gehend warten)" (Notizbuch 23, December 11, 1979, 36).

36. "Warten, bis alle guten Wörter ^auf leben" (Notizbuch 24, December 31, 1979, 42).

37. See also Heuß, *Handkes Bildpoetik*, 249–50.

38. "schön ist die Leichtigkeit, und doch ärgert die fehlende Erdenschwere, -mühsal, -langsamkeit" (Notizbuch 19, February 2, 1979, 27).

39. "Cézanne konnte sich an die Dinge hängen ~~mit~~ in der Kraft seiner Verzweiflung [. . .] die anderen geben den Dingen zu früh Ausdruck, er wartet auf die Zeit jedes Dinges" (Notizbuch 20, July 6, 1979, 133–34).

into movement; tree as rain, air as stone; Cézanne almost always creates <u>the marriage of everything</u> (like the wedding of the trees in the right foreground) [;] 'Chateau Noir': dance and quietude in one: showing and letting-be (also the '5 bathers'); everything strives toward each other."[40] Cézanne did not merely represent the "marriage" and "wedding" of things; instead he actively produced it, "setting the world into motion." Using the same colors and brushwork techniques to paint "tree as rain" and "air as stone," Cézanne proposes the ontological connectedness and continuity of all things, capturing it in the materiality of his painting. In *Le Château Noir*, Handke senses a "dance and quietude in one," a balance of dance-like vitality and stillness. In an ontological sense, Cézanne's painting "shows" (*zeigt*) and "lets be" (*Sein-lassen*), revealing the world and granting being to things.[41] Reminiscent of the "marriage of everything" and "wedding of the trees" in *La Mer à L'Estaque*, Handke notes a gravitational pull of things to each other: "everything strives toward each other."

These dynamics of Cézanne's painting resonate in Handke's description of the dance scene from *The Grapes of Wrath*: "danger, dance, solidarity, warmth—these were the components of my feeling of 'nearness'" (LMSV 177). Many other notes describe a spe-

---

40. "'La Mer à l'Estaque': Der Maler setzt / die Welt in Bewegung; Baum als Regen, / Luft als Stein; Cézanne schafft fast immer / <u>die Hochzeit von allem</u> (wie die Vermählung / der Bäume des rechten Vordergrunds)/'Chateau Noir': Tanz und Ruhe in / einem: Zeigen und Sein-Lassen (auch / die '5 Badenden'); es strebt alles zuein- / ander" (Notizbuch 20, June 30, 1979, 120).

41. On Handke's engagement with Heidegger, see Ulrich von Bülow, "Raum Zeit Sprache: Peter Handke liest Martin Heidegger," in *Peter Handke: Stationen, Orte, Positionen*, ed. Anna Kinder (Berlin: De Gruyter, 2014), 111–40; reproduced (with minor revisions) as "Heidegger-Lektüren," in *Das stehende Jetzt: Die Notizbücher von Peter Handke*, ed. Dietmar Jaegle (Marbach am Neckar: Deutsche Schillergesellschaft, 2018), 85–123. On Handke's Heidegger reception in relation to *The Lesson* specifically, see Ingeborg Hoesterey, "Mit Cézanne auf der Hochebene des Philosophen: Der visuelle und der philosophische Intertext in Handkes *Die Lehre der Sainte-Victoire*," in *Verschlungene Schriftzeichen: Intertextualität von Literatur und Kunst in der Moderne/Postmoderne* (Frankfurt am Main: Athenäum, 1988), 101–29; Jacob Haubenreich, "'My whole being fell silent, and read': Handke's Hölderlin and Heidegger Reception," in *Friedrich Hölderlin's Philosophy of Nature*, ed. Rochelle Tobias (Edinburgh: Edinburgh University Press, 2020), 178–95.

cifically vibrational or dancelike energy emanating from Cézanne's paintings. Handke describes an "eternal vibration of things for C." in comparison to "the heaviness of things" in Modersohn-Becker's still lifes.[42] After traveling the *route Cézanne* for the second time, Handke noted the "dance of freedom in C.'s last pictures."[43] In an earlier note, recalling the "trembling" effect he had first observed of Cézanne's painting *Bibémus* in the 1978 Paris exhibit, Handke directly connected the dancelike vibrational energy emanating from Cézanne's paintings with his method of realization: "And again C.'s pictures tremble in quiet / presence ("represent . . . nature")."[44]

In other notes Handke reflects on how to achieve the "dance and quietude in one" he sensed in Cézanne's painting. Here Handke recorded another quote from Ludwig Hohl on Cézanne: "'yes, the danger of confusing the actual exhilaration with the clarity of language, which alone can enliven . . .' (Nuances and Details) [;] how do I create drama and maintain stillness? (The Lesson of St Victoire)."[45] Hohl noted that his own intoxication or exhilaration must not interfere with the "clarity" of his language, the means of transmitting this enlivening effect to others (that is, to readers). Handke's challenge of achieving a balance of drama and calm is echoed several pages later: "'full power, yes, but without innervation, without exhaustion'—how to achieve that?"[46] Handke directly connects these notions to dance when he describes Hohl as the "the dervish of poetry (L.H.)"[47] and posits such a dance as an essential feature of poetry: "on poetry: does this dervish-ness, this maddish dancing thing also belong, as a means

---

42. "ewiges Schwingen der Dinge bei C."; "die Schwere der Dinge" (Notizbuch 23, December 9, 1979, 26).
43. "der Tanz der Freiheit der letzten Bilder C.'s" (Notizbuch 24, January 7, 1980, 57).
44. "Und wieder zittern die Bilder C.'s in ruhiger / Gegenwart ('representer . . . la nature')" (Notizbuch 20, July 7, 1979, 134).
45. "'Ja, die Gefahr, den eigenen Rausch zu verwechseln mit der Klarheit der Sprache, die allein den andern Belebung bringen kann . . .' (Nuancen und Details) [;] Wie schaffe ich Dramatik und behalte die Ruhe? (Die Lehre der Ste Victoire)" (Notizbuch 24, December 19, 1979, 4).
46. "'volle Kraft, ja, aber ohne Enervation, ohne Erschöpfung'—wie das erreichen?" (Notizbuch 24, December 21, 1979, 12).
47. "der Derwisch der Poesie (L.H.)" (Notizbuch 24, December 20, 1979, 6).

of preserving the quietude that is to be created, and that has already been created (L.H.)."[48] The description of the whirling dance as a "means of preserving" again echoes Handke's description of the dance scene in Ford's *Grapes of Wrath*: mother and son whirling about each other in a dance of warmth and solidarity that serves to protect and defend a place of refuge.

Etymologically, the term "dance" (French *danse,* German *Tanz*) denotes the rhythmic movement of the feet or body; a leaping or hopping motion, including as emotional expression; and trembling or quivering, including the vibrations of inanimate things.[49] Whereas medieval courtly dance involved choreographed steps, the folk dance or farmers' dance was a jumping dance that took place outdoors in the form of a roundel.[50] The verb "dance" can also be used transitively—to "give a dancing motion to" something.[51] Closely related semantically is the notion of choreography, literally "dance writing," derived from the Greek *khoros* (Latin *chorus*)—meaning "dance in a circle," "grasp, enclose," and "rejoice"—and the Greek *graphia* or *graphein*, signifying writing, description, or drawing with lines.[52]

These meanings resonate both in Handke's descriptions of the dance in Ford's *Grapes of Wrath*—the farmers dance together, taking pause to rejoice, encircling and protecting their small patch of land, an expression of warmth or solidarity—as well as in Handke's notes on Cézanne's realization. Cézanne grasped the inner vitality and vibrational energy of things in nature, giving expression to their interconnectivities, by actively "dancing" them in his paintings, unifying them in "Hochzeit" (marriage)" or "Vermählung" (wedding). Such descriptions also echo throughout *The Lesson*: in *Le grand pin*, the twisted tree limbs rise out of the earth and reach into the sky,

---

48. "Zur Poesie: gehört auch dieses Derwisch-hafte, das verrückt-anmutig Tanzende, als Bewahr-Mittel der zu schaffenden, auch schon geschaffenen, Ruhe (L.H.)" (Notizbuch 24, December 20, 1979, 6).
49. "Dance," *Online Etymology Dictionary,* https://www.etymonline.com/word/dance.
50. "Dance," *Online Etymology Dictionary.*
51. "Dance," *Online Etymology Dictionary.*
52. "Choreography," *Online Etymology Dictionary,* https://www.etymonline.com/word/choreography#etymonline_v_11323.

"mak[ing] the empty space around it vibrate" (LMSV 151); the fruits and vessels of Cézanne's still lifes appear as "enchanted things, which in another moment will come to life" (LMSV 179). Handke describes the "celebrated subjects" of Cézanne's late paintings, and landscape forms that come together in "unison" (*LSV* 35). Once again recalling the farmers' dance in *The Grapes of Wrath*, Handke describes the "nameless peasants" as "heroes" of Cézanne's portraits, who enthrone (*thronen*) "an earth-colored ground, which is their land, their country" (LMSV 155; *LSV* 35). Handke even captures the interaction between painter and viewer, coming together not on a dance floor (*Tanzfläche*) but instead on the picture surface: an "experience of a leap, in which two pairs of eyes, separate in time, come together on a picture surface" (*LSV* 36). In a similar way, the surface of the text (*Schriftfläche*) forms a stage on which writer and reader meet, the reader drawn into motion by the dance of characters across the page, and by the slow, rhythmic flow of Handke's prose.[53]

In multiple respects, then, we might view Handke's experiment in writing as a choreographic experiment: the cultivation of a slow, attentive mode of moving through the world and transforming it into writing, a mode grounded at once in the movement of the feet across the earth and the hands across the page. This conceptualization is evoked most explicitly in Handke's description of his "even gait" through the Provençal landscape as a "dance." A lengthier excerpt from the passage is translated here:

> My pace was deliberately slow, as I walked in the whiteness of the mountain.... Freed from all expectation, I was far from ecstasy. My even gait [*das gleichmäßige Gehen*] became a dance. I was an outstretched body, carried by its own steps as on a litter [*Sänfte*]. In this perfect hour the walking dancer, who happened to be me, expressed "extension as a form of existence and the idea of this form of existence," which, according to the philosopher, are one and the same thing, expressed in different ways.

---

53. Compare Morton's description of the medial element of ambient poetics, which is surprisingly apt in this case; namely, that it "reinforce[s] the illusion that the dimension of reading is the same as inscription: that reader and writer inhabit the same dimension, the same place." Timothy Morton, *Ecology without Nature: Rethinking Environmental Aesthetics* (Cambridge, MA: Harvard University Press, 2007), 38.

But the walking dancer expressed them in one and the same way.... The philosopher's work, after all, had been an Ethics.

A photograph shows Cézanne leaning on a heavy cane, carrying his painting materials tied to his back, with the mythical legend: "Setting out for the motif." (LMSV 163–64)

Handke experiences his own body, that of "this walking dancer," as extending outward into the landscape, his steps effortless and unwilled.[54] This image is juxtaposed with a photograph of Cézanne preparing to set out into the same landscape, his painting tools strapped to his back, and leaning on a walking stick—an image reminiscent of a brush or pen with which he will also trace the landscape. But Cézanne and Handke are not the only figures in this passage. Handke quotes from the *Ethics* of Baruch Spinoza, whom Handke refers to several times in *The Lesson* as "the philosopher." Handke's understanding of Cézanne's realizations as "constructions and harmonies parallel to nature" (LMSV 178) that reveal nature's unity and vitality was informed by Handke's reading of Spinoza.[55] For Spinoza, everything in Nature is made of the same substance—in that everything is a "mode" of God/Nature—and bears within it a fundamental animacy, which he described as *natura naturans*, the ceaseless generativity of nature.[56] As Jane Bennett summarizes,

---

54. On Handke's movement through the landscape, compare Honold: "The wanderer follows like a bodily measuring instrument the relief formations of the traversed landscape and draws its irregularities in one-to-one ratio into the rhythm of his own walking." Honold, *Der Erd-Erzähler*, 172.

55. Volker Graf, Ulrich von Bülow, and Georg Schiffleithner all characterize Handke's appropriation of Spinoza as somewhat liberal and unsystematic. Graf writes, "With his quotes, Handke does not take up Spinoza's 'system,' not even the Spinozist meaning of individual quotes; instead he searches for a context within which they can assume relevant meaning today, which is influenced by Spinoza, but not identical with his perspective." Volker Graf, "'Verwandlung und Bergung der Dinge in Gefahr': Peter Handkes Kunstutopie," in *Peter Handke*, ed. Raimund Fellinger (Frankfurt am Main: Suhrkamp, 2004), 300. See also Georg Schiffleithner, "Wege zu Peter Handkes *Die Lehre der Sainte-Victoire*" (MA thesis, University of Vienna, 2012), 14, 42–45; Ulrich von Bülow, "'The Philosopher's Stone?' Peter Handkes Spinoza-Lektüren in den Jahren 1980 and 1983," *Gegenwartsliteratur* 12 (2013): 91–112.

56. Jane Bennett, *Vibrant Matter* (Durham, NC: Duke University Press, 2010), x, 117. On the notion of *natura naturans* for Cézanne and/or Handke, see Fischer, *Poet as Phenomenologist*, 164–65; Kurz, *Bild-Verdichtungen*, 92–97; Ralph Köhnen,

Spinoza ascribes a power, called *conatus*, to everything, suggesting that "conative bodies . . . strive to enhance their power of activity by forming alliances with other bodies," or assemblages of simpler bodies.[57] Citing Deleuze, Bennett writes that "in the case of a complex body or mode, conatus refers to the effort required to maintain the specific relation of 'movement and rest' that obtains between its parts."[58] Deleuze and Guattari, Bennett continues, "put this spin on *natura naturans*: Nature is a 'pure plane of immanence . . . upon which unformed elements and materials dance.'"[59]

These concepts of Spinozist philosophy are reflected in Handke's description of Cézanne's paintings, in which, like conative bodies, "everything strives toward each other." Spinoza's conception of the ontological unity of all things becomes realized on the material level of paint, where things are unified through Cézanne's use of the same materials, colors, and bodily gestures ("tree as rain, air as stone"). The equilibrium of "movement and rest" achieved through conatus recalls the sense "dance and quietude in one" of the *Château Noir* painting.

Handke also indirectly stages a dialogue between Cézanne and Spinoza through the notion of parallelism. The section of the *Ethics* that Handke references in the above quote is the so-called parallelism doctrine (or "2P7 doctrine")—namely, the proposition: "The order and connection of ideas is the same as the order and connection of things." In Handke's view, though, what is at stake for Cézanne is not the relationship between things and ideas but instead the relationship between things and their representation in art. Cézanne's realizations were constructions that were "parallel" to reality, not in the geometrical sense (as two planes that never intersect), but through their sameness: the relationships and interaction of things in/of Cézanne's paintings are *the same as*, and thereby express and capture, the relationships and interaction of things in nature. At the same time—and this, I believe, is equally crucial for

---

"Zwischen Zeichenspiel und Wahrheit/en: Peter Handkes Cezanne-Rezeption," in *Intermedialität: Vom Bild zum Text*, ed. Ulf Bleckmann (Bielefeld: Aisthesis, 1994), 199.

57. Bennett, *Vibrant Matter*, x, 117.
58. Bennett, *Vibrant Matter*, 22.
59. Bennett, *Vibrant Matter*, 117.

Handke's Slow Making 43

comprehending Handke's project—Handke, as "the walking dancer" before the "philosopher's plateau," experiences this parallelism of thought and extension, mind and body: the movements of the mind and the body operating and expressed "in one and the same way," in this perfect, complete hour (*vollkommenen Stunde*).

In the next paragraph, Handke directly connects his "even gait," which "became a dance," to Cézanne's realization, emblematized in the photograph of the painter with walking stick and painting tools setting out for his motifs. At the same time, we can read this passage as a reflection on Handke's own project of *writerly* realization. "The walking dancer" in the text is always 'the *writing* dancer,' the "whiteness of the mountain" evoking the white of the page. Handke's description of his body extending into the landscape ("Der ganz ausgedehnte Körper, der ich war"), interacting with the things of nature as part of them, recalls his description of note-taking as "co-writing [*Mit-Schreiben*] with the daily and nightly happenings."[60] "Freed from all expectation," he traverses the landscape in the same way that his hand traverses the notebook page, a space of "spontaneous recording of aimless perceptions."[61] Indeed, the interconnection of walking and writing is essential to Handke's poetological project; as Honold writes, "Going by foot [*Das Zu-Fuß-Gehen*] and recording in exposed locations [*in exponierter Lage*] remain for him the Ur-forms of a literally *topo-graphic* poesis."[62] The description of feeling "carried by its own steps as on a litter" describes not only Handke's "even gait" but also the automatic nature of writing. Like walking, writing occurs through the coordination of learned manual gestures, the stringing together of choreographed strokes—of the hand guiding the pencil, or the fingers striking the keys—through the seamless coordination of mind and body that leaves a written trace in its wake: dance-writing.

A similar conceptualization of writing underlies contemporary scholarship on the scene of writing. Campe, for instance, defines

---

60. Peter Handke, *Gestern Unterwegs: Aufzeichnungen November 1987 bis Juli 1990* (Salzburg: Jung und Jung, 2005), 5.
61. Handke, *Das Gewicht*, 5.
62. Honold, *Der Erd-Erzähler*, 11.

writing as a "non-stable *ensemble* of language, instrumentality, and gesture."[63] Playing with Roland Barthes's notion of the "engaged" writer, Martin Stingelin considers writing as an interactive dance between the writer and their writing implements: "But what about when the writer is 'engaged' by the surrounding circumstances of his writing, e.g., by the chosen writing implements? 'Engaged' in literal sense, i.e., according to the *Foreign Word Lexicon* both to 'employ' someone as well as 'to invite to dance.' And so again a scene is constituted in that writing in general, the writing tool specifically, employs a writer in its service, by 'inviting him to dance.'"[64] From this perspective, the writer is no longer the director of the scene; rather, the writing instrument, writing as such, takes the writer into its service, inviting the writer to dance.

In such conceptualizations, authorship—the agency of textual production—is dispersed from the human mind and body onto an array of heterogeneous interactants; in other words, an assemblage. The notion of writing as assemblage brings us back to Spinoza's theory of conative bodies and its new materialist reverberations. In fact, Jane Bennett employs a description of a scene of writing—the writing of "this," her own book—as *the* illustrative example in first defining assemblage: "The sentences of this book also emerged from the confederate agency of many striving macro- and microactants: from 'my' memories, intentions, contentions, intestinal bacteria, eyeglasses, and blood sugar, as well as from the plastic computer keyboard, the bird song from the open window, or the air or particulates in the room, to name only a few of the participants. What is at work here on the page is an animal-vegetable-mineral-sonority cluster with a particular degree and duration of power. What is at work here is what Deleuze and Guattari call an assemblage."[65] In the formulation "animal-vegetable-mineral-sonority cluster," the orthographic linking

---

63. Campe, "Writing," 973. On the diversity of ontologically heterogeneous factors that interact in the act of inscription, see Vilém Flusser, "Die Geste des Schreibens," in *Gesten: Versuch einer Phänomenologie* (Düsseldorf: Bollmann 1991), 40.

64. Martin Stingelin, "Schreiben," introduction to *"Mir ekelt vor diesem tintenklecksenden Säkulum": Schreibszenen im Zeitalter der Manuskripte*, ed. Martin Stingelin, Davide Giuriato, and Sandro Zanetti (Munich: Fink, 2004), 13.

65. Bennett, *Vibrant Matter*, 23.

of terms through hyphenation (*Durchkopplung*) visually performs the conceptual interlinking (*Kopplung*) of interactant categories. With the hyphenated formulation "things-picture-script-stroke-dance," Handke similarly grasps Cézanne's realization as dynamic ensemble of interacting elements, through which Cézanne's brush danced across both the ontological boundary between art and world and the mediatic boundary between image and writing. This is what made Cézanne, for Handke, "*the* teacher of mankind in the here and now [*Menschheitslehrer der Jetztzeit*]" (LMSV 176).

Just like the scene of writing can be understood as a kind of dance, the "scene of reading" can be conceived of as an interactive ensemble of language (semantically, structurally, even rhythmically), the materiality and mediality of the text (the typography of the page, the visual, material form of the book), and the gestural, bodily dimensions of reading (the movements of the eyes over the text, the hand turning the page, the affective experience induced by the rhythm of prose).[66] Both the rich, reflective, vividly descriptive nature of Handke's language, as well as the often-described montage-like, somewhat fragmentary quality of *The Lesson*—composed of extensive intertextual references, including self-citations of his own notes and texts—*decelerate* the reading pace: Handke's texts are slow reads by design. As such, they also demand a high degree of *activity* on the part of the reader. Calvin Jones, for example, describes Handke's text as a "collage-like arrangement of disparate parts" that "often seems on the verge of disintegration."[67] The reader, then, becomes an active participant in navigating the pieces: "the textual difficulties resulting from the lack of transitions, rather than excluding readers, actually serve to incorporate them by making their active part in the re-creation of the text a sort of common experience."[68] In this way the reader becomes incorporated into a kind of readerly dance

---

66. On the notion of the "scene of reading," see Irina Hron, Jadwiga Kita-Huber, and Sanna Schulte, eds., *Leseszenen: Poetologie—Geschichte—Medialität* (Heidelberg: Universitätsverlag Winter, 2020).

67. Calvin N. Jones, "Learning to See, to Experience, to Write: Peter Handke's *Die Lehre der Sainte-Victoire* as Narrative," *Germanic Review* (2001): 150.

68. Jones, "Learning to See," 153.

choreographed by the writer; the actual "dance" that takes place, the individual scene of reading, will vary from reader to reader.

Handke's choreography of the reading experience, however, consists not only in the production of structural, semantic textual effects. The collage-like quality of the text, as I will examine in more depth, emerges directly out of Handke's material process of composing the text out of notes. Handke's choreography of the scene of reading, moreover, extends into the typographic form of the page and the material, mediatic form of the book.

But books are not paintings. In attempting to apply Cézanne's method of realization by translating it into his writing, in all its dimensions—narrative, typographic, bibliographic—Handke encountered certain *intermedial* problems. In and through Cézanne's paintings, Handke came to perceive the ontological interconnectedness of things, a truth that Cézanne was able to realize in his art through specific habits and techniques of seeing and depicting. By cultivating a practice of note-taking, Handke trained himself in a Cézannean mode of seeing—slowing down, pausing, taking note—a perceptual attentiveness mediated through certain material practices of inscription. But Handke's notebooks also were not paintings. Whereas Cézanne created a string of realizations of a given motif, resulting in numerous works, Handke would have to convert the Cézannean mode into another medium—to somehow transfer, via other material operations, his own process of perceiving and note-taking into a single printed work. Before examining the techniques that Handke developed to do so in constructing *Die Lehre*, however, it will be useful to look more closely at how Handke understood Cézanne's material techniques themselves.

Thing-Picture

So far I have not addressed one detail of the dance scene in *The Grapes of Wrath*—the "danger" against which the dancers protect their "refuge." Toward the end of the chapter titled "The Picture of Pictures," Handke returned to this notion, describing Cézanne's belief that humanity faced imminent danger: "In a few hundred years, the painter had written from L'Estaque, the whole world would be flattened. He had added: 'But the little that remains is still very dear to the heart and eye.' And thirty years later, he said: 'Things are in a bad way. We shall have to hurry if we want to see anything. Everything is vanishing'" (LMSV 179).

Handke shared Cézanne's sense of urgency about the need to counteract this disappearance of things. Like the dancers encircling their "refuge" (*Bleibe*), Cézanne's realizations could preserve and protect that which remains ("das bleibt") by grasping and transforming it into paint: "That is how I see Cézanne's 'realizations [*Verwirklichungen*] . . . a transformation and sheltering of things endangered" (*LSV* 84). For Handke, the question was at once how Cézanne accomplished this—his material techniques, his use of color, his brushwork, and his deconstruction of perspectival space would emerge as particularly significant—and in turn, how Handke could accomplish something similar in his own work, analogizing Cézanne's methods through media-specific techniques of writing.

Handke understood Cézanne's realization to be, in essence, a mode of *ontography*. In *Alien Phenomenology, or What It's Like to Be a Thing* (2012), Ian Bogost defines ontography as "a general inscriptive strategy" that "[reveals or] uncovers the repleteness of units and their interobjectivity."[69] What Bogost describes as "ontological repleteness" or "the rich variety of beings," Handke calls "the richness of the world [*das Reich der Welt*]" (LMSV 179). A result of his material techniques of painting, Cézanne's "picture[s] of pictures" describe a deeper, truer picture of things and their interrelationships, in which, Handke noted, "everything strives to each other."

Handke thus saw Cézanne's paintings as more than mere depictions (*Abbilder*); rather, they reveal an underlying, truer picture of the interconnectedness of all things: "the others make pictures; Cézanne shows, the sole one!, the pictures behind the pictures (<u>the pictures of pictures</u>), the earth-colors, and he shows one thing in another, one person in another, the people in the things ('la vieille

---

69. Ian Bogost, *Alien Phenomenology, or What It's Like to Be a Thing* (Minneapolis: University of Minnesota Press, 2012), 38.

aus chaplet').">[70] Handke uses the term *Bild* (picture) in two senses: surface image and depth image, artificial image and true image, *Abbild* and *Bild*. Cézanne's painting shows the "pictures behind the pictures," a truer image of things behind their superficial appearances. Consider the following comparison to van Gogh: "van Gogh: reveals [*zeigt*] this ^his landscape; C. reveals this landscape—and reveals, how it is [*wie es ist*], in C.'s pictures there is always a lesson."[71] Whereas van Gogh's painting shows his individual, subjective view, Cézanne's reveals things *as they are*, their underlying being or essence, penetrating the boundary between art(-ifice) and reality: "C. broke through the boundary between picture and reality, revealing the picture."[72] The underlying structure of Cézanne's pictures, the "picture *behind* the pictures," is one of ontological connectedness: "one thing in another, one person in another, the people in the things."

Handke often registered the ontographic nature of Cézanne's realization through comparison to other painters, especially the Impressionists: "with the impressionists it's often picture-appearance [*Erscheinung*], with C.: picture-extraction [*Gewinnung*]."[73] Whereas the Impressionists were concerned with surface perception, Cézanne captures, through extracting or mining—all senses of the German *gewinnen*—a true picture of things, buried deep beneath the surface. Cézanne's perception (*Wahrnehmung*), is thus a literal "truth-taking" (*Wahr-Nehmung*), taking or grasping a hidden truth (*Wahrheit*) and transforming it into paint. This transformation, crucially, remains visible: "the English pictures: the transformation is lacking, or rather: there is only the transformed, without the transformation being experienced, formed ... always only pictures of pictures [*Bilder von*

---

70. "Die anderen machen Bilder; Cézanne zeigt, als einziger!, die Bilder hinter den Bildern (die Bilder der Bilder), die Erdfarben, und er zeigt ein Ding im anderen, einen Menschen im anderen, die Menschen in den Dingen ('la vieille aus chaplet')" (Notizbuch 20, May 15, 1979, 59).

71. "van Gogh: zeigt diese ^seine Landschaft; C. zeigt diese Landschaft—und zeigt, wie es ist, in C.'s Bildern ist immer eine Lehre" (Notizbuch 22, November 10, 1979, 6).

72. "C. hat die Grenze zwischen Bild und Wirklichkeit durchbrochen, zeigend das Bild" (Notizbuch 22, December 27, 1979, 24).

73. "bei den Impressionisten ist es oft Bild-erscheinung, bei C.: Bild -Gewinnung" (Notizbuch 23, December 9, 1979, 31).

Bildern]."⁷⁴ Handke distinguishes the *depiction* of transformed things from Cézanne's *transformation of things* through realization—a transformation that can in turn be experienced by the viewer in the act of viewing. Rather than "Bilder *von* Bildern," Cézanne's realizations are "Bilder *der* Bilder."

Handke conceived of Cézanne's realization in explicitly religious terms.⁷⁵ He recorded an almost mystical experience before Cézanne's *Dans le parc du Château-Noir* and *Aix, Paysage rocheux*: "the complete picture; 'all is one', 'all in one' . . . one can worship such pictures."⁷⁶ In *The Lesson*, Handke compares the things of Cézanne's paintings to reliquaries, containers of presence. In the final section of the chapter, Handke directly compares Cézanne's realization to the transubstantiation during the Catholic mass, describing the communion chalice, containing the host, as another "picture of pictures": "Didn't I, very early in my life, have a 'picture of pictures'? . . . This picture was an object in a receptacle in a large room. The room was the parish church, the object was the chalice with the white wafers, the receptacle was a gilded tabernacle, which opened and closed like a revolving door and was kept in a recess in the altar.—This so-called holy of holies was for me the *reality of realities*" (LMSV 181).⁷⁷ In the Eucharist, the mundane matter of bread and wine is transformed into sacred matter, the living body and blood of Christ. In Cézanne's realizations, the mundane materiality of paint is imbued with the divine vitality of nature. The viewing experience, in turn, becomes an act of communion: "the mass: 'a réalisation'[;] connectedness with things."⁷⁸

After describing the dance scene from *The Grapes of Wrath*, Handke recalls another image that enabled him to grasp a further

---

74. "die englischen Bilder: es fehlt die Verwandlung, oder: es gibt nur das Verwandelte, ohne daß die Verwandlung erlebt, geformt ist . . . immer nur Bilder von Bildern" (Notizbuch 23, December 9, 1979, 31).

75. On Cézanne's religiosity, compare Kurt Badt, *Die Kunst Cézannes* (Munich: Prestel, 1956), 108–19.

76. "das vollkommene Bild; 'alles ist eins', 'alles in eins' . . . solche Bilder kann man anbeten" (Notizbuch 20, May 15, 1979, 59).

77. Translation modified.

78. "die Messe: 'eine réalisation' [;] Die Verbundenheit mit den Dingen" (Notizbuch 23, December 9, 1979, 31).

dimension of his experience before Cézanne's *Rochers près de grottes*: "Once, when Cézanne was asked to explain what he meant by a *motif*, he 'very slowly' joined the outspread fingers of his two hands together, folded, and interlocked them. Reading about this, I remembered that in looking at this picture I had seen the pines and rocks as intertwined letters [*verschungene Schriftzeichen*], their meaning as clear as it was indefinable" (LMSV 178).[79] In considering Cézanne's relationship to his motifs, Handke presents not an explanation, but a visual, bodily image. How might we read this image? We might see the outstretched fingers as capturing the relationship of objects in the world, which appear to be isolated but are actually "fest verschränkt" (firmly entangled). Cézanne's motifs, then, would be sites in which the entanglement of things was particularly palpable. But Cézanne describes not only a state but also a process, an entangling that occurs "very slowly." In turn, we might simultaneously see the clasping hands to capture Cézanne's process, in which the seemingly isolated domains become entangled through Cézanne's "thing-picture-script-stroke-dance," the five elements like the five fingers of each hand.

Cézanne's relationship to things, and the thing-picture relationship enacted through his realizations, was a crucial part of the "lesson" that Handke learned from Cézanne; Handke noted, for example: "from C. learning objectivity above all" and "only in narrating can I get at the real things [*an die wirklichen Sachen herankommen*]."[80] Resonating with his comparison of realization to transubstantiation, Handke envisions a narration with the power to resurrect: "the colors and forms must be resurrected in the narrative."[81] In "applying" Cézanne's realization in his writing, Handke similarly strove to preserve and protect the things of the world: "My subject (like C.'s

---

79. This scene is described by Joachim Gasquet in Paul Cézanne, Joachim Gasquet, and Walter Hess, *Über die Kunst* (Hamburg: Rowohlt, 1957), 8.

80. "von C. vor allem die Sachlichkeit lernen" (Notizbuch 25, March 9, 1980, 23); "Nur im Erzählen kann ich an die wirklichen Sachen herankommen" (Notizbuch 23, December 8, 1979, 26).

81. "In der Erzählung müssen die Farben und Formen wiederauferstehen" (Notizbuch 25, May 15, 1980, 188–89).

subject) would have to wholly strengthen the things of the world / (the peace-things)."⁸²

Techniques of *Wahr-Nehmung*

Handke understood the philosophical, metaphysical, ethical dimensions of the "thing-picture" relationship in Cézanne's painting to be rooted in his material practice. In November 1978 at the Metropolitan Museum of Art (the Met) in New York City—Handke's next encounter with Cézanne after the Paris exhibition several months prior—Handke took notes on numerous features of Cézanne's practice. He noted Cézanne's use of color to effect a unity of things in his paintings: "Cézanne: the houses belong to the landscape, are landscape-colored."⁸³ Handke also noticed Cézanne's gestural method of applying paint: "In the course of the years he brought the colors ever more into the pictures, pressed them into, no longer on as in the beginning ('Oncle Dominic'); the surfaces still remain thick (sheets) [;] the bodies increasingly flat (apples)."⁸⁴ Finally, Handke noticed the unusual edges of objects in Cézanne's paintings: "The edges of the objects for Cézanne were mourning edges."⁸⁵

Handke examined these material features of Cézanne's painting firsthand in museums, but also engaged with art historical scholarship, above all Kurt Badt's *The Art of Cézanne* (*Die Kunst Cézannes*, 1956); he recorded numerous quotes from Badt about "the

---

82. "Mein Subjekt müßte (wie C.'s Subjekt) ganz die Dinge der Welt verstärken / (die Friedensdinge)" (Notizbuch 24, January 1, 1980, 45).
83. "Cézanne: die Häuser gehören zur Landschaft, sind landschaftsfarben" (Notizbuch 18, November 30, 1978, 5).
84. "im Lauf der Jahre trug er die Farben immer mehr in die Bilder hinein, trieb sie hinein, nicht mehr auf wie am Anfang ('Oncle Dominic'); die Flächen bleiben noch dick (Tücher) [;] die Körper werden immer flächiger (Äpfel)" (Notizbuch 18, November 30, 1978, 5). On the materiality of Cézanne's thick strokes, compare Aruna D'Souza, *Cézanne's Bathers: Biography and the Erotics of Paint* (University Park: Pennsylvania State University Press, 2008).
85. "Die Ränder der Objekte bei Cézanne waren Trauerränder" (Notizbuch 18, December 1, 1978, 7).

wisdom of his picture construction."[86] Badt wrote, for example, that like Nicolas Poussin, Cézanne endowed everything with the same sense of weight: "Badt on Poussin: 'He had . . . followed classical antiquity itself, had applied its method of constructing bodies to the picture composition by organizing it such that <u>each supporting part was simultaneously a weighty one</u> (as with C.'s late pictures).'"[87] This effect was generated in part through Cézanne's techniques of spatial construction. Shortly after his second trip to travel the *route Cézanne*, Handke noted: "Badt: C.—<u>end of the ENFILADES</u> [;] C.'s is the <u>art of humans (the fluidity</u> of the air, the human air around the things) . . . 'everything in the middle ground.'"[88] Abandoning linear perspective, an abstract system of spatial organization, Cézanne's painting involved an interrogation of visual perception itself; objects that would be perspectivally isolated into separate planes resolve into elementary forms and color fields that meet and interact on the surface of the canvas.[89] This interaction, achieved in part through Cézanne's spatial construction, lends his paintings a script-like quality:[90] "Then, taught by the canvas itself, I realized that in that historical moment the pines and rocks, on a plain surface but—irreversibly dispelling the spatial illusion!—in colors and forms bound to the actual spot ('above the Chateau Noir'), had become entangled into a coherent picture writing unique in the history of mankind" (LMSV 178, translation modified). Cézanne's deconstruction of perspective produces what is often experienced as a flattening of representational space. This effect is also achieved through Cézanne's material application of

---

86. Notizbuch 24, January 8, 1979, 58.
87. "Badt zu Poussin: 'Er war . . . der klassischen Antike selbst gefolgt, hatte ihre Methode des Körperaufbaus auf die Bildkomposition angewendet, indem er diese so organisierte, <u>daß jeder tragende Teil zugleich ein lastender war</u> (wie bei C.'s späten Bilder)'" (Notizbuch 24, July 1, 1980, 57).
88. "Badt: C.—<u>Ende der RAUMFLUCHTEN</u> [;] C.'s ist die <u>Kunst des Menschen (das Fluidum</u> der Luft, der Menschenluft um die Dinge) . . . 'Alles im Mittelgrund'" (Notizbuch 24, December 27, 1979, 34).
89. Compare Badt, *Die Kunst Cézannes*, 124.
90. On the textual/script-like quality of Cézanne's painting, see also Ralph Köhnen, "Zwischen Zeichenspiel," 189; Kurz, *Bild-Verdichtungen*, 162–63; Badt, *Die Kunst Cézannes*, 130.

paint, as Handke observed in New York: "the surfaces [*Flächen*] still remain thick (sheets) [;] the bodies become increasingly flat [*flächig*] (apples)." As the facture of the painted objects becomes thicker materially, the space they occupy becomes flattened representationally; philosophically, in turn, Cézanne's pictures project what Bogost describes as a "flat ontology," in which all things equally exist.[91]

Handke also saw color as a means through which Cézanne unified and connected things in his paintings. At the Met, Handke had noted that the houses belong to the landscape, indeed are painted in landscape colors. The German *Farbe* signifies not only color, but also paint. The connection of the houses and landscape in Cézanne's painting parallels that of the houses in the Provençal landscape: not only would the building materials (wood, brick, stucco) have been derived from the landscape, from the earth, so too would many of Cézanne's pigments, producing paintings *of* the landscape both representationally and materially. Like his treatment of space, Cézanne's use of color was also informed by his interrogation of visual perception. Consider another comparison to van Gogh: "Are v. Gogh's colors not too obvious; too much: 'the orange bed', 'the yellow window', 'the blue door'? (too much the things already?)."[92] Van Gogh's colors appear too obvious to Handke, as if preselected or predetermined, "zu sehr schon die Dinge" *before* he begins to paint. For Cézanne, by contrast, colors were not merely attributes of things, a painterly means of depicting them; rather, Cézanne actively constructed things out of colors. As Handke noted from Badt, "'He lets things emerge from color forms and formulas and simultaneously makes their connectivity comprehensible' (Badt on C.)."[93] In this way, we can understand Cézanne's realization as a mode of ontography: not representation, but instead de*scription* of things, a

---

91. Bogost, *Alien Phenomenology*, 11.
92. "Sind bei v. Gogh die Farben nicht zu offensichtlich; zu sehr: 'das orange Bett', 'das gelbe Fenster', 'die blaue Tür'? (zu sehr schon die Dinge?)" (Notizbuch 24, December 19, 1979, [IV]).
93. "'Aus farbigen Formen und Formeln läßt er Dinge hervorgehen und macht zugleich ihren Zusammenhang verständlich' (Badt zu C.)" (Notizbuch 23, December 9, 1979, 32).

"picture-script [*Bilderschrift*]" that, in Heideggerian terms, brings things into being.[94]

In Cézanne's *painting of* things, the "edges of objects" were particularly charged sites. In New York, Handke had detected something unusual about these zones, describing them as "mourning edges." A year later, having returned from his second trip to Provence, Handke noted: "'<u>transition</u>'; not '<u>boundary</u>' (Badt) [;] 'the <u>shadow paths</u> bring the separated objects of reality together in unison' [;] by ~~(wanting to)~~ seeing unity, C.'s pictures are philosophic."[95] In Cézanne's paintings, things are not separated by borders; instead they meet and interact at sites of transition or exchange. Instead of creating sharp lines, Cézanne builds up "shadow paths"— what Handke had earlier perceived as "mourning edges"—where objects interact or merge together in the perceptual field. Cézanne interrogated these transition zones intensely with the eye and the brush, capturing the vibration or dynamism experienced in the visual field; this often resulted in a material buildup of paint, rendering these zones thicker than the central surfaces of bodies themselves.

Sichtliche Striche (Visible Strokes)

During his visit to the Met, Handke was struck in particular by Cézanne's gestural technique of pressing (*hineintreiben*) into the material surface. Over the next year and a half, Handke would increasingly come to see Cézanne's stroke-work as a central element of Cézanne's "praxis of the canvas [*Praxis der Leinwand*]" (*LSV* 78). Indeed, as I will explore in the next section, the stroke (*Strich*) would become a pivotal concept in Handke's translation of Cézanne's technique into writing.

---

94. Martin Heidegger, "Die Frage nach der Technik," in *Gesamtausgabe* vol 1, pt. 7 (Frankfurt am Main: Vittorio Klostermann, 2000), 7–36.

95. "'<u>Übergang</u>'; nicht '<u>Grenze</u>' (Badt) [;] 'die <u>Schattenbahnen</u> bringen die getrennten Objekte der Wirklichkeit miteinander in Einklang' [;] indem sie die Einheit sehen ~~(wollen)~~, sind die Bilder C.'s philosophisch" (Notizbuch 23, December 16, 1979, 62).

After his second trip to Provence, Handke took notes on three portraits in Zurich that he would later describe in *The Lesson*—"the painter himself, his wife, and the boy with the red vest" (LMSV 179):

[The one] eye of the boy is as though involuntarily black, used, visible strokes [*sichtliche Striche*], "stroked on" [*zugestrichen*], the one eye of the woman as though "voluntarily black," from the beginning on; the black comes from inside; for the boy as a black arrow from outside; for the others: the brushstrokes <u>follow</u> the thing (body)forms (<u>never for C.!</u>) [Fragonard: Mme Fragonard; nose, cheeks]X C., grasping his people, <u>through painting</u>, <u>defends</u> them x for Ingres, in the surfaces, one does not see the strokes at all; strokes always only then when there are things "like strokes [*wie Striche*]" (hair ornaments on the garments) XX ("driven out") [. . .] his figures are in danger- that's why he <u>raises</u> them, makes them impenetrable.

[Das eine] Auge des Jungen ist wie unfreiwillig schwarz, verwendet, sichtliche Striche, "zugestrichen", das eine Auge der Frau wie "freiwillig schwarz", von Anfang an; das Schwarz kommt von innen; bei den Jungen als ein Schwarzpfeil von außen [;] bei den andern: die Pinselstriche <u>folgen</u> den Ding (Körper)formen (<u>bei C. nie!</u>) [Fragonard: Mme Fragonard; Nase, Wangen]X C., seine Leute angreifend, <u>malend</u>, <u>verteidigt</u> sie x bei Ingres, in den Flächen, sieht man die Striche gar nicht; Striche sind immer nur dann, wenn es Dinge "wie Striche" sind (Haare Ornamente am Gewand) XX ("vertrieben") . . . seine Figuren sind in Gefahr- darum <u>errichtet</u> er sie, macht sie undurchdringlich.[96]

Unlike some painters (Fragonard), who traced the contours of bodies with their brush, Cézanne gradually produced things, such as the eyes of the boy in the red vest, through an accumulation of "visible strokes." For other painters (Ingres), individual strokes are visible only in the service of illusionistic representation—to depict things that are stroke-like in appearance. Cézanne strengthens his "figures in danger" with thick strokes, making them "impenetrable."

Handke took extensive notes on the dynamism and (in)visibility of brushwork during visits to the Louvre and the Jeu de Paume in the spring of 1979, when he first encountered Cézanne's *Rochers près*

---

96. Notizbuch 24, December 21, 1979, 16.

de grottes. Handke noted the "gestures of so many modern pictures,"[97] but contrasted the "lightness" of Impressionist brushwork with Cézanne's effects of slowness and groundedness: "the lightness is nice, but the lack of earth-heaviness, -toil, -slowness still irritates; so often one sees the movement of the stroke."[98] Consider the contrast with van Dyck: "V. Dyck: Man with child; . . . For some pictures one completely forgets that they had once been made."[99] And a note on Poussin from a follow-up visit: "Like on the old pictures (Le jeune Pyrrhus sauvé, Poussin) the brushstrokes are invisible; only some tree leaves are one individual brushstroke."[100] Like Fragonard's strokes in the painting of Madame Fragonard, Poussin's strokes are visible only in the service of illusionistic representation—for instance, to depict the occasional leaf. The visibility or legibility of Cézanne's stroke-work, allowing his process of seeing and painting to remain visible, was essential to the "lesson" Handke learned from Cézanne, as he noted in the following comparison to Picasso: "there is nothing to learn from Picasso; he has something that one does not have (:C.);| ~~artist but~~ artiste (C. is an | artist); his pictures are like processes."[101]

Handke not only described this phenomenon in his notes, he also sketched passages from Cézanne's paintings and drawings in order to grasp Cézanne's gestural technique. In a detail sketch of Cézanne's *Le Pilon du Roi*, Handke overlays multiple pen strokes, pressing deeply into the paper to capture the shadowed area where the mountain ridge meets the sky (figure 1.1). The following page reveals

---

97. "Gestik so vieler Bilder der Moderne (kein 'Schwerfall') [:] Das Weizenfeld von Berttie Morisot" (Notizbuch 19, February 25, 1979, 28).

98. "schön ist die Leichtigkeit, und doch ärgert die fehlende Erdenschwere, -mühsal, -langsamkeit; so oft sieht man die Bewegung des Strichs" (Notizbuch 19, February 25, 1979, 27).

99. "V. Dyck: Mann mit Kind; . . . Bei manchen Bildern vergißt man ganz, daß sie einmal gemacht worden sind" (Notizbuch 19, February 25, 1979, 26).

100. "Wie auf den alten Bildern (Le jeune Pyrrhus sauvé, Poussin) die Pinselstriche unsichtbar sind; nur manche Baumblättern sind ein einzelner Pinselstrich" (Notizbuch 23, December 16, 1979, 63).

101. "Von Picasso ist nichts zu lernen; er hat etwas, was man nicht hat (:C.);| ~~Künstler aber~~ Artist (C. ist ein | Künstler); seine Bilder sind wie Prozesse" (Notizbuch 23, December 17, 1979, 67).

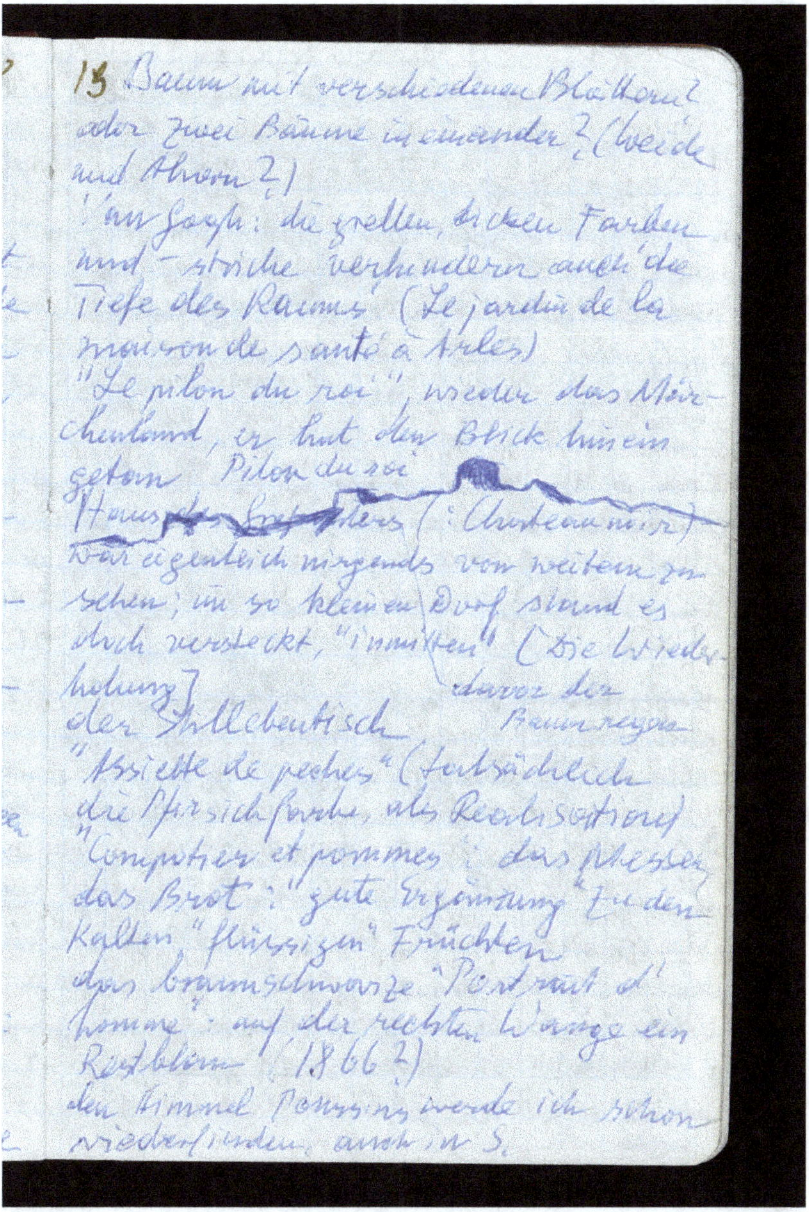
13 Baum mit verschiedenen Blättern? oder zwei Bäume ineinander? (Weide und Ahorn?)
Van Gogh: die grellen, dicken Farben und -striche verhindern auch die Tiefe des Raums (Le jardin de la maison de santé à Arles)
"Le pilon du roi", wieder das Märchenland, er hat den Blick hineingetan
Pilon du roi
Haus (: Château noir) war eigentlich nirgends von weitem zu sehen; im so kleinen Dorf stand es doch versteckt, "inmitten" (Die Wiederholung)
davor der Baumreigen
der Stillebentisch
"Assiette de pêches" (tatsächlich die Pfirsichfarbe, als Realisation)
"Compotier et pommes": das Messer, das Brot: "gute Ergänzung" zu den kalten "flüssigen" Früchten
das braunschwarze "Portrait d'homme": auf der rechten Wange ein Rotblau (1866?)
den Himmel Poussins werde ich schon wiederfinden, auch in S.

Figure 1.1. Peter Handke, "Ohne Titel. 19.12.1979 bis 01.03.1980" (= Notizbuch 24), December 22, 1979, 19. HS.2007.0010.00024. Deutsches Literaturarchiv, Marbach.

two further sketches (figure 1.2). At the top, in a detail sketch of a Saint-Victoire watercolor, Handke renders an area of high contrast where light strikes the surface of the mountain, casting a dark shadow on the rock face behind it. Handke noted the concentration of blue watercolor ("eine viel dunklere Blau-Schliere") against the blank, white space of the paper, as well as Cézanne's use of pencil strokes: "with the pencil: he does not make unilinear contours, instead often multiple, quasi parallel strokes x (crest lines) . . . his pencil strokes were never decisive; at most here and there a watercolor stroke; they were then form-body-certitude-(reassuredness-?) strokes."[102] Below is a sketch of the "mighty stems" (*mächtige Stiele*) of the pears depicted in Cézanne's *Nature morte aux fruits*; here Handke wonders, "Did he always begin to paint from the middle? [*Hat er von der Mitte jeweils angefangen zu malen?*]." In each sketch, Handke zeros in on areas of sharp contrast, zones of "transition" (*Übergang*) where two areas meet, and mimics Cézanne's technique with his pen: the short, compact strokes of the mountain contour, the loose pencil-work of the watercolor sketch, the forceful, high-pressure strokes used to render the pear stems.

Handke put these drawing lessons into practice in his own notebook sketches. After arriving in Salzburg the following week, Handke produced a drawing of the Kapuzinerberg mountain spanning two pages (figure 1.3). Rather than a single outline, Handke uses multiple strokes to build up the contour zone where earth meets sky, pressing intensely into the paper with numerous tiny strokes to render the forested mountainside. Below the sketch, Handke notes: "It is in fact the shadow paths, that ^draw the forms of bodies, a connection of shadow-paths creates <u>places</u> (in the placeless) . . . and in fact I saw the Kappuziner mountain with dock houses in front of it and the river with its swells as a <u>house mountain.</u>"[103]

---

102. "mit dem Bleistift: er macht nicht einlineare Konturen, sondern oft mehrere, quasi parallele Striche x (Gipfellinien) . . . seine Bleistiftstriche waren nie eindeutig; höchstens dann hier und da ein Aquarell-Strich; es waren dann Gestalt-Körper-Gewißheits-(Vergewisserungs -?) Striche" (Notizbuch 24, December 22, 1979, 20).

103. "Es sind tatsächlich die Schattenbahnen, die die Gestalt der Körper ^zeichnen, eine Verbindung von Schatten-bahnen schafft <u>Orte</u> (im Ortlosen). . . . Und

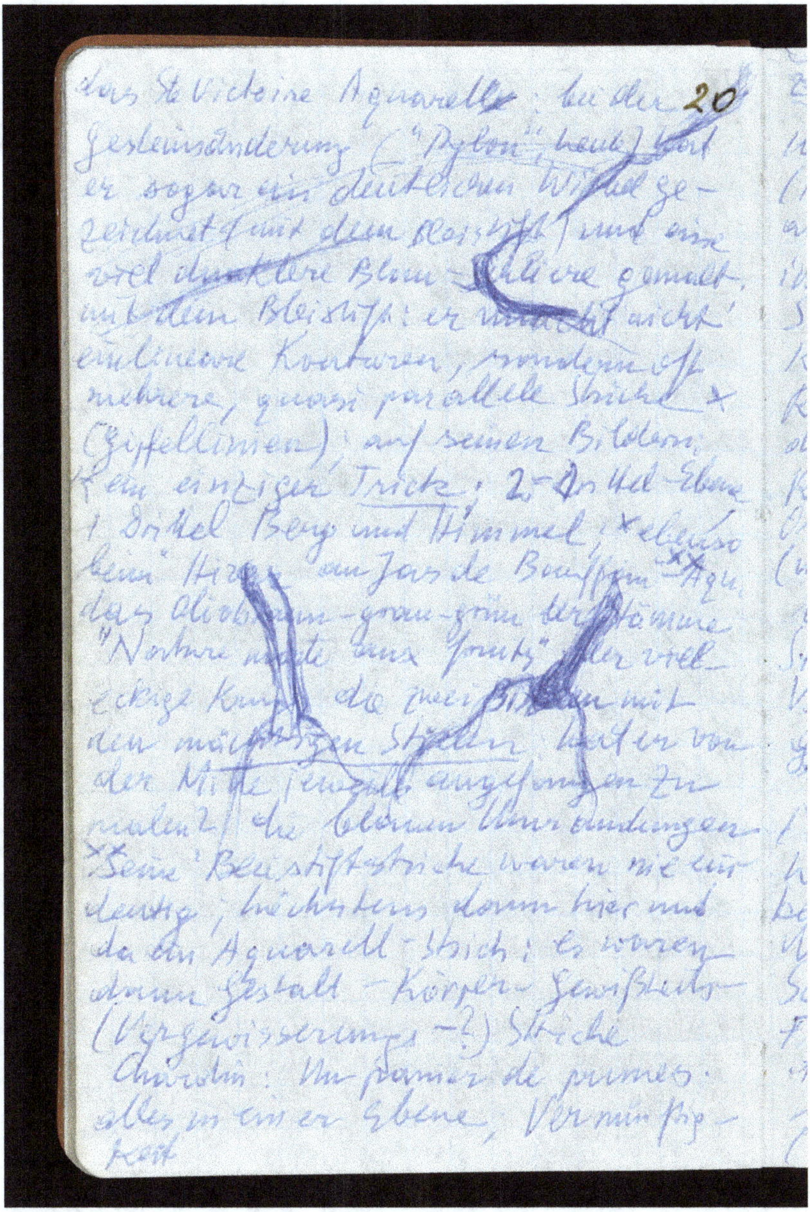

Figure 1.2. Peter Handke, "Ohne Titel. 19.12.1979 bis 01.03.1980" (= Notizbuch 24), December 22, 1979, 20. HS.2007.0010.00024. Deutsches Literaturarchiv, Marbach.

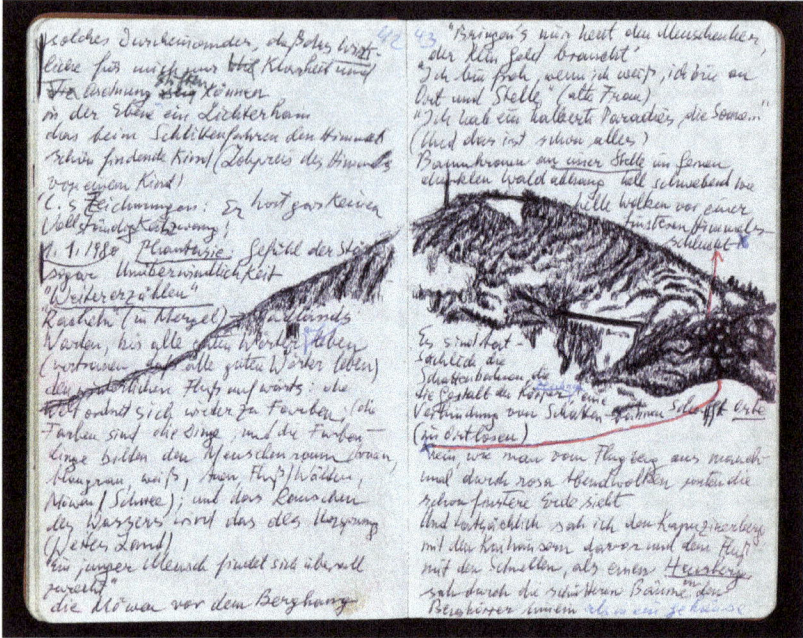

Figure 1.3. Peter Handke, "Ohne Titel. 19.12.1979 bis 01.03.1980" (= Notizbuch 24), January 1, 1980, 42–43. HS.2007.0010.00024. Deutsches Literaturarchiv, Marbach.

It is through these *material* techniques that Cézanne's paintings are "philosophical": they offer a particular view of the ontology of things, one that for Handke was informed by Spinoza and Heidegger, but which also resonates with Ian Bogost's "alien phenomenology." This ontology of things is proposed, indeed produced, through an *ontographic* mode of painting, a mode of painting that does not merely depict or reproduce things, as *Abbild*, but instead pictures the underlying unity of things and their interconnections, preserving and protecting them, as Handke saw it, by transforming them into art.

In the first two sections of this chapter I have focused on Handke's notebooks and the "lesson" as it appeared to Handke in paint.

---

tatsächlich sah ich den Kapuzinerberg mit den Kaihäusern davor und dem Fluß mit den Schwellen, als einen Hausberg" (Notizbuch 24, January 1, 1980, 43).

But while Handke could note down these media-specific techniques in his notebooks, how to translate Cézanne's mode into writing through the techniques of *textual* production was another matter.

Stroke

> Do I not need to bring the <u>gesture</u> of writing
> into every work? (:painting) [continuity]
>
> Muß ich nicht die <u>Geste</u> des Schreibens in jede
> Arbeit mithineinnehmen? (: Malerei) [Kontinuität][104]

How exactly did Handke translate his insights into Cézanne's process, as it materialized on his notebook pages, into the generation of *The Lesson*? Cézanne's realization can be thought to have enacted a certain theory or philosophy of art.[105] Similarly, Handke's process of generating *The Lesson*—a process that unfolded through multiple drafts and rounds of page proofs—enacted a specific theory of writing, reflecting what he had learned from Cézanne, but using the materials and procedures of textual production. Examining the different versions of the in-process text, in turn, reveals something of how Handke was thinking about and attempting to implement a Cézannean mode as a *writerly* method rather than a painterly one.

More than any other material feature of Cézanne's painting, it was Cézanne's brushwork, his gestural method of applying paint, that most struck Handke. Indeed, all of the features discussed thus far—physical and metaphysical, material and spiritual—emerged directly out of Cézanne's brushwork. Handke writes in the chapter "The Picture of Pictures" that "Cézanne's rocks and trees were more than such written symbols [*Schriftzeichen*]; more than pure forms without earthly traces—in addition, they were woven into incantations by the dramatic *stroke* (and dashes) of the painter's hand. At first my only thought was: 'So near!' Now they seem to me related

---

104. Notizbuch 24, March 2, 1980, 49.
105. Renner, *Peter Handke*, 131.

to the first cave paintings.—They were things, they were images, they were script; they were strokes—and all these were in harmony" (LMSV 178).[106] In Cézanne's paintings, we will recall, things were not "placed" into an illusionary three-dimensional space; instead they were laid onto the same plane, onto the surface of the canvas, evoking the placement of written signs on the two-dimensional surface of the page. More than this, however, the nature of Cézanne's brushwork appeared to Handke to bring the things of his paintings into dynamic interaction, making them commune together in solidarity in a way that registered as a feeling of proximity. The description of trees and boulders becoming bound together, entangled into invocations or incantations, evokes the Eucharistic ceremony, where individual supplicants become bound together in communion. Like the Words of Consecration pronounced by the priest, which initiate the transubstantiation of bread and wine into the body and blood of Christ, Cézanne's stroke effects a kind of transubstantiation—a realization—of worldly things into painted things.

Cézanne's stroke was pivotal for Handke not only in these metaphysical dimensions, but also in a much more material way. The German term *Strich*, like the English term "stroke," denotes both an action and a thing, a physical gesture and a material trace. Through the gesture of the stroke, moreover, painting, drawing, and writing are unified: the stroke of the brush, of the pencil or pen, of the typewriter keys. To understand how Handke "applied" Cézanne's method of realization, we must examine Handke's writing on the same level: the "*Strich* (und dem Gestrichel) der *Schreiber*hand"—the stroke and the dashes of the writer's hand. In various and complex ways, as I will explore, Handke approximated and analogized Cézanne's painterly stroke technique in composing *The Lesson*. To see how he did this, we must look closely at the earlier versions of the text. In the published version, traces of this process remain in the narrative and syntactic "texture" of the text—which is often described as being somewhat fragmentary or montage-like—in ways that might be thought to resemble the facture of Cézanne's paintings, built up out of individual, visible strokes.

---

106. Translation modified.

Handke also analogized Cézanne's stroke technique in the visual, *typographic* form of the text—most prominently in the punctuation, which includes various kinds of typographic strokes.

In what follows, I show how Handke translated Cézanne's painterly stroke technique into a writerly stroke technique by examining the generation of the chapter "The Picture of Pictures." After first returning to the earliest notes on the painting *Rochers près de grottes* in Handke's notebooks, I trace the production of the chapter, through its numerous typescript and typeset versions, to see how Handke ultimately arrived at the final version of the text, and particularly the composite term "thing-picture-script-stroke-dance" as itself a patchwork of "strokes."

Schriftliche Striche (Written Strokes)

During his first encounter with Cézanne's *Rochers prè des grottes* in the Jeu de Paume museum, Handke recorded the following notes: "'Rochers près de grottes au-dessus de Chateau-Noir' (1904): having dreamed oneself into the landscape; its forms; so near (seems to me the best picture in the whole Jeu de Paume): the landscape is already distant and still there; and afterward almost only the abstract remains, without the glorious anguish of attraction; (and before it was still too much depiction [*zu sehr Abbild*]?) somber, hefty masterwork [one still sees the blue behind the trees] (and yet not too much sky for the earth)."[107] Handke was clearly struck by the painting, describing it as "the best picture" and a "somber, heavy masterwork." Two small words—"so near"—record his initial experience; in *The Lesson* he attempts to reconstruct "the feeling of nearness," even quoting verbatim from the notebook: "At first my

---

107. "'Rochers près de grottes au-dessus / de Chateau-Noir' (1904): sich eingeträumt / in die Landschaft, deren Formen; so nah / (scheint mir das beste Bild im ganzen / Jeu de Paume): die Landschaft ist / schon weg und noch da; und nachher / gibt es fast nur noch das Abstrakte, / ohne der glorreichen Schmerz der / Attraktion (und vorher war es noch zu / sehr Abbild?) düsteres, heftiges Meister- / werk [noch sieht man das Blau hinten / den Bäumen] (und doch nicht zu viel / Himmel für die Erde)" (Notizbuch 19, February 25, 1979, 28).

only thought was: 'So near!' Now they seem to me related to the first cave paintings" (LMSV 178).

Handke viewed *Rochers* a second time in late June 1979, just before his first trip to the *route Cézanne*, taking notes on this and other paintings: "'Pont de Maincy': the moment in which the world FINALLY closes up (C. paints this permanence-moment); nature BOWS down, and becomes rich; the world gives itself back to the painter (and after that to the viewer)—until there are (before nature) only pictures (as written symbols (Rochers prés de grottes . . .)."[108] In *Pont de Maincy*, Cézanne captures a moment of permanence, in which the world bows down, presenting itself to the painter, and in turn the viewer, in its fullness; in *The Lesson*, Handke will write that Cézanne's painting "permanently held open the richness of the world [*das Reich der Welt*]" (*LSV* 79). What are revealed, what remain, are "pictures (as written symbols) [*Bilder (als Schriftzeichen)*]"; Handke connects this directly to *Rochers près de grottes* as well, placing the title in parentheses.

Though the chapter "The Picture of Pictures" focuses on a single work, Handke's reading of it was informed by encounters with numerous other paintings, including other paintings of the Château-Noir. At the National Gallery London in May 1979, Handke noted: "'Dans le parc du Chateau-Noir': the complete picture; 'all in one', 'all is one'ˣ just as for 'Aix, Paysage rocheux'-rocks, houses, hills, wing-tree x again spot sky belongs to the forest body; such pictures one can worship (they also have <u>the necessary emptiness</u>; they are pictures <u>of my home</u> (which wait for me, in emptiness) the others make pictures; Cézanne reveals, as the sole one!, the pictures behind the pictures (<u>the pictures of pictures</u>)."[109] Handke notes the effect

---

108. "'Pont de Maincy': Der Moment, da sich / die Welt ENDLICH zusammenschließt (diesen / Dauer-Moment malt C.); die Natur / BIEGT sich, und wird reich; die Welt / gibt sich dem Maler (und danach dem / Betrachter) zurück—bis es nur / (vor der Natur) die Bilder gibt (als / Schriftzeichen (Rochers prés de grottes . . .)" (Notizbuch 20, June 28, 1979, 118–19).

109. "'<u>Dans le parc du Chateau-Noir</u>': das vollkommene Bild; 'alles ist eins', 'alles in eins'ˣ ebenso wie 'Aix, Paysage rocheux' -Felsen, Häuser, Hügel, Flügelbaum x wieder Fleck Himmel zum Waldkörper gehört; solche Bilder kann man anbeten (sie haben auch <u>die nötige</u> Leere; es sind die Bilder <u>meiner Heimat,</u> (die auf mich

of unity and completeness in *Dans le parc du Château-Noir* (1900–1904), comparing it to that of *Aix, Paysage rocheux* (1890–92) at the Tate Gallery. Handke observed a sacred quality of Cézanne's painting—"one can worship such pictures"—that is echoed in his comparison of realization to transubstantiation in *The Lesson*. It was also here that Handke first formulated the notion "picture of pictures."

To compose the first version of the text, Handke paged back through his notes of the previous year and a half, gathering and incorporating into the typescript version. In the process, Handke's notebook also served as a place to collect notes and experiment with formulations. On the pages in figures 1.4 and 1.5, Handke plays with a number of key formulations for the chapter "The Picture of Pictures" (figures 1.4 and 1.5):

C.'s <u>picture-writing</u>, thing-script-pictures
<u>Script-picture</u>
Forest + rocks: no more <u>Illusion</u> (of
space)
THE PICTURE OF PICTURES
. . .
as letter: heart-joy
face, thing of fantasy
not just written characters, more a
human stroke, dashes
picture of pictures of a thing: script
picture of pictures <u>many things</u>
dance, danger, heart-joy
accessories, tabernacle, gold,
transformation, parallelism, the
tabernacle was a holy thing
<u>with</u> the chalice, the d[oor] opened
itself up and turned itself away, with
the chalice in it, secret of
faith, accessory, not kneeling

---

wartet, in Leere) [;] Die anderen machen Bilder; Cézanne zeigt, als einziger!, die Bilder hinter den Bildern (<u>die Bilder der Bilder</u>)" (Notizbuch 20, May 15, 1979, 59).

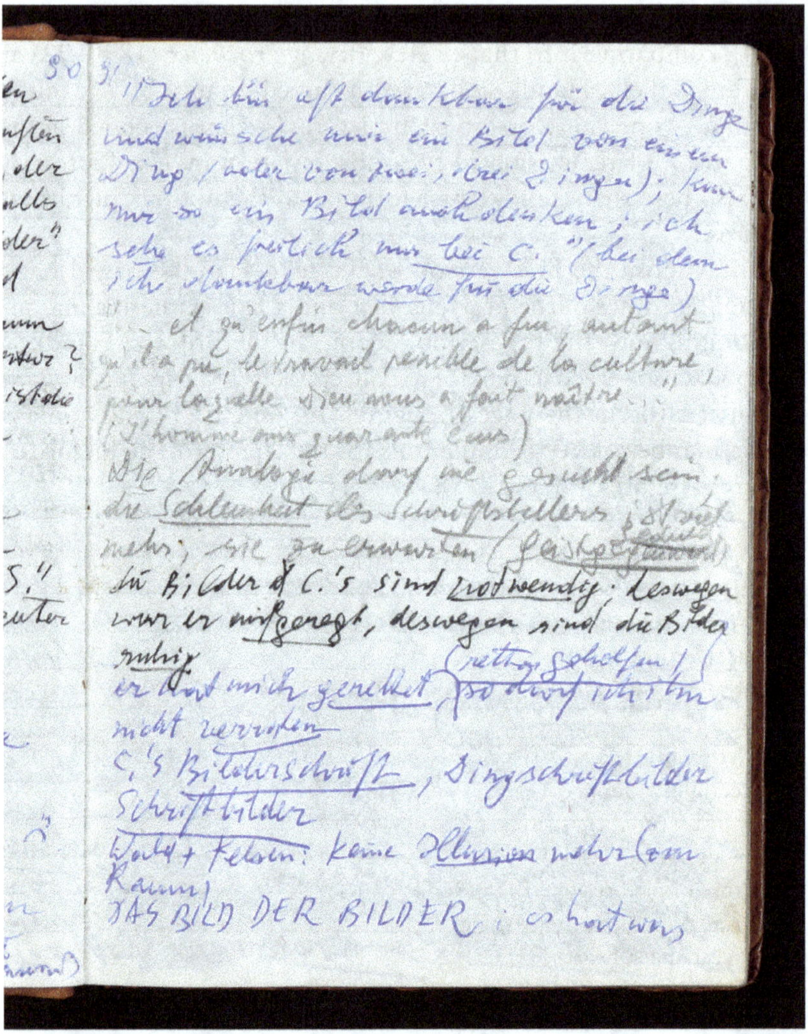

Figure 1.4. Peter Handke, "Die Lehre der Sainte-Victoire; Kindergeschichte; Die Geschichte des Bleistifts; Bleistiftgeschichte, 02.03.1980 bis 22.01.1981" (= Notizbuch 25), March 29, 1980, 91. HS.2007.0010.00025. Deutsches Literaturarchiv, Marbach.

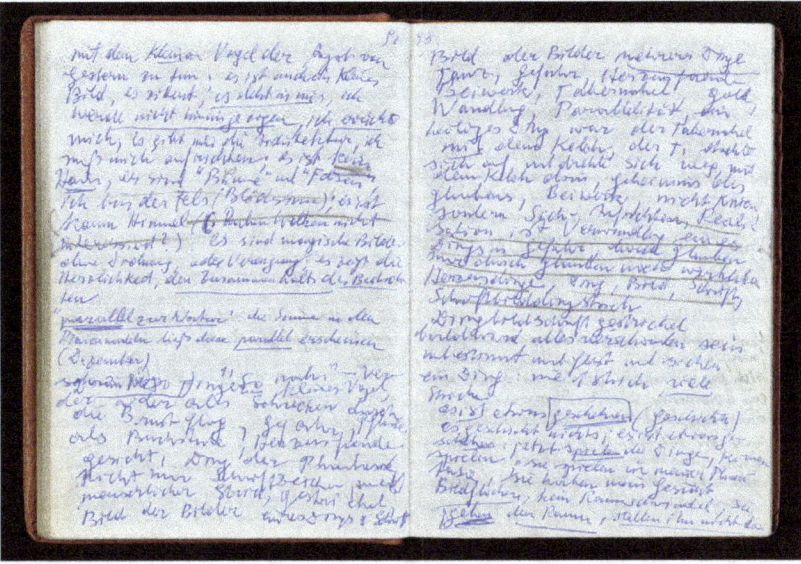

Figure 1.5. Peter Handke, "Die Lehre der Sainte-Victoire; Kindergeschichte; Die Geschichte des Bleistifts; Bleistiftgeschichte, 02.03.1980 bis 22.01.1981" (= Notizbuch 25), March 29, 1980, 92–93. HS.2007.0010.00025. Deutsches Literaturarchiv, Marbach.

rather sitting upright, <u>Realization is transformation of a thing in danger, through faith only through faith still real heart-things, thing, picture, script</u> script-picture-thing-stroke thing-picture-stroke-dashing soon everything will have disappeared indefinite and secure and safe one thing: never 1 stroke, <u>many</u> strokes . . .

C.'s <u>Bilderschrift</u>, Dingschriftbilder <u>Schriftbilder</u>
Wald + Felsen: keine <u>Illusion</u> mehr (von Raum)
DAS BILD DER BILDER

> ...
> als Buchstabe: Herzensfreude
> Gesicht, Ding der Phantasie
> nicht nur Schriftzeichen, mehr
> menschlicher Strich, Gestrichel
> Bild der Bilder eines Dings: Schrift
> Bild der Bilder <u>mehrere Dinge</u>
> Tanz, Gefahr, Herzensfreude
> Beiwerk, Tabernakel, Gold,
> Wandlung, Parallelität, ein
> heiliges Ding war der Tabernakel
> <u>mit</u> dem Kelch, der T. drehte
> sich auf und drehte sich weg, mit
> dem Kelch darin, Geheimnis des
> Glaubens, Beiwerk, nicht Knien
> sondern Sich- Aufrichten, <u>Realisation ist Verwandlung eines Dings in Gefahr, durch Glauben nur durch Glauben noch wirklich Herzensdinge, Ding, Bild, Schrift, Schriftbilddingstrich</u>
> Dingbildschriftgestrichel
> bald wind alles verschwunden sein
> unbestimmt und fest und sicher
> ein Ding: nie 1 Strich, <u>viele</u>
> Striche.... [110]

On these pages Handke notes down words and concepts that he will incorporate into the text, concerning in this instance Cézanne's deconstruction of perspectival space, the notion of the "picture of pictures," the metaphor of the communion chalice, and the definition of realization as "transformation of a thing in danger." But this is more than a mere outline. We see Handke experimenting with a mode of thinking and construction informed by Cézanne's mode of building up representations out of individual "small strokes." This is clearest in the combinations of "picture," "script," "thing," and so forth—"thingscriptpicture,"

---

110. Notizbuch 25, March 28, 1980, 91–93.

"scriptpicturethingstroke," "thingpicturestrokedashes"—where Handke attempts to grasp Cézanne's realization with a composite concept that lays bare Cézanne's mode. The small format of the notebook pages, which do not lend themselves to the elaboration of lengthy and complex linguistic formulations, is itself conducive for fostering this mode of formulating. As we will see, Handke draws this patchwork mode into his process of drafting and editing *The Lesson* across its multiple iterations.

While correspondences between notes and the printed text make it clear that Handke drew explicitly from his notes in constructing *The Lesson*, there is also material evidence for Handke's process of gathering from earlier notes.[111] For example, on the notebook page on which Handke first formulated the notion "picture of pictures," in May 1979, the phrase is underlined, *not* in the black ink Handke used to pen these notes at the time, but instead in *blue* ink, the color he was using to compile notes and sketch formulations for the first version in March 1980 (figure 1.6).

Version 1

In examining the first version, we see traces of Handke's initial attempts to incorporate notes into coherent text, joining them together by embedding and elaborating them into connected clauses and sentences.[112] The first version of the text is a single-spaced typescript with very narrow margins; there are no paragraph, section, or chapter breaks, and chapter titles were added by hand. Despite the limited space for corrections, Handke edited the version heavily, squeezing typewritten and handwritten additions carefully into the margins and between lines. As a result, the text is visually dense, such that deciphering certain passages can be difficult—all the more

---

111. Compare Pektor, "Wartet nur," 304–7.
112. In discussing the text versions, I use the numbering system proposed in Handke*online*. https://handkeonline.onb.ac.at/node/122/material (8.3.2022). Schiffleithner ("Wege," 89–102) also offers descriptions of the typescript versions housed at the Literaturarchiv der Österreichischen Nationalbibliothek, but not those from the Suhrkamp Verlag archive, which is now housed at the DLA Marbach.

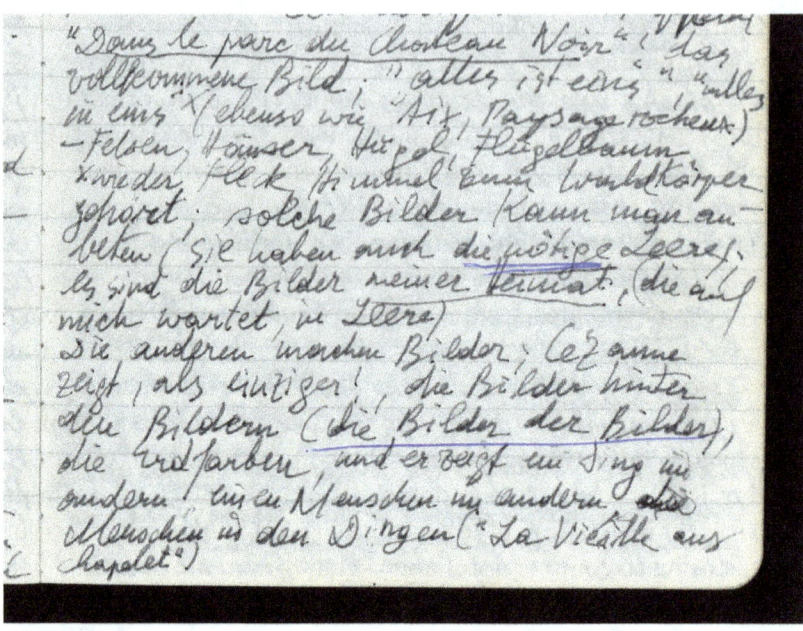

Figure 1.6. Peter Handke, "Langsame Heimkehr (Eine Geschichte unter Freunden); Die Wiederholung Notizbuch, 26.04.1979 bis 08.07.1979" (= Notizbuch 20), May 15, 1979, 59. HS.2007.0010.00020. Deutsches Literaturarchiv, Marbach.

so because the only extant version is a photocopy, produced by Handke himself.[113]

Figure 1.7 shows a passage from the chapter "The Picture of Pictures" containing various combinations of "picture," "script," and "thing." After quoting Cézanne's definition of his motifs as "Konstruktionen Harmonien und Harmonien parallel zur Natur" (constructions and harmonies parallel to nature), Handke types "Bild, Schrift" (picture, script), then strikes these words out; "Dinge" (things) is inserted before "Kiefern und Felsen" (pines and rocks) on the same line. Handke originally described these elements as "nebeneinandergestellt"

---

113. Christoph Kepplinger-Prinz and Katharina Pektor, "Die Lehre der Sainte-Victoire (Textfassung 1)," Handke*online*, https://handkeonline.onb.ac.at/node/873.

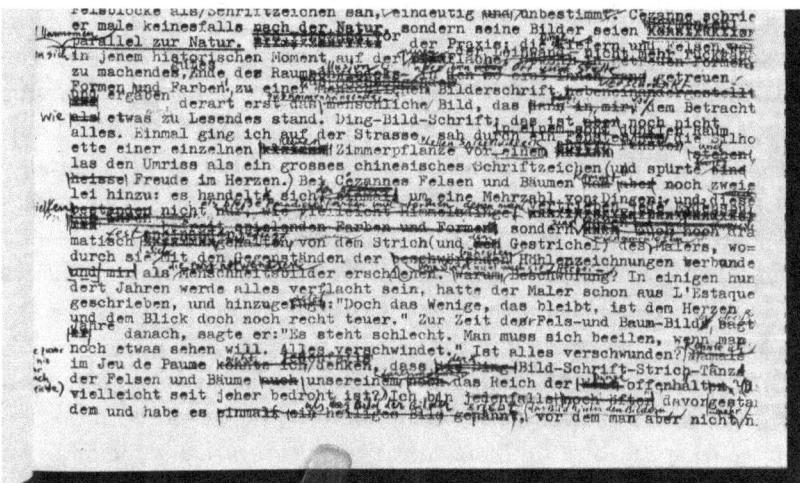

Figure 1.7. Peter Handke, first version of *Die Lehre der Sainte-Victoire*, 16. ÖLA SPH/LW/W19. Literaturarchiv der Österreichischen Nationalbibliothek, Vienna.

(juxtaposed, placed side by side), but struck this term and replaced it with "verschränkt" (entangled). Scanning the page, the eye tracks various appearances and combinations of "Bild" (picture), "Schrift" (script), and "Ding" (thing), which ultimately give rise to the pluralized form "Ding-Bild-Schrift-Strich-Tänze" (thing-picture-script-stroke-dances). "Ding" (thing) is struck from the formulation and moved one line below ("Reich der W̶e̶l̶t̶" [richness of the world] becomes "Reich der Dinge" [richness of things]), and the pluralization of "Tänze" (dances) is canceled, yielding "Bild-Schrift-Strich-Tanz" (picture-script-stroke-dance). Among other differences from the printed version, Handke originally described Cézanne's painting as "das heilige Bild" (the holy picture) before replacing it with "das Bild der Bilder" (the picture of pictures), even adding the formulation "das Bild hintern den Bildern" (the picture behind the pictures) that he had noted in the National Gallery.[114]

---

114. The latter formulation was eliminated in the second version.

Handke's method of piecing terms together into conceptual composites, which we observed in the notebooks, extends into the drafting of the text, unfolding across the surface of the page. This mode of thinking, in turn, is transferred into the syntactic and narrative structure of the text. Over the course of the chapter, Handke narrates a process of piecing together an understanding of Cézanne's realization in terms of "thing-picture-script-stroke-dance"—one that is not identical to, but parallels, the process as it unfolds across the multiple versions of the text.

Handke opens his narration of this process as follows: "Today, in my need to communicate my experience after long 'reflection on things seen' [*Bedenken des Gesehenen*] (it would be more accurate to speak of a thinking-storm [*Denksturm*]), a scene in a film comes to mind" (modified LMSV 177). But Handke's "long 'reflection on things seen,'" the journey he took in and with his notebooks, did not conclude only to *then* be represented in writing; rather, it extended into the material construction of the text. The process of *Bedenken des Gesehenen* was thus also, crucially, one of *Be-schreiben des Gesehenen*, de-scription of things seen: of *Kopfarbeit* as *Papierarbeit*, mental-work *as* paper-work.

Version 2(a/c)

The second version of *The Lesson* looks strikingly different from the first. Handke increased the line spacing from single to double, set wider margins, and introduced paragraph, section, and chapter breaks. Visually, the text thus begins to approximate more closely the appearance of the printed text. There is not just one second version, however; there are several variants. Additionally, numerous so-called *Abfallblätter* (waste pages) have been archived; draft pages that Handke abandoned that were recovered (literally from the waste bin) by Hans Widrich, with whom Handke was living in Salzburg while he wrote *The Lesson*. In constructing the draft, Handke also sometimes pasted pieces of corrected text onto the original typescript, which is referred to as version 2a. Before sending version 2a to Siegfried Unseld, editor in chief at Suhrkamp Verlag—"so that I can finally be rid of it" (*damit ich es schon einmal los habe*)[115] —Handke produced a photocopy of it, which he continued to edit in pencil; this palimpsest version is referred to version 2c. A carbon copy of the version 2a, prior to Handke's additional edits, is also extant, referred to as version 2b.

In version 2c, one can distinguish edits made in version 2a (reproduced in photocopy) from subsequent edits introduced in version 2c. Teasing apart these correction layers enables us to see just how fluid certain formulations were during the process of constructing the text. The formulation "Bild-Schrift-Strich-Tanz" (picture-script-stroke-dance) from version 1 appears as "Bild-Schrift-Strich-Tanz-Klang" (picture-script-stroke-dance-sound) in version 2a, and the modifier "gewaltiger" (mighty) was also added. In version 2c, Handke struck out "gewaltiger" and replaced it with "machtvoller" (powerful); he then struck out "machtvoller" (powerful) and moved it down two lines, where it appears as an adverb modifying "dauernd" (lasting) ("unsereinem *machtvoll* dauernd"), and returned "gewaltiger" to the text with a dashed underline (per conventions of editorial markup). Similarly, Handke struck through "zuvor und nie mehr danach geschaffter" (before and never thereafter achieved again) and "der Felsen und Bäume" (the rocks and trees) in version 2c, and then reversed these cancellations with dashed underlines. The formulation "Bild-Schrift-Strich-Tanz" (picture-script-stroke-dance) from version 1 was changed to "Bild-Schrift-Strich-Tanz-Klang" (picture-script-stroke-dance-sound) in version 2a; in version 2c, Handke struck out "Tanz-Klang" (dance-sound) and replaced it with "Einklang" (harmony) yielding "Bild-Schrift-Strich-Einklang" (figure 1.8).

Handke's narration in the chapter proceeds by describing an experience or image and then distilling the insights about Cézanne's painting that he gleaned from it. This too, I suggest, represents an effort to approximate Cézanne's method in writing. After describing something, Handke distills or draws out the key linguistic/conceptual "strokes," enabling them to remain visible. For example, after describing the "Strich (und dem Gestrichel) der Malerhand" (stroke [and the dashes] of the painter's hand) and drawing a

---

115. Peter Handke and Siegfried Unseld, *Der Briefwechsel*, ed. Raimund Fellinger (Frankfurt am Main: Suhrkamp, 2012), 408.

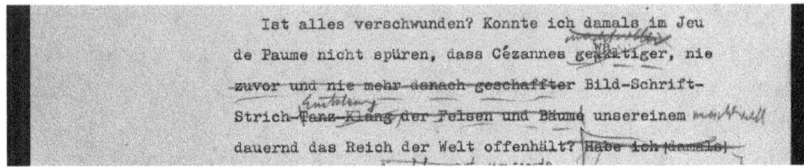

Figure 1.8. Peter Handke, version 2c of *Die Lehre der Sainte Victoire*, 55. ÖLA SPH/LW/W18. Literaturarchiv der Österreichischen Nationalbibliothek, Vienna.

comparison to earliest cave paintings, Handke adds the following by hand: "es waren die <u>Dinge</u>, es waren die <???> Bilder, es war die menschliche Schrift, und es war der Strich" (they were <u>things</u>, they were <???> pictures, it was human script, and it was stroke).

Examining this passage in the typescript version enables us to see how Handke developed this mode of narration, integrating notes and thoughts into coherent text, while at the same time attempting to preserve the brevity and concentratedness of his notes in the expanded text. We can see this by comparing the first two versions: In version 1, notes from the tiny notebook pages are integrated into lengthier clauses and sentences that expand over the spacious surface of the A4 page. In the second version, Handke then pulls back, editing to make the text more concise, even choppier and more fragmentary at times—an effect that ultimately carries over into the printed version.

Not only does the linguistic form of the text shift through Handke's edits to version 2c; Handke's material process of editing also shifts. Given the limited interlinear and marginal space in version 1, Handke had to make strike-throughs and additions relatively neatly, with a controlled hand and small script, for the text to remain legible. In version 2a, the clean copy intended to be read by his editor, the few handwritten edits are also very neatly and legibly inscribed. Handke's pencil edits in version 2c, by contrast, become visually and materially messier; the handwriting is not as neat, the strike-throughs less even. In the excerpt reproduced as figure 1.9, for example, Handke struck through several lines of text (beginning

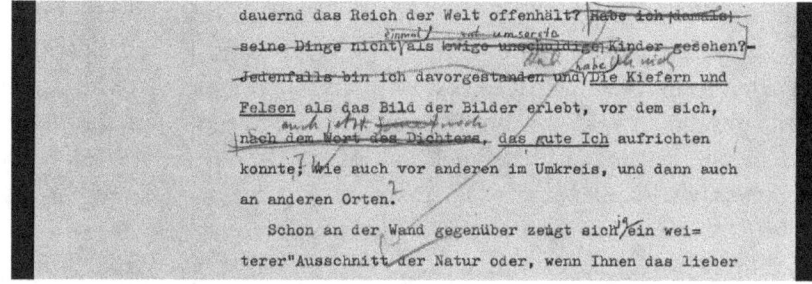

Figure 1.9. Peter Handke, version 2c of *Die Lehre der Sainte Victoire*, 55. ÖLA SPH/LW/W18. Literaturarchiv der Österreichischen Nationalbibliothek, Vienna.

with "Habe ich damals") with relatively quick gestures, and drew an arrow from this the first line down to the next paragraph, indicating a paragraph-level syntactic change (figure 1.9).

These different material editing techniques are engendered, in part, by the different visual form of the typescripts. It has been suggested that Handke used single-spacing in the first version to limit his corrections. This very well could be the case; but Handke nonetheless edited the draft quite extensively. The limited marginal and interlinear space, I would alternatively suggest, was intended to *slow* the writing process, demanding careful pre-formulation before typing and requiring neat strike-throughs and additions and edits for the text to be legible. In this way, Handke pulls the *slowness* of his note-taking into his editing procedure, preserving in the text itself not only the semantic content of the notes but also the process of their making. In version 2a, a clean copy, Handke uses a similarly neat and precise hand. Once he took up the pencil to revise version 2c, the increased interlinear space and wider margins—resembling those of the printed page, but more specifically of the galley proofs, which have even more marginal space for corrections—enabled edits with a much looser hand.

One could argue that none of this is particularly significant. Many writers who used the typewriter similarly typed to the very edges of the paper because changing sheets would disrupt the flow of writing.[116] Moreover, typescript versions of *The Lesson* do not look that different from those of other Handke typescripts from the period, which also had single-spaced first versions and double-spaced second and subsequent versions. But this regularity, I would suggest, is itself significant: it speaks to a defined, routinized method. Each version of the text constituted a new visual, material preparation of it, a different *Schriftbild*. Each revision was a re-vision, a different view of the text, enabling Handke to see and approach it differently. The visual differences between Handke's typescripts, and the material differences in his techniques of editing, become all the more significant when we consider how intensively Handke was grappling with Cézanne's method— one of slow, careful observation and rendering through specific stroke techniques, which he saw as script-like ("picture script" / "written symbols")—and attempting to apply these to his writing. By varying the appearance of the text (the *Schriftbild*, in German), Handke *engineered* different stroke techniques into his generation of the text, quite literally by altering the machine settings of the typewriter: a slower, more precise, more deliberate stroke technique for the production of the first version, a looser, quicker technique for the second.[117] This shift, engineered into Handke's process, also reflects something of the evolution of Cézanne's technique (beginning in the 1880s, Cézanne began using increasingly loose brushwork).[118] Of Cézanne's drawing technique, Handke noted: "C.'s drawing: he has no compulsion for completion at all!"[119] Of a Saint-Victoire watercolor sketch, Handke noted that Cézanne employed "at most here and there a watercolor stroke."[120]

---

116. Catherine Viollet, "Mechanisches Schreiben, Tippräume: Einige Vorbedingungen für eine Semiologie des Typoskripts," trans. Davide Giuriato and Sandro Zanetti, in *"Schreibkugel ist ein Ding Gleich Mir: Von Eisen"—Schreibszenen im Zeitalter der Typoskripte*, ed. Davide Giuriato, Martin Stingelin, and Sandro Zanetti (Munich: Fink, 2005), 36.

117. Compare the description of Sorger's drawing technique in *Slow Homecoming*: "His lines [*Striche*], first almost fussily close together, began to diverge; they were aiming at something beyond physical reality." Peter Handke, *Slow Homecoming*, trans. Ralph Mannheim (New York: New York Review Books, 2009), 74–75.

118. Badt, *Die Kunst Cézannes*, [x].

119. "C.'s Zeichnungen: Er hat gar keinen Vollständigkeitszwang!" (Notizbuch 24, December 31, 1979, 42).

120. "höchstens dann hier und da ein Aquarell-Strich" (Notizbuch 24, December 22, 1979, 20).

Version 3

Handke produced a third typescript version (3a), implementing many of the edits made to version 2c while also introducing many additional changes; this version served as the template for the production of page proofs. The format is similar to that of version 2, double-spaced with wide margins for corrections. A carbon copy prior to further editing exists (version 3b), and numerous *Abfallblätter* were also left in its wake.

Handke was now multiple versions into the process of generating the text; nonetheless, we see him actively wrestling with the composite term that is at the center of his conceptual and methodological engagement with Cézanne. In version 2c, the formulation had settled at "Bild-Schrift-Strich-Einklang"; in version 3a, "Tanz" replaced "Einklang" (yielding "Bild-Schrift-Strich-Tanz"), and "Einklang" was moved up to a preceding paragraph, part of a newly added clause: "und es war das alles im Einklang" (and it was all in harmony). In the text, Handke narrates the process of coming to understand Cézanne's realization in a way that allows the reader to witness the linguistic piecing-together of the composite concept. Though narrated in the past tense, this process of grappling with Cézanne's method extended into the present tense of writing, taking place on the page. Examining Handke's process of editing enables us to trace this narrative—namely, Handke's material-conceptual process of working out the relationship of his own work to Cézanne's process—which is not directly represented in the text but nonetheless is entangled within it.

Galley Proofs

Version 3a served as the copy-text for the production of the first set of galley proofs, which was corrected and followed by two additional rounds of galleys. Here, Handke encountered the text in yet another visual incarnation—type*set* rather than type*script*, and prepared by others' hands. At this stage the visual appearance of the text becomes even more significant: further linguistic changes were made to the proofs, but the majority of edits are orthographic and typographic.[121]

The visual effect of certain orthographic and typographic features is highlighted by errors introduced during typesetting. When the words "Dinge," "Bilder," and "Schrift" were italicized on page 79 of the galleys, the semicolons (*Semikolon* or *Strichpunkte* in German) following them were also italicized (these words were underlined in version 3a; there is no way to italicize on a typewriter) (figure 1.10). The mistakenly italicized semicolons were underlined and annotated with the correction instruction "gerade" (straight). Additionally, the wrong kind of stroke is used following the word "Strich": a hyphen (*Bindestrich*), rather than an em dash (*Gedankenstrich*). The hyphen was canceled with a vertical strike-through, and the correct stroke was drawn in the margin, its length exaggerated for clarity. The word "L'Estaque" is also inappropriately hyphenated: the hyphen (here a *Trennstrich* or "dividing stroke" in German) had been mistakenly placed in the middle of a syllable ("L'Esta-que"). There are two corrections to justification on this page: a bracket around "Einklang" (harmony) instructs the typesetter to make the paragraph break visible, and the markup between the words "Zeit der Fels-und-Baum-Bilder, dreißig" (time of the rock-and-tree-pictures, thirty) indicates that the excessive, visually distracting space between words needs to be eliminated. While these corrections may seem insignificant, certain annotations indicate just how important the typographical appearance of the text was for Handke: an emphatic justification correction in the third and final set of proofs reads "*Absatz unbedingt!!!*" (paragraph necessary!!!) (figure 1.11).[122]

When corrections to the first set of proofs were implemented in a second set, new typographical errors were introduced. Handke had

---

121. Handke's edits to the proofs were communicated by telephone to Handke's reader, Raimund Fellinger (who later was editor in chief of Suhrkamp Verlag), who implemented them by hand (in dark-blue ink). One also finds more routine typographical edits implemented by a corrector (in light-blue ink). Christoph Kepplinger-Prinz, "Die Lehre der Sainte-Victoire: Druckfahnen 1. Lauf, Exemplar von Raimund Fellinger, 71 Blatt, [23.05.1980 bis] 27.05.1980," Handke*online*, https://handkeonline.onb.ac.at/node/2152.

122. This correction was not implemented in the published version.

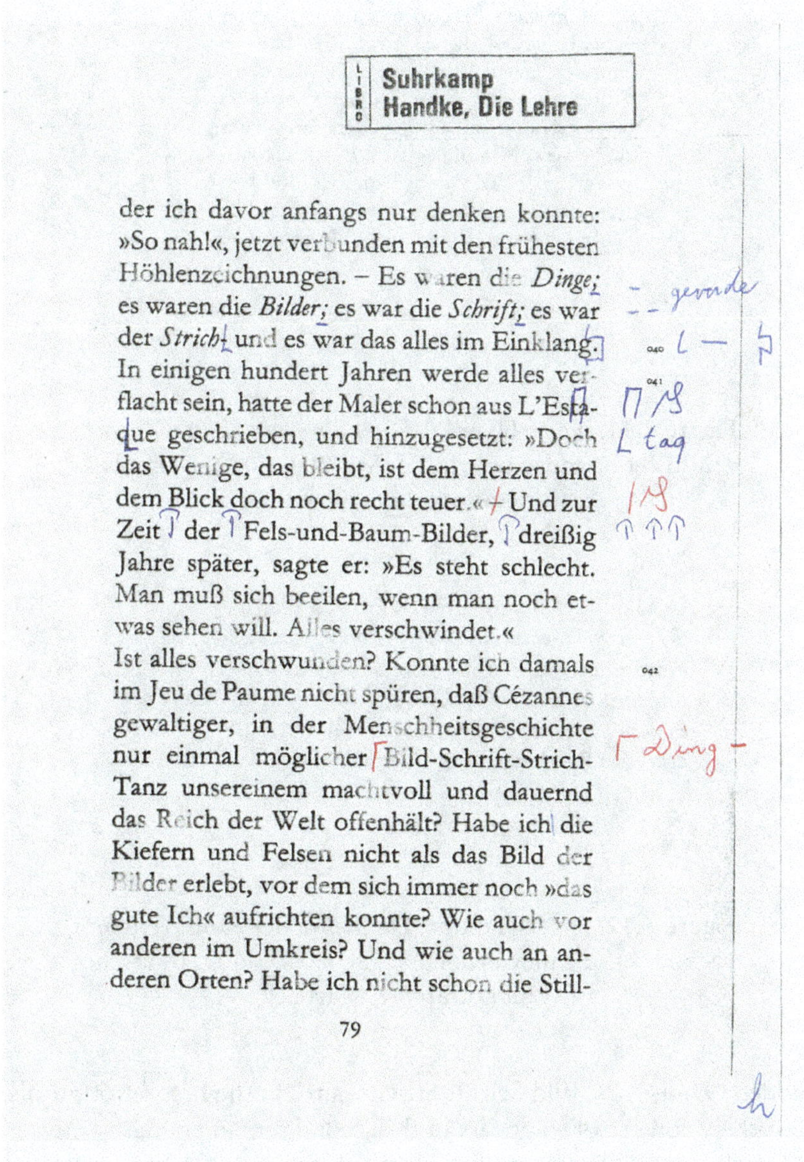
Suhrkamp
Handke, Die Lehre

der ich davor anfangs nur denken konnte: »So nah!«, jetzt verbunden mit den frühesten Höhlenzeichnungen. – Es waren die *Dinge*; es waren die *Bilder*; es war die *Schrift*; es war der *Strich*; und es war das alles im Einklang. In einigen hundert Jahren werde alles verflacht sein, hatte der Maler schon aus L'Estaque geschrieben, und hinzugesetzt: »Doch das Wenige, das bleibt, ist dem Herzen und dem Blick doch noch recht teuer.« Und zur Zeit der Fels-und-Baum-Bilder, dreißig Jahre später, sagte er: »Es steht schlecht. Man muß sich beeilen, wenn man noch etwas sehen will. Alles verschwindet.«
Ist alles verschwunden? Konnte ich damals im Jeu de Paume nicht spüren, daß Cézannes gewaltiger, in der Menschheitsgeschichte nur einmal möglicher Bild-Schrift-Strich-Tanz unsereinem machtvoll und dauernd das Reich der Welt offenhält? Habe ich die Kiefern und Felsen nicht als das Bild der Bilder erlebt, vor dem sich immer noch »das gute Ich« aufrichten konnte? Wie auch vor anderen im Umkreis? Und wie auch an anderen Orten? Habe ich nicht schon die Still-

79

Figure 1.10. Peter Handke, *Die Lehre der Sainte-Victoire*, first set of galley proofs, 79. SU.2010.0002. Deutsches Literaturarchiv, Marbach.

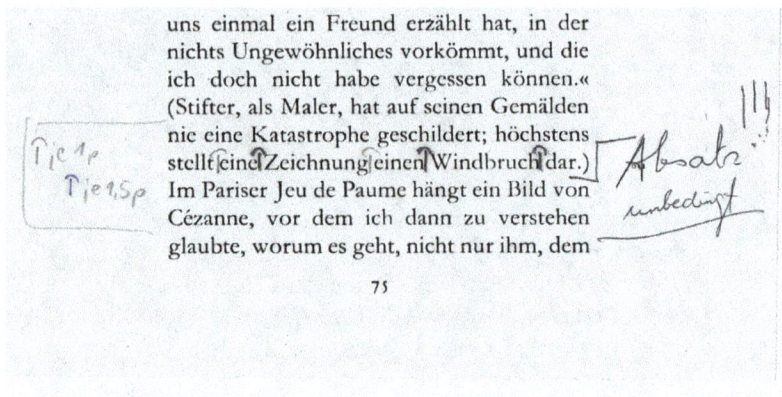

Figure 1.11. Peter Handke, *Die Lehre der Sainte-Victoire*, third set of galley proofs, 75. SU.2010.0002. Deutsches Literaturarchiv, Marbach.

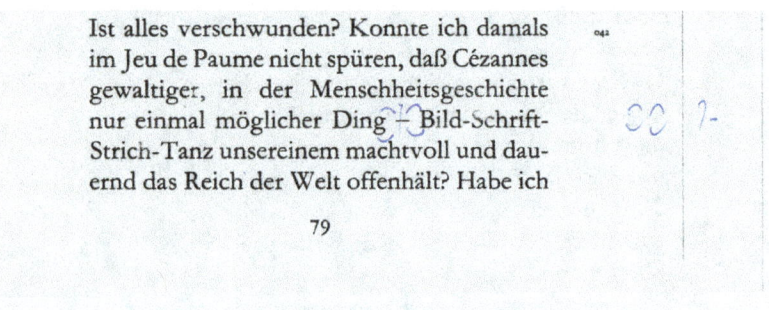

Figure 1.12. Peter Handke, *Die Lehre der Sainte-Victoire*, second set of galley proofs, 79. SU.2010.0002. Deutsches Literaturarchiv, Marbach.

added "Ding-" to "Bild-Schrift-Strich-Tanz" in the first set of proofs, but the wrong stroke appears in the second set: an em dash between "Ding" and "Bild" rather than a hyphen (figure 1.12). In the third set of galleys, the correct stroke is used. It is thus not until the third and final set of proofs that the formulation "Ding-Bild-Schrift-Strich-Tanz"—Handke's conglomerate conceptualization of Cézanne's realization—becomes conceptually-linguistically-orthographically-typographically set. The result not only reflects the slowness of realization, engineered by Handke into his own writerly realization process; it is also itself the product of numerous strokes.

Visible Strokes (Redux)

The introduction of erroneous strokes in the galley proofs was not the result of carelessness. On the typewriter, the only dash available is the hyphen, which Handke employed as both *Bindestrich* (binding-stroke) and *Gedankenstrich* (thought-stroke). Printed *Striche*, by contrast, include hyphens, en dashes, and em dashes. In this respect the typewriter is a limited tool, and as we have seen, slippages could occur in the translation of typescript to typeset text, particularly given Handke's excessive and idiosyncratic use of typographic *Striche*. Visual *Striche*, a crucial feature of Cézanne's method, are also crucial for the visual, typographical form of Handke's text, its *Schriftbild*. The limited features of the typewriter, however, required Handke to work closely with an editor to achieve the intended typographical form; the challenges of doing so, the errors generated in the process of translating typescript to printed text, underscore just how significant the typographical *Striche* are in the text.

When we compare the punctuation of the text across its multiple versions, we discover that in the third typescript version Handke added *numerous* hyphens, performing the function of *Gedankenstriche* (em dashes); these become rendered with em dashes in the proofs. In many cases these *Striche* are additional punctuation marks, separating sentences that are also punctuated by periods. Strictly speaking, they are unnecessary, if not ungrammatical, but they function performatively: these pages of *The Lesson*, on which Handke narrates flashes of insight into Cézanne's stroke-work, display more typographic "strokes" than any others in the book. Handke's "'reflection on things seen' (more like a thought-storm [*Denksturm*])" is performed visually as a "*Strich*sturm," the *Gedankenstriche* punctuating the text like lightning bolts. Visualizing conceptual flashes of insight, cognitive leaps and springs, these *Striche* leap out at the reader, bringing the surface of the page into motion as a kind of typo-graphic choreo-graphic dance.

These *Gedankenstriche*, however, do more than represent the dynamic nonlinearity of thought: as I explore in more detail in the next section, they also frequently separate pieces of text that were based on separate notes. They thus refer to, or represent visually, points of disjuncture in the *temporal* generation of the text: pieces of text that were originally composed at different moments—like different viewpoints on a motif—then joined together in the text. As such, the *Gedankenstriche* function something like faults (*Bruchstellen*) in the earth's crust, where distinct geological layers, formed over the *longue durée* of the earth's geological history, come into contact.[123] This geological phenomenon captivated both Cézanne and Handke. In observing Cézanne's paintings of Mont Sainte-Victoire, Handke over time notices a "fault [*Bruchstelle*] between two strata of different kinds of rock" (LMSV 195) that reappears in Cézanne's paintings, and to which Cézanne devoted particular energy in attempting to capture it: "This point, which in nature cannot be discerned with the naked eye, nevertheless recurs time and again in Cézanne's paintings, where it is indicated by a shadow line of varying length and thickness" (LMSV 195). This fault line ultimately led Handke to return for a second time to the mountain: "It was this spot more than anything else—I was about to start working—that impelled me to repeat the trip to Provence. From this new trip I expected the key" (LMSV 195).

In addition to em dashes, hyphens also play a crucial role in the chapter "The Picture of Pictures." The interconnectedness of all things, "paralleled" in the materiality and visuality of Cézanne's realization, becomes analogized in the hyphenation of composite terms, a result of his own material process of textual construction. Handke narrates a step-by-step process of piecing together, as through an accumulation of "small strokes," an understanding of Cézanne's painting. Over the course of the text's generation, "Bild und Schrift" merge into "Bilderschrift"; with the addition of "Ding", hyphens are introduced to punctuate the composite concept, linking and separating the

---

123. On the *Bruchstelle* for Handke in relation to poststructuralist concepts of *rupture* and *Riß*, see Hoesterey, "Mit Cézanne," 112–13. In relation to Handke's "geological gaze," see Honold, *Der Erd-Erzähler*, 123–24.

individual terms at once. "Dinge," "Bilder," and "Schrift" become ultimately entangled (*ineinandergefügt*) through "Strich" into the conceptual ensemble "Ding-Bild-Schrift-Strich-Tanz." This entanglement is visualized through Handke's use of hyphens, which function here not as *Trennstriche* (separating dashes—for instance, to hyphenate words split over the end of a line) but instead as *Bindestriche* (binding dashes)—more specifically, as *Durchkopplungsbindestriche*, entangling or intertwining binding dashes.[124] Handke's narration of his piece-by-piece process of thinking through Cézanne's realization thus is performed not only on the level of narrative structure, but also orthographically and typographically, on the surface of the printed page, embodying a process of thinking that, for Handke himself, took place in large part on his own notebook and typescript pages.

These typographic features draw attention to the *visual* surface of the page, contributing to what Hoesterey describes as an effect of "frontality."[125] Though not identical, the effects can be compared to those of Cézanne's treatment of space. Cézanne's construction of objects in paint disrupts the illusion of perspectival space; they become pressed into a single plane, interacting materially on the surface of the canvas, pushed to the front of the visual field.[126] But the illusion of space is not entirely destroyed; rather, one observes an oscillation between two- and three-dimensionality.[127] The "flattening" of space into two dimensions, such that objects appear as "verschlungene Schriftzeichen" (intertwined letters) is part of what gives Cézanne's paintings a script-like quality of "Bilderschrift" (picture writing). In *The Lesson*, the reader is continually confronted by the text's *Schriftbildlichkeit*; the typographical surface becomes visible, indeed meaningful, interacting with the verbal text in the process of reading.

---

124. "Bindestrich oder Gedankenstrich?," Federwerk, https://federwerk.de/bindestrich-gedankenstrich/. The same orthographic convention, to the same ends, is employed by Jane Bennett in formulating the "animal-vegetable-mineral-sonority cluster" (*Vibrant Matter*, 23).

125. Hoesterey, "Mit Cézanne," 117; Ralph Köhnen, "Ein Möbiusband von Wort und Bild: Peter Handkes Cézanne-Lektüren als Lebensform," in *Gemäldereien: Zur literarischen Diskursivierung in Bildern*, ed. Konstanze Fliedl, Bernhard Oberreither, and Katharina Serles (Berlin: Erich Schmidt 2013), 98.

126. Compare Badt, *Die Kunst Cézannes*, 125.

127. Compare Badt, *Die Kunst Cézannes*, 128.

84   Chapter 1

Handke's use of punctuation also operates in sync with the often-described fragmentary or montage-like structure of the text. Alongside Handke's own reflections and reconstructions of lived experiences, the text is filled with numerous intertextual references to works by other writers, philosophers, and painters, as well as *self*-citations of Handke's own published works and notebooks (such as "'The picture has begun to tremble,' I jotted down at the time" [LMSV 155]). Ralph Köhnen has described the resulting abundance of quotation marks in the text, which Handke not only uses to demarcate intertextual references but also applies—seemingly inexplicably—to "normal thing-designations."[128] In many cases, words and phrases that appear inside quotation marks for no ostensible reason are actually quotations from Handke's notebooks. The typographic structure, in this way, not only contributes to the pastiche-like structure of the text, but also *indexes* the process of the text's composition from individual notes, one akin to Cézanne's composition through the accumulation of "small strokes."

Script

Not a text-maker, rather a
text-seeker (-searcher)

Kein Schriftsteller, sondern ein
Schrift-Sucher (-suchender)[129]

In the fifth chapter of *The Lesson*, Handke narrates a climactic moment of transformation that he experienced on the path to the summit of Mont Sainte-Victoire, in which his self expands into and burrows among the things of the landscape: "In the great painter's territory I had grown more invisible from day to day. . . . I felt, not that I had vanished or dissolved into the landscape, but that I was well hidden [*verborgen*] among its objects (Cézanne's objects)"

---

128. Köhnen, "Ein Möbiusband," 99.
129. Notizbuch 21, October 5, 1979, 154.

(LMSV 173). When Handke reemerges, he is infused with a new conviction about writing:

> once again imbued with my justification for writing; once again convinced of writing and narration. . . . and all this in the midst of silence in which my usual self became strictly No One, and I, in a sudden transformation, became something more than merely invisible, namely, a *writer* [*Schriftsteller*]. . . . In addition to innocently uniting the fragments of my own life with the mulberry spots on the dust, the moment of fantasy . . . revealed to me anew my kinship with other, unknown lives, thus acting as an unspecified love and striving to communicate itself in a form conducive to fidelity, namely, as a justified project aimed at the cohesion of my never-to-be-defined nation as our common form of existence. (LMSV 174–75)[130]

The particles of dust along the path become connected with all of the "fragments" of his life, an experience of unity with everything that he becomes compelled to transmit (*weitergeben*) to a "never-to-be-defined nation" (*nie bestimmbaren, verborgenen Volk*) (LMSV 175): a "nation of readers" (*Volk der Leser*) (LMSV 184).

The question for Handke became *how* exactly to transmit Cézanne's lesson, how to achieve Cézanne's realization in the medium of writing, *Schrift*. Such an intermedial translation was by no means one-to-one. One the one hand, certain features of Cézanne's realization could be seen to lend themselves more readily to analogization in writing: for example, the script-like appearance of the pines and rocks in Cézanne's *Rochers près des grottes*. Fritz Novotny wrote that Cézanne *inscribed* his objects into the surface of the canvas, yielding a kind of "surface picture" (*Flächengemälde*) that suspends the illusion of space and approximates the phenomenon of writing.[131] Ralph Köhnen has described the way that individual patches of paint on the canvas surface thus appear to interact like written characters.[132] Kurt Badt described an increasing effect of "unification" (*Vereinheitlichung*) in Cézanne's paintings in the 1880s, resulting from

---

130. Translation modified.
131. Fritz Novotny, *Cézanne und das Ende der wissenschaftlichen Perspektive* (Vienna: A. Schroll, 1938), 142. Cited in Kurz, *Bild-Verdichtungen*, 162–63.
132. Köhnen, "Zwischen Zeichenspiel," 189.

that fact that "all parts of the picture are of the same thickness and the motif is grasped from the edges of the picture, such that the picture surface is completely filled or, in any case, the middle is no longer emphasized."[133] This method of gradually covering the canvas with small patches of paint "from the edges" resembles somewhat the process of covering a page with writing from one end to the other (left to right, top to bottom).[134] Cézanne himself, moreover, conceived of his method of realization as a process of "reading nature": "Let us read nature ... The best will be whoever has seen most deeply and completely realized ... Reading nature means seeing through the veil of interpretation with the means of colorful blotches, which follow each other according to a law of harmony.... To paint is to record [*aufzeichnen*] one's colored sensations."[135] On the one hand, the notion of "reading nature" implies that nature itself is textlike, a "book of nature" or *Schrift der Natur*.[136] Cézanne's realizations, in turn, as "harmonies parallel to nature," might be understood as translations or transformations of the *Schrift der Natur* into a *Bilderschrift*. Just as Cézanne's works are made up of visible strokes, so too is writing; and in various ways, as we have seen, Handke attempted to translate something of Cézanne's painterly *Bilderschrift* into the typographic *Schriftbild* of *The Lesson*.

What proved to be the greatest challenge for Handke was Cézanne's habit of repeatedly realizing the same motifs, which gave rise to numerous paintings and drawings. Handke had been struck by this already at the 1978 exhibit in Paris. In *The Lesson*, Handke narrates his experience of the room full of paintings of Mont Saint-Victoire, emphasizing Cézanne's method of repeatedly rendering the mountain from similar, but always slightly different, vantage points: "In a separate room, which seemed circular, one picture after another showed the top of Mont Sainte-Victoire, which the painter depicted from different angles, but always from below, from the plain and from a distance. He himself said: 'The same motif, seen

---

133. Badt, *Die Kunst Cézannes*, [x].
134. Badt, *Die Kunst Cézannes*, 130.
135. Emile Bernard, "'Paul Cézanne' (1904)," in *Gespräche mit Cézanne*, ed. Michael Doran (Zurich: Diogenes, 1982), 54. Cited in Kurz, *Bild-Verdichtungen*, 79.
136. Kurz, *Bild-Verdichtungen*, 80–81.

from different angles, offers an object of study of such extreme interest and such diversity that I believe I could keep busy for several months in the same spot, just turning now a little more to the right, now a little more to the left'" (LMSV 156). After his so-called small world trip (*kleine Weltreise*), several years of nearly constant traveling, Handke settled in Salzburg, where he would write *The Lesson* and began to put this method of repeated observation and recording into practice.[137] During the months he worked on the text, Handke took routine walks to and through the Morzg forest—which became his "motif"—recording extensive notes on these repeated walks. These notes became the basis for the final chapter of *The Lesson*, titled "The Great Forest" (*Der große Wald*). In scholarship on *Die Lehre*, this final chapter has been the most overlooked. In considering the printed text alone, this is perhaps understandable: the chapter has been read as an attempt to create a Cézannean description of another landscape, and in this sense it can be seen as an "application" of the lesson, but otherwise it departs thematically from the previous nine chapters.[138] When examined closely through the lens of its production, however, this chapter stands out as the theoretical and poetological pinnacle of the entire work: here Handke attempts to put the "lesson" into practice—specifically, through an extended material experiment in writerly realization.

But Cézanne's method, which resulted in *multiple* realizations of a motif, did not lend itself in an obvious way to the generation of a *singular* printed work. This would require that Handke somehow select, whittle down, and integrate into a single text many notes recorded on many walks. The method Handke ultimately devised, we will see, is a kind of "patchwork" technique—comparatively long and difficult, but also characterized by the slowness and repetition of Cézanne's realizing—in which individual notes are gathered and deployed to form a textual montage. Cézanne's stroke technique, in

---

137. "Clamart, 53 rue Cécile Dinant (1976–1978)," Handke*online*, https://handkeonline.onb.ac.at/node/1567.
138. See Hans Höller: "'Der große Wald' bei Salzburg," Handke*online* (2012), http://handkeonline.onb.ac.at/forschung/pdf/hoeller-2002.pdf.

this way, would become reflected in the syntactic structure of the text, composed out of individual notes like "small strokes."

Such a method evokes poststructuralist notions of text as an intertextual fabric of quotations, and to a degree this is accurate. Such notions of intertextuality, however, often imply that a text is something immaterial: for Roland Barthes, the "work" can be "held in the hand," whereas the text is "held in language."[139] For Handke, text, writing, *Schrift* were decidedly *material*; the text Handke would construct out of his notes, *The Lesson of Mont Sainte-Victoire*, would take the form of a printed book. As we have begun to see, the typographic—the visual—features of the printed page played a crucial role. But the typographic is only one dimension of the bibliographic—the visual, material structure of the book.

Patchwork

In the penultimate chapter, Handke narrated his struggle to find an adequate textual form through which to transmit the "lesson." Handke considered presenting his experiences as a fragmentary text: "For a time I thought of treating particular aspects—the mountain and me, the pictures and me—and setting them down side by side as unconnected fragments. But then I rejected such fragmentary treatment because it would have resulted not from a possibly unsuccessful striving for unity but from a deliberate method, known in advance to be safe" (LMSV 190). Although Cézanne built up forms in paint through an accumulation of "small strokes," individual strokes that remain visible in the final product, Cézanne's paintings did not have a fragmentary feeling; on the contrary, Cézanne's pictures revealed to Handke the inner unity and connection of things. Handke worried that the "lessons" he had learned through his experiences with Cézanne would not cohere for the reader of a

---

139. Roland Barthes, "From Work to Text," in *Image Music Text*, ed. Stephen Heath (London: Fontana, 1977), 157. Critical bibliographers employ these terms differently; compare G. Thomas Tanselle, *Rationale of Textual Criticism* (Philadelphia: University of Pennsylvania Press, 1989), 14–15.

fragmentary narrative. Handke would thus have to identify and distill the unifying principles of the lesson, so that he could impart them to his readers. Handke writes in *The Lesson*, "Then, in Grillparzer's *The Poor Minstrel*, I read: 'I trembled with a longing for unity.' A desire for the One in All was rekindled in me. For I knew that unity is possible. Every single moment of my life hangs together with every other—without intermediate links. I need only reconstitute them with the help of my imagination" (LMSV 190).

This poetological problem compelled Handke to undertake a second journey to travel the *route Cézanne*. In *The Lesson*, Handke is accompanied by a travel companion named "D.," based on Handke's friend Domenika Kaesdorf, a clothing and costume designer. In D(omenika), Handke found a secondary teacher; in her patchwork method of textile construction he found the final piece he needed to translate Cézanne's realization into his writing.[140] Handke writes of D.'s garments, "Her pictures are her 'creations,' each one of which represents an idea of its own," and recounts her comments on the challenges of constructing one particular coat: "Once, she told me, she decided to create the 'coat of coats.' . . . in the end she had been defeated by the problem of 'connections,' which I 'as a writer must have come up against.' . . . But the unfinished coat of coats had been so beautiful that people who had seen it on the Métro had been stricken with awe" (LMSV 192). Kaesdorf's "coat of coats" is thus another "picture of pictures," and in key respects D.'s patchwork (*Stückwerk*) method resembles Cézanne's "stroke-work" (*Strichwerk*): both involve gradual production through the accumulation or assemblage of individual units—tiny strokes of paint, individual patches of fabric. This method of textual patchwork was a long, difficult process, as is underscored by the failures D. experienced in attempting to implement it. D.'s articulation of the "problem of connections and transition," however, was ultimately clarifying for Handke in his own effort to create the sense of textual cohesion necessary to analogize Cézanne's

---

140. In the first and second versions of *The Lesson*, Handke in fact describes her as "Lehrmeister" (TF1, 21; TF2c, 73).

realization in writing. The final pages of the chapter present a lengthy monologue in which D. describes her process of envisioning and realizing the coat. "Once again D. had thought with me and was immediately able to answer my question about the problem of connections and transition. She had even brought samples of the different materials intended for her coat: brocade, satin, damask. 'So you want me to tell you about the coat. It began with my calling what I had thought up the Great Idea. The coat was to embody it'" (LMSV 199). D. goes on to describe the experience of finding, losing, and rediscovering the "Great Idea," the principle of cohesion, and her difficulties in determining the size and arrangement of fabric pieces and creating transitions between them: "the form determines the color and must solve the problem of transition. 'A transition [*Übergang*] must clearly divide and at the same time bring together'" (LMSV 200). D.'s descriptions of the problems of "connection" and "transition," in turn, recall Badt's discussion of the edges of things in Cézanne's paintings: not as borders but instead "transitions" (Übergänge), sites of interaction and interconnection captured through his "shadow path" technique.

In the "picture of pictures" and the "coat of coats," Handke found intermedial models for both a narrative technique *and* a material process of constructing a text (*Schrift*) out of "small strokes," out of individual pieces (*Stücke*) patched together. Handke gathered bits and pieces not only from his own notebooks, but also from texts by many other writers and philosophers. D.'s description of her patchwork method is a case in point. Whereas "D." accompanies Handke in *The Lesson*, the actual Domenika Kaesdorf did not accompany Handke to Provence—at least, not physically. The two did, however, exchange letters about the difficulties of their respective creative processes. The "coat of coats" is no mere fiction: housed at the Austrian Literature Archive is an advertisement for a 1980 exhibition of Kaesdorf's designs featuring a patchwork coat of multiple striped and floral patterns, as well as a letter to Handke from March 23—midway through his process of writing the first version of *The Lesson*—onto which fabric samples for the coat are attached. On March 26, after receiving the letter, Handke noted: "'<u>Hill of spinning tops</u>' in the narration of the <u>connection</u>, of which <u>D.'s</u>

letter will form the final part, word for word."¹⁴¹ In *The Lesson*, Handke reproduces the majority of Kaesdorf's two-and-a-half-page letter almost verbatim. As such, it constitutes the largest intertextual "patch" in Handke's patchwork text.

While Handke narrates the challenges he faced in finding an adequate textual form, and indicates that D.'s patchwork method provided an instructive model, Handke does not actually narrate his process of constructing the text out of notes. Cézanne never explicitly explained of his theory of realization, which can only be gleaned by studying his "praxis of the canvas." Similarly, Handke does not fully explain his theory of writing as textual patchwork, as *Schriftstellen*. Instead, this theory is *inscribed into his practice* of writing and editing the text, and as such, can only be comprehended by examining that practice closely.

The Great Forest

The final chapter of *The Lesson* opens neither in Provence, nor in Salzburg, but instead at the Vienna Kunsthistorisches Museum, with a description Jacob van Ruisdael's painting *The Great Forest*. Handke names the general subject—"It shows a spacious deciduous forest with mighty oak trunks" (LMSV 200)—and notes that, although titled *The Great Forest*, only a small part of this forest is pictured. Handke posits that the vantage point is not from outside the forest, but instead that of a viewer who has entered *into* the forest and turns outward—in other words, a view from the *Schwelle* (threshold). Handke describes the figures that populate the scene: a hiker with a hat, hiking stick, and small bundle beside him, reminding of the photograph of Cézanne evoked in juxtaposition with Spinoza's *Ethics*, and a pair walking together, resembling Handke and D. Standing before the painting, Handke is overcome by an intense sense of expansiveness, a "Weitgefühl" (feeling of spaciousness) that contrasts with "Das Gefühl Nähe" (feeling of nearness) he experienced before Cézanne's painting: "The feeling of spaciousness is further intensified

---

141. "'Hügel der Kreisel' in der Erzählung von der Verknüpfung, von der D.'s Brief der Schlußteil sein wird, wörtlich" (Notizbuch 25, March 26, 1980, 81).

by a peculiarity of seventeenth-century Dutch landscapes: for all the minuteness of their forms, they nevertheless, with their patches of water, their roads over dunes, their dark woods (under spacious skies), begin to grow as one beholds them. The trees grow perceptibly, and with them grows a quiet, overall twilight. Even the two horsemen who have stopped to rest grow as they stand there" (LMSV 201). Forming a "transition" between Mont Sainte-Victoire and the Morzg forest, Handke's description of Ruisdael's forest is less an objective description than a reading of the painting and a narration of his subjective experience viewing it. With this reading, Handke primes his reader to see his "great forest" similarly, as a textual picture. Handke transitions as follows: "There is a forest of this kind near Salzburg; it is not one of those great forests one finds at the edge of large cities; it is no forest of forests; yet it is wonderfully real" (LMSV 201). Even in its negation, the phrase "forest of forests" nonetheless draws Handke's textual realization into relationship with Cézanne's "picture of pictures" and Kaesdorf's "coat of coats." The description of the forest as wonderfully "real" also evokes Cézanne's notion of realization.

All the while he was composing *The Lesson*, Handke took routine walks through the Morzg forest—no fewer than fifteen are accounted for in his notebooks—and recorded extensive notes and sketches, all in the single notebook that accompanied him through the duration of his work on *The Lesson*.[142] In constructing the chapter, Handke employed a patchwork method, gathering notes and suturing them together into what reads as a unified representation of a single walk, presented in enough detail that it can still be retraced.[143] Close examination of the final page of the first version reveals that on this single page alone, no fewer than twenty-eight

---

142. Likely by coincidence, fifteen is the number of Saint-Victoire paintings that were displayed in the 1978 exhibition in Paris. These walks took place on March 8, 11, 12, 14, 18, 23, 25, 26, 31, and April 2, 3, 6, 10, 11, 12. Of these, the most significant concentration of notes that reappear in *The Lesson* were recorded on March 8, 25, 26, and April 10, 11, 12.

143. For a photographic documentation of the route, see Katharina Pektor, "Der Morzger Wald bei Salzburg," Handke*online*, https://handkeonline.onb.ac.at/node/1574.

chunks of text can be traced to distinct notes or groups of notes dispersed over some 150 notebook pages, stitched together onto the space of a single A4 format page (figure 1.13).

Closer examination of a particular passage can offer a more detailed sense of this patchwork process.

> In time, the green of the empty field below becomes warm and deep, and extends far beyond the city. Across it cuts a path on which a child once ran after a man, jumped up on his back, and was carried from there on. Another time, a real horseman merged with his horse in the darkness, to form a single gigantic creature. From a distance, the dialect of the people walking down below sounds like all the languages in the world rolled into one.
> On the hilltop the village children are about the only passersby. With their varied costumes, they are the bright color in the forest. The forest is their big playground, and they are bursting with information about it. Question: "Do you know the forest well?" Answer: "Sure do!" Even if you don't hear a thing and there's no one in sight, the hill is certain to be full of them. At the first peal of thunder, figures can be seen running homeward between the trees.
> The pale-gray crest road running straight westward looks something like a military highway. Bare saplings screech as they rub together in the wind, or send out muffled messages in Morse code. The resinous spots on the bark of the trees mark bullet holes. Lightning has struck off the main branch of a solitary beech, and the bare trunk shows three bright patches of color: white where the limb broke off, the blue-gray of the southern lee side, the rust-yellow of the windward side (black in the rain). The white flowers in the grass turn out to be animal teeth. And maybe a dog will come running out of the thicket, his tongue flapping from side to side like a whiplash, and silently sniff at the hollows of your knees from behind. The sharp-edged nagelfluh niches along the road repeat the pattern of the ancient cliff tombs. But they are empty. Light-brown beech leaves have blown in. With their ovals and parallel lines, they radiate eternal peace. (LMSV 208–9)

> Das Grün des leeren Feldes unten wird mit der Zeit warm und tief, und streckt sich dann weit jenseits der Stadt. In seiner Diagonale verläuft ein Weg, wo einmal ein Kind hinter einem Mann herrannte, ihm auf den Rücken sprang und weitergetragen wurde.[144] Ein anderes Mal wuchs da ein tatsächlicher Reiter in der Dunkelheit mit seinem Pferd zu einem

---

144. Compare Notizbuch 25, March 18, 1980, 50; April 10, 1980, 137; April 21, 1980, 156.

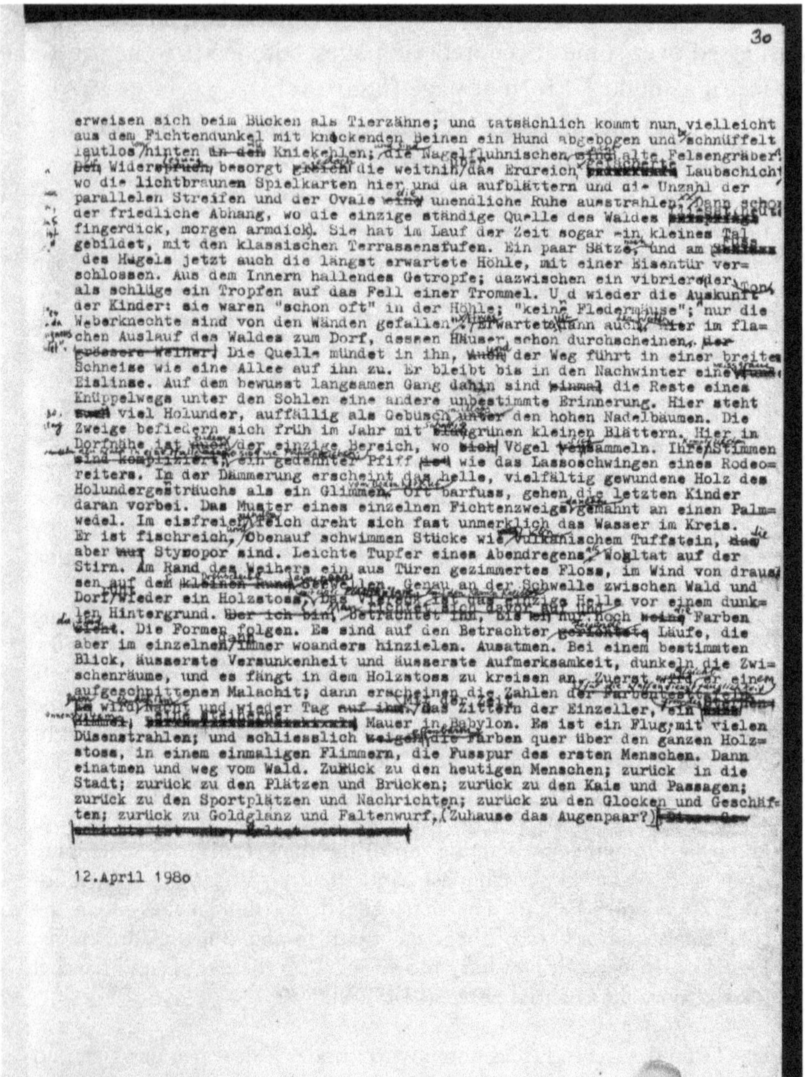

erweisen sich beim Bücken als Tierzähne; und tatsächlich kommt nun vielleicht
aus dem Fichtendunkel mit knöckenden Beinen ein Hund abgebogen und schnüffelt
lautlos hinten in den Kniekehlen; die Nagelfluhnischen sind alte Felsengräber,
den Widerspruch, besorgt zwisch die weitnin/das Erdreich Laubschicht
wo die lichtbraunen Spielkarten hier und da aufblättern und die Unzahl der
parallelen Streifen und der Ovale wirft unendliche Ruhe ausstrahlen. Dann schon
der friedliche Abhang, wo die einzige ständige Quelle des Waldes
fingerdick, morgen armdick. Sie hat im Lauf der Zeit sogar -in kleines Tal
gebildet, mit den klassischen Terrassenstufen. Ein paar Sätze, und am
des Hügels jetzt auch die längst erwartete Höhle, mit einer Eisentür ver=
schlossen. Aus dem Innern hallendes Getropfe; dazwischen ein vibrierender
als schlüge ein Tropfen auf das Fell einer Trommel. Und wieder die Auskunft
der Kinder: sie waren "schon oft" in der Höhle; "keine Fledermäuse"; nur die
Weberknechte sind von den Wänden gefallen. Erwartet dann auch, hier im fla=
chen Auslauf des Waldes zum Dorf, dessen Häuser schon durchscheinen. Der
Die Quelle mündet in ihn, und der Weg führt in einer breiten
Schneise wie eine Allee auf ihn zu. Er bleibt bis in den Nachwinter eine
Eislinse. Auf dem bewusst langsamen Gang dahin sind einmal die Reste eines
Knüppelwegs unter den Sohlen eine andere unbestimmte Erinnerung. Hier steht
viel Holunder, auffällig als Gebüsch unter den hohen Nadelbäumen. Die
Zweige befiedern sich früh im Jahr mit hellgrünen kleinen Blättern. Hier in
Dorfnähe ist auch der einzige Bereich, wo sich Vögel versammeln. Ihre Stimmen
sind kompliziert; ein gedehnter Pfiff ist wie das Lassoschwingen eines Rodeo=
reiters. In der Dämmerung erscheint das helle, vielfältig gewundene Holz des
Holundergesträuchs als ein Glimmen. Ort barfuss, gehen die letzten Kinder
daran vorbei. Das Muster eines einzelnen Fichtenzweigs gemahnt an einen Palm=
wedel. Im eisfreien Teich dreht sich fast unmerklich das Wasser im Kreis.
Er ist fischreich. Obenauf schwimmen Stücke wie vulkanischem Tuffstein, die
aber nur Styropor sind. Leichte Tupfer eines Abendregens, Wohltat auf der
Stirn. Am Rand des Weihers ein aus Türen gezimmertes Floss, im Wind von draus=
sen auf dem kleinen Teich Wellen. Genau an der Schwelle zwischen Wald und
Dorf, wieder ein Holzstoss. Der ich bin, betrachtet ihn, bis er nur noch Farben
Die Formen folgen. Es sind auf den Betrachter gerichtete Läufe, die
aber im einzelnen immer woanders hinzielen. Ausatmen. Bei einem bestimmten
Blick, äusserste Versunkenheit und äusserste Aufmerksamkeit, dunkeln die Zwi=
schenräume, und es fängt in dem Holzstoss zu kreisen an. Zuerst wird er einem
aufgeschnittenen Malachit; dann erscheinen die Zahlen der
Tag auf ihm, das Zittern der Einzeller,
Mauer in Babylon. Es ist ein Flug; mit vielen
Düsenstrahlen; und schliesslich walzen die Farben quer über den ganzen Holz=
stoss, in einem einmaligen Flimmern, die Fussspur des ersten Menschen. Dann
einatmen und weg vom Wald. Zurück zu den heutigen Menschen; zurück in die
Stadt; zurück zu den Plätzen und Brücken; zurück zu den Kais und Passagen;
zurück zu den Sportplätzen und Nachrichten; zurück zu den Glocken und Geschäf=
ten; zurück zu Goldglanz und Faltenwurf. (Zuhause das Augenpaar?)

12.April 1980

Figure 1.13. Peter Handke, first version of *Die Lehre der Sainte Victoire*, 30. ÖLA SPH/LW/W19. Literaturarchiv der Österreichischen Nationalbibliothek, Vienna.

einzigen Riesengeschöpf zusammen.[145] Der Dialekt der dort unter Gehenden hört sich von weitem wie alle Sprachen in einer an.[146]
Oben auf der Kuppe kommen fast nur die Dorfkinder vorbei. Mit ihren wechselnden Kostümen sind sie das Bunte im Wald.[147] Dieser ist ihr großer Spielgrund, und sie können über ihn viele Auskünfte geben. Frage: ‚Kennt ihr den Wald?'—Antwort: ‚Und wie!'[148] Auch wenn es still ist und kein Mensch sichtbar, ist der Hügel gewiß mit ihnen bevölkert. Beim ersten Donnerschlag eines Gewitters laufen überall zwischen den Bäumen Gestalten nach Hause.[149]
Der Kammweg, indem er gerade und fahlgrau ostwärts fährt, erinnert flüchtig an eine Heerstraße. Das kahle Gestänge, das hier aufwächst, reibt sich im Wind schrill aneinander oder gibt dumpfe Morsezeichen.[150] Die harztränenden Stellen in den Baumrinden rühren von Einschüssen? Von einer einzelnen Buche hat der Blitz den Hauptast abgeschlagen, so daß der nackte Stamm der leuchtende Fahnenbahnen zeigt: das Weiß der Bruchstelle, das Blaugrau der windabgekehrten Südseite, das Rostgelb der Wetterseite (bei Regen ein Schwarz).[151] Die weißen Blüten im Gras erweisen sich als Tiergebiß.[152] Und wirklich kommt aus dem Dickicht mit knickenden Beinen ein Hund abgebogen, vor dem die Zunge lang hin und herschwingt wie eine Peitsche, und beschnüffelt lautlos vor hinten die Kniekehlen.[153] Die scharfkantigen Nagelfluhnischen am Weg sind wieder die alten Felsengräber.[154] Aber sie sind leer. Die lichtbraunen Buchenblätter sind hineingeweht und strahlen mit ihren Ovalen und Parallelen die unendliche Ruhe aus.[155] (*LSV* 134–36)

The majority of this passage can be traced to specific notes (individual correspondences are footnoted). For example, the description of a beech tree split by a lightning strike ("Von einer einzelnen Buche . . .") is based on these notes from March 8: "another banner:

---

145. Compare Notizbuch 25, April 21, 1980, 156.
146. Compare Notizbuch 25, May 8, 1980, 181.
147. Compare Notizbuch 25, April 9, 1979, 131.
148. Compare Notizbuch 25, April 3, 1980, 114.
149. Compare Notizbuch 25 April 3, 1980, 114.
150. Compare Notizbuch 25, April 2, 1980, 108; April 3, 1980, 113.
151. Compare Notizbuch 25, March 8, 1980, 19.
152. Compare Notizbuch 25, March 23, 1980, 67.
153. Compare Notizbuch 25, March 23, 1980, 66–67.
154. This sentence is not based on a particular note; descriptions of "Nagelfluh" and "Felsengräber" are found on notebook pages 146 and 143, respectively.
155. Compare Notizbuch 25, February 4, 1980, 108; March 4, 1980, 113; April 9, 1980, 129; April 12, 1980, 143–44.

beech: underneath green-yellow brown, white path of the split-off thick branch, black path of the nuts, actual color-paths, also the green yellow [;] the BANNER-TREE [*FAHNENBAUM*] [;] mightily colorful [;] noticeably different from the rest."[156] Handke also sketched the tree, indicating the colors of the wood: "white (very)"; "normal grey (blue) gleaming distinctly but not"; "yellow-green"; and "black (white)" (figure 1.14.)[157] In this case the published description is based on notes from one specific walk, on one notebook page, but other descriptions can be linked to multiple notes in which Handke described the same phenomenon. Take, for example, Handke's description of the light-brown-colored beech leaves, with visible rills, that cover the forest floor: "With their ovals and parallel lines, they radiate eternal peace."[158] On April 2, Handke sketched the rills of one such leaf, captioning it "the beach leaf floor of the forest, the radiating rills," noting that "in this way the whole forest is striped."[159] On the following page, which is dominated by a sketch of "thick alder rods [*dichten Erlenstänge*],"[160] Handke notes the "lightness of the beech foliage [*Helligkeit des Buchenlaubs*]" and the "beautiful, eternal light brown (that is the color of the forest); shimmering brown, with the many parallel rills of the leaves after the storm."[161] On another walk the next day (April 3), Handke noted

---

156. "eine andere Fahne: Buche: unter grüngelb braun, weiße Bahn des abgesplitterten dicken Aste, schwarze Bahn der Nüsse, tatsächlich Farbenbahnen, auch das Grüngelb [;] der FAHNENBAUM [;] kräftigfarbig [;] deutlich unterschieden von den anderen" (Notizbuch 25, March 8, 1980, 19).

157. "Weiß (sehr)"; "normalgrau (blau) leuchtend eindeutig aber nicht knallig"; "gelbgrün"; "Schwarz (weiß)" (Notizbuch 25, March 8, 1980, 19).

158. "strahlen mit ihren Ovalen und Parallelen die unendliche Ruhe aus." Compare Notizbuch 25, February 4, 1980, 108; March 4, 1980, 113; April 9, 1980, 129; April 12, 1980, 143–44.

159. "der Buchenblattboden des Waldes, die Strahlenrillen"; "so ist der ganze Wald gestreift" (Notizbuch 25, April 2, 1980, 108).

160. Handke also notes on this page, "ein paar schwarze Stangen liegen als tote Monster im lieb ovalen Laubreich"; these are described in the published text on pages 131–32.

161. "schönes, ewiges Lichtbraun (das ist die Farbe des Waldes); schimmerndes Braun, mit den vielen parallen Rillen der Blätter nach dem Sturm" (Notizbuch 25, April 2, 1980, 109).

"the parallelism of the beech leaf rills: soothing."[162] And on April 9 Handke noted "the light brown of the fallen beech leaves: the color of the forest the form + the rills."[163] A schematic pencil sketch at the bottom of this page, faintly visible after the word "rills" (*Strahlen*), shows the rills of a beech leaf; the edge of the leaf is not depicted, as if the rills could in fact expand to fill the page—which itself is a lined *Buchblatt* (book leaf, or page), the lines of which resemble the rills of the *Buchenblatt* (beech leaf). Finally, on April 12—the day Handke finished the first version—we find several other descriptions of the beech-leaf-littered forest floor, inscribed in pencil and in some cases difficult to decipher, particularly as lines of writing frequently overlap and the faint pencil is now only barely legible: "light brown and the radiating card game across the soil"; "in contrast the light brown radiating ovals across the soil"; "the still playing cards, every now and then fluttering on their own"; "radiating striped ovals of the ~~cards~~ playing cards, which provide calm."[164]

These are just a few examples of the hundreds of notes that Handke pieced together to construct the first version of the chapter titled "The Great Forest," making numerous revisions—edits to formulations, strike-throughs, and additions—along the way. In generating the subsequent versions, Handke continued to edit the text extensively, making not only linguistic and syntactic changes to the individual pieces of text, but also *rearranging* them. A comparison of the three typescript versions of the passage shows that Handke repositioned several pieces in version 2, but reordered them much more extensively in version 3.

---

162. "die Parallelität der Buchenblattrillen: besänftigend" (Notizbuch 25, April 3, 1980, 108).

163. "das Lichtbraun der abgefallenen Buchenblätter: die Farbe des Waldes die Form + die Strahlen" (Notizbuch 25, April 9, 1980, 129).

164. "Lichtbraun und des weithin am Erdreich strahlenden Kartenspiels"; "Im Wiederspruch weithin auf dem Erdreich die lichtbraunen Strahlenovale"; "der still liegenden, sich manchmal wie selbstsätig auf blätternden Spielkarten"; "ausstrahlende Streifenovale der ~~Karten~~ Spielkarten, die für Ruhe sorgen" (Notizbuch 25, April 2, 1980, 143–44).

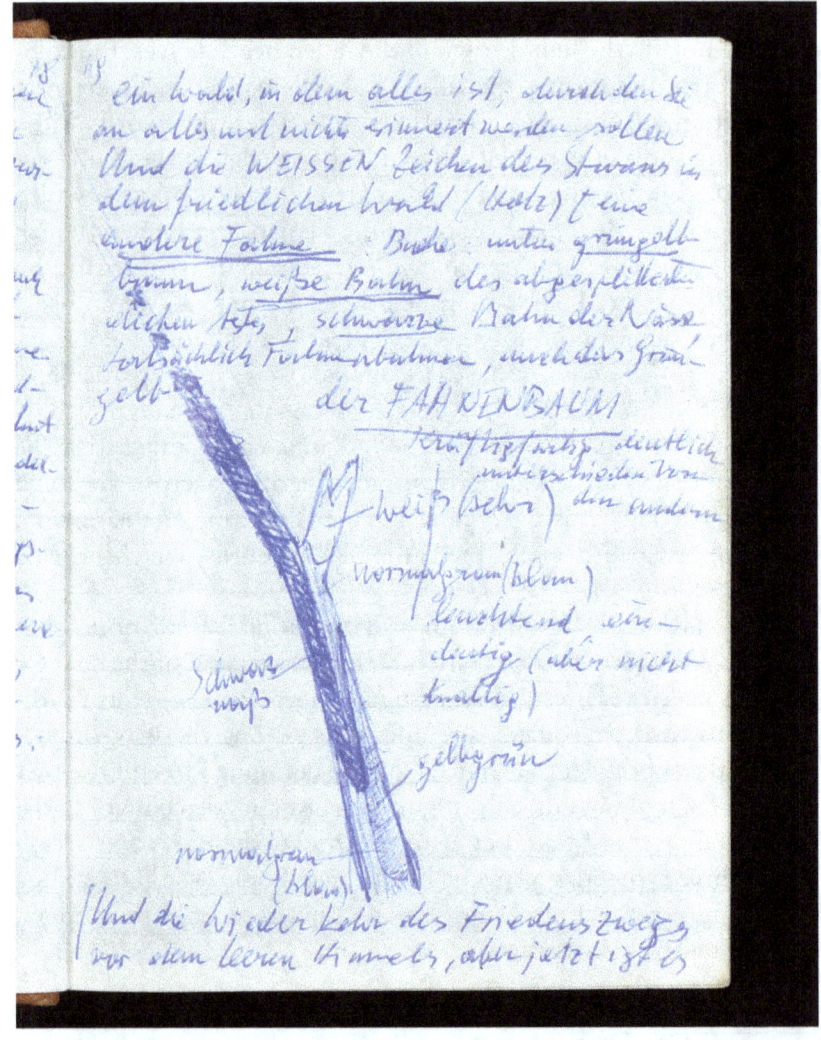

Figure 1.14. Peter Handke, "Die Lehre der Sainte-Victoire; Kindergeschichte; Die Geschichte des Bleistifts; Bleistiftgeschichte, 02.03.1980 bis 22.01.1981" (= Notizbuch 25), February 2, 1980, 19. HS.2007.0010.00025. Deutsches Literaturarchiv, Marbach.

To get a better sense of what happened in this rearranging process, I focus on a smaller piece of text from the larger passage cited above. Consider the following section from the first version.

Auffällig ~~noch~~ der Fahnenbaum:^{von} einer einzelnen Buche~~, von der~~ ^{ist} der Hauptast abgesplittert, ~~ist~~^{und} ^{ihr} Stamm zeigt drei leuchtende Farben~~bahnen~~: das Weiss der Bruchstelle, das Blau^{grau} der windgeschütz= ten Südseite,^{und} das Gelb der Wetterseite(bei Regen ~~ein S~~schwarz). Das Grün des ^{leeren} Feldes unten wird mit der Zeit warm$^{und\ tief,}$ ^{und} ~~D~~das Feld erstreckt sich dann ^{weit} jenseits der Stadt. In seiner Diagonale verläuft ein Weg, wo einmal ein Kind ~~hinter~~ einem Mann ^{nach}~~her~~lief, ihm ~~auf den~~ ~~Rücken~~ ^{hintenauf} sprang und so weiter *auf dem Rücken* getragen wurde. Ein andres Mal, in der Dunkelheit, bewegte sich da ein Reiter ~~in einem~~ lang= samen Schritt^{es} und wuchs$^{dann?}$, ~~von hinten gesehen~~$^{bei\ zunehmender\ Entfernung}$, mit ~~dem~~^{seinem} Pferd in dem ^{nächtlichen} ~~Finsternis=~~ Licht zu einem ~~einzigen~~ Riesengeschöpf zusammen. Darüber zog der ^{mondlose} Sternenhim= mel ~~als~~ $^{wie\ ein\ einziger}$ Raumschiff, und? ?aus den/^{vereinzelten} Feldwegpfützen blitzten vollständige ^{Sternbilder}

Striking ~~still~~ the <u>color-streaked tree</u>: ^{of} a solitary beach tree, from ~~which~~ the main branch ^{has} split open, ~~is~~ and its trunk shows three bright color~~s~~patches: the white of the splitting point, the blue^{grey} of the wind-protected southern side,^{and} the yellow of the weather side (~~a~~ black in the rain). The green of the ^{empty} field below becomes warm $^{and\ deep}$ in time, ^{and} ~~T~~the field extends then ^{far} beyond the city. Across it cuts a path on which a child once ran ~~behind~~ ^{after} a man, jumped up ~~on his back~~ $^{up\ on}$ him and was carried *on his back* from there on. Another time, in the darkness, a rider ~~with a~~ with slow steps was moving there and $^{then?}$ ~~seen~~ from ~~behind~~ $^{from\ an\ increasing\ distance}$ grew together with ~~the~~ ^{his} horse in the ^{nighttime} ~~darkness~~ light into a ~~single~~ gigantic creature. The ^{moonless} starry sky stretched above this ~~as~~ $^{like\ a\ single}$ spaceship, and? entire ^{constellations} flashed ?from the/^{scattered} puddles in the path

Among other things, Handke describes here the "color-streaked tree [*Fahnenbaum*]," a single "beech tree [*Buche*]" with its split trunk displaying different colors: "the white of the splitting point, the blue^{grey} of the wind-protected southern side,^{and} the yellow of the weather side (~~a~~ black in the rain)." In version 2a, among other changes, Handke altered the description of the beech tree, deleting "color-streaked tree," and changing "beech" to "linden [*Linde*]," which he later canceled and replaced again with "beech." He also changed the color of the "weather side [*Wetterseite*]" from "yellow" to "bird-throat-red [*Vogelkehlenrot*]." Moreover, the entire sentence has been repositioned, placed after the description of the child that sprang onto the man's back. The descriptions of the rider and the starry sky disappear entirely in version 2a.

> Das Grün des leeren Feldes unten wird mit der Zeit warm und tief, und erstreckt sich dann weit jenseits der Stadt. In seiner Diagonale verläuft ein Weg, wo einmal ein Kind hinter einem Mann her~~xxxx~~^{rannte}, ihm hinten aufsprang und so weitergetragen wurde. Auf= fällig/^{unter allen Bäumen} die einzelne ~~Linde~~^{Buche}, von der ein Blitz den Hauptast abgespalten hat, so dass der nackte Stamm drei leuchtende Farbbahnen zeigt: das Weiss der Bruch= stelle, das Blaugrau der Südseite, das ^{Vogelkehlenrot} ~~Gelb~~ der Wetter= seite(bei Regen ein Schwarz).

> The green of the empty field below becomes warm and deep in time, and then extends far beyond the city. Across it cuts a path on which a child once ^{ran} after ~~xxxx~~ behind a man, jumped up on him and was carried from there on. Striking /^{of all the trees} the individual ~~linden~~ ^{beech,} from which lightning has split open the main branch such that the bare trunk shows three bright patches of color: the white of the splitting point, the blue-gray of the southern side, the ^{bird-throat red} ~~yellow~~ of the weather side (a black in the rain)., ~~is~~ ^{and its} trunk shows three bright colorspatches: the white of the splitting point, the blue^{grey} of the wind-protected southern side,^{and} the yellow of the weather side (a black in the rain).

In version 2c, the description of the beech shifts yet again. Handke adds the word "banner tree" back to the text, and twice more changes the color of the "weather side [*Wetterseite*]" first to "rust brown [*Rostbraun*]" and then to "rust yellow [*Rostgelb*]." He also adds the description of the rider back into the text with the interlinear addition "another time [*Ein andres Mal*] (156 Nb.)" (figure 1.15). The parenthetical annotation refers to notebook page 156, where the following correction note indicating the order of pieces to be executed in the version can be found: "the green field: once a child ran after a man jumped up on his back, and rode on from there. Another time, a real horseman merged with his horse in the darkness, to form a single gigantic creature."[165]

---

165. "das grüne Feld: lief ein mal ein Kind einem Erwachsenen nach, sprang ihmauf den Rücken und ritt so weiter. Ein tatsächliche Reiter mit seinem Pferd

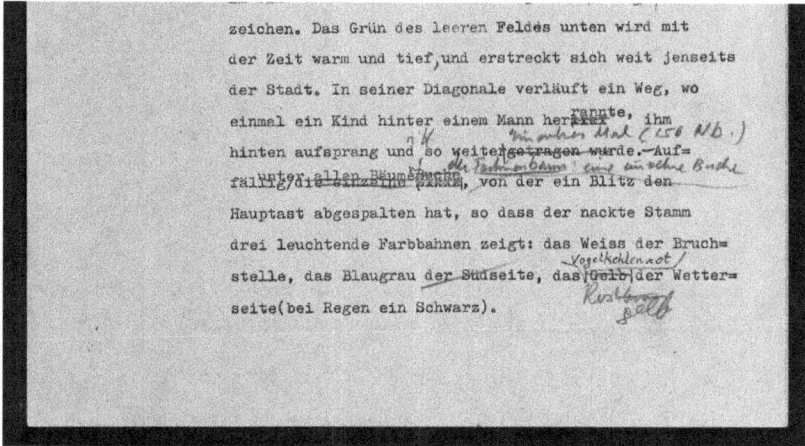

Figure 1.15. Peter Handke, version 2c of *Die Lehre der Sainte Victoire*, 97. ÖLA SPH/LW/W18. Literaturarchiv der Österreichischen Nationalbibliothek, Vienna.

Das Grün des leeren Feldes unten wird mit der zeit warm und tief, und erstreckt sich dann weit jenseits der Stadt. In seiner Diagonale verläuft ein Weg, wo einmal ein Kind hinter einem Mann her~~xxxx~~ ^{rannte}, ihm hinten aufsprang und ^{ritt} so weiter~~getragen wurde.~~^{Ein andres Mal (156 Nb.)} ~~Auf=~~ fällig/^{unter} ^{allen Bäumen} ~~die einzelne xxx~~^{Buche}, von *der* ^{Fahnenbaum: eine einzelne Buche} der ein Blitz den Hauptast abgespalten hat, so dass der nackte Stamm drei leuchtende Farbbahnen zeigt: das Weiss der Bruch= stelle, das Blaugrau ~~der Südseite~~, das ^{Vogelkehlenrot}~~Gelb~~rot_{Rostbraungelb} der Wetter= seite (bei Regen ein Schwarz).

The green of the empty field below becomes warm and deep in time, and then extends then far beyond the city. Across it cuts a path on which a child once ^{ran} after ~~xxxx~~ behind a man, jumped up on him and rode ~~was carried~~ from there on. ^{Another time (156 Nb.)} Striking /^{of all the trees} ~~the individual xxx~~ ^{beech,} from *the* ^{color-streaked tree: an individual beech} that lightning had split open the main branch of, such that the bare trunk shows three bright patches of color: the white of the splitting point, the blue-gray ~~of the southern side~~, the ^{bird-throat red} ~~yellow~~ red _{rust-brown-yellow} of the weather side (a black in the rain).

---

wuchs da ein anderes Mal in der Dunkelheit von hinten zu einer Riesengeschöpf" (Notizbuch 25, April 22, 1980, 156).

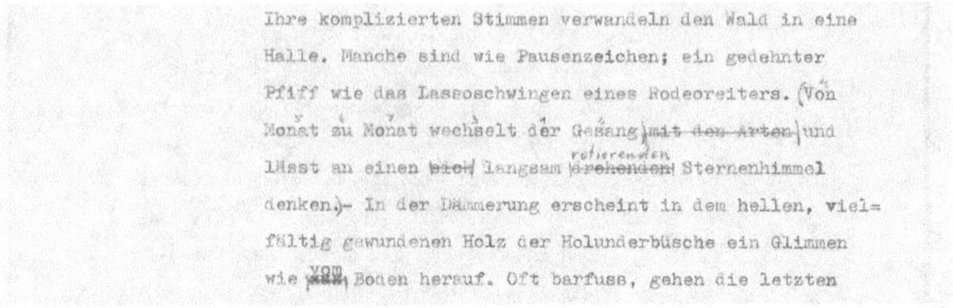

102   Chapter 1

> Ihre komplizierten Stimmen verwandeln den Wald in eine
> Halle. Manche sind wie Pausenzeichen; ein gedehnter
> Pfiff wie das Lassoschwingen eines Rodeoreiters. (Von
> Monat zu Monat wechselt der Gesang mit den Arten und
> lässt an einen sich langsam drehenden *rotierenden* Sternenhimmel
> denken.)— In der Dämmerung erscheint in dem hellen, viel=
> fältig gewundenen Holz der Holunderbüsche ein Glimmen
> wie vom Boden herauf. Oft barfuss, gehen die letzten

Figure 1.16. Peter Handke, third version of *Die Lehre der Sainte-Victoire*, 99. SU.2010.0002. Deutsches Literaturarchiv, Marbach.

We cannot know why Handke decided to make these changes. Was the replacement of "beech" with "linden" accidental or intentional? Regardless, the change draws attention to the type of tree, which is not insignificant, given that *Buche* (beech) is connected etymologically to *Buch* (book); in the medieval period, beech wood was commonly used to bind books, which then as now contain *Blätter*, the standard German word for both page and leaf (botanically and bibliographically). We might also wonder if Handke intentionally removed the description of the rider in the second version, and then decided to return it; or, if he accidentally deleted it in the patchwork process, adding it back once he discovered the omission. Regardless of his motivations, these changes highlight Handke's patchwork method of working, arranging and rearranging over the course of the text's generation.

The syntactic reorganization of the passage examined above occurred on the level of text-syntax: sentences or groups of sentences were reordered, paragraphs shaped and reshaped. But Handke also rearranged syntactically within individual sentences. Consider this sentence from the third version, which in fact appears for the first time there (figure 1.16).

> From month to month the songs change, ~~with the kinds~~ and one is reminded of the slowly ~~turning~~ *rotating* starry sky.

> (Von^4 Monat^5 zu^6 Monat^7 wechselt^3 der^1 Gesang^2, ~~mit den Arten~~ und

lässt an einen sich langsam ~~drehenden~~*rotierenden* Sternenhimmel denken.*)*-

Instead of striking through and rewriting, or retyping the entire page, Handke instructed typesetters to rearrange the words of the sentence by numbering them.

Handke even employed a material patchwork technique. Several pages of both versions 2a and 3 are physical montages, with strips of corrected text pasted on the original typescript, or two or more larger pieces of text pasted together. In version 3, one such patch is found before the description of the "beginning tree [*Anfangsbaum*]" (figure 1.17). In one particularly striking example, three patches are pasted onto a sheet to form an individual page, the middle patch of which itself contains a patch (figure 1.18). In version 1 as well, there is also evidence of this material patchwork, although it is more difficult to discern in the extant photocopy. At the bottom of page 29, for example, the final three lines, which appear to be slightly further indented than the preceding lines, were pasted over the original text of the typescript.[166] If one looks closely, tiny bits of the tops of letters on the top line, and a shadow of the text beneath the final line, remain visible (figure 1.19).

The patchwork nature of Handke's text-work extends into the typeset versions as well. Punctuation marks visually punctuate text, breaking it into units (clauses, sentences, and so on), but also function as "transitions" and "connections" between these units, signaling and visualizing semantic relationships between them. Semicolons separate clauses that are somewhat connected conceptually, in contrast to those punctuated with a period (*Punkt*); phrases or clauses parenthetically bracketed are both visually and semantically set "aside" from the main text. Similarly, paragraph breaks segment text into units not only visually but also semantically, guiding the cognitive and affective flow of reading.

These typographic features, of course, apply generally to printed text. But Handke actively mobilized punctuation as a component of

---

166. Traces of cut-and-paste operations are also found on pages 4 and 7 of the first text version.

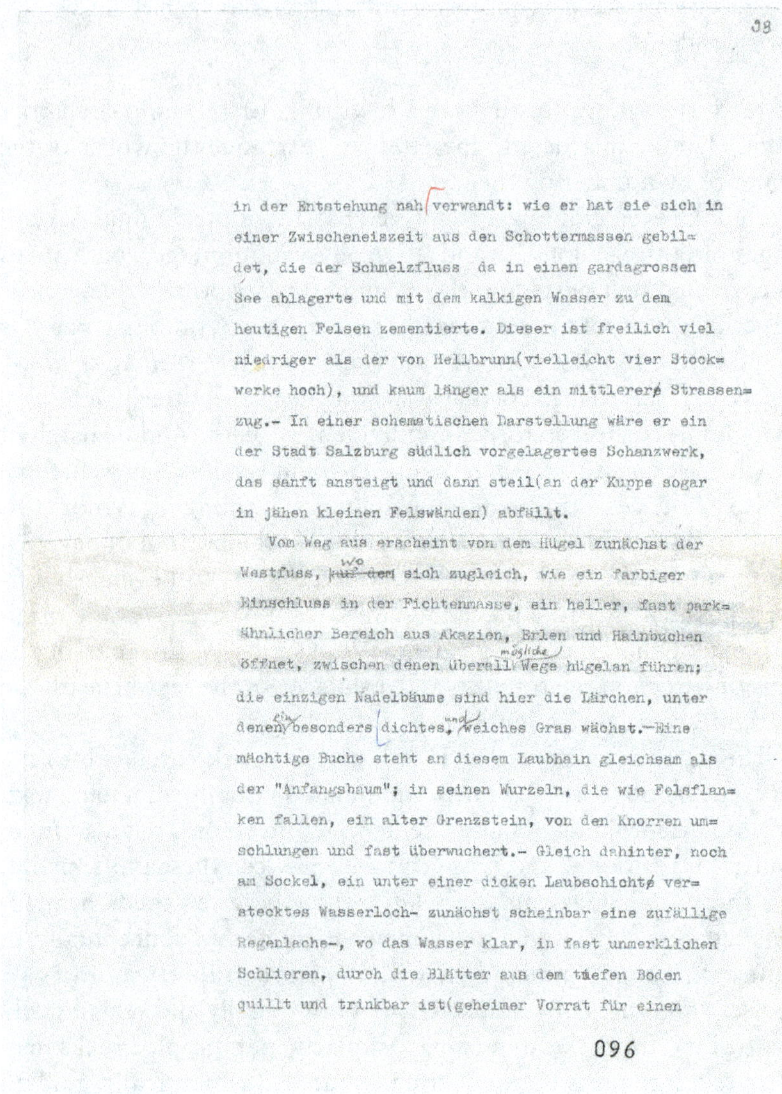

in der Entstehung nah verwandt: wie er hat sie sich in
einer Zwischeneiszeit aus den Schottermassen gebil=
det, die der Schmelzfluss da in einen gardagrossen
See ablagerte und mit dem kalkigen Wasser zu dem
heutigen Felsen zementierte. Dieser ist freilich viel
niedriger als der von Hellbrunn(vielleicht vier Stock=
werke hoch), und kaum länger als ein mittlerer Strassen=
zug.- In einer schematischen Darstellung wäre er ein
der Stadt Salzburg südlich vorgelagertes Schanzwerk,
das sanft ansteigt und dann steil(an der Kuppe sogar
in jähen kleinen Felswänden) abfällt.

Vom Weg aus erscheint von dem Hügel zunächst der
Westfuss, auf dem sich zugleich, wie ein farbiger
Einschluss in der Fichtenmasse, ein heller, fast park=
ähnlicher Bereich aus Akazien, Erlen und Hainbuchen
öffnet, zwischen denen überall Wege hügelan führen;
die einzigen Nadelbäume sind hier die Lärchen, unter
denen besonders dichtes, weiches Gras wächst.-Eine
mächtige Buche steht an diesem Laubhain gleichsam als
der "Anfangsbaum"; in seinen Wurzeln, die wie Felsflan=
ken fallen, ein alter Grenzstein, von den Knorren um=
schlungen und fast überwuchert.- Gleich dahinter, noch
am Sockel, ein unter einer dicken Laubschichte ver=
stecktes Wasserloch- zunächst scheinbar eine zufällige
Regenlache-, wo das Wasser klar, in fast unmerklichen
Schlieren, durch die Blätter aus dem tiefen Boden
quillt und trinkbar ist(geheimer Vorrat für einen

096

Figure 1.17. Peter Handke, third version of *Die Lehre der Sainte-Victoire*, 93. SU.2010.0002. Deutsches Literaturarchiv, Marbach.

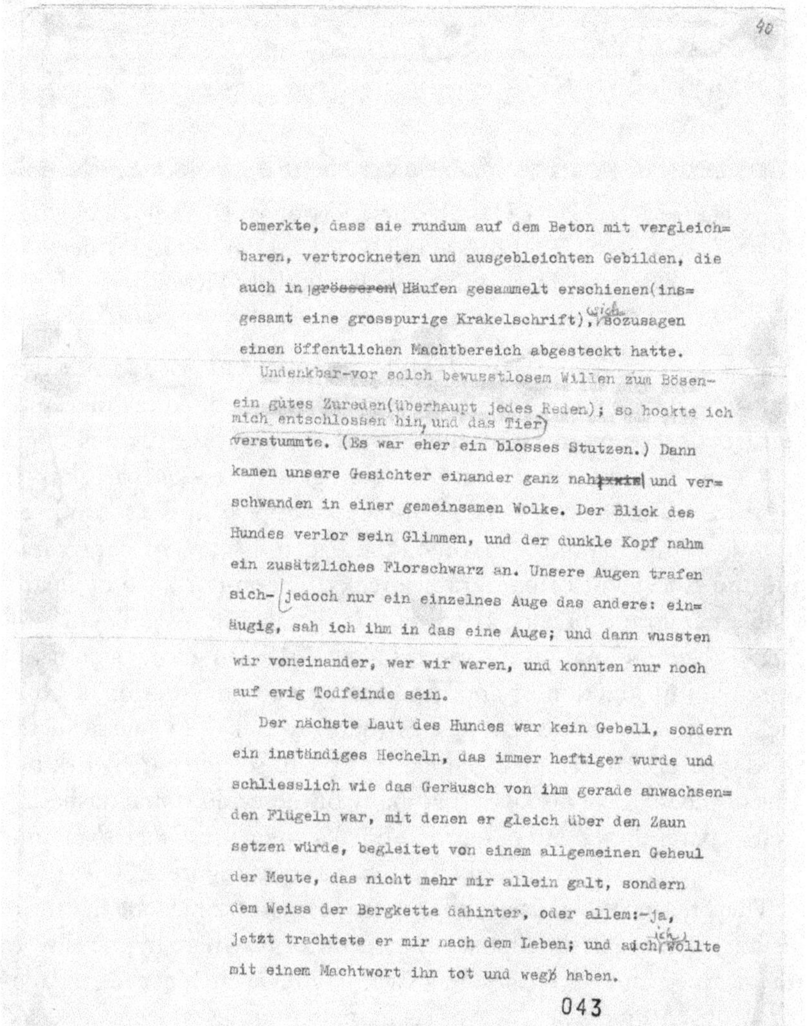

bemerkte, dass sie rundum auf dem Beton mit vergleich=
baren, vertrockneten und ausgebleichten Gebilden, die
auch in ~~grösseren~~ Häufen gesammelt erschienen(ins=
gesamt eine grosspurige Krakelschrift), sich sozusagen
einen öffentlichen Machtbereich abgesteckt hatte.

Undenkbar-vor solch bewusstlosem Willen zum Bösen—
ein gütes Zureden(überhaupt jedes Reden); so hockte ich
mich entschlossen hin, und das Tier)
verstummte. (Es war eher ein blosses Stutzen.) Dann
kamen unsere Gesichter einander ganz nah~~xxxx~~ und ver=
schwanden in einer gemeinsamen Wolke. Der Blick des
Hundes verlor sein Glimmen, und der dunkle Kopf nahm
ein zusätzliches Florschwarz an. Unsere Augen trafen
sich- jedoch nur ein einzelnes Auge das andere: ein=
äugig, sah ich ihm in das eine Auge; und dann wussten
wir voneinander, wer wir waren, und konnten nur noch
auf ewig Todfeinde sein.

Der nächste Laut des Hundes war kein Gebell, sondern
ein inständiges Hecheln, das immer heftiger wurde und
schliesslich wie das Geräusch von ihm gerade anwachsen=
den Flügeln war, mit denen er gleich über den Zaun
setzen würde, begleitet von einem allgemeinen Geheul
der Meute, das nicht mehr mir allein galt, sondern
dem Weiss der Bergkette dahinter, oder allem:—ja,
jetzt trachtete er mir nach dem Leben; und auch ich wollte
mit einem Machtwort ihn tot und weg haben.

Figure 1.18. Peter Handke, third version of *Die Lehre der Sainte-Victoire*, 40. SU.2010.0002. Deutsches Literaturarchiv, Marbach.

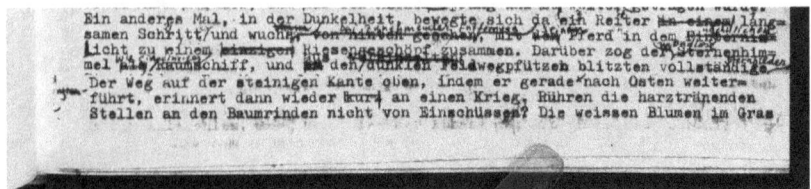

Figure 1.19. Peter Handke, first version of *Die Lehre der Sainte-Victoire*, 29. ÖLA SPH/LW/W19. Literaturarchiv der Österreichischen Nationalbibliothek, Vienna.

the typographic form (*Schriftbild*) to create specific visual, affective, and semantic effects. As we have seen, Handke edited orthographic features of the text in significant ways throughout the various stages of its production: there were *no* paragraph, section, or chapter breaks at all in the first version; these first appear in the second version. In editing, Handke modified the size and shape of paragraphs and the placement of paragraph breaks. The importance of clearly visible paragraph breaks, as we saw, is signaled in his galleys ("*Absatz unbedingt* [paragraph necessary]!!!"). Even more significant were the introduction of and modifications to punctuation, such as the addition of numerous dashes (here hyphens) en masse in the third typescript version. When we are able to see the patchwork origins of the text, we discover that many of these additional dashes, as well as parentheses and paragraph breaks, in fact *visualize the seams* between pieces of text based on different notes (figure 1.20).

The presence of these typographic seams becomes all the more visually striking in the first set of galley proofs, where hyphens were transformed into em dashes. In a sweeping reversal, however, the majority of the em dashes, as well as many parentheses, were canceled in the first set of proofs (figure 1.21). One wonders: Might the hyphens introduced in typescript version 3a have been intended to visualize, as "visible strokes [*sichtliche Striche*]" the patchwork origins of the text, the transitions between chunks based on separate notes—perhaps in keeping with D.'s dictum that "The transition must clearly divide *and* at the same time bring together"? Might these textual seams, once rendered typographically as em dashes in

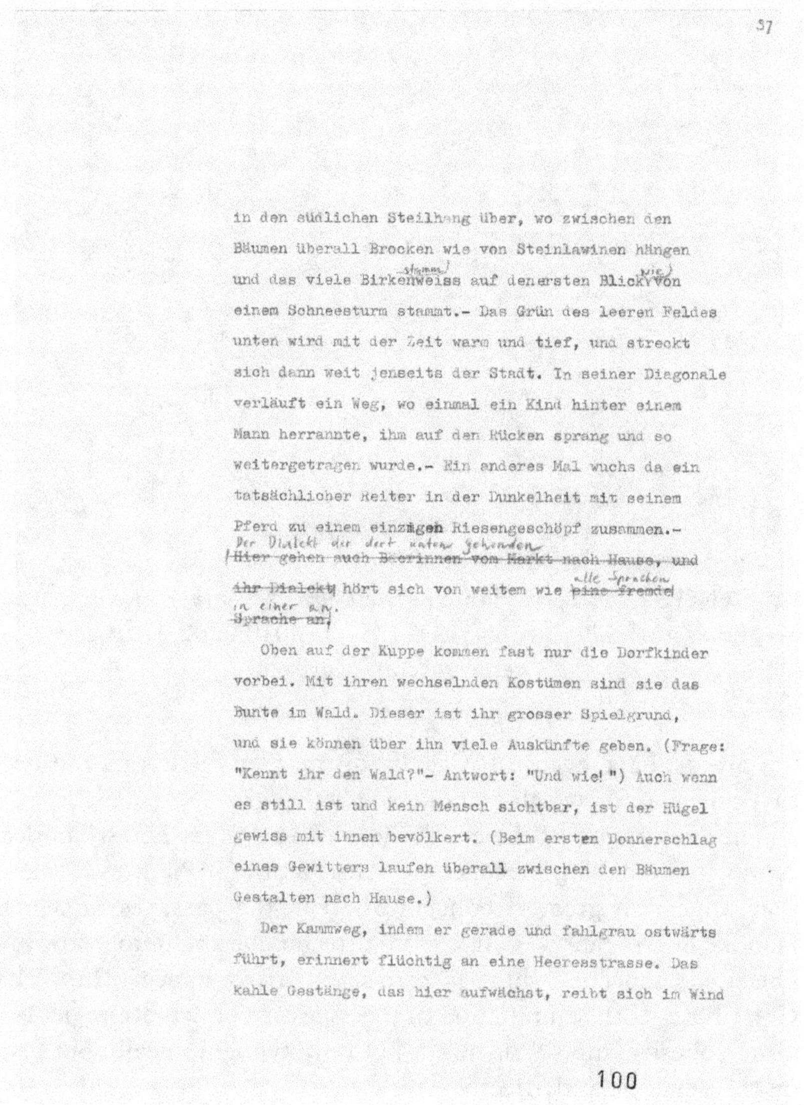

in den südlichen Steilhang über, wo zwischen den
Bäumen überall Brocken wie von Steinlawinen hängen
und das viele Birkenweiss auf den ersten Blick von
                      ˢᵗᵃᵐᵐᵗ⁾   ʷⁱᵉ⁾
einem Schneesturm stammt.- Das Grün des leeren Feldes
unten wird mit der Zeit warm und tief, und streckt
sich dann weit jenseits der Stadt. In seiner Diagonale
verläuft ein Weg, wo einmal ein Kind hinter einem
Mann herrannte, ihm auf den Rücken sprang und so
weitergetragen wurde.- Ein anderes Mal wuchs da ein
tatsächlicher Reiter in der Dunkelheit mit seinem
Pferd zu einem einzigen Riesengeschöpf zusammen.-
Der Dialekt der dort unten gehenden
[Hier gehen auch Bäuerinnen vom Markt nach Hause, und
                                       alle Sprachen
ihr Dialekt hört sich von weitem wie eine fremde
in einer an.
Sprache an]

   Oben auf der Kuppe kommen fast nur die Dorfkinder
vorbei. Mit ihren wechselnden Kostümen sind sie das
Bunte im Wald. Dieser ist ihr grosser Spielgrund,
und sie können über ihn viele Auskünfte geben. (Frage:
"Kennt ihr den Wald?"- Antwort: "Und wie!") Auch wenn
es still ist und kein Mensch sichtbar, ist der Hügel
gewiss mit ihnen bevölkert. (Beim ersten Donnerschlag
eines Gewitters laufen überall zwischen den Bäumen
Gestalten nach Hause.)

   Der Kammweg, indem er gerade und fahlgrau ostwärts
führt, erinnert flüchtig an eine Heeresstrasse. Das
kahle Gestänge, das hier aufwächst, reibt sich im Wind

100

Figure 1.20. Peter Handke, second version of *Die Lehre der Sainte-Victoire*, 97. SU.2010.0002. Deutsches Literaturarchiv, Marbach.

Chapter 1

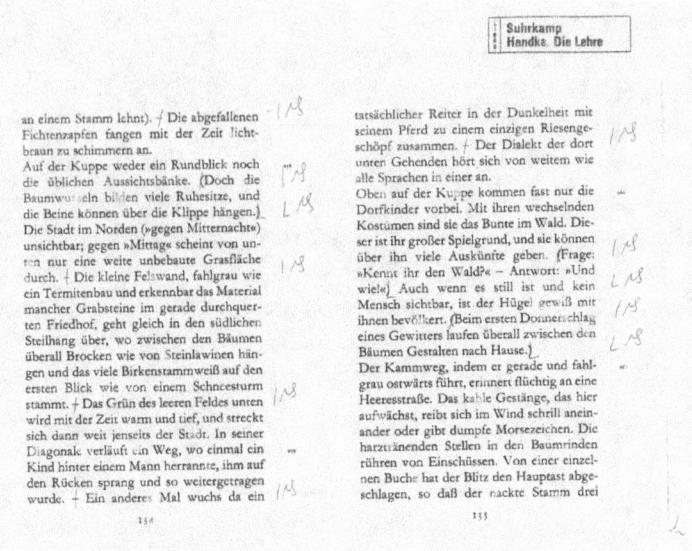

Figure 1.21. Peter Handke, *Die Lehre der Sainte-Victoire*, first set of galley proofs, 134–135. SU.2010.0002. Deutsches Literaturarchiv, Marbach.

the proofs, have been *too* visually distracting, disrupting the textual cohesion for which Handke was striving?

The elimination of the em dashes in "The Great Forest" underscores their striking presence in "The Picture of Pictures," where they appear in greatest concentration in the passages in which Handke interrogates Cézanne's stroke technique and unfolds the hyphenated concept "thing-picture-script-stroke-dance." In "The Great Forest," the elimination of the excessive punctuation yields a more cohesive, fluid *Schriftbild*, not only typographically but also on the semantic and affective levels.

Handke's text, then, is a patchwork through and through: a typographical patchwork composed of patches (chapters, sections, paragraphs) that are themselves patchworks of smaller patches (individual notebook notes). At the same time, these patches are like "small strokes" that together generate a cohesive picture, a picture produced through a *Strichwerk* of writing and striking through.

With a process reminiscent of Kaesdorf's *Stückwerk*, Handke modified the size and shape of these textual patches, their order and arrangement, over the course of the text's production.

In and of themselves, many of the features of Handke's writing and editing may not seem particularly noteworthy. Indeed, much that we have seen was common to writing and editing in the age of the typewriter. But when we consider Handke's process in relation to his interrogation of Cézanne's *Strichwerk* and Kaesdorf's *Stückwerk*, certain visual and material features of the text and its production take on added significance, as sites for Handke's material experimentation with the medium of writing (*Schrift*). Confronting the printed text alone, the reader cannot discern the seams between pieces of text—at least, not at first glance. Handke's narrative realization reads as a cohesive walk through the forest. When we examine the production of the text closely, however, we can see how this single walk through the forest is constructed from numerous walks, notes taken from numerous "viewpoints" that have been pieced together, the disjunctions smoothed over through the application of writerly strokes. This, in fact, is also a feature of Cézanne's painting. The objects of Cézanne's still lifes, as Meyer Schapiro (among others) has suggested, are not pictured from a single position, but instead are the products of a "shifting" gaze; multiple viewpoints bump up against one another, generating what appear to be visual distortions and misalignments.[167] What appear as "mistakes," however, are the result of an attempt to picture the fundamental interconnection of things, as well as their meetings and overlaps in the experience of visual perception. Through an analogous, textual "patchwork" process, Handke attempts to preserve and transmit what he has seen and experienced: the fundamental cohesion and interconnectedness of nature.

The *Strich*, however, constitutes one dimension of Handke's theory and practice of *Schrift*. Similarly, the *typo*graphic forms one dimension of the *biblio*graphic. Whereas the pen and notebook were the key tools of Handke's note-taking, the typewriter

---

167. Meyer Schapiro, *Paul Cézanne* (New York: Harry N. Abrams, 1952), 18–19.

was a crucial tool for the process of drafting. But the completion of a typescript version was not, of course, the end of the process; the patchwork text would need to assume *bibliographic* form, as a printed book. The material and visual features of the first edition, from binding to font size, were deliberately selected to produce certain effects in the experience of reading. In the process of drafting *The Lesson*, Handke had clear visions of the material form that his to-be-published text would take. In the first letter to Unseld in which he mentions the work (March 22, 1980), Handke writes: "I've been working on a story for a few weeks and often enjoy it immensely. It's called 'The Lesson of Sainte-Victoire.' . . . If it becomes a book, then I'd like it to be paperback [*broschiert*], but not a pocketbook [*Taschenbuch*; that is, a Suhrkamp Taschenbuch]. . . . The cover should be like that of "The Left-Handed Woman," only with a small mountain silhouette as signum instead of the bull."[168] Per Handke's specifications, the first edition of *The Lesson* is a paperback. The materiality of the cover, made of grey laid paper, evokes the aura of the handmade. Designed by Willy Fleckhaus, who designed the majority of Handke's Suhrkamp covers during this period, the cover presents the work title, author's name, and publisher's name in a "typewriter font [*Schreibmaschinenschrift*]," which Handke had also specified for the covers of *Slow Homecoming* and *The Moment of True Feeling* (*Die Stunde der wahren Empfindung*).[169] The cover also features an illustration, a facsimile of a pencil sketch of Mont Sainte-Victoire taken from one of Handke's notebooks.[170] The cover thus re-presents the multimediality of the printed text's production: the drawing indexes the manuscript notebooks that accompanied Handke along the *route Cézanne*, whereas the typewriter font references

---

168. Handke and Unseld, *Briefwechsel*, 392.
169. Handke and Unseld, *Briefwechsel*, 361.
170. In the June 12, 1980, letter to Unseld, Handke wrote, "It should not be indicated anywhere that the sketch was made by the writer [Handke]. It was just so that I could become calmer before the mountain" (Handke and Unseld, *Briefwechsel*, 409).

Handke's practice, at this time, of composing text drafts on the typewriter.[171]

In addition to the cover design, the font size selected for the text of *The Lesson*—which is unusually large, reminiscent of that used more frequently for printed poetry—is also particularly significant.[172] Along with other typographical features discussed, the larger font size itself has a defamiliarizing effect, causing the reader to *perceive* it as text, as written marks on the page. While there is no documentation of Handke's selection of this font size for *The Lesson*, we might glean its intended effect from Handke's requests regarding the font size of other texts. For Handke's second novel, *The Peddler* (*Der Hausierer*), for example, Handke specified the following: "The font size should be maximally larger than in *The Hornets* [*Die Hornissen*], so that each sentence has the effect of a 'blow' [*Schlag*]. Each sentence should be perceptible as an individual sentence, not as a sentence in a succession of sentences. (It should also be this). That would also make reading easier, because the text demands a change in reading habits, and the attempt of the reader to read the novel 'like a novel' would then immediately be met with resistance and the reader would become tired and frustrated."[173] Here, the larger font size is intended to slow the reading pace, such that each sentence will "strike" the reader, causing the reader to perceive each sentence *as a sentence*; that is, to actually *see* the text as written text. Handke intends the font size to interact with the linguistic text, which, Handke states, cannot be read as a typical novel but instead requires a shift in reading habits. Although the genre and aesthetics of the text are quite different, the larger font size of *The Lesson* functions in a similar way: it causes the reader to *see* the text in its visuality, effecting a slower reading pace, which allows the reader, if not to "stumble," then to perceive each sentence, each image, in and of itself as they traverse the topography of the page.

---

171. Beginning with *Versuch über die Jukebox* (Frankfurt am Main: Suhrkamp,1989), Handke shifted to constructing his prose texts entirely in pencil.
172. Hoesterey, "Mit Cézanne," 101.
173. Handke and Unseld, *Briefwechsel*, 62–63.

These typographic dimensions *interact with* Handke's vividly descriptive, slow rhythmic language, as well as the montage-like structural dimensions of the work—which, as we have seen, result not only from the text's extensive intertextuality, but also from the process of its patchwork composition—to *slow* the reading pace. In this way, the slowness of Handke's walking, note-taking, and text production is brought into the experience of reading the printed book. Through all of these dimensions at once—the semantic and structural dimensions of the text, the visual and material dimensions of the book—Handke attempted to capture and transmit Cézanne's experience of seeing and grasping the world, such that the reader can experience this "lesson" for themselves.

Hidden Writing

Once we reverse engineer Handke's process, we can see that traces of it do shine through in the published version of *The Lesson*; in some cases they are quite literally visible in the text's typographical surface. In other words, the process of constructing the text remains entangled within its material and visual form, as well as its content. To show this, I examine a final passage, in which Handke describes the entry into the forest, to suggest that Handke's narration of the walk to and through the Morzg forest and back is not only a "realization" of this motif, but simultaneously reflects his theoretical method of *Schrift* generally and his construction of *The Lesson* specifically.

Like the rest of the chapter "The Great Forest," this passage is also composed of numerous notes that have been patched together. In what follows, instead of analyzing the construction of this passage in great detail, I will focus on a host of details that stick out notably, now that we are familiar with Handke's process.

> At the edge of this deciduous copse there is an enormous beech tree that serves as a kind of "beginning tree"; its roots rise like cliffs, twining around an old boundary stone and almost concealing it. Directly behind it, still at the bottom of the hill, a water hole is partially hidden beneath a thick layer of leaves. At first sight, one takes it for a rain puddle, but this water is clear and rises in almost imperceptible jets through the blackish leaves from deep underground. It is drinkable (a secret supply

in case of emergency). One is struck by the rounded stones under the grass, ordered as regularly and compactly as cobbles in a road. They are many-colored, and on each one the lichens have etched a distinct picture script, as different from one to the next as traditions originating in different continents. A red, bell-shaped hump is a replica in miniature of Ayer's Rock in Australia, the largest monolith on earth. Another shows an Indian hunter's tale. At dusk, when the vegetation above them disappears, these stones reveal their secret writing and become a somber-white Roman road, leading into the forest. (LMSV 205–6)

Eine mächtige Buche steht an diesem Laubhain gleichsam als der "Anfangsbaum"; in seinen Wurzeln, die wie Felsflanken fallen, ein alter Grenzstein, von den Knorren umschlungen und fast überwuchert.[174] Gleich dahinter, noch am Sockel, ein unter einer dicken Laubschicht verstecktes Wasserloch—zunächst scheinbar eine zufällige Regenlache–, wo das Wasser klar, in fast unmerklichen Schlieren, durch die schwärzlichen Blätter aus dem tiefen Boden quillt und trinkbar ist (geheimer Vorrat für einen Notfall).[175] Auffällig, schon auf dem Weg dahin, die rundlichen Steine unter dem Gras, regelmäßig und dichtgefügt, wie ein Kopfsteinpflaster. Sie sind vielfarbig, und die Moosflechten haben in jeden einzelnen eine deutliche Bilderschrift geätzt, von einem zum anderen völlig verschieden, wie Überlieferungen aus getrennten Erdteilen.[176] Ein roter glockenförmiger Buckel wiederholt im kleinen

---

174. On March 25, Handke produced a sketch of the roots of the beech tree, labeling it "Im Wurzelwurk der Waldausgangsbuche" (Notizbuch 25, March 25, 1980, 77). Ten days later he noted: "beim Anblick der breitgegabelten alten Buche am Waldeingang: man möchte ewig leben; |der in den Wurzeln halb verschwundene Grenzstein|; von den W. überflossen" (Notizbuch 25, April 3, 1980, 113).

175. Compare the following: "Unter dem Laub die Quelle (Schwärze unter dem Laub); leichtes Heben und Senken des Laubs unter dem Wasser; Schwanken der Laubfäden (sonst ist die Quelle nicht sichtbar); aber es rinnt unten doch stetig Wasser ab; die Quelle ist sehr tief; in der Laubschicht ist also ein Wasserloch von fast im Tiefe; nach dem Stochern auch lang schwärzliche, beinah tintige Schlammschwaden; sehr komplizierte Vogelrufe, vielfältige Sprache (über der Quelle); es ist mehr, wie sich herausstellt, ein Wasserloch (wie geheimer Vorrat)" (Notizbuch 25, April 2, 1980, 107–8). On the same pages, Handke sketched a beech leaf with its radiating grooves—noting "der Buchenblattboden des Waldes, die Strahlenrillen"—which stands in for the beech leaves that covers the entire forest floor: "so ist der ganze Wald gestreift" (Notizbuch 25, April 2, 1980, 108). In the printed version, Handke writes that the "Laubschicht" makes it difficult to spot the water hole ("ein unter dickem Laubschicht verstecktes Wasserloch," [129]). The day before he drafted this passage, Handke noted "das Wasser der Quelle: wie ein geheimer Vorrat" (Notizbuch 25, April 9, 1980, 129).

176. Notes on the the moss-etched stones were recorded on multiple walks: "die runden Steine auf dem Waldweg, man kann sich in sie vertiefen (das Geräusch

einmal den australischen Ayers Rock, den größten Einzelberg der Erde; auf einem anderen steht eine indianische Jagderzählung.[177] In der Dämmerung, wenn das Pflanzenwerk darüber verschwindet, offenbaren sich diese Steine als Geheimschrift und leuchten als eine düsterweiße, waldeinwärts führende Römerstraße.[178] (*LSV* 129–30)

Marking the threshold of the forest, as a "beginning tree [*Anfangsbaum*]," is a beech tree with visibly protruding roots.[179] What at first glance appears to be a puddle, barely visible beneath a layer of leaves (*Laubschicht*), is the source of a spring that will eventually flow into "finally hoped-for pond [*endlich erhoffte Weiher*]," a pond that for Handke marks the end of the path through the forest. Stones on the ground, also partially obscured beneath the grass, have been "etched" by lichens with a "picture writing [*Bilderschrift*]." Although

---

der Steine, auf einander fallend, im zwischen den Bäumen [;] Im Wald gibt es von den runden Steinen hier und das wirklich eine Ast Kopfsteinpflaster (Römerweg)" (Notizbuch 25, March 15, 1980, 40). This note is followed by a note connecting Cézanne's painting *Le grand pin*, Ruisdael's *Der große Wald*, and the Morzg forest: "'die große Kiefer' und Ruysdaels 'Der große Wald' (das ist Verschränkung Verknüpfung); im M.ger Wald vergeht einem jede Lust, dafür ist Freude möglich" (Notizbuch 25, March 15, 1980, 40). On March 26, Handke notes that the stones appear as a Roman path: "der Weg im M.ger Wald mit den runden Steinen ist ein Römerweg (O→W); es sind Steine, an denen man mit einem Blick alles sehen kann" (Notizbuch 25, March 16, 1980, 83). The day before Handke drafted this section in the first text version, Handke again noted the leaves covering the forest floor with their parallel rills (Notizbuch 25, April 9, 1980, 131).

177. Compare the following notes: "der kleine Stein im Wald, und der Ayers Rock im Australien |9.4.1980|... im Herbst die Blätter im Hohlweg" (Notizbuch 25, April 8, 1980, 128); "der Stein glockenförmig im Weg, mit parallelen Rillen; kann den Ayers Rock darstellen, den einzigen Berg Australiens" (Notizbuch 25, April 9, 1980, 131). The reference to the *Jagderzählung* emerged in the second draft; compare the following correction notes: "X An dem glockenförmigen Stein wiederholt sich einmal der Ayers Rock" (Notizbuch 25, April 21, 1980, 155); "X Ayers Rock: wiederholten sich die Höhlenzeichnungen vom^{austrat} Ayers Rock, dem größten Einzelberg der Welt, und auf einem ... stand |dichtgefügt| eine Jagderzählung nordamerikanischer Indianer)" (Notizbuch 25, April 21, 1980, 157).

178. Compare the following correction note: "X Römerweg: in der Dämmerung verschwinden die Pflanze; und der Rw. schimmert erscheint wie eine Geheimschrift" (Notizbuch 25, April 21, 1980, 156).

179. In earlier versions Handke described an "Eingangsbaum," marking a *spatial* entry point; the term "Anfangsbaum" emphasizes a *temporal* beginning point—that is, of a narrative or journey unfolding in time.

it recalls Cézanne's *Bilderschrift*, this picture writing is produced, not by human hands, but by nature itself, a *Bilder-Schrift der Natur*. These stones tell stories: one repeats in its form Ayers Rock in Australia; another is inscribed with characters resembling Indian hunting stories. Together, these individual texts form a mosaic-like "hidden writing [*Geheimschrift*]"—a material *Schrift der Schriften*. The picture-writing of each stone is so unique that it seems the stones have been gathered from all the "continents [*Erdteilen*]" into a Pangea-like mosaic.[180] Veiled beneath the layer of leaves, this hidden text becomes visible in special conditions, appearing simultaneously as a cobblestone path or Roman road.[181]

In narrating his hike to the peak of Mont Sainte-Victoire, Handke describes Cézanne's own fascination with Roman roads: "Consequently, I didn't stay long but started on the westward descent, taking pleasure in the upland meadows, the valleys, and the Provençal roads, which Cézanne had praised for being Roman roads. 'The roads of the Romans are always admirably placed. They had a feeling for landscape. At every point, there's a picture'" (LMSV 172). Like these Provençal roads, now part of the *route Cézanne*, the path through the Morzg forest is a similar kind of path—the *route Handke*—along which, at which, at every point, a different picture of nature is revealed.

Once could analyze the entire material production of this passage with the same degree of detail demonstrated in the preceding analysis, tracing each sentence back to its notebook source. But when we step back and view this passage from a distance, another image begins to appear. Through the leaves of the book (*Buchblätter*), largely obscured from view, lies a "hidden writing"—a mosaic, patchwork text composed of notes—that shines through in certain places, becoming visible under certain conditions. This secret writing,

---

180. Handke described "Kontinenten" in earlier versions, replacing this with "Erdteilen," the root "Teilen" (parts/pieces) emphasizing the mosaic quality of the path.
181. On the concept of the Book of Nature for Cézanne, see Kurz, *Bild-Verdichtungen*, 80–81; Fischer, *Poet as Phenomenologist*, 146. In relation to Handke, see also Köhnen, "Zwischen Zeichenspiel," 197, 204, 216; Hoestery, "Mit Cézanne," 114.

however, is not only a visual mosaic, it is also a path. The text realizes the path to and through the Morzg forest, one that Handke took many times, not only physically but also in the process of constructing the text, leafing back through his notes, repeating the journey with each revision—a journey that the reader also repeats in the act of reading, traversing the topography of the page, the cobblestone typography of the printed text.

In addition to the path narrated *in* the text, the path to and through the Morzg forest, the text *itself* is a kind of path. But there also a third path that lies beneath the surface, entangled within these two: the path of the text's production. As we have seen, Handke constructed the text gradually and in stages, with great deliberation and care, making many modifications along the way. Though some revisions were quite dramatic, transformations of the work into an entirely different *Schriftbild*, the majority of edits that Handke made were relatively small, "small strokes" that together generated constantly shifting pictures of his motif.

The path of the text's production began on the pages of Handke's notebooks, inscribed *in* the forest that would eventually become realized in print. Examining the process of the text's production, from the notebooks to published version, enables this secret writing to shine through in Handke's narration. The preprint pages of *The Lesson*—from notebooks to typescripts to galley proofs—remain enmeshed within the pages of the printed book. The path through the Morzg forest leads from "*beginning* tree [*Anfangsbaum*]" toward "*finally* hoped-for pond [*endlich erhoffte Weiher*]" in the same way that reading proceeds from the beginning to the end of the chapter, and of the book.[182] The "beginning tree," however, though marking the beginning of the forest, was not the beginning of the journey: prior to arriving at this beginning tree, Handke narrates the path *to* the Morzg forest. In a similar way, the beginning of the printed text is not the "beginning" of the work. The path to the forest, as Handke describes it, passes through three

---

182. The final paragraph of the text—the rush from the forest back to civilization—could be thought to represent the closing of the book, when the reader is whooshed back from their absorption in the book to their everyday world.

prominent meadows, three main stations along the way, which parallel the three main text versions on the way to the published text. "First comes an urban sort of 'meadow,' traversed by concrete walks and resounding with footsteps"—reminding of the first version covered in strike-throughs, resounding with interstitial additions—"and then a 'quiet zone'" (LMSV 202). "The road across the plain rises gently.... The slight increase in altitude makes it possible to speak of a plateau. There is nothing citified about the meadow here; it is an open field" (LMSV 202). Like version 2a, a clean copy of the text, this second meadow looks quite different from the first; it is a spacious, open field. From this meadow, Handke's path proceeds through a large, open cemetery, from which the third meadow is visible: "The paths are long and narrow, and in the archway at the end of them the approach to the Morzg Forest shimmers green" (LMSV 203). Similarly, Handke proceeded from version 2a through another revision, version 2c, with version 3, and the forest beyond it, in sight: "This approach is the third meadow along the way: no longer a citified meadow, but also not an agricultural area, instead a wide, almost treeless a wide, almost treeless plot" (*LSV* 125). Before the "beginning tree," Handke describes his entry into the forest, a threshold zone like the typeset proofs to the text: "Only utility paths and disorderly trails traverse this space" (*LSV* 128).

Like the reader, who follows along the path of Handke's textual forest, the hiker through Morzg forest proceeds from "beginning" to "finally hoped-for pond." The roots of the beech tree, however, like the roots of the book, protrude upward, flowing over its surface. At one point, in proceeding through the forest and observing the fallen beech leaves, Handke notices some leaves that are caught in the bushes: "For a moment, playing cards seem to be hanging on the bushes—and then they are lying on the ground all over the forest, sparkling and fluttering in the slightest breeze, reappearing wherever you go.... This network catches the leaves, which in retrospect stand for the whole forest" (LMSV 207). These *Buchenblätter*, with their prominent rills, are like the lined pages of Handke's *Notiz-Buchblätter*, entangled within the *Buchblätter* of Handke's textual forest.

When one encounters the published version alone, various features of the text remind of Cézanne's realization: Handke's slow, detailed description of the forest that seems to penetrate through superficial appearances to capture vibrancy and vitality, the forest's mystery and allure, which "shine through" in various spots. With this narration, Handke aims to transform the reader's own view of the world. Yet by examining the *longue durée* of the text's production, examining its buried layers, we can see that Handke's application of Cézanne's method was not only about creating textual effects. For Handke was also experimenting with a material, intermedial method of writing, a choreographic-ontographic-typographic-bibliographic *Schriftwerk* informed by Cézanne's *Strichwerk* and Kaesdorf's *Stückwerk*.

When we examine Handke's process as closely as Handke examined Cézanne's, we can discern in it a theory of *Schrift*, one parallel to Cézanne's theory of realization. Cézanne spoke of this theory, but never articulated it fully or directly; it becomes legible only in his material process. Similarly, Handke gestures to his theoretical method of writing in *The Lesson*; it only fully visible, legible as a theoretical method, when we examine his material writing process. While Handke's theoretical method of patchwork writing can be put into dialogue with poststructuralist notions of *bricolage*,[183] the structural and semantic effects grasped through such metaphors in fact result from Handke's patchwork process of constructing *The Lesson*, which remains entangled within, inscribed into, the form and content dimensions of the work. Part of what makes Handke's experimental interrogation writing so unique, I suggest, was its philosophical and ethical dimensions: the way in which, *through writing*, Handke sought to develop and cultivate a relationship to things, to put into practice Cézanne's method of realization as a "transformation and sheltering of things endangered" (LMSV 181). For Cézanne, it was essential to realize "*devant la nature*," "in the open," "hanging" onto things, waiting for them to express themselves so that he could capture and transform them through painting. For Handke, the transformation and preservation of things similarly began with note-taking in nature. But once Handke captured them on his notebook pages, they had to undergo another of additional

---

183. See Hoesterey, "Mit Cézanne," particularly 114.

steps—steps that were not part of Cézanne's process—in their transformation into printed text. To "preserve" the things of the world through this process, Handke stayed as close to his notes as possible, engaging in a slow, repetitive, patchwork method of writing as text-making, *Schrift-stellen*. As Handke noted in late May 1979, "I must learn to love the words (one at a time [*einzeln*]) (like the colors for Cézanne), so that I can repeatedly place [*setzen*] them."[184] In Handke's writerly realization, a textual picture of a great forest, we can also see, when viewed from a certain angle, a picture of his own *Schriftwerk*, a forest of *Buchblätter*.

---

184. "Ich muß die Wörter (einzeln) lieben lernen (so wie Cézanne die Farben), damit ich sie wiederholt setzen kann" (Notizbuch 20, May 28, 1979, 75).

2

Bernhard's Productive Destruction

In an essay titled "Als ich 'Verstörung' von Thomas Bernhard las" (When I read *Gargoyles* by Thomas Bernhard), Peter Handke recounts his experience of reading Bernhard's second novel.[1] While waiting for a friend at a café in the Hannover train station, Handke describes attempting to read the newspaper, but exhausted though he was, "the book left me no peace."[2] Handke goes on to recount aspects of the story as he internalized it, in a somewhat disorganized flow. Toward the end of the short essay, Handke moves from the café to a park, and from the park to another restaurant, all the while continuing to read. His narration oscillates between the content of Bernhard's text and his physical surroundings: "The prince could not lead the two of them into the house, because everything was in

---

1. Peter Handke, "Als ich 'Verstörung' von Thomas Bernhard las," *Manuskripte* 7, no. 3 (1967–68): 14–15.
2. Handke, "Als ich 'Verstörung' von Thomas Bernhard las," 14.

disorder. I got up in the restaurant and continued to read, accompanied by the music of a café violinist. I tried to make a phone call a few more times, in vain. I drank something and continued to read. The prince had been constructed entirely against reality. He froze from the inside out. I read and read and read...."[3] In this essay, Handke describes the scene of his reading: sitting at a table in the train station café, sipping a coffee, browsing the newspaper, exhausted; later standing in a another restaurant, reading in unison with the music of a violinist. But this "scene" also includes the language of the text itself that pulls Handke to keep reading, his attention shifting between its content and his physical surroundings. Concluding with an ellipsis, the final sentence points beyond the boundaries of the text in a double sense: it not only gestures to the fact that the act of reading continues, but also refers intertextually to another text by Bernhard, the short story "Die Mütze" (The cap), which similarly ends with an ellipsis: "He wrote and wrote and wrote . . ." (W 14:34).

This experience of the pull or suction of Bernhard's language has been echoed by numerous readers. Franz Eyckeler famously describes a "Sprachsog," a linguistic suction or undertow, that derives less from the content than from the rhythmic style of Bernhard's writing.[4] In this chapter I explore how key stylistic and affective features of Bernhard's writing emerged out of his highly bodily process of writing, for which the typewriter was his primary instrument. I draw particular attention to the agential participation of Bernhard's writing materials in his writing process. In particular, I center his use of the typewriter as an instrument of production, and his use of the space of the page as a productive constraint to shape the text. The materiality and visuality of Bernhard's writing produced recursive effects on how and what he wrote, directly shaping the linguistic form of the text and becoming figured in its contents. In this way—through the language of the text, in its material and semiotic dimensions—the scene of writing is connected to the scene of reading. In other words, the entanglement of the scene of writing and the scene of reading, broadly conceived, is

---

3. Handke, "Als ich 'Verstörung' von Thomas Bernhard las," 15.
4. Franz Eyckeler, *Reflexionspoesie: Sprachskepsis, Rhetorik und Poetik in der Prosa Thomas Bernhards* (Berlin: Schmidt, 1995), 76.

premised on the micro-entanglements of materiality and meaning at each stage of, and rippling across, the entire textual production process. The material experience of reading—"He read and read and read . . ."—is thus shaped in part, and in direct, concrete ways, by the material process of writing—"He wrote and wrote and wrote . . ."

As Austria's most notorious *Nestbeschmutzer* (nest beschmircher) and self-proclaimed "Geschichtenzerstörer" (story destroyer),[5] Thomas Bernhard is known for his radical critiques of the conservatism and complacency of Austrian society, critiques that he enacts through highly experimental, postmodernist linguistic structures and narrative forms. Constructed of highly repetitive, rambling, hyperbolic, often self-contradictory clauses that can proceed for pages upon pages without pause, Bernhard's language is often experienced as musical and rhythmic, but also as assaulting and maddening, overflowing the boundaries of sense-making discourse. The reader is confronted with, as Derek Attridge puts it, "writing as writing, in all its uncertainty, prolixity, contradictoriness, and materiality."[6] Scholars have examined the prominent theme of destruction throughout Bernhard's work, as well as the performative linguistic, narrative strategies of destruction that characterize Bernhard's prose.[7] But these structural/stylistic features are also generated, I explore, through specific writerly methods and techniques of textual composition—the material techniques of Bernhard's *Geschichtenzerstören*.

Bernhard's convention-destroying writing is thus fundamentally disorienting: it works to destabilize language and narrative, the basic epistemological forms/structures though which humans construe—and all too frequently misconstrue—the world. Whereas Handke believed in the power of language to capture external truth, Bernhard

---

5. Thomas Bernhard, "Drei Tage," in *Der Italiener* (Frankfurt am Main: Suhrkamp, 1989), 83–84.

6. Derek Attridge, *Peculiar Language: Literature as Difference from the Renaissance to James Joyce* (Ithaca NY: Cornell University Press, 1988), 228. Cited in Samuel Frederick, *Narratives Unsettled: Digression in Robert Walser, Thomas Bernhard, and Adalbert Stifter* (Evanston, IL: Northwestern University Press, 2012), 14.

7. On Bernhard as *Geschichtenzerstörer*, see Bianca Theisen, *Silenced Facts: Media Montages in Contemporary Austrian Literature* (Amsterdam: Rodopi, 2003), esp. 43–46; Frederick, *Narratives Unsettled*, esp. 102–6.

was under no such illusion: in contrast with Handke's poetics of restoration, Bernhard's poetics of destruction is characterized by profound nihilism and deep linguistic skepticism. It is telling, in this respect, that many of Bernhard's protagonists are readers of the German Romantic poet Novalis. In his 1798 "Monologue," Novalis suggests that language can refer only to itself, not to any exterior world: "There is really something very foolish about speaking and writing; proper conversation is merely a word game. One can only marvel at the ridiculous mistake that people make when they think—that they speak for the sake of things. The particular quality of language, the fact that is concerned only with itself, is known to no one.... If one could only make people understand that it is the same with language as with mathematical formulae. These constitute a world of their own."[8] Something similar could be said of Bernhard's writing.[9] Although his writing contains references to extratextual figures, places, and events, these signifiers are incorporated into the self-propagating machinery of Bernhard's prose in a way that divorces them from anything signified. Bernhard's writing is highly hermetic and frequently thematizes itself, its own linguistic and narrative form becoming recursively entangled within its semantic, thematic dimensions. Highly self-reflexive, Bernhard's depictions of writing and other creative practices at times display striking similarity to his own practices, which sometimes seem to be as "mad" as those of his famed protagonists. But though self-reflexive, Bernhard's texts do not offer clear, faithful images of his actual creative practices and process; instead they present ironic, hyperbolic, distorted depictions: like reflections in a funhouse mirror. Many of Bernhard's protagonists are so-called *Geistesmenschen* (intellectuals), writers who generate entire studies in their minds but are unable to put any words to paper; ironically, this thematized inability to write becomes the material for novels that go on for hundreds of pages. Examining the material production of

---

8. Novalis, "Monologue," in *Philosophical Writings*, trans. and ed. Margaret Mahony Stoljar (Albany: SUNY Press, 1997), 83–84.

9. Compare here Frederick, who notes that Prince Saurau's monologue in *Verstörung* "reveals the workings of narrative discourse on a level that parallels how Novalis conceived of the generative power of language itself" (Frederick, *Narratives Unsettled*, 121).

these texts reveals that the unusual, idiosyncratic features of Bernhard's writing—its repetitive, rambling, rhythmic dimensions—emerged out of a writing process that was itself extraordinarily generative, in which the typewriter played a crucial role: as primary instrument of writing and as agential participant.

On the face of it, the material generativity of Bernhard's process would seem antithetical to a "poetics of destruction" as described above.[10] But as we will see, production and destruction are intimately entangled, both in Bernhard's process and in the resultant textual products. While this dialectic is thematized in many of Bernhard's novels—most obviously in *Auslöschung* (*Extinction*, 1986)—I will be focusing on it primarily with regard to *Korrektur* (*Correction*, 1975), Bernhard's most self-reflexive work with respect to his material production process.[11] The character Roithamer corrects his work so excessively, producing draft upon draft, that he ultimately edits it down to nothing, essentially destroying it, as Roithamer himself sees it. The destruction of the work, however, leaves behind a massive amount of material text in its wake. From the perspective of the narrator, who has been charged with organizing and editing Roithamer's textual Nachlass after his death, Roithamer did not destroy his work through correction, but instead actually created an entirely new work—one generated out of the destructivity of material correction:

> he destroyed it again by starting to make corrections in it and correcting it over and over again until in the end he destroyed it entirely by his incessant corrections during his stay in Höller's garret after his sister's death, he felt he had corrected it to death and so destroyed it, but as I know now, as I have ascertained in the shortest possible time of my stay here in Höller's garret, he did not really destroy it by his utterly ruthless, hence utterly perfect corrections, but turned it into an entirely new work, because the destruction of his work by his own hand, by his keen mind which dealt most ruthlessly with his work was, after all, merely synonymous with the creation of an entirely new piece of work, he had gone on correcting his work until his work was not, as he thought, destroyed but rather a wholly new piece of work had been created. (C 61–62)

---

10. Compare Theisen, *Silenced Facts*, 46.
11. Martin Huber and Wendelin Schmidt-Dengler, commentary to Thomas Bernhard, *Korrektur*, ed. Martin Huber and Wendelin Schmidt-Dengler (W 4:321).

In attempting to edit Roithamer's unfinished work for publication, the narrator becomes so overwhelmed that he decides to send *all* versions of the text to an editor to be published together, as a "whole" (*das Ganze*): "for all three versions belong together, each deriving from the previous one, they compose a whole, an integral whole of over a thousand pages in which everything is equally significant [*alles die gleiche Bedeutung hat*] so that even the most minor deletion would reduce it all to nothing ... *all this together is the complete work* [*alles zusammen ist das Ganze*]" (C 130–31). At the heart of this conception of generative destructivity, or destructive generativity, is a notion of *das Ganze*, the whole: namely, that *all* of the writing produced in the process of generating a work, is *itself* a work, a kind of whole. A similar conception of a textual "whole" guides my examination of Bernhard's writing in this chapter. This whole, however, is not a finite material totality—either for myself, or for Bernhard. As Bernhard famously stated in Ferry Radax's 1970 film portrait of him, titled *Drei Tage* (*Three Days*), "There can be nothing whole; you've got to smash it to pieces. The successful, the beautiful becomes ever more suspicious. At the most unanticipated point possible you've got to abandon.... So it is wrong, too ... to write a *so-called chapter* in a book really to the end. And the *biggest mistake* is when an author writes a book to the end."[12] A programmatic statement of his *Geschichtenzerstören*, Bernhard's skepticism regarding the completeness of the work also informs my conception of the textual whole. One can never have all possible traces of the textual production process, and thus can never reconstruct a "complete" picture. In this respect, the conception of the "whole" that guides my considerations resembles Morton's notion of the entangled mesh of interconnected entities and forms.[13] It is the notion that everything matters—that "everything is equally significant" (C 130)—that all *avant-texte* and paratext is also part of "the text." Examining the traces of Bernhard's process reveals just how extensively the material, visual, and bodily dimensions of

---

12. Thomas Bernhard, *Three Days*, trans. Laura Lindgren (New York: Blast Books, 2016), 132–35.
13. Timothy Morton, "The Mesh," in *Environmental Criticism for the Twenty-First Century*, ed. Stephanie LeMenager, Teresa Shewry, and Ken Hiltner (London: Routledge, 2011), 22.

writing remain entangled within his published texts, and in the scene of reading. In turn, the process of writing itself can be considered a crucial component of Bernhard's overarching *project* of writing.

Bernhard's writing process differed radically from Handke's. Slow, ritualistic, and highly methodical, Handke's working method in producing *The Lesson* left behind a chronological series of traces that register his movement between dated notebook entries, typescript text versions, and typeset page proofs. Bernhard, by contrast, wrote rapidly and explosively on his typewriter, producing pages and pages and pages of typewritten text that often stood in uncertain relationship to one another.[14] While certain aspects of Bernhard's process were highly routinized, the material traces of this process—typescripts in some cases virtually free of corrections, in others corrected so extensively that the became virtually illegible—offer a much more vexing picture of how he actually constructed his works.

I have organized this chapter around four concepts that represent key thematic dimensions of Bernhard's works while simultaneously encapsulating defining features of his compositional process: *Korrektur* (correction), *Verrücktheit* (madness), *Rhythmus* (rhythm), and *Vernichtung* (destruction). Each section of this chapter centers on one specific notion, but these concepts are highly interconnected in Bernhard's work—Roithamer *corrects* his work so extensively that he believes himself to have *destroyed* it, driving himself *mad* in the process—and thus cannot be entirely disentangled. The first three sections focus on the novel *Correction* in order to show how the material, visual, and bodily dimensions of Bernhard's writing process became incorporated into the thematic and stylistic dimensions of this text. The final section brings these insights to bear on the reading of another work, which has one of the most complex production histories of Bernhard's works: the autobiographical novella *Wittgensteins Neffe* (*Wittgenstein's Nephew*, 1982).[15] This text is much less

---

14. On the chaos of Bernhard's *Schreibwerkstatt* and the material state of his Nachlass prior to archiving, see Stefano Apostolo, *Thomas Bernhards unveröffentlichtes Romanprojekt Schwarzach St. Veit: Das Konvolut, die Fassungen und ihre Deutung* (Mattighofen: Korrektur, 2019), 21–22.

15. Thomas Bernhard, *Wittgensteins Neffe* (Frankfurt am Main: Suhrkamp, 1982).

obviously about destruction than other works by Bernhard, but approaching it as a "whole"—examining its early versions and material production history alongside the published form—reveals how the material dynamics of creation and destruction are enmeshed within the text's thematics. This can only become visible, however, when we examine the scene of the work's generation. Expanding the scope to consider the work as a "whole" thus enables us to understand and appreciate the material-semiotic complexity of not only this text but also, by extension, Bernhard's writing more broadly.

Correction

Published in 1975, Bernhard's fourth novel, *Correction*, represents a radicalization of the aesthetic program that Bernhard began developing in his earlier prose works, and thereby establishes many characteristic features of his late work. These include: its distinct prosodic rhythmicality; a repetitiveness bordering at times on perseveration; lengthy, meandering sentences that can continue for pages without pause; and an all-but-complete lack of paragraph or section breaks, yielding uniform rectangles of text that proceed for page after page without relief. On the level of plot, the novel is the most thematically self-reflexive of any work by Bernhard with respect to his textual production process and the engagement with Nachlass materials.[16] Examining the novel's actual production enables us to see how the content not only reflects, but also was directly generated out of, this material process.

On the first page of the novel, the reader encounters an unnamed, first-person narrator who has been entrusted with overseeing the Nachlass of his deceased friend, the scientist and mathematician Roithamer. Roithamer's Nachlass encompasses thousands of manuscript pages and scraps, including numerous versions of an unpublished study titled "Über Altensam und alles, das mit Altensam zusammenhängt, unter besonderer Berücksichtigung des Kegels"

---

16. Huber and Schmidt-Dengler, commentary to Thomas Bernhard, *Korrektur* (W 4:321).

(About Altensam and everything connected with Altensam, with special attention to the Cone). Filled with hatred for his ancestral home, the Altensam palace in a region by the same name, Roithamer had ultimately left Austria to live and teach in Cambridge.[17] Expressing condemnation of Altensam—an anti-Austrian sentiment shared by many of Bernhard's protagonists—the work "About Altensam" consists primarily of Roithamer's conceptualization and documentation of the construction of the Cone, a conical structure he had built in the middle of the Kobernaußer forest.

The narrator first describes "dragging [*schleppen*]" Roithamer's massive Nachlass from England back to "Höller's garret" (*die höllersche Dachkammer*), an attic room, in the house of a taxidermist named Höller, where Roithamer had lived while designing and overseeing construction of the Cone, and where he composed much of his study "About Altensam."[18] Roithamer designed the highly idiosyncratic structure to be the perfect dwelling for his sister; that is, to correspond (*entsprechen*) to her perfectly and thus produce an experience of "perfect happiness" (*vollkommenes Glück*) (C 165). When she enters the Cone upon its completion, however, it produces the opposite effect—a "devastating" (C 267), literally "vernichtende Wirkung" (destructive effect) (W 4:313)—and she dies on the spot. Soon thereafter, Roithamer commits suicide.

The story of Roithamer's fictional manuscript, Bernhard's *Correction* is itself also a manuscript fiction. In the second sentence, the narrator declares his intention to write about the process of "sifting and sorting" (*sichten und ordnen*) Roithamer's Nachlass in Höller's garret, "as I have here begun to do" (C 3). The text we read in *Correction*, then, corresponds to this fictional manuscript, written

---

17. In these and other respects, Roithamer can be read as a thinly veiled fictionalization of Ludwig Wittgenstein. See, for example, Fatima Naqvi, "Conclusion—Demolition and Restoration in *Correction* (1975)," in *How We Learn Where We Live: Thomas Bernhard, Architecture, and Bildung* (Evanston, IL: Northwestern University Press, 2015), 129–52.

18. The fictionalized depictions the Höller family and house are based in reality. For documentation of Alfred Höller's taxidermy practice and house, see Richard Pils, ed., *Thomas Bernhard und der Tierpräparator Höller* (Weitra: Bibliothek der Provinz, 2009). A museum, the Salzkammergut Tierwelten Höller, and shop are still operational.

by the narrator. Höller's "Dachkammer" (attic room, garret), which served as Roithamer's "*Denk*kammer" (thought-chamber) and "Korrekturzelle" (correction cell) thus becomes the site where the narrator will read and organize Roithamer's Nachlass (with the intent to possibly publish his work "About Altensam"), at the same time documenting the whole experience in writing (C 15, 243) . Höller's garret, then, is thus at once a scene of writing, archiving, editing, and reading.

In examining the versions of Roithamer's work "About Altensam," the narrator discovers a correction process so excessive—"correction of the correction of the correction of the correction" (C 270)—that it ultimately "destroyed" the work altogether: "he'd tackled and finished it . . . but soon afterward . . . he destroyed it again by starting to make corrections in it and correcting it over and over again until in the end he destroyed it entirely by his incessant corrections . . . he felt he had corrected it to death and so destroyed it" (C 61). Whereas correction is typically understood to improve a text through modification, thereby bringing it toward a state of fullness or completion, Roithamer's correction goes awry. Unbridled correction devolves into destruction, revealing the inherent destructivity that lies within the act of correction itself: that which was written is canceled, negated, destroyed, sometimes through materially destructive acts (such as erasure, strike-through). Through this process of correction, Roithamer reduces his original manuscript from 800 pages to 400 to 150 to 80 to fewer than 20 pages, until "nothing" of the work is left at all (W 4:158). For Roithamer, correction is destruction: "When I make corrections, I destroy [*zerstöre*], when I destroy, I annihilate [*vernichte*], so Roithamer. What I used to consider an improvement, formerly, is after all nothing but deterioration [*Verschlechterung*], destruction, annihilation. Every correction is destruction, annihilation, so Roithamer" (C 266). This conception of correction not only applies to textual production, but also constitutes a life principle: Roithamer conceives of existence as a process of perpetual correction—which ultimately culminates in his suicide, a final act of "correction" (W 4:268). In the narrator's view, however, Roithamer's correction was not only destructive but also generative; he ultimately determines that Roithamer did not destroy the work, but in fact "completed" it by transforming it into something entirely new: "he had gone on correcting his work until his work was not, as he thought, destroyed but rather a wholly new piece of work had been created" (C 61–62).[19]

"Everything together is the whole"

As we are beginning to see, *Correction* is a wildly self-reflexive work, not only with respect to writing process, but also with respect to the whole of literary production and reception, from writing and correcting to editing and archiving to publishing and reading. A manuscript fiction penned by the narrator, *Correction* is about a fictional manuscript: the numerous versions of Roithamer's monumental work "About Altensam." This work is about the conception and execution of another work, not textual but architectural: the Cone. Roithamer's manuscript is thus an *Entstehungsgeschichte* (origin story) of sorts that both documents the generation of the Cone and simultaneously is part of that genesis. The narrator's text, in addition to constituting an *Entstehungsgeschichte* of both Roithamer's work and the Cone, is also a *Rezeptionsgeschichte* (history of reception). That is, akin to a reader of a textual work, Roithamer's sister is the intended recipient of his architectural masterwork, which was designed to prompt a response of "perfect happiness." "Readerly" response—a literally destructive effect produced when the sister views the Cone—entirely diverges from "authorial" intention (namely, the response Roithamer intended to generate).

But Roithamer's sister is not the only reader-figure in *Correction*. As estate overseer, quasi-archivist, and would-be editor, the narrator is also a reader of Roithamer's work. Roithamer, like all writers,

---

19. The depiction of Roithamer's corrective destruction has particularly strong resonances with that of Wertheimer in *The Loser*: "He wanted to publish a book, but it never came to that, for he kept changing his manuscript, changing it so often and to such an extent that nothing was left of the manuscript, for the change in his manuscript was nothing other than the complete deletion of the manuscript, of which finally nothing remained except the title, The Loser. From now on I have only the title, he said, it's better that way." Thomas Bernhard, *The Loser*, trans. Jack Dawson (New York: Knopf, 1991), 53–54. See Theisen, *Silenced Facts*, 52.

is also his own first reader during the process of writing.[20] The narrator, moreover, is also a writer, whose text—corresponding to the text of *Correction*—indirectly posits the existence of a fictional editor. In the second half of the novel the narrator increasingly weaves quotations from Roithamer's manuscripts into his own, only sometimes demarcating them with formulas such as "so Roithamer" or descriptions of Roithamer's material correction marks (for instance, "'must make her happy' again underlined" [C 165]). In their absence, however, it can be difficult or impossible to determine whether certain words are the narrator's or Roithamer's. In his recent analysis of the posthumously published story "Leichtlebig," Paul Buchholz mobilizes the figure of undergrowth (*Gestrüpp*)—another concept of entanglement or enmeshment—to describe the metaleptic structure of the narrative: "*Gestrüpp* serves both as a descriptive term for the complex environments surrounding the characters but also for the emergent structure of the text itself, as it is increasingly dominated and densified by the chaotic intergrowth of two narrative contextures (Leichtlebig's and the Doctor's)."[21] When we return to examine closely the material scene of writing, however, this metaleptic undergrowth is revealed to be even more intricate: in the case of *Correction*, Roithamer's writing and correcting marks, described and partially rendered by the narrator, also closely mirror Bernhard's own. In the scene of writing, then, Roithamer's (fictional) writing, the narrator's writing about that writing (namely, the text *Correction*), and the Bernhard's own material writing, are all entangled within one another. This entanglement occurs not only on the level of person/discourse (author, narrator, character), but also, in this case, in the representation of writing and its material underpinning.

In *Correction*, Bernhard offers the reader another concept to account for the confounding relationships between all of these

---

20. Compare Almuth Grésillon, *Literarische Handschriften: Einführung in die "critique génétique,"* trans. Franke Rother und Wolfgang Günther (Bern: Peter Lang, 1999), 183.

21. Paul Buchholz, *Private Anarchy: Impossible Community and the Outsider's Monologue in German Experimental Fiction* (Evanston, IL: Northwestern University Press, 2018), 143.

materials, which is evoked by the name Höller—*Hölle* (hell). Sequestered in this hellish garret, the narrator quickly becomes overwhelmed, pushed to the brink of insanity (*Verrücktheit*) through his attempts to order Roithamer's manuscripts. He ruminates obsessively on whether he has the "right" to publish Roithamer's work and the implications of doing so (C 127). Disgusted by the prospect of editing Roithamer's manuscripts—"the mere word *edit* [*bearbeiten*] or *edition* [*Bearbeitung*] was always enough to nauseate me" (C 132)—he decides that editing the "hundreds of thousands of fragments" (C 132) into an artificial whole would be criminal: "other people come along and proceed to edit such fragments, shreds of ideas [*Brüchstücke, Fetzen, Geistesfetzen*] that have been abandoned and left lying around, thinking they must edit and publish them, no matter where, publicize them, all these publications are criminal acts every single time, perhaps the greatest crime there is" (C 128). The narrator ultimately resolves not to edit the work at all, but instead to deliver the Nachlass in its entirety to the publisher, stating that all the drafts together constitute a whole: "I shall pass it on to his publisher untouched, just as I found it, the first eight-hundred-page draft, and the second three-hundred-page revision of this first draft, and the third version, boiled down to only eighty pages, of the second version, *all three of these versions of Roithamer's handwritten manuscript*, for all three versions belong together, each deriving from the previous one, they compose a whole, an integral whole of over a thousand pages in which everything is equally significant so that even the most minor deletion would reduce it all to nothing ... *all this taken together is the complete work*" (C 130–31). This whole consists of all of the versions of Roithamer's manuscript, the exact number and lengths of which are not entirely clear. Here, versions of 800, 300, and 80 pages are mentioned, but at other points the narrator describes versions of 800, 400, 150, and fewer than 20 pages, and that effectively nothing of the work was left at all in the end. Roithamer believes that he has destroyed his work through the process of correction; but though he may have destroyed the *work*, he did not physically destroy his *texts*, the manuscript notes and pages covered in strike-throughs that remain and now overwhelm the narrator in their volume and disarray.[22]

The notion that Roithamer's manuscripts, though destroyed through correction, still constitute part of the "whole" of the work prompts us to consider the status of Bernhard's drafts and earlier versions, as well as his own correction process, in relation to the published version of the text. In other words, what does Bernhard's work look like when we examine it as a whole?

"Sometimes I type things out"

Whereas Handke has frequently commented on his writing process in interviews, and directly mediated the scene of writing in his published work in various ways (for instance, by producing facsimiles of notebook pages and drawings), Bernhard spoke relatively little about his writing process. When he did, the known *Übertreibungskünstler* (artist of exaggeration) often toyed with his interviewers, describing his method in a characteristically stylized, hyperbolic, or deliberately misleading manner. In his interview with Krista Fleischmann, for example, Bernhard stated that he wrote with an "old stylus" inherited from his grandfather on the "most expensive paper" possible, inscribing each page with "only a *single* sentence"; and for each individual sentence, it would take him "four to five weeks" of thinking and ruminating before he could finally write it down. When asked about his use of the typewriter, Bernhard replied sarcastically, "Sometimes I type things out"[23] (W 22.2:316–17).

---

22. The contradiction at play here—canceled versions as part of the "whole"—resonates with conceptions of the work from contemporary editorial theory that negate the separation of the "finished" work from its production or genesis. See Rüdiger Nutt-Kofoth, "'Schreiben und Lesen': Für eine produktions- und rezeptionsorientierte Präsentation des Werktextes in der Edition," in *Text und Edition: Positionen und Perspektiven*, ed. Rüdiger Nutt-Kofoth (Berlin: Erich Schmidt, 2000), 169–70; Peter Schillingsburg, *Resisting Texts* (Ann Arbor: University of Michigan Press, 1997), 101.

23. Thomas Bernhard, "'Die Ursache bin ich selbst': Interview von Krista Fleischmann," in *Journalistisches, Reden, Interviews*, ed. Wolfram Bayer, Martin Huber, and Wendelin Schmidt-Dengler (W 22.1:316–17).

Nothing could be further from the truth. Bernhard's primary instrument of writing was the typewriter—and not the vintage Underwood typewriter, in fact, that Bernhard famously inherited from his grandfather, morphed into the figure of an "old stylus" in the interview description. Instead, Bernhard typed much more frequently on small travel typewriters than on the antique machine. Bernhard was known to type extremely rapidly and forcefully, often on the cheapest, thinnest of papers—a far cry from the "porcelain paper" he described writing on in the Fleischmann interview. Instead of one sentence per page, Bernhard's typescript pages are typically filled to the very edges with text, almost obsessively.[24] As we will see, Bernhard's composition in so-called page-episodes—written episodes completely filling the space of one or several pages—were a defining feature of his method.[25]

Unlike Handke, who began his writing process in his manuscript notebooks, Bernhard employed the typewriter as his primary instrument of composition from the beginning. Bernhard rarely made detailed notes or outlines of his texts. Accompanying typescript versions in Bernhard's Nachlass are troves of preparatory sketches or draft pages, more or less obviously associated with one text or another, that were gathered into bundles, sometimes by archivists, sometimes by Bernhard himself.[26] In the case of *Correction*, for example, an approximately ninety-page bundle of papers is stuffed in an envelope that is labeled in Bernhard's hand "lose Blätter zu

---

24. On typing to the page edges, see Catherine Viollet, "Mechanisches Schreiben, Tippräume: Einige Vorbedingungen für eine Semiologie des Typoskripts," trans. Davide Giuriato and Sandro Zanetti, in *"Schreibkugel ist ein Ding gleich mir: Von Eisen": Schreibszenen im Zeitalter der Typoskripte*, ed. Davide Giuriato et al. (Munich: Fink, 2005), 36–37.

25. Bernhard himself commented on this method of filling pages in a discussion with Kurt Hofmann: "Well, I was already writing novels by then, long ones, three hundred pages long, impossible stuff, you know. One was called 'Peter Goes to the City,' and there I was, already on page one hundred, and he was still at the train station. So I stopped, the idea was wrong. He wasn't even sitting in the streetcar and there were already 150 pages. Zero economy." Kurt Hofmann, *Aus Gesprächen mit Thomas Bernhard* (Munich: Deutsche Taschenbuch, 2001), 50. Cited in Frederick, *Narratives Unsettled*, 101.

26. On the state of Bernhard's Nachlass upon his death and its archiving, see Apostolo, *Thomas Bernhards unveröffentlichtes Romanprojekt* , 27–29.

Korrektur" (loose pages for *Correction*).[27] The status of these pages is different from that of the so-called *Abfallblätter* (waste pages) that Handke discarded in the process of typing his texts. In typing a new text version, Handke would abandon a page if he decided to make more than the most minimal of corrections, and would retype it from the beginning on a fresh sheet. One can match the *Abfallblätter* to corresponding pages in the completed versions. In examining Bernhard's *lose Blätter*, one finds passages that echo or appear to be earlier versions of a given passage from a printed text; however, Bernhard rarely ever directly copied or transcribed from these quasi-draft pages in generating his text versions. At the same time, for the majority of texts, there is only one complete version, and there is no evidence that Bernhard systematically destroyed drafts or prewriting materials.[28] Many works, particularly his late works, appear to have been produced "in einem Zug"—at one go—uninterrupted.[29]

Unlike Handke's method of text construction, which involves repetitively combing through notebooks and manuscript versions and is defined by a high degree of recursiveness, Bernhard's "method" was more straightforward, literally so. Rather than taking notes and drafting "before" beginning to compose a text, Bernhard, I argue, was always just—writing. What he wrote became part of a text version, or was discarded. Whereas Handke frequently retyped pages in generating the second and third versions of *The Lesson*, generating extremely clean copies easily legible for his editors, Bernhard rarely retyped a page to implement corrections; rather than producing distinct iterations of the text, he would make corrections on the *same* sheet. In turn, whereas Handke's process of manuscript note-taking was distinct from his process of writing his texts, there is no such clear distinction between the pages of Bernhard's text versions and the loose draft pages associated with them. One can observe the same kind of phenomena—the same material/visual features, and

---

27. "Lose Blätter zu Korrektur," ÖLA 563/W4/1c, 23. Literaturarchiv der Österreichischen Nationalbibliothek, Vienna.
28. Martin Huber and Wendelin Schmidt-Dengler, commentary to Thomas Bernhard, *Frost* (W 1:348).
29. Martin Huber and Wendelin Schmidt-Dengler, commentary to Thomas Bernhard, *Alte Meister* (W 8:230).

the same entanglements of these features in the formal, stylistic, semantic dimensions of the typed text—transpiring on these draft typescript pages as in the complete text versions. In examining these dimensions of Bernhard's writing, I use a similar approach for the draft materials/loose pages and the pages of his text versions, all of which can be seen as part of a "whole." For while in some cases there are direct correlations between the semantic content of a printed passage and the material/visual dimensions of a corresponding typescript page, there are also aspects of Bernhard's writing that manifest more diffusely in the published work—aspects that are just as discernible, and at times more discernible, in the draft material.

Examining Bernhard's material correction process in more detail underscores a lack of clear distinction between the preparatory sketches and the "final" text versions. Bernhard made some edits by hand, but the majority of corrections were made directly on the typewriter. Bernhard's typewritten corrections included both "immediate corrections" and "late corrections."[30] Making immediate corrections in the process of typing typically involved adjusting the carriage to the left, overtyping text to be canceled with strings of Xs or Ms and Ns—a common method in the era of typewriting[31]—and proceeding on the same line or in the interlinear space; later typewritten corrections could involve feeding the page back into the machine. In the finalized text versions sent to the publisher, Bernhard often reinforced typewritten strike-throughs with a thick black marker, rendering the canceled text completely illegible. Bernhard typically used 1.5 line spacing, leaving room for interlinear corrections and additions. At times these were so excessive that it is difficult to determine what line precedes the next; or lines of text began to overlap, rendering the text nearly, if not entirely, illegible (figure 2.1). In such cases, correction tips into destruction and the text is essentially "destroyed" through the process of correction; in the novel *Correction*, the inherently destructive potential of correction becomes the defining feature of Roithamer's writing process. But Bernhard also expanded the text through corrections: not infrequently, he would return to a passage and insert the same clause and/or variations thereof in multiple places,

---

30. Grésillon, *Literarische Handschriften*, 94.
31. Grésillon, *Literarische Handschriften*, 94.

one of the techniques by which he achieved and intensified the repetitive, rhythmic quality of his prose.³² In some cases Bernhard expanded the text beyond the physical limits of the sheet, adhering text flaps onto the left margin or onto the bottom of the page. The visual messiness of many of Bernhard's pages is evoked in the narrator's increasingly dismayed descriptions of Roithamer's Nachlass in *Correction*. In one passage, for example, the narrator describes how "hundreds and thousands of plans . . . millions of lines and numbers and figures" cover the walls of Höller's garret; that is to say, writing has proliferated so excessively and uncontrollably that it becomes completely overwhelming, literally unmanageable, not to mention unreadable (C 14). Here too, a fundamental feature of Bernhard's writing—its generativity and repetitiveness, at times nearly overwhelming the reader's ability to make sense of it—becomes transformed in *Correction* into the nightmarish encounter with Roithamer's Nachlass in Höller's garret.

Dense, illegible typescript passages were not only the product of earlier drafting sessions. Bernhard's editors sometimes encountered great difficulty in deciphering the typescript versions, which were sometimes far from "clean" copies and contained extensive corrections. A foreboding note on the title page of *Der Untergeher* (*The Loser*) warns of the difficulty that in-house copyists will face: "The manuscript is difficult to read in parts, we have not been given a better copy. Please do the most you can. [Ursula] Julkowski."³³ In preparing Bernhard's typescripts for typesetting, copyists routinely produced in-house fair copies of particularly difficult-to-read pages. One copyist working on *Correction* left this defeated note in the margin of a passage found to be altogether indecipherable: "Zusammenhang ist nicht eindeutig zu rekonstruieren!" (Coherency cannot be clearly reconstructed!) (figure 2.2).³⁴

---

32. Catherine Marten identifies this as one manifestation of Bernhard's "Baukastensystem." Marten, *Bernhards Baukasten: Schrift und sequenzielle Poetik in Thomas Bernhards Prosa* (Berlin: De Gruyter, 2018), 156–57. See also Renate Langer, commentary to Thomas Bernhard, *Das Kalkwerk* (W 3:249).

33. "Das Manuskript ist teils schlecht lesbar, es liegt uns aber keine bessere Kopie vor. Bitte Ihr Möglichstes tun [Ursula] Julkowski" (Thomas Bernhard, "Der Untergeher," 1. SU.2010.0002. DLA Marbach).

34. Thomas Bernhard, "Korrektur," 92. SU.2010.0002. DLA Marbach.

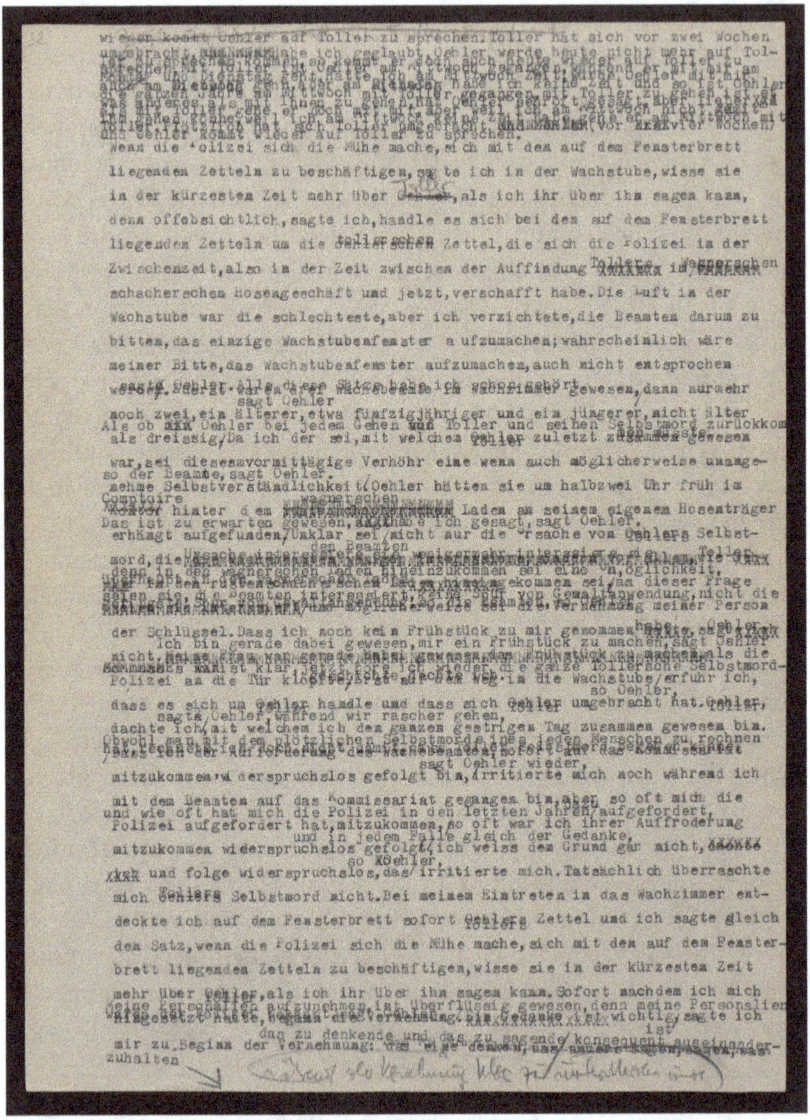

Figure 2.1. Thomas Bernhard, typescript fragment from *Gehen*, ÖLA 563/W19/2, 22. Literaturarchiv der Österreichischen Nationalbibliothek, Vienna.

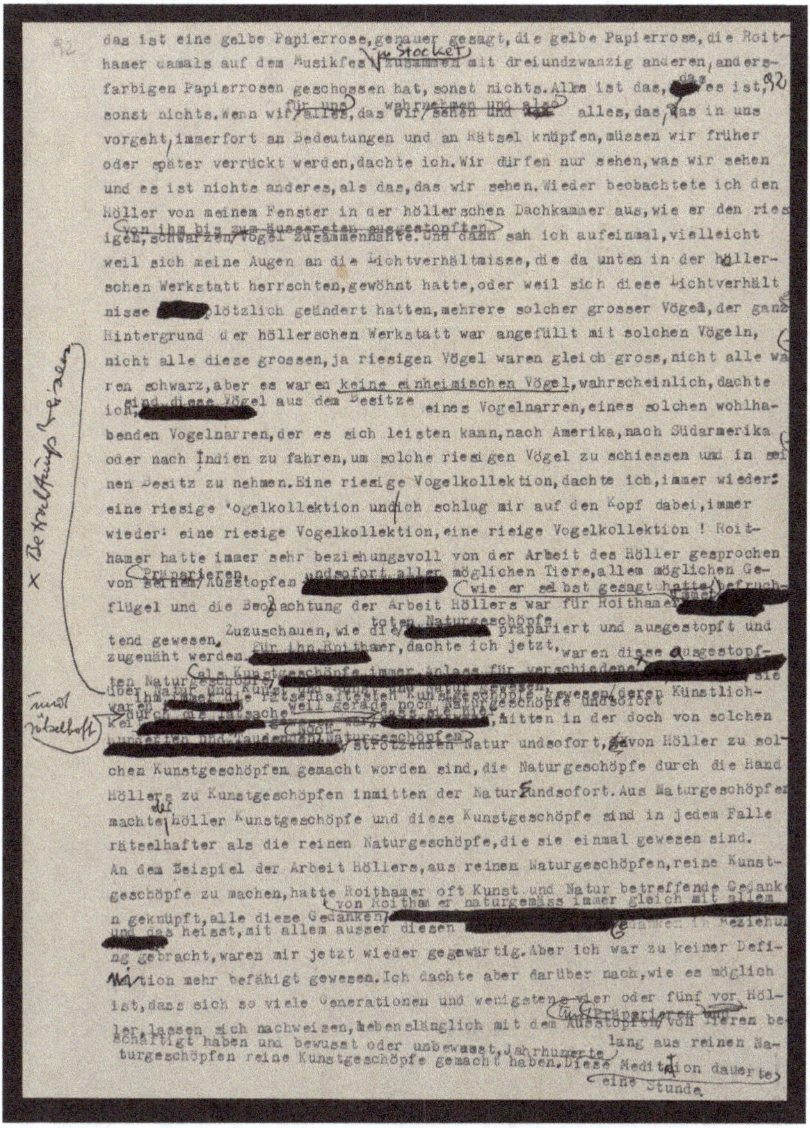

Figure 2.2. Thomas Bernhard, typescript of *Korrektur*, ÖLA 563/W4/2, 92. Literaturarchiv der Österreichischen Nationalbibliothek, Vienna.

dass sie jetzt alle zu Stifter pilgern zu Hunderttausenden und
sich niederknien vor jedem einzelnen seiner Bücher, als wäre jedes
einzelne ein Altar. Gerade in solchem Pseudoenthusiasmus ist
mir die Menschheit widerlich, sagte Reger, ist sie mir absolut
abstossend. Schliesslich fällt am Ende alles der Lächerlichkeit
oder wenigstens der Armseligkeit anheim, es mag so groß und
bedeutend sein, wie es will, sagte er. Tatsächlich erinnert mich
Stifter immer wieder an Heidegger, an diesen nationalsozialistischen Pumphosenspiesser. Hat   Stifter die hohe Literatur auf
die unverschämteste Weise verkitscht, so hat Heidegger, der
Schwarzwaldphilosoph Heidegger, die Philosophie verkitscht auf
einer sehr hohen Ebene, sicher, wie Stifter auch auf einer sehr
hohen Ebene die Literatur, aber doch verkitscht. Heidegger, dem
die Kriegs- und die Nachkriegsgenerationen nachgelaufen sind und
den sie mit widerwärtigen und stupiden Doktorarbeiten überhäuft
haben schon zu Lebzeiten, sehe ich immer auf seiner Schwarzwaldhausbank sitzen neben seiner Frau, die ihm ununterbrochen Winterstrümpfe strickt mit der von ihr selbst von den eigenen Heideggerschafen heruntergeschorenen Wolle. Heidegger kann ich nicht anders
sehen, als auf der Hausbank seines Schwarzwaldhauses, neben sich
seine Frau, die ihn zeitlebens total beherrscht und die ihm alle
Strümpfe gestrickt und alle Hauben gehäkelt hat und die ihm das
Brot gebacken und das Bettzeug gewebt und die ihm selbst seine
Sandalen geschustert hat. Heidegger war ein Kitschkopf, sagte
Reger, genauso wie Stifter, aber doch noch viel lächerlicher als
Stifter, der ja tatsächlich <u>eine tragische Erscheinung</u> gewesen
ist zum Unterschied von Heidegger, der <u>immer nur komisch</u> gewesen
ist, ebenso kleinbürgerlich wie Stifter, ebenso grössenwahnsinnig,
ein Voralpenschwachdenker, wie ich glaube, gerade recht für den
deutschen Philosophieeintopf. Den Heidegger haben sie alle mit
Heisshunger ausgelöffelt jahrzehntelang, wie keinen anderen und
sich den deutschen Germanisten- und Philosophenmagen damit vollgeschlagen. Heidegger hatte ein gewöhnliches, kein Geistesgesicht,
sagte Reger, war durch und durch ein ungeistiger Mensch, bar jeder
Phantasie, bar jeder Sensibilität, ein urdeutscher Philosophiewiderkäuer, nachgerade eine Philosophiekuh, sagte Reger, die auf
der deutschen Philosophie geweidet hat und darauf ihre koketten
Fladen fallen gelassen hat im Schwarzwald. Heidegger war ein
philosophischer Heiratsschwindler, sagte Reger, dem es gelungen
ist, eine ganze Generation von deutschen Geisteswissenschaftlern
auf den Kopf zu stellen. Heidegger ist eine abstoßende Episode

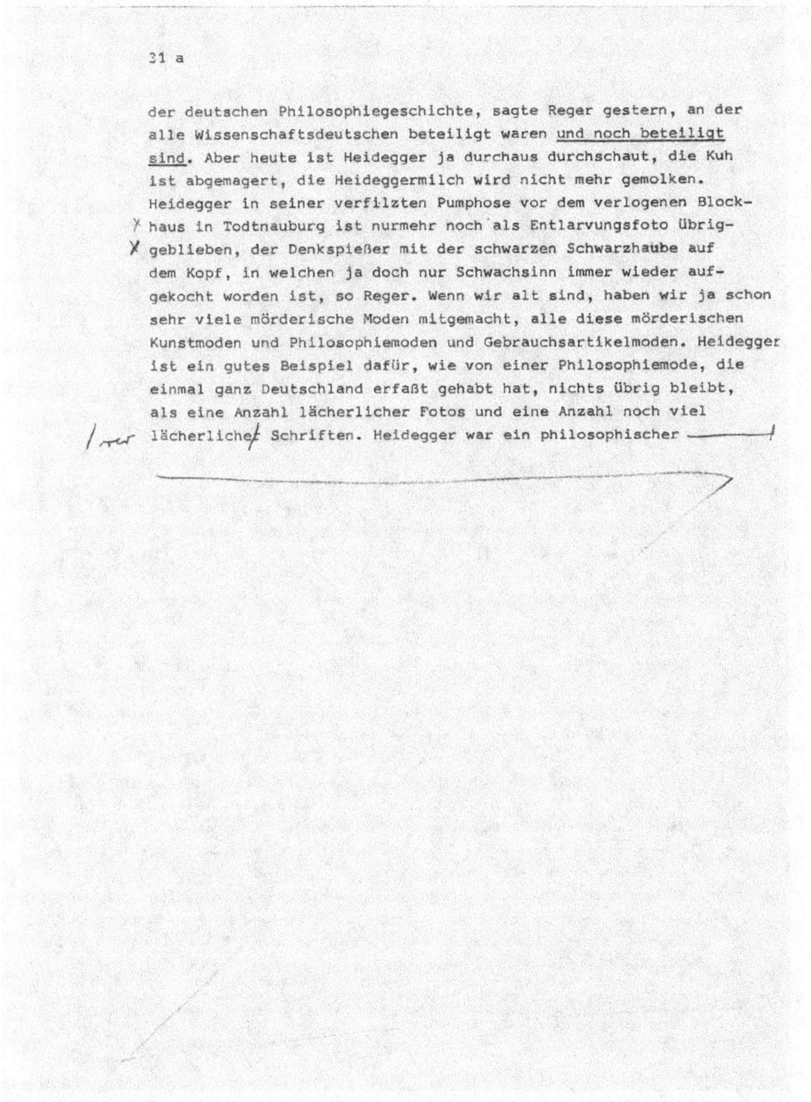

31 a

der deutschen Philosophiegeschichte, sagte Reger gestern, an der
alle Wissenschaftsdeutschen beteiligt waren und noch beteiligt
sind. Aber heute ist Heidegger ja durchaus durchschaut, die Kuh
ist abgemagert, die Heideggermilch wird nicht mehr gemolken.
Heidegger in seiner verfilzten Pumphose vor dem verlogenen Block-
haus in Todtnauburg ist nurmehr noch als Entlarvungsfoto übrig-
geblieben, der Denkspießer mit der schwarzen Schwarzhaube auf
dem Kopf, in welchen ja doch nur Schwachsinn immer wieder auf-
gekocht worden ist, so Reger. Wenn wir alt sind, haben wir ja schon
sehr viele mörderische Moden mitgemacht, alle diese mörderischen
Kunstmoden und Philosophiemoden und Gebrauchsartikelmoden. Heidegger
ist ein gutes Beispiel dafür, wie von einer Philosophiemode, die
einmal ganz Deutschland erfaßt gehabt hat, nichts übrig bleibt,
als eine Anzahl lächerlicher Fotos und eine Anzahl noch viel
lächerlicher Schriften. Heidegger war ein philosophischer ———/

Figure 2.3. Thomas Bernhard, copy of the typescript of *Alte Meister*, 31–31a. SU.2010.0002. Deutsches Literaturarchiv, Marbach.

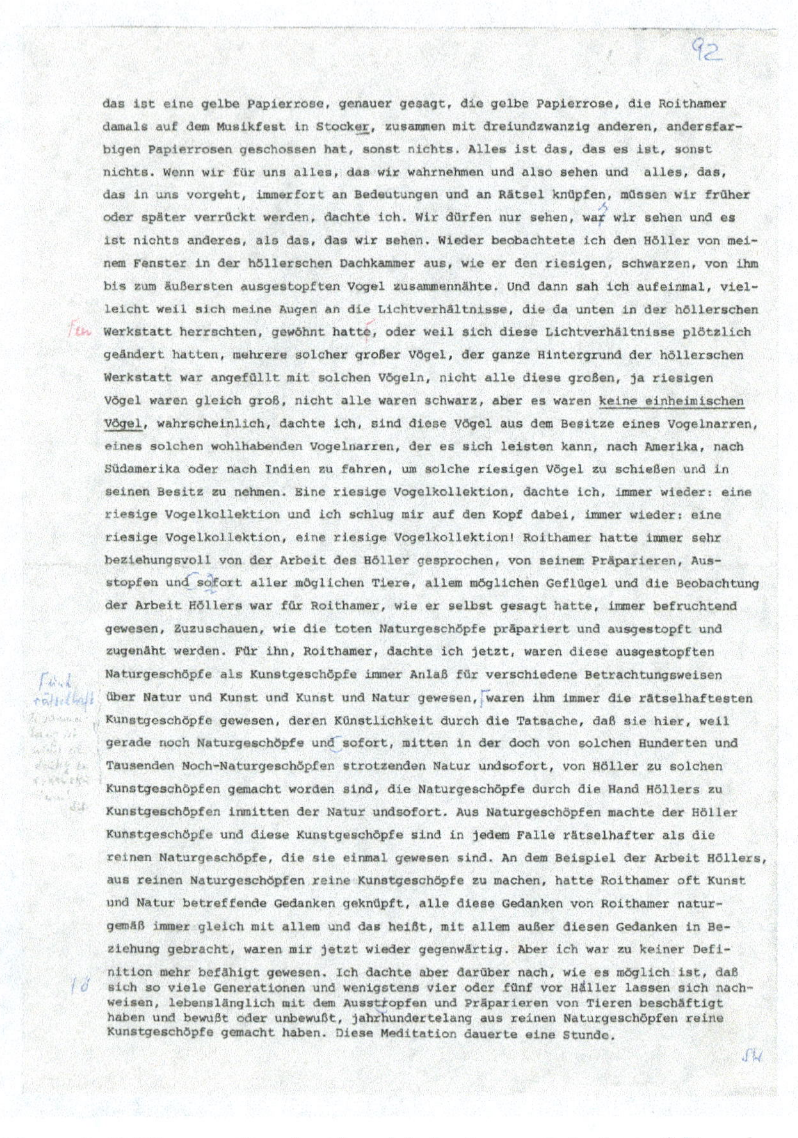

das ist eine gelbe Papierrose, genauer gesagt, die gelbe Papierrose, die Roithamer
damals auf dem Musikfest in Stocker, zusammen mit dreiundzwanzig anderen, andersfar-
bigen Papierrosen geschossen hat, sonst nichts. Alles ist das, das es ist, sonst
nichts. Wenn wir für uns alles, das wir wahrnehmen und also sehen und alles, das,
das in uns vorgeht, immerfort an Bedeutungen und an Rätsel knüpfen, müssen wir früher
oder später verrückt werden, dachte ich. Wir dürfen nur sehen, was wir sehen und es
ist nichts anderes, als das, das wir sehen. Wieder beobachtete ich den Höller von meinem Fenster in der höllerschen Dachkammer aus, wie er den riesigen, schwarzen, von ihm
bis zum äußersten ausgestopften Vogel zusammennähte. Und dann sah ich aufeinmal, vielleicht weil sich meine Augen an die Lichtverhältnisse, die da unten in der höllerschen
Werkstatt herrschten, gewöhnt hatte, oder weil sich diese Lichtverhältnisse plötzlich
geändert hatten, mehrere solcher großer Vögel, der ganze Hintergrund der höllerschen
Werkstatt war angefüllt mit solchen Vögeln, nicht alle diese großen, ja riesigen
Vögel waren gleich groß, nicht alle waren schwarz, aber es waren keine einheimischen
Vögel, wahrscheinlich, dachte ich, sind diese Vögel aus dem Besitze eines Vogelnarren,
eines solchen wohlhabenden Vogelnarren, der es sich leisten kann, nach Amerika, nach
Südamerika oder nach Indien zu fahren, um solche riesigen Vögel zu schießen und in
seinen Besitz zu nehmen. Eine riesige Vogelkollektion, dachte ich, immer wieder: eine
riesige Vogelkollektion und ich schlug mir auf den Kopf dabei, immer wieder: eine
riesige Vogelkollektion, eine riesige Vogelkollektion! Roithamer hatte immer sehr
beziehungsvoll von der Arbeit des Höller gesprochen, von seinem Präparieren, Ausstopfen und sofort aller möglichen Tiere, allem möglichen Geflügel und die Beobachtung
der Arbeit Höllers war für Roithamer, wie er selbst gesagt hatte, immer befruchtend
gewesen, zuzuschauen, wie die toten Naturgeschöpfe präpariert und ausgestopft und
zugenäht werden. Für ihn, Roithamer, dachte ich jetzt, waren diese ausgestopften
Naturgeschöpfe als Kunstgeschöpfe immer Anlaß für verschiedene Betrachtungsweisen
über Natur und Kunst und Kunst und Natur gewesen, waren ihm immer die rätselhaftesten
Kunstgeschöpfe gewesen, deren Künstlichkeit durch die Tatsache, daß sie hier, weil
gerade noch Naturgeschöpfe und sofort, mitten in der doch von solchen Hunderten und
Tausenden Noch-Naturgeschöpfen strotzenden Natur undsofort, von Höller zu solchen
Kunstgeschöpfen gemacht worden sind, die Naturgeschöpfe durch die Hand Höllers zu
Kunstgeschöpfen inmitten der Natur undsofort. Aus Naturgeschöpfen machte der Höller
Kunstgeschöpfe und diese Kunstgeschöpfe sind in jedem Falle rätselhafter als die
reinen Naturgeschöpfe, die sie einmal gewesen sind. An dem Beispiel der Arbeit Höllers,
aus reinen Naturgeschöpfen reine Kunstgeschöpfe zu machen, hatte Roithamer oft Kunst
und Natur betreffende Gedanken geknüpft, alle diese Gedanken von Roithamer natur-
gemäß immer gleich mit allem und das heißt, mit allem außer diesen Gedanken in Beziehung gebracht, waren mir jetzt wieder gegenwärtig. Aber ich war zu keiner Definition mehr befähigt gewesen. Ich dachte aber darüber nach, wie es möglich ist, daß
sich so viele Generationen und wenigstens vier oder fünf vor Höller lassen sich nach-
weisen, lebenslänglich mit dem Ausstopfen und Präparieren von Tieren beschäftigt
haben und bewußt oder unbewußt, jahrhundertelang aus reinen Naturgeschöpfen reine
Kunstgeschöpfe gemacht haben. Diese Meditation dauerte eine Stunde.

Figure 2.4. Thomas Bernhard, publisher's transcription of *Korrektur*, 92. SU.2010.0002. Deutsches Literaturarchiv, Marbach.

Comparing these publisher's fair copies to Bernhard's original typescript pages underscores significant visual features of Bernhard's writing. The visually uniform lines produced on the publisher's electric typewriters contrast with the highly irregular lines generated on Bernhard's small travel typewriters. A single Bernhardian page could be expanded to cover as much as one and a half clean-copy pages, underscoring the visual density of Bernhard's typed lines (figure 2.3). In some cases, rather than allowing the text to expand onto a second sheet, copyists adopted Bernhard's technique of decreasing the line spacing at the bottom in order to contain the text on a single page (figure 2.4). In rare cases, particularly messy passages were excised and replaced with pieces of clean copy through a surgical cut-and-paste operation—a method similarly reminiscent of Bernhard's occasional cut-and-paste practice of correction.

What happened in the proofs stage could vary. In some cases Bernhard's revisions of his work extended well into the proofs stage, which display extensive corrections.[35] In other cases Bernhard made hardly any edits to the proofs at all. Occasionally Bernhard continued to make numerous corrections—primarily additions, an extension of his generative mode—to the proofs. The process of correction could even extend beyond the publication of first editions: in so-called *Strichexemplare* (correction copies) Bernhard made further alterations to the text—frequently orthographical, but also sometimes lexical—that were then implemented in subsequent print runs.[36] This would suggest that although he asserted much less control of its typographic form than did Handke (in the case of *The Lesson*), the printed form of the work—part of the work as "the whole"—was significant for Bernhard. Though the rhythmic/musical dimensions of his writing are often understood to be its most significant aspects—as we will discuss below—the visual dimensions

---

35. Apostolo characterizes Bernhard's attempts to achieve "completion and perfection," reflected in the predicaments of his protagonists, as Sisyphean (Apostolo, *Thomas Bernhards unveröffentlichtes Romanprojekt*, 15).

36. Bernhard's story *Ja* is a particularly striking example. See Hans Höller and Manfred Mittermayer, "Anmerkungen zur Textgestaltung," in Thomas Bernhard, *Erzählungen III* (W 13:358–73, here 358–59).

of Bernhard's printed pages play a no less crucial role in conditioning the readerly/affective experience of his works.

Madness

On August 8, 1975, after receiving the proofs of *Correction*, Bernhard was so impressed with the typesetting that he requested that a bottle of champagne be sent to the compositor: "As for the proofs of 'Correction,' I have never seen any so exquisitely set, and I ask you to convey my admiration to the typesetter for this very outstanding, almost unbelievable, superhuman work!, for I know the manuscript, it is a masterful achievement. And I ask you to send a bottle of champagne to the typesetter of 'Correction' (i.e. by charging my account!)! And please do not forget this wish on my part!!!"[37] This acknowledgment of the "outstanding, almost unbelievable, superhuman work" indicates that Bernhard was well aware of the challenges that his typescripts posed to editors. As we saw in the previous section, Bernhard's typescripts did cause serious problems for editors attempting to decipher them. These challenges are directly reflected in *Correction*: utterly overwhelmed with the task of sorting and possibly editing Roithamer's monstrous Nachlass, the narrator wonders whether Roithamer in fact intended to "destroy" him by bequeathing it to him. He writes that his "mental state and entire constitution were extremely vulnerable to every kind of injury from Roithamer's papers" (C 24) and begins to suspect Roithamer of sadistic intentions: "what else could he have meant by making me his literary executor than to destroy me" (C 116). Ultimately, this activity of reading and attempting to order Roithamer's manuscripts begins to drive him mad: "millions of lines and numbers and figures covered these walls and at first I thought I would go mad or at least get sick if I looked at these millions of lines and numbers and figures ... so that at first I thought I'd go

---

37. Thomas Bernhard and Siegfried Unseld, *Der Briefwechsel*, ed. Raimund Fellinger et al. (Frankfurt am Main: Suhrkamp, 2010), 481.

mad or at least get sick from looking at these millions of lines and numbers and figures" (C 14).

In *Correction*, the thematization of madness is not only connected to the narrator's activity of sorting Roithamer's Nachlass; it is also directly connected to Roithamer's material processes of conceptualizing and writing itself. Madness is a pervasive theme throughout Bernhard's oeuvre, which is populated by figures whose behavior and speech are nonsensical and disorderly and who are pushed to the margins of society. Madness is not only thematized, but also figured mimetically in highly repetitive sentences that can meander so endlessly as to defy comprehensibility, even grammaticality. In such ways, the cognitive, affective experience of reading Bernhard's writing can also be—literally—maddening.

This readerly experience is intensified by the typographical form of Bernhard's printed text. In stark contrast to the often-chaotic state of Bernhard's typescripts, the printed pages of Bernhard's published texts are highly regularized. Aside from a single section break roughly halfway through *Correction*, there are no paragraph or chapter breaks in this novel of over 300 pages. The writing completely fills the text block to form perfectly uniform rectangles, walls of text that repeat incessantly, page after page, offering the reader no relief from the onslaught of Bernhard's language.

Scholars have explored the interconnection of the poetics and thematics of madness in Bernhard's work. In *Narratives Unsettled*, for example, Samuel Frederick considers Bernhard's "digressive tactics" and plotless narration to be analogous to madness, particularly in *Verstörung*.[38] But these dimensions are intertwined within an even more complex material-textual mesh. For the poetics and thematics of madness are also entangled in, literally produced out of, the visuality and materiality of Bernhard's own process of writing and correcting, in ways that manifest in the typographical form of the printed text. In the next section I examine Bernhard's *material* techniques for both representing and generating madness, which remain inscribed within the formal and stylistic features of Bernhard's

---

38. Frederick, *Narratives Unsettled*, 21, 106.

language and, in turn, specific affective, cognitive phenomena that characterize the scene of reading.

"My writing table has transformed into a drafting table in the most horrible way"

Before beginning to sift and sort Roithamer's Nachlass, the narrator first describes "dragging" it to Höller's garret: "and I have to say dragged it, because it's a matter of thousands of pages, however, as I know, it's a case of hundreds of thousands of fragments, interrelated ones on the one hand, but completely unrelated ones on the other hand" (C 131). In a most horrifying way, the narrator dumps the thousands of papers from his Mary Poppins-esque knapsack into the room. Confounded by its material mass—an unstable, shifting mountain of papers that threatens to collapse—he is pushed to the "edge of despair" (C 132) and begins stuffing the papers haphazardly into drawers to get them out of sight:[39] "I went over to the sofa and grabbed handful after handful of the Roithamer legacy [*Nachlass*] and crammed the desk drawers full of it. Again and again I grabbed a handful of papers and crammed it into a drawer.... But what matters, I thought, is that those remains [*Nachlass*] are now out of sight, that I don't have to see those papers anymore.... And since Roithamer's papers are hardly ever dated or numbered or anything, as I know for a fact, there was no hope at all that I could ever put them in order again, even to try to put them in order would drive me crazy [*verrückt*], I thought, over and over, putting them in order would drive me crazy" (C 133). Here, the physical state of the papers and the narrator's mental state become intertwined through Bernhard's unusual syntax and repetitive word play—particularly with the word *verrückt* and its thematic opposite, *ordnen/Ordnen/Ordnung*—ultimately swelling into perseverative fit: "So there I stood and said over and over that such a hopeless effort to put them in order would actually drive me crazy.... I had apparently in a

---

39. Bernhard's Nachlass was found in a similar state upon his death, dispersed in relative disorder among various desk drawers in the writer's various residences. See Huber and Schmidt-Dengler, commentary to *Frost*, 348.

moment of total confusion lost my mind altogether and grabbed the knapsack and dumped its contents on the sofa and got all the papers so thoroughly mixed up they could never be straightened out again. So there I sat on that old chair and again said sort and sift, sift and sort, several times" (C 133). A towering mass of paper, text is reduced to its materiality, to stuff stuffed into drawers. The disordered pile-up of paper, overwhelming the narrator's abilities to organize it, is captured syntactically in the pile-up of repetitive clauses that will go on, in this case, for pages, forming sentences that buckle under their own weight, overwhelming readers' efforts to make sense of them. The narrator is driven mad, "verrückt." The German term *verrückt* commonly is translated as "crazy," "mad," or "insane," but literally means disturbed, off-kilter, displaced, shifted out of place. The material *Verrückung* (displacement) of the teetering paper mountain that threatens to collapse is directly transposed or transferred into a type of mental *Verrückung*. The materiality of Roithamer's texts is thus equated with the mental response it induces.

It was not just the material mass of Roithamer's Nachlass that distressed the narrator so greatly, but also the visual appearance of Roithamer's manuscripts. When the narrator returned to Höller's garret with the Nachlass, he found that the walls of the room itself were still covered in notes, drawings, and other scraps of Roithamer's process, "millions of lines and numbers and figures" (C 14). Among the "loose pages for Correction," one finds a page on which this experience is described in even greater detail—not from the narrator's perspective, but from Roithamer's. Roithamer expresses dismay at how quickly his walls became covered after he initially conceived of the Cone:

> [I] had [hundre]ds of drawings, sketches, plans on my room walls, so many sketches I had made immediately ... and above all made in my increasingly more stubborn and sleep-deprived nights, that all at once and already, as I said, a few days after the idea, the walls of my room had still only been covered with these plans, there were hundreds and thousands of ground plans and numbers and digits corresponding to these ground plans, which I had inscribed on these ground plans, I was locked in my room, now only occupied with sketch- and plan-making.

[Hunder]te von Zeichnungen, Skizzen, Pläne an meinen Zimmerwänden hatte [ich], soviele Skizzen hatte ich sofort . . . gemacht, und vor allem in meinem immer hartnäckiger schlaflos werden Nächten gemacht, dass aufeinmal und schon wie gesagt wenige Tage nach der Idee, meine Zimmerwände nur noch ~~von~~ mit diesen Plänen bedeckt gewesen waren, es handelte sich um Hunderte und Tausend Grundrisse und zu diesen Grundrissen gehörende Zahlen und Ziffern, die ich au[f] diesen Grundrisse eingetragen hatte, ich war in mein Zimmer eingeschlossen, nur mehr noch mit ~~solchen~~ Skizzen- und Plänemachen beschäftigt.[40]

"Hundreds and thousands" of sketches proliferate day after day, legible forms devolving into an illegible mess of "millions" of indecipherable, crisscrossing lines, driving Roithamer mad:

> I woke up in my room, just two days in fact after the idea . . . and was horrified at the hundreds and thousands of lines that suddenly crisscrossed my walls and I after a few minutes I had to stop looking at them in order not to go crazy, when you look longer at these pages with these thousands of lines, which overnight had in fact become millions of lines, as you've just looked at them, you are insane.

> tatsächlich wachte ich schon zwei Tage nach der Idee . . . in meinem Zimmer auf und war erschrocken über die Hunderte und Tausende von Linien, die plötzlich meine Wände kreuzten, und deren Betrachtung ich nach wenigen Minuten abzubrechen hatte, um nicht verrückt zu werden, wenn du diese Blätter mit diesen Tausenden von Linien, die in der Nacht tatsächlich Millionen Linien gewesen waren, länger betrachtest, als du sie jetzt betrachtest hast, bist du verrückt.[41]

In a horrifying moment, Roithamer's writing table (*Schreibtisch*) appears to morph into a drafting or drawing table (*Zeichentisch*): the visuality of his notes and drawings surges so overwhelmingly into the foreground of perception that he can no longer read them, their semiotic contents obscured by their materiality.[42] Roithamer is

---

40. Thomas Bernhard, *Korrektur*, ÖLA 563/W4/1c, 37, Literaturarchiv der Österreichischen Nationalbibliothek (LÖN), Vienna.
41. Bernhard, *Korrektur*, ÖLA 563/W4/1c, 37, LÖN.
42. My reading of this passage is informed in part by Craig Dworkin's analysis of Charles Bernstein's *Veil* in "Reducing Redness," in *Reading the Illegible* (Evanston, IL: Northwestern University Press, 2003), 50–70.

thrust into a perseverative fit similar to that which befalls the narrator in the printed version as he attempts to sort these papers:

> finally it was a sudden onslaught of exhaustion, which me at my writing desk, which, I suddenly found, turned into a drafting table, my writing table turned into a drafting table in the most horrible way, I thought, over and over my writing table a drafting table and this discovery depressed me most disconcertingly, out of my writing desk, mind you, a drafting table, mind you, I said over and over to myself, out of my writing table a drafting table, out of the science-table a drafting table, over and over I, very loudly, without worrying about the fact that I possibly . . .

> schliesslich war es eine plötzlich eingetretene Erschöpfung, die mich am Schreibtisch, der, wie ich aufeinmal feststellte ein Zeichentisch geworden ist, mein Schreibtisch ist auf die fürchterlichste Weise ein Zeichentisch geworden, dachte ich, immer wieder mein Schreibtisch ein Zeichentisch und diese Feststellung deprimierte mich auf das ~~ungeheuerlich~~ unberuhigendste, aus meinem Schreibtisch wohlgemerkt, ein Zeichentisch wohlgemekrt, mehrere Male sagte ich vor mich hin, aus meinem Schreibtisc[h] ein Zeichentisch, aus dem Wissenschaftstisch ein Zeichentisch . . . [43]

In the published version of the text, Roithamer's experience of his own manuscripts, as described on this draft sheet (fictional scene of writing), becomes transformed and transposed into the *narrator's* experience of Roithamer's manuscripts (fictional scene of reading)—which in turn becomes transposed into the reader's experience (actual scene of writing). In the published version, Bernhard also describes Roithamer himself being driven to the brink of insanity in the process of composing his study: "This manuscript too is nothing but a mad aberration [*Verrücktheit*], just as . . . the erection of the Cone was nothing but a mad aberration, those who always regarded the building of the Cone as a mad aberration . . . it was absolute madness [*die größte Verrücktheit*], so Roithamer, to build the Cone and to write this manuscript about Altensam, and these two crazy acts [*diese beide Verrücktheiten*] . . . have done me in, 'have done me in' underlined" (C 266–67). Roithamer realizes that the construction of the Cone was *verrückt*, that everyone who observed it thought he was *ver-*

---

43. Bernhard, *Korrektur*, ÖLA 563/W4/1c, 37, LÖN.

rückt, and that writing his manuscript was *verrückt* as well. These *Verrucktheiten*, Roithamer believes, would ultimately destroy him.

In *Correction*, the narrator's plight of working with Roithamer's Nachlass—as a reader, archivist, and would-be-editor figure at once—is directly connected to the scene of Roithamer's writing, such that the reader comes to understand the narrator's maddening task as conditioned by Roithamer's process. But there are also clear overlaps between the ways Bernhard conceptualizes Roithamer's process and his own. In Bernhard's typescripts, lines of excessively corrected text, overlapping so densely at times that they become illegible, similarly confront the reader—be it the twenty-first-century scholar, the Suhrkamp Verlag editor, or Bernhard himself in the act of writing—in their materiality and visuality. The way that Bernhard's own methodology is figured in the text allows us to look back across his materials—the whole of the text's production—and see how textual features and motifs emerged out of this process.

"Thin spots"

The relationship between Roithamer and the narrator thus reflects the relationship between Bernhard and the editors and readers of his texts. But there are subtler, less obviously self-reflexive ways in which textual motifs originate in visual and material features of Bernhard's writing—and not only in *Correction*, but throughout Bernhard's oeuvre. One of the best-known of Bernhard's mad characters is the psychiatric patient Karrer from the novella *Gehen* (*Walking*, 1971). On the draft page in figure 2.5, (from a bundle of sketches similar to the "loose pages for *Correction*"), the gait of this figure—here named Oehler, but renamed Karrer later in the writing process—is described as a "Humpeln" (limping or hobbling) in a way that mimics the "hobbling" movement of the typed text across the page.[44]

---

44. On Bernhard's habit of renaming and reassigning attributes of characters in the process of writing, see Hans Höller and Manfred Mittermayer, commentary to Thomas Bernhard, *Erzählungen II* (W 12:269–70). In the published version, Bernhard adds a further layer of narrative focalization, renaming Oehler "Karrer" and assigning the name "Oehle" to a third figure who reports to the unnamed narrator on his walks and conversations with Karrer.

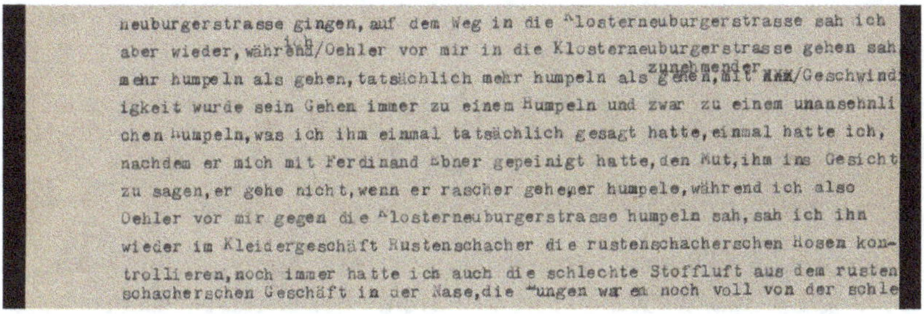

neuburgerstrasse gingen, auf dem Weg in die ^losterneuburgerstrasse sah ich
aber wieder, während/Oehler vor mir in die Klosterneuburgerstrasse gehen sah
mehr humpeln als gehen, tatsächlich mehr humpeln als gehen, mit zunehmender xxx/Geschwind
igkeit wurde sein Gehen immer zu einem Humpeln und zwar zu einem unansehnli
chen Humpeln, was ich ihm eimmal tatsächlich gesagt hatte, einmal hatte ich,
nachdem er mich mit Ferdinand Ebner gepeinigt hatte, den Mut, ihm ins Gesicht
zu sagen, er gehe nicht, wenn er rascher geheer humpele, während ich also
Oehler vor mir gegen die ^losterneuburgerstrasse humpeln sah, sah ich ihn
wieder im Kleidergeschäft Rustenschacher die rustenschacherschen Hosen kon-
trollieren, noch immer hatte ich auch die schlechte Stoffluft aus dem rusten
schacherschen Geschäft in der Nase, die ^ungen war en noch voll von der schle

Figure 2.5. Thomas Bernhard, typescript fragment from *Gehen*, ÖLA 563/W19/2, 7. Literaturarchiv der Österreichischen Nationalbibliothek, Vienna.

Like the limping of the traveling figure, the text produced on Bernhard's travel typewriters visually jumps and jolts, producing uneven lines (figure 2.5).[45] Through the mechanical misalignment of the type hammers (such as the H, K, and L), the text breaks out of the regular horizontality prescribed by the typewriter,[46] becoming literally "verrückt," dislodged or shifted out of place—a material marker of madness simultaneously depicted in textual representation. The herky-jerky motion of the travel typewriter thus becomes embodied in the description of the character's hobbling, uneven movement. Similar visual irregularities could emerge from the misalignment of type ribbon or arms, in combination with variations in the force used to depress the keys (figure 2.6). That is, the visuality of Bernhard's typescript text, although regularized through the production of the printed version, still finds resonance within the space of representation, or even embodiment in its contents.

At the bottom of the page in figures 2.5 and 2.6, Oehler's hobbling accelerates to the point that it is no longer "walking" at all: "with ever quicker steps in an ever quicker hobbling, that for some

45. On the graphic individuality of patterns produced on a specific manual typewriter, which will be as unique a human's handwriting, see Davide Giuriato, "(Mechanisiertes) Schreiben: Einleitung," introduction to Giuriato, Stingelin and Zanetti, *"Schreibkugel ist ein Ding,"* 15.

46. Compare Viollet, "Mechanisches Schreiben," 36.

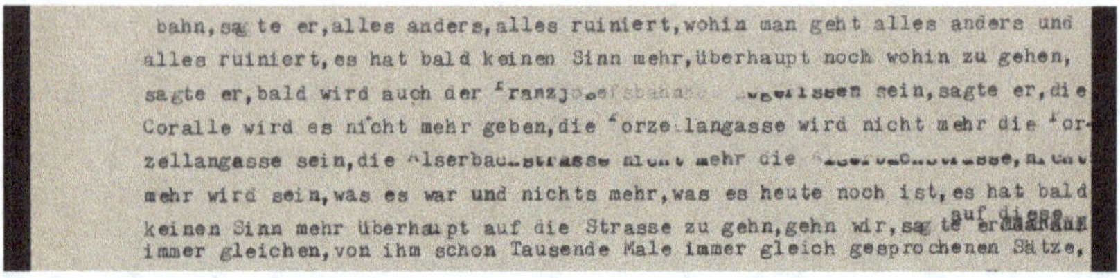
bahn, sagte er, alles anders, alles ruiniert, wohin man geht alles anders und
alles ruiniert, es hat bald keinen Sinn mehr, überhaupt noch wohin zu gehen,
sagte er, bald wird auch der Franzj[illegible] [illegible]ssen sein, sagte er, die
Coralle wird es nicht mehr geben, die Porze[illegible]langasse wird nicht mehr die Por-
zellangasse sein, die Alserbau[illegible]strasse [illegible] mehr die [illegible]
mehr wird sein, was es war und nichts mehr, was es heute noch ist, es hat bald
keinen Sinn mehr überhaupt auf die Strasse zu gehn, gehn wir, sagte [illegible] auf diese
immer gleichen, von ihm schon Tausende Male immer gleich gesprochenen Sätze,

Figure 2.6. Thomas Bernhard, typescript fragment from *Gehen*, ÖLA 563/W19/2, 7. Literaturarchiv der Österreichischen Nationalbibliothek, Vienna.

time now was no longer walking at all."[47] Bernhard describes Oehler's fondness for the word *schütter* (thin) and obsession over the threadbare fabric at Rustenschacher's pants store. In the published version, "schüttere Stellen" (thin spots) in the low-quality "tschechoslowakische Ausschußware" (Czechoslovakian rejects)—which the owner claims are first-class English fabric—induce a mental breakdown: Karrer (previously named Oehler) falls into a fit of perseveration—perhaps the most iconic scene of perseverative speech and writing in Bernhard's oeuvre—repeating "*these thin spots, these thin spots*" (*W* 12:202–3).

Karrer's walking and speaking become *ver-rückt*, transgressing the norms of rational, sensible behavior and communication. Karrer's descriptive breakdown in *Walking* is similar to the breakdowns of Roithamer and the narrator in *Correction*: Roithamer is driven mad by the visuality of his manuscripts, repeating over and over "my writing table has transformed into a drafting table in the most horrible way." Similarly, the narrator's archival and editorial work plunges him into a fit of madness, leaving him repeating over and over "sorting and sifting [*ordnen und sichten*], sifting and sorting" (*C* 134). In each case, "Ver-rücktheit" is triggered by a material encounter: with textile in *Walking*, with text in *Correction*.

47. "mit immer rascherer Schritten in einem immer rascherer Humpeln, das schon lange kein Gehen mehr gewesen ist." Thomas Bernhard, typescript fragment from *Gehen*, ÖLA 563/W19/2, 7. Literaturarchiv der Österreichischen Nationalbibliothek, Vienna.

By expanding the scope of interpretation to include the visuality and materiality of Bernhard's production of these passages, as part of the entangled whole, an even more complex picture is revealed. For these scenes of materially generated madness were themselves generated materially, through Bernhard's idiosyncratic method of type-writing. Unlike the lines of the printed text, Bernhard's typing did not proceed in neat linear fashion. Corrections, interlinear insertions, and overtyping were at times so excessive that they not only interfered with legibility, but materially damaged the paper, which was rendered prone to punctures through the pounding of the type hammers—a material state recalling the "thin spots" in the threadbare fabric in *Walking*. In analyzing the printed text, the prominent role of fabric might be connected interpretively to the concept of text, which is rooted in the Latin *texere* (weaving). Nothing in the published version, however, suggests that this passage can be connected to the specific materiality of Bernhard's paper; this dimension of the text's intertextuality becomes discernible only when we open the frame of reference to the materiality of the text in the process of its production.

The edges of Bernhard's typescript pages are particularly charged sites of material-semiotic entanglement. In approaching the bottom edge of the sheet, Bernhard commonly decreased the line spacing in order to fit as much text as possible onto the page. As mentioned above, this visual feature stems from Bernhard's method of composition in so-called *Seitenepisoden* (page-episodes), material-thematic-narratological-process units that filled the full space of one or more pages, and that were produced in discrete writing sessions.[48] Bernhard would begin a page-episode with a new sentence at the top of a fresh sheet and bring the episode to a close, ending it with a period, at the bottom margin of either the same, or a second or third, sheet (in turn yielding an episode of writing that completely

---

48. For reference to Bernhard's composition in page-episodes, see Martin Huber, "'Schrieb und schrieb und schrieb . . .': Anmerkungen zur Arbeitsweise Thomas Bernhards," in *Thomas Bernhard und seine Lebensmenschen: Der Nachlaß*, ed. Martin Huber, Manfred Mittermayer, and Peter Karlhuber (Frankfurt am Main: Suhrkamp, 2002), 78; Huber and Schmidt-Dengler, commentary to *Frost*, 351; Langer, commentary to *Das Kalkwerk*, 249; Marten, *Bernhards Baukasten*, 186–89.

fills the space of two or three pages). In some cases the final sentence fits nearly perfectly onto the final line, a testament to Bernhard's controlled coordination of the "shape" of the linguistic text and the space of the page. In others, Bernhard went to great lengths to contain the text on the page, decreasing the line spacing at the bottom and occasionally continuing in the top margin to bring the episode to a close. This technique enabled Bernhard to order and reorder episodes through a kind of "building-block system" in constructing his texts; and in some cases Bernhard even transferred units of writing *between* work projects.

Bernhard's method of obsessively filling pages with text can be observed both in Bernhard's sketches and draft pages, and in the complete typescript versions of his texts. On more than a few occasions, the semantic content of the lines crammed into the bottom margin, or sloping off the edge of the page, peculiarly reflects their material, visual form. In one such passage from the "loose pages for *Correction*," Roithamer is crippled with fear that his madness will be discovered; he lays his head on the tabletop (*Tischplatte*)—alternatively described as the drafting tabletop (*Zeichentischplatte*) and the writing desk tabletop (*Schreibtischzeichentischplatte*)—and pressed (*presste*), indeed crushed (*zerdrückte*), his head so intensely onto the surface that he worries his skull will shatter and its contents (*Inhalt*) will spill out. This image resonates with Bernhard's notoriously violent typing, pounding the type hammers against the cylindrical platen—the "Schreibmaschinenplatte," or simply "Platte"—and destroying multiple typewriters in the course of his career.[49] Roithamer's perseveration reaches a climax at the bottom edge of the page, where Bernhard decreases the line spacing as if to "press" the text into the remaining space and prevent its contents from spilling over (figure 2.7). The final lines of the page read, "Die Architekten, dachte ich immer wieder, halten mich für verrückt, für verrückt, für ver-

---

49. Compare Karl Ignaz Hennetmair, *Ein Jahr mit Thomas Bernhard: Das notariell versiegelte Tagebuch 1972* (Salzburg: Residenz, 2000), 325.

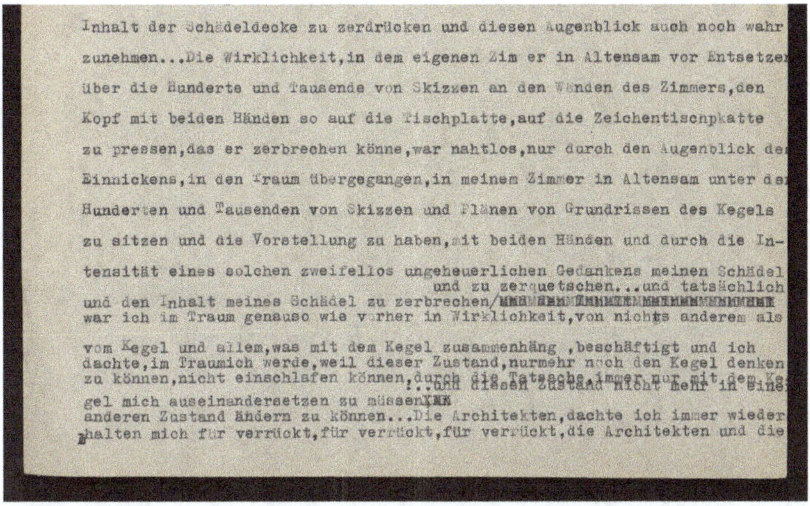

Figure 2.7. Thomas Bernhard, from the "lose Blätter zu Korrektur," ÖLA 563/W4/1c, 39. Literaturarchiv der Österreichischen Nationalbibliothek, Vienna.

rückt . . . [The architects, I thought again and again, think I'm crazy, crazy, crazy . . .]."[50]

In addition to being compressed through reduction of line spacing, the final lines of Bernhard's pages often become literally *verrückt*. At the very bottom edges of many pages, so little paper was left that the typewriter arms could no longer grasp onto the sheet, which would begin to pull away from the platen. The text becomes uneven, sinking and sloping and occasionally running off the page, a visual state sometimes reflected in the text's contents. In one instance from the "loose pages," Roithamer compares his attempts to flee Altensam with a struggle to escape a swamp; the narration of sinking into the swamp mimics the visual sinking of the final lines on the page (figure 2.8).[51] In another example, the narration of an "Überwindung der Widerstände" (an overcoming of obstacles) in

---

50. Bernhard, *Korrektur*, ÖLA 563/W4/1c, 39, LÖN.
51. Bernhard, *Korrektur*, ÖLA 563/W4/1c, 23, LÖN.

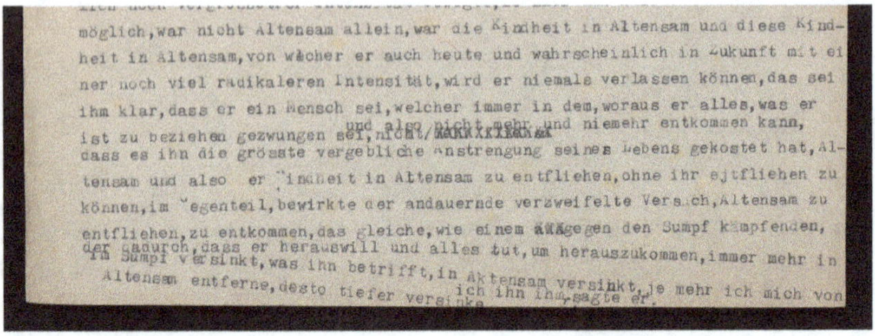

Figure 2.8. Thomas Bernhard, from the "lose Blätter zu Korrektur," ÖLA 563/W4/1c, 23. Literaturarchiv der Österreichischen Nationalbibliothek, Vienna.

Figure 2.9. Thomas Bernhard, from the "lose Blätter zu Korrektur," ÖLA 563/W4/1c, 85. Literaturarchiv der Österreichischen Nationalbibliothek, Vienna.

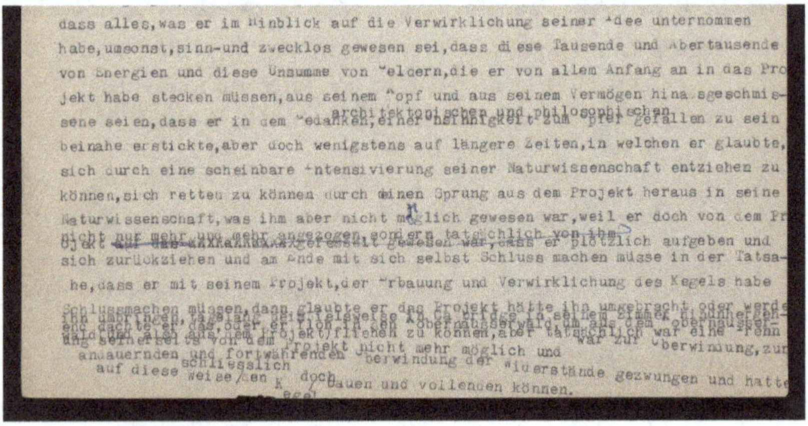

Roithamer's attempt to complete the construction of the Cone corresponds directly to Bernhard's attempts to overcome the resistance posed by the mechanics of the typewriter and the spatial limits of the page—registered in decreased spacing and uneven lines at the bottom edge—in completing the episode (figure 2.9). The end of the sentence, the end of the narrative episode, and the end of the page coincide. This happens not by chance, but instead through

Bernhard's efforts to overcome the tension between the physical space of the page, the mechanical features of the typewriting, and the "shape" of the linguistic text.[52]

"A monstrous movement"

Through the publication process, all of these unique material and visual dynamics of Bernhard's typescripts would seem to be entirely effaced, transformed into a typographical *hyper*-regularity of perfectly repeating rectangles.[53] In many contexts, regularity produces a calming effect; in Bernhard's texts, however, it quickly becomes anything but. The typographical form of the printed text, hyper-regular walls of text that repeat monotonously page after page, providing no paragraph or section breaks, no respite in the process of reading, contributes to, indeed intensifies, the maddening affective experience of Bernhard's language.[54]

The visual dynamics of Bernhard's printed pages are reflected in Bernhard's comparison of the walls of his house with the pages of his books in *Three Days*: "My house is also actually a vast prison. Which I like very much—the walls the barest possible. It is bare *and* brisk. This has a very good effect on my work. The books, whatever I write, *are as is* the place I live [*sind wie das*, worin ich hause]. Sometimes I find that the individual chapters in a book are like different rooms in this house."[55] What first appear to be cold, bare walls, however, are actually riddled with visual disruptions. Bernhard continues: "The walls are alive—right? So—the pages are like walls.... You only need to *examine* them intently [*intensiv anschauen*]. If you *scrutinize* a white wall, you find that it isn't white at all, it *isn't bare*.... In the

---

52. On writing and the overcoming of *Widerstände*, see Martin Stingelin, "Schreiben," introduction to *"Mir ekelt vor diesem tintenklecksenden Säkulum": Schreibszenen im Zeitalter der Manuskripte*, ed. Martin Stingelin, Davide Giuriato, and Sandro Zanetti (Munich: Fink, 2004), 11–18.

53. On editing as typographical translation, see Roland Reuß, "Spielräume des Zufälligen: Zum Verhältnis von Edition und Typographie," *Textkritische Beiträge* 11 (2006): 57.

54. Compare Eyckeler, *Reflexionspoesie*, 78, 91–92.

55. Bernhard, *Three Days*, 98.

wall you discover cracks, little chinks, bumps, bugs. There is a *tremendous* activity (*ungeheuere Bewegung*) on the walls. Really, the wall and the book page are perfectly alike."[56] At first glance, the pages of Bernhard's books may appear to be completely uniform, perfect rectangles of text that repeat page after page, "bare and cold." The longer one spends with Bernhard's pages, however, the more one notices disruptions of the typographical surface not unlike those in the narration; visually, the pages begin to vibrate with a kind of "ungeheuere Bewegung" (monstrous movement). Because the text is left- and right-justified—as is quite standard for printed prose in contemporary publishing—the lack of paragraph or section divisions means that there are no visual breaks in the text; this, in combination with the repetitiveness of Bernhard's prose, gives rise to visual fissures, accidental typographical arrangements that jump out from the "wall" of uninterrupted text. In other words, the macro-uniformity of Bernhard's printed pages, repeating rectangles of text, amplifies micro-typographical patterns. Clauses repeated at regular syntactic intervals may fall into accidental alignment (figure 2.10), rendering visible the rhythmic structuring of Bernhard's language produced by the stringing together of repetitive clauses that at times are (nearly) identical in syntactic length.[57] Something similar occurs when blank spaces between words end up stacked one atop the next during justification, producing typographical "rivers" or "canyons" of white space that wind between words. Typesetters generally attempt to eliminate such features, thought to be visually unpleasing and distracting. The perfect rectangularity of Bernhard's text blocks makes these visual disturbances all the more noticeable; the reader is thrust momentarily out of the immersive experience of reading and onto the surface of the page in a kind of visually induced *Ver-rückung* in the reading experience.[58] Without the respite typically provided by

---

56. Bernhard, *Three Days*, 98–100.

57. Compare Reuß, "Spielräume," 59–60; Marten, *Bernhards Baukasten*, 114; Alfred Gelbmann, "Beobachtungen zur Genealogie des Schreibens bei Thomas Bernhard" (Master's thesis, University of Vienna, 2012), 10–11.

58. Marten describes this similarly as a "Moment des Kippens" or "Kippvorgang" between "sukzessives Lesen" into "synoptischen Wahrnehmung" (Marten, *Bernhards Baukasten*, 7).

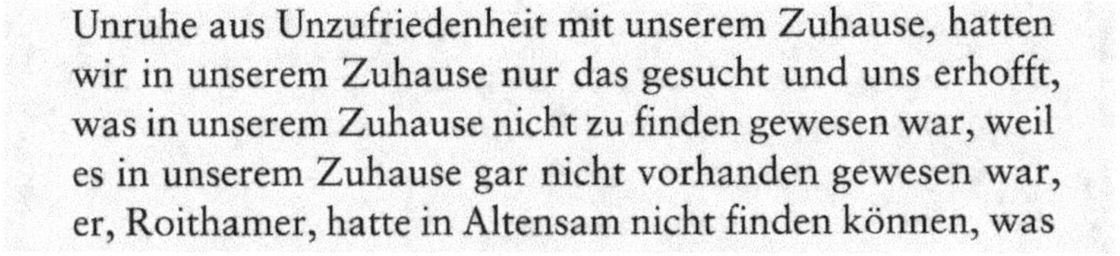

Unruhe aus Unzufriedenheit mit unserem Zuhause, hatten wir in unserem Zuhause nur das gesucht und uns erhofft, was in unserem Zuhause nicht zu finden gewesen war, weil es in unserem Zuhause gar nicht vorhanden gewesen war, er, Roithamer, hatte in Altensam nicht finden können, was

> **Figure 2.10.** Thomas Bernhard, *Korrektur* (2005), 72. © Suhrkamp Verlag, Berlin.

paragraph or chapter breaks, the reader can become overwhelmed by the Bernhardian deluge of language; as Eyckeler writes, "the reader himself (like in *Verstörung*) risks being driven mad."[59]

These typographical glitches were generated in the process of typesetting; but similar visual phenomena are observable in Bernhard's typescripts (figures 2.11 and 2.12). In turn, these visual and material phenomena had the potential to affect recursively how and what Bernhard wrote, and even to become figured in the space of representation. Descriptions of the "Unordnung der Blätter" (disorder of those pages) (W 13:181) or of the "Irritationsintensität" (intensity of irritation) (W 13:308) conducive for Roithamer's writing refer not only to Roithamer's fictional pages and writing process, but also to the actual disorder and visual irritations of Bernhard's typescripts, or to the frenetic process through which these pages were sometimes produced (figure 2.11).[60] Typographic canyons also resemble traces of the activity of the "Holzwürmer" (book worms)—one recalls the "Ungeziefer" (bugs) that Bernhard described on the walls of his house—that eat through the attic floorboards and drawers stuffed with Roithamer's manuscripts (figure 2.12). Like the "Hohlräume" (hollow spaces) in Roithamer's vertical tower of text that destabilize it, causing it to shift and teeter, the typographical canyons within the vertical rectangle of the printed text block—stacks of lines like stacks of pages—perpetually disrupt the absorptive experience of reading.

---

59. Eyckeler, *Reflexionspoesie*, 91–92.
60. Compare Theisen's discussion of "irritation words," which often take the form of repeated italicized words in passages of Bernhard's writing (Theisen, *Silenced Facts*, 49, 66).

> vollendet,ich habe es in der grössten Irritation~~ intensität ~~verwirklichen
> und vollenden können,denn alles ist nur auf Irritation angelegt,so Roit-
> hamer.Jede Idee hat ihre grösste Irritation,so Roithamer.Des Planers und
> Erbauers Kopf,so Roithamer,muss in der grössten Irritation sein Ziel errei-
> chen und vollenden, so Roithamer.Zuerst hatte ich von den sogenannten Geolo-
> gen,die heran~~ziehen~~ *für uns, denn sie begleitete hatten*, die grösste Irritation und Geringschätz-
> ung,dann von den sogenannten Architekten die grösste,die äusserste Irrita-
> tion und Geringschätzung,dann auch von den Handwerkern die grösste Irrita-
> tion und Geringschätzung,aber diese grösstmögliche Irritation und höchst-
> mögliche Geringschätzung war notwendig gewesen,so Roithamer,um den Kegel
> verwirklichen und vollenden zu können,ohne diese Irritation~~ und ~~Gering-
> schätzung hätte ich mein Ziel niemals erreichen können,dann wäre ich ganz
> einfach zu schwach gewesen dazu.Dass mir alle Voraussetzungen für die Ver-
> wirklichung,geschweige denn Vollendung meines Vorhabens fehlten,war mir
> von allen Seiten gesagt worden,aber jetzt darf ich sagen,dass ich genau
> alle diese Voraussetzungen gehabt habe,~~ denn der ~~ Kegel vollendet.Wenn
> auch die Wirkung der Vollendung des Kegels eine andere ist,als die erwar-

Figure 2.11. Thomas Bernhard, typescript of *Korrektur*, ÖLA 563/W4/2, 188. Literaturarchiv der Österreichischen Nationalbibliothek, Vienna.

> was wir wissen und kommen gut voran,so Roithamer.In der Nacht habe er immer
> den Holzwurm gehört in Altensam,die Gefrässigkeit der Holzwürmer habe ihn
> in der Nacht nicht schlafen lassen,überall und in der Nacht naturgemäss durch
> seine Hellhörigkeit und Überempfindlichkeit seines Kopfes am deutlichsten den
> Holzwurm an der Arbeit,in den Fussbodenbrettern und unter den Fussbodenbret-
> tern,in den Kasten und Kommoden,in allen Schubladenkasten vor allem,so Roit-
> hamer,in den Türen und Fensterstöcken,ja in den Türen und in den Sesseln und
> Fauteuils,er habe immer genau unterscheiden können,wo und in welchem Gegen-
> stand,Möbel,ein Holzwurm arbeite,tatsächlich hatte sich der Holzwurm auch scho
> n in sein eigenes Bett hineingefressen gehabt,während des Wachliegens im Bet
> die ganze Nacht,so Roithamer,habe er die Arbei*t* der Holzwürmer verfolgt,ver-
> folgen müssen,in höchster Aufmerksamkeit,~~ den süssen ~~ Geruch des frischen Holz-
> mehls habe er ~~   ~~ eingeatmet und es sei ihm bedrückend gewesen,
> festzustellen zu müssen,dass sich im Laufe der Jahre Tausende,möglicherweise
> Zehntausende und Hunderttausende von Holzwürmern an Altensam herangemacht
> hatten,um,wie er in der Nacht immer habe denken müssen,Altensam aufzufressen
> ,solange Altensam anzufressen und aufzufressen,bis es in einem einzigen,mög-
> licherweise gar nicht mehr so lange auf sich warten lassenden Augenblick in
> sich zusammenfällt.Es gab keinen einzigen Gegenstand in Altensam,so Roithame

Figure 2.12. Thomas Bernhard, typescript of *Korrektur*, ÖLA 563/W4/2, 180. Literaturarchiv der Österreichischen Nationalbibliothek, Vienna.

Thus far I have focused primarily on visual aspects of Bernhard's writing that remain legible in various ways in his published texts, transformed into figurative descriptions or even reappearing unexpectedly on the visual surface of printed page. Yet there are other fissures in Bernhard's work through which the material scene of writing surges into the scene of reading. Aspects of Bernhard's writing—the rhythmic, bodily dimensions of his typing, for example—left a material trace on his typescript pages. These are rendered *invisible* in the printed text, but they remain nonetheless perceptible, incorporated not only into the representational content but also into the cognitive and bodily-affective experience of reading.

Rhythm

All of the material traces we have seen up to this point were generated on the typewriter. As his primary instrument for composing texts, Bernhard's typewriter was much more than a mere tool: it conditioned the writing itself, directly shaping the characteristic textual features of Bernhard's language in ways that scholars have generally correlated (the relationship between navigating type keys and piano keys, for instance) but not examined in detail from a media-theoretical vantage point. In this section I examine the interaction of the typewriter as a writing technology and the page as a unit in shaping the bodily, rhythmic dimensions of Bernhard's writing practice, which in turn manifest, I will show, in the rhythmic, affective dimensions of Bernhard's prose.

As mentioned above, Bernhard was known to type extremely rapidly and forcefully, often filling his pages to the very edges; but the material effects of this mode also had an auditory component. Bernhard is reported to have typed so loudly that his neighbors complained, and so forcefully that he destroyed multiple typewriters throughout his career. As Karl Hennetmair recalls,

> When I arrived in Nathal at 7:30 the gates and doors were open. Already in the courtyard I heard Thomas typing on the typewriter, such that from a distance it sounded like machine-gun fire. Thomas can only write on

models from the 20s or early 30s, because he thrashes [*hindrischt*] on the keys in such a way that on later models they fly away, just break off, after a few days. He writes mostly on the machine of his grandfather Freumbichler. But he additionally bought a second such model, because he has also thrashed to pieces [*zusammendreschen*] the old, strong machine several times, and during the repair his modern travel typewriter regularly broke down.[61]

Though the antique Underwood typewriter that Bernhard famously inherited from his grandfather is often evoked in mythologization of Bernhard as an author, Bernhard used small travel typewriters far more frequently than Hennetmair suggests. As Peter Fabjan, Bernhard's half-brother and overseer of the writer's estate, noted in an interview with Marek Kędzierski, "He had a small travel typewriter, which he carried around with him everywhere in a leather bag, and which he mistreated [*malträtiert*], he was a two-finger-writer."[62] Bernhard's "mistreatment" and abuse of his typewriters registers haptically in the impressions left by the type hammers striking the page, impressions that, in the case of manual typewriters, directly index the bodily intensity of typing. At times Bernhard typed so forcefully that he punctured the paper.

The speed and intensity of Bernhard's typing were conditioned, in part, by the mechanics of the typewriter. Typing enabled writers to compose more rapidly than by hand,[63] and multiple copies could be created simultaneously with the use of carbon paper, a method that Bernhard himself sometimes employed, and that required typing with sufficient force to ensure that the impression of the hammers would register on multiple sheets. In comparison to handwriting and electronic typing, transitioning from one line to the next is most cumbersome on a manual typewriter, requiring interrupting the flow of typing at every line end to manually return the cylindrical carriage. If one takes seriously the suggestion that "Denken" (thought)

---

61. Hennetmair, *Ein Jahr*, 325.
62. Peter Fabjan and Marek Kędzierski, "Jeder Tag war inszeniert: Krankheit, Einsamkeit, Literatur—Erinnerungen an Thomas Bernhard," *Lettre International* 92 (2011): 90.
63. Viollet, "Mechanisches Schreiben," 35.

was for Bernhard "Musizieren" (music making),[64] or Bernhard's statement that "how" was more important than "what" he wrote, then one must account for the fact that the mediality of typewriting, which necessarily conditioned Bernhard's process, always had the potential to produce recursive effects on textual form and content.[65] These, however, are difficult dimensions to access, either from anecdotal accounts or from directly examining Bernhard's typescripts. We have no audio recordings of Bernhard's typing, the soundtrack that always accompanied his writing; even if we did, these would not necessarily tell us anything about the degree to which the phenomenological experience of writing shaped Bernhard's texts.

Bernhard himself asserted that rhythm and musicality are key to understanding "how" he wrote: "I see the subject matter proper as entirely secondary.... To come back to how I write my books: I would say, it's a question of rhythm and has a lot to do with music. Yes, one can only understand what I write when one realizes that *the musical components* matter first and foremost, and that *what* I narrate only comes second.... The problem lies in *how*."[66] Scholars have devoted significant attention to the musical structuring of Bernhard's writing, which has been compared to the fugue, Schönberg's twelve-tone principle, and techno.[67] Bernhard's voice training

---

64. Manfred Jurgensen, "Die Sprachpartituren des Thomas Bernhard," in *Bernhard: Annäherungen*, ed. Manfred Jurgensen (Bern: Franke, 1981), 115.

65. Klaus Hurlebusch describes the "processual reflexiveness of writing upon itself" in "Den Autor besser verstehen: Aus seiner Arbeitsweise—Prolegomenon zu einer Hermeneutik textgenetischen Schreibens," in *Textgenetische Edition*, ed. Hans Zeller und Gunter Martens (Tübingen: Niemeyer, 1998), 46. Compare also Marshall McLuhan: "Because he is an audience for his own mechanical audacities, he never ceases to react to his own performance. Composing on the typewriter is like flying a kite." McLuhan, *Understanding Media: The Extensions of Man* (Cambridge, MA: MIT Press, 1994), 284.

66. Jean-Louis de Rambures, "Aus zwei Interviews mit Thomas Bernhard," in *Antiautobiografie: Zu Thomas Bernhards "Auslöschung,"* ed. Hans Höller and Irene Heidelberger-Leonard (Frankfurt am Main: Suhrkamp, 1995), 13–14.

67. Eyckeler, *Reflexionspoesie*, 11–12; Manfred Mittermayer, "Ein musikalischer Schriftsteller: Thomas Bernhard und die Musik," in *Sprachmusik: Grenzgänge der Literatur*, ed. Gerhard Melzer and Paul Pechmann (Vienna: Sonderzahl, 2003), 63–87; Andreas Herzog, "Thomas Bernhards Poetik der prosaischen Musik," in Höller and Heidelberger-Leonard, *Antiautobiografie*, 132–47. Regarding Bernhard's use of specific rhetorical structures, see Martina Ochs, *Eine Arbeit über meinen Stil*,

at the Mozarteum in Salzburg is often evoked in analyses of the simulated orality of his prose.[68] Scholars have also related the musical structuring of Bernhard's prose to readerly affect: as theorists from Merleau-Ponty to Kristeva to Nancy have discussed, the musicality, intensity, and rhythm of language is experienced first and foremost in the body, which participates in meaning production.[69]

Bernhard himself characterized his prose as fundamentally bodily: "Of course everything that I write is prose, and prose is always necessarily something earthly, something corporeal . . . something tangible, something that defies total dissolution [*das keine gänzliche Auflösung zuläßt*]."[70] The bodily responses to Bernhard's prose thus constitute a key dimension of his work. But Bernhard also produced

---

sehr interessant: Zum Sprechverhalten in Thomas Bernhards Theaterstücken (Frankfurt am Main: Peter Lang, 2006). On Bernhard's use of specific music-compositional structures, see Gudrun Kuhn, *"Ein philosophisch-musikalisch geschulter Sänger": Musikästhetische Überlegungen zur Prosa Thomas Bernhards* (Würzburg: Königshausen und Neumann, 1996). On Schönberg as a model, see Karin Marsoner, "Musikalische Gestaltungsvorgänge in Thomas Bernhards Roman *Auslöschung*," in *Die Musik, das Leben und der Irrtum: Thomas Bernhard und die Musik*, ed. Otto Kolleritsch (Vienna: Universal Edition, 2000), 153–68. On the fugue-like structure of Bernhard's writing, see Benjamin Henrichs, "Der Triumph des Untergehers: Thomas Bernhard ist tot—es lebe Thomas Bernhard!," in *Thomas Bernhard: Portraits*, ed. Sepp Dreissinger (Weitra: Bibliothek der Provinz, 1993), 305; and Manfred Jurgensen, "Die Sprachpartituren," 118. On techno as model, see Johannes Windrich, *TechnoTheater: Dramaturgie und Philosophie bei Rainald Goetz und Thomas Bernhard* (Munich: Fink, 2007).

68. On Bernhard's prose as a kind of textualized *Redefluß*, see Christoph Kappes, *Schreibgebärden: Zur Poetik und Sprache bei Thomas Bernhard, Peter Handke und Botho Strauß* (Würzburg: Königshausen und Neumann, 2006), 25. On the voice as instrument in Bernhard, see Jurgensen, "Die Sprachpartituren"; Kappes, *Schreibgebärden*; Gudrun Kuhn, "Der Stimmenhörer," in *Sprachmusik: Grenzgänge der Literatur*, ed. Gerhard Melzer and Paul Pechmann (Vienna: Sonderzahl, 2003), 101. Elfriede Jelinek described Bernhard's prose as "eine Literatur des Sprechens (in Gegensatz zum Denker Handke), der Endlos-Tiraden. . . . Und wenn man längst kannte, was da gesagt wurde—in ihrer Musikalität, in ihrer rhythmischen Gliederung, einer Endlos-Sinuskurve, waren die Texte unerreicht, mußte man, selbst los geworden, immer weiter lesen." Jelinek, "Atemlos," in *Thomas Bernhard: Portraits*, ed. Sepp Dreissinger (Weitra: Bibliothek der Provinz, 1993), 311.

69. Kappes, *Schreibgebärden*, 12.

70. Martin Huber, "Von Schwarzach St. Veit nach Weng: Zur Vorgeschichte von Thomas Bernhards literarischem Durchbruch mit seinem Roman 'Frost,'" *Thomas Bernhard Jahrbuch* 4 (2005/2006), 43.

his prose through a highly bodily process of writing, one defined by its own rhythms. Fleischmann described Bernhard as a thoroughly "musikalischer Mensch" (musical person), noting that he tapped his foot like a metronome while speaking.[71] Bernhard was known to write with extraordinary bodily intensity; Peter Fabjan characterized Bernhard's writing as "an almost eruptive process": "When he had written a novel, he was around a kilo lighter, downright exhausted."[72] It has been suggested that Bernhard preferred the typewriter because of its similarity to the piano, and Bernhard himself described the similarity between the two instruments.[73] Typing rapidly and elaborating motifs through repetitive variations, Bernhard's "Musizieren" might at times be compared to a kind of jazz-like improvisation, in which he would sit at the typewriter and begin to "play," riffing on a rhetorical or thematic motif until the page was filled.[74] Bernhard described this compositional technique in similar terms: "One day I sit myself down and just write some prose and then again something else. . . . I don't have any concept. . . . You want to make something good, you have an interest in what you're making, like a pianist. He starts the playing, then he once tries out three notes, then he can do twenty . . . and I do like they do with notes, just with words."[75] Seen from this perspective, "what" Bernhard wrote, "the subject matter proper," becomes secondary with respect to "how" he wrote, the performance of writing itself: "only the *process* interests him, not its results."[76]

---

71. Thomas Bernhard, *Thomas Bernhard, eine Begegnung: Gespräche mit Krista Fleischmann*, ed. Krista Fleischmann (Vienna: Edition S, 1991), 134–35.
72. Fabjan and Kędzierski, "Jeder Tag," 90.
73. Kurt Hofmann, *Aus Gesprächen*, 22–23. On relationships between typewriting and piano playing in general, see Viollet, "Mechanisches Schreiben," 25, 30–31.
74. Sandro Zanetti describes improvisation as a combinatorial method drawing on a repertoire of "gestures and forms of articulation." Sandro Zanetti, "Improvisation," in *Medien der Literatur: Ein Handbuch*, ed. Natalie Binczek, Till Dembeck, und Jörgen Schäfer (Berlin: De Gruyter, 2014), 221.
75. Hofmann, *Aus Gesprächen*, 22. Compare also Fabjan and Kędzierski, "Jeder Tag," 90; Eyckeler, *Reflexionspoesie*, 82.
76. Peter von Becker, "Bei Bernhard: Eine Geschichte in fünfzehn Episoden (1978)," in Dreissinger, *Thomas Bernhard: Portraits*, 126.

In addition to its rhythmic, musical dimensions, scholars and critics have also detected a notable "mechanical" quality of Bernhard's writing, characterized in terms of a sinister "Intensität" (intensity) and "Dichte" (density), an experience of "Betroffenheit" (shock) and a capacity "zu fesseln" (to captivate).[77] Descriptions of the "machine-like, self-reproductive mechanics" of Bernhard's writing not only echo Hennetmair's comparison of Bernhard's typing to "machine-gun fire"; the language generated through this process, which "mercilessly hammers away at the reader's nerves," emerged directly from Bernhard's ferocious typewriting.[78] Bernhard's characterization of the bodily "shocks" his texts produce might similarly be tied to the physical shocks of his hammering into the page: "Read my books, it's an accumulation of millions of shocks. It's a stringing together not only of sentences, but of shock impressions. A book should also be a shock, a shock that is not visible from the outside."[79]

How much interpretative pressure can these relationships between the physical intensity of typing, the formal intensity of Bernhard's prose, and the bodily intensities of reading bear? One can imagine that particularly intense, scathing passages sometimes emerged through intense writing sessions that were particularly intense physically; or that particularly vehement, destructive tirades resulted from a psychosomatic writerly process so furious that it physically punctured the page. Bernhard himself commented on the feedback between style, semantics, and the bodily intensity of writing during his production of the novel *Holzfällen* (*Cutting Timber*, 1984), which bears the subtitle *Eine Erregung* (an irritation): "Yes, because the style, understood musically, is also a somewhat irritated

---

77. Eyckeler, *Reflexionspoesie*, 11, 78; Wendelin Schmidt-Dengler, "Von der Schwierigkeit, Thomas Bernhard zu lesen: Zu Thomas Bernhards *Gehen*," in *Bernhard: Annäherungen*, ed. Manfred Jurgensen (Bern: Franke, 1981), 125; Claudia Albes, *Der Spaziergang als Erzählmodell: Studien zu Jean-Jacques Rousseau, Adalbert Stifter, Robert Walser und Thomas Bernhard* (Tübingen: Francke, 1999), 296; Kappes, *Schreibgebärden*, 25, 149.

78. Heinz Kuehn, "On Reading Thomas Bernhard," *Sewanee Review* 105, no. 4 (1997): 550–51; Herzog, "Thomas Bernhards Poetik," 140.

79. Bernhard, *Thomas Bernhard, eine Begegnung*, 250. For a discussion of "shocks" as part of Bernhard's techniques of *Geschichtenzerstören*, see Theisen, *Silenced Facts*, 38–45.

one in the book, seen from the content one doesn't write something like that calmly, [but] rather in a certain irritated mood . . . so you set yourself down and are at once irritated from the *idea*, and when you begin to *write*, the style already irritates you. It is always written in an irritated style."[80] Material analysis alone cannot confirm whether the deep, destructive impressions of the type hammers of any given passage resulted from an "irritated mood" translated into the intensity of typing. But regardless, the musical, rhythmic *language* of Bernhard's texts necessarily emerged through media-specific, bodily *processes* of writing, which had their own musicality and rhythm. This is not to say that Bernhard's style is technologically determined—at least not entirely. It *is* to acknowledge, however, that the *"mechané* of the Bernhardian text"[81] is co-constituted by the mechanics of his compositional process.

The prosaic rhythms generated through this process, in turn, directly guide the rhythms of reading, producing "fluctuations in intensity, acceleration, deceleration, or atmosphere shifts."[82] Bernhard stated, "When I have reached my working tempo, nothing can distract me."[83] This pace resurfaces in the tempo of reading: "one always reads Bernhard too quickly," owing to Bernhard's ability to bring his writing "auf ein solches Tempo" (to such a pace)."[84] Of course, the rhythms of reading and the sonic, rhythmic dimensions of Bernhard's prose do not directly reproduce the rhythms and sounds of typing. Yet, as a result of the feedback between idea, style, and the bodily intensity of typing that Bernhard described, the reader senses the reverberations of the intensity and noise of Bernhard's hammering in the affective experience of reading. The language of Bernhard's texts is a conduit for not only the transmission

---

80. Bernhard, *Thomas Bernhard, eine Begegnung*, 168.
81. Reuß, "Spielräume," 60.
82. Christian Klug, *Thomas Bernhards Theaterstücke* (Stuttgart: Metzler, 1991), 189ff. Cited in Mittermayer, "Ein musikalischer Schriftsteller," 79.
83. Rambures, "Aus zwei Interviews," 15.
84. Andreas Maier, "Es gab eine Zeit, da hab ich Thomas Bernhard gemocht: Über Bernhards Willen zum rhetorischen Effekt," in *Rhetorik und Sprachkunst bei Thomas Bernhard*, ed. Joachim Knappe and Olaf Kramer (Würzburg: Königshausen und Neumann, 2011), 147.

of meaning, but also a kind of material transfer: the materiality and corporeality of writing remain entangled within the written product, and are in turn transferred into the embodied, material experience of reading, where form and meaning are most immediately processed. This material circulation or feedback loop, moreover, was already operating during the process of writing itself, when Bernhard was producer and recipient at once, with all the possibilities for material-semantic recursion that entails.

The rhythms and sounds of Bernhard's typing also manifest more directly in the representational space of Bernhard's texts. Although it may seem surprising, given its pronounced self-reflexivity, that there are no explicit representations of *type*writing in *Correction*, reexamining the work through the lens of its production suggests how thoroughly infused representational content is with the sounds and rhythms of typing. The characters populating *Correction* and the spaces they inhabit are defined by rhythm, music, and noise. Roithamer's progress in writing is dependent on and spurred by listening to music; his "Redeweise" (way of speaking) displays a kind of musicality; and his life in general possesses its own unique rhythm. The text is permeated with descriptions of machines and mechanistic processes, such as the rattling of Mrs. Höller's sewing machine, which reverberates, along with other noises, through Höller's garret: "The rattle of the sewing machine above and the roar of the Aurach [River] below combined in a quite definite musical rhythm" (C 109). Together these noises blend into a kind of soundtrack that pervades the attic, in concert with and incorporated into the "mechanism of his thought" (C 5).

In descriptions of the mechanics of Roithamer's thought, in the sounds of the sewing machine flooding Roithamer's scene of writing, one hears the music of another machine: the omnipresent clattering of Bernhard's typewriter. The overwhelming affective experience that Bernhard's language can produce in the reader's body—"shock effects" of a "machine-like" language that "mercilessly hammers away" at the reader's nerves—evokes not only the "destructive effect" (W 4:313) produced when Roithamer's sister enters his architectural work, the Cone, but also the exhaustion experienced by the narrator, who felt "vulnerable to every kind of injury from Roithamer's papers" (C 24) and questioned whether Roithamer intended to physically destroy him by bequeathing him his Nachlass (C 116). Just like the narrator becomes a part of Roithamer's work—"because I was so entirely part of his development" (C 117), integrated into it—the reader becomes incorporated into the structure of Bernhard's work. Traces of the bodily scene of writing are activated in the bodily dimension of reading, whether one experiences them as rhythmic and musical, or violent and machine-like. Transformed into a surface of inscription, the reader's body becomes a component of the work's mediality and a constitutive site for its generation—part of its structure, part of the whole.

Mental-Manual Labor

In characterizing writing process, a distinction is sometimes drawn between writing as intellectual labor (*Kopfarbeit*) and writing as material labor (*Papierarbeit*). Martin Huber writes of Bernhard's process, "Starting from the rough division of authors into head- or paperworkers [*Kopf- oder Papierarbeiter*], one quickly determines that these drawers aren't suitable to fit Bernhard into precisely."[85] The productive interaction of the intellectual and material in Bernhard's process distinguishes it from that of his prototypical protagonists, so-called *Geistesmenschen* (intellectuals) who construct in their heads entire texts that they cannot materialize on paper (in this respect, Roithamer is fairly anomalous). Bernhard succeeds where his protagonists fail, one might argue, because of the interaction of material and mental activity, *Handarbeit* and *Kopfarbeit*, in his compositional process.[86]

The juxtaposition of intellectual labor and manual labor also structured Bernhard's working routine. Fabjan described Bernhard's work on his Ohlsdorf farmhouse as a means of "structuring the everyday": "The house, this building, he as a builder, that meant for him a structuring of the everyday. He didn't have to contemplate and fear, 'When

---

85. Huber, "'Schrieb,'" 77.
86. Compare Marten, *Bernhards Baukasten*, 26–28; Wieland Schmied, *Auersbergers wahre Geschichte* (Weitra: Bibliothek der Provinz, 2014), 140.

will I start the novel?'; instead that gave him contact with the ground.... This voluntary connection to simple reality was important to him. In his head he was already working on the next novel, completely independently."[87] Bernhard himself described an oscillation between mental and manual labor as crucial for his work: "For each of my books I'm torn back and forth between passion and hate toward the subject that I'd chosen. Each time when the second feeling gains the upper hand, I decide to abandon intellectual things entirely and instead to devote myself to entirely material tasks, such as chopping wood or cleaning a wall, in order to find my way back to amusement. But after a more or less lengthy space of time I start hating myself again for my unproductivity and flee, out of despair at the cause, once again into my brain."[88] Bernhard frames his experience of writing here as a multilayered rhythmic counterpoint structure. During the writing process, he is perpetually "hin- und hergerissen" between "passion" and "hatred," an experience resonating with the description of "Erregung" (irritation) while writing *Cutting Timber*. The rhythmic oscillation between "intellectual things" and "material tasks" also structured his work routine. The productive interruption of writerly work with more bodily concerns is also thematized in *Correction*: Höller knocked from below on the floor of the attic chamber "at quite definite times and at quite regular intervals," signaling for Roithamer to break from his writing and join the family to eat (C 82). This periodic interruption was not a "disturbance"; instead "it often came as a liberation from some blind alley he had constructed, speculated, thought himself into, and so forth" (C 83). The routine interruption also engendered a distinct "rhythm" to Roithamer's work: "I can imagine that Roithamer greatly valued their adherence to this routine [*Rhythmus*] as a ritual" (C 82). The narrator experienced this "behavior mechanism" himself in Höller's attic: "the moment I had moved into Höller's garret I had become locked into the mechanism of their behavior with Roithamer, everyone who now lives in Höller's garret after Roithamer is probably locked into the same behavior mechanism that functioned for Roithamer" (C 83).

---

87. Fabjan and Kędzierski, "Jeder Tag," 90.
88. Rambures, "Aus zwei Interviews," 13–14.

In considering the material rhythms of Bernhard's writing, we can distinguish multiple interconnected levels: On the one hand, there are the rhythms of typing, through which a highly musical prose was generated, the rhythms of which are felt in the bodily experience of reading. On the other, Bernhard's working routine can be described as episodic in nature, with intense, eruptive writing sessions punctuated by other forms of manual labor, forming a kind of working rhythm.

Page-Episodes

There is one place where all these dimensions—the typewriter as tool and the page as unit, the rhythms of writing and the rhythms of reading—come together: Bernhard's composition in "page-episodes."[89] While not all of Bernhard's pages of writing are page-episodes, those that are emphasize the interaction between the two material considerations—the typewriter as tool, and the page as unit—as constraints on Bernhard's writing. This compositional mode may simply stem from a principle of economy: writers employing the typewriter commonly filled pages to the edges because switching out sheets disrupted the flow of writing.[90] For Bernhard, something more was at play. It appears that he willfully allowed, even encouraged, the page space to shape and constrain what he wrote. The page served as a material stage on which to play with a thematic and/or rhythmic motif, expanding it through variations and elaborations until reaching the bottom edge. This method yielded single-page or multipage units that could be (re)ordered through a montage-like building block system of textual construction—a method reflected in the activity of "sifting and sorting" Roithamer's Nachlass in *Correction*. Bernhard rearranged page-episodes not only within a single work, but also between work projects; episodes originally composed for one novel could be transposed into another.

---

89. Huber, "'Schrieb,'" 78; Huber and Schmidt-Dengler, commentary to *Frost*, 351; Langer, commentary to *Das Kalkwerk*, 249.
90. Viollet, "Mechanisches Schreiben," 34–37.

Whereas the typewriter engendered certain dimensions of rhythm in Bernhard's writing, the method of composing in page-episodes also points to *sequential structuring* of the writing process itself into distinct writing sessions, or episodes. And although this "rhythmic arrangement in episodes" has been observed as part of Bernhard's writing process, scholars have not interrogated the degree to which key stylistic and structural features of Bernhard's texts are specifically rooted in this method.[91] Easy to spot in Bernhard's typescript versions—when the line spacing is decreased toward the bottom edge before the last sentence is brought to a close, followed by the beginning of a new sentence on the next page—junctures between page-episodes are, in theory, invisibly sewn together in print. Once we become attentive to Bernhard's process, however, we can detect the "fissures" between episodes, and the reasons such fissures exist in the published text. In some cases, an abrupt thematic shift indexes a break between page-episodes. In others, the reader senses rhythmically when one episode concludes and another begins, like transitions between symphonic movements. In one passage of *Correction*, a lengthy meditation on Höller's taxidermic creation of "purely art(ificial) creatures" from "purely natural creatures" closes with an unusually *short* sentence: "This meditation lasted an hour" (C 127). The narration shifts abruptly into angst-ridden rumination on the task of sifting and sorting: "Pacing the floor [*Hin und her gehend*] in Höller's garret I thought that I need only *approach* Roithamer's legacy, *approach* it to begin with . . ." (C 127). In the typescript version, the meditation ending "Diese Meditation dauerte eine Stunde" (This meditation lasted an hour) comes to a close in the bottom line of a page, the final words squeezed into the corner.[92] The next page starts with the sentence beginning "Hin und her gehend . . ."[93] In print, nothing signals this transition visually; but in the typescript, it is clear that the thematic shift from one narratological episode to another, which the reader discerns cognitively, corresponds to a transition between page-episodes, products of two distinct writing episodes.

---

91. Huber, "'Schrieb,'" 78.
92. Bernhard, *Korrektur*, ÖLA 563/W2, 92, LÖN.
93. Bernhard, *Korrektur*, ÖLA 563/W2, 93, LÖN.

Material-semiotically, the sentence "This meditation lasted an hour" is thus particularly charged: it refers to the culmination of the represented meditation on the taxidermic transformation of nature into art, but also, it seems, to the culmination of Bernhard's actual, writerly meditation on that topic, transpiring over some time span, the precise duration of which (an hour? longer?) we cannot know. It is a double reference, a metaleptic transgression that disturbs the ontological boundary between fictional and actual, between text as representation and text as process.

The reader may also sense fissures between episodes affectively. In a passage about Roithamer's attempts to escape Altensam, structured linearly through the addition of successive clauses, the narrator shifts suddenly to an oppositional, seesaw-like structure constituted by a slew of antithetical yet syntactically analogous statements: "Whereas Roithamer took advantage of *every opportunity to get out of Altensam*, I took *every opportunity to get into Altensam*, that I had the opportunity *to go to Altensam* and be allowed inside, inside the Absolute Other, *in order to come to life*, for Roithamer it was the other way around, he had to *get out of Altensam* and down into the villages, *in order to come to life* in the villages and most frequently in our house, in the house of my parents . . ." (C 77). Here, the beginning of a new syntactic-rhythmic structure corresponds to the beginning of a new episode; this is registered not cognitively, but instead affectively, when, unconsciously proceeding from one episode to the next, the reader is swept into the rhythmic structure of a new episode, in this case pulled back and forth by the counterpoint thematic-syntactic structure of the passage.

Looking intensively (*intensiv anschauen*) at the printed text, interrogating the "Risse, kleine Sprünge, Unebenheiten" in its linguistic surface, reveals how significantly Bernhard's process of constructing his texts remains entangled in their semantic-material-affective dynamics. The rhythmic structuring of Bernhard's episodic composition manifests itself in the narratological structure of the text and the affective experience of reading. In effect, this method of construction can be thought to constitute a technique of *Geschichtenzerstören*: as Frederick writes, "plot has been disenthroned, shifted away from its central rule, leaving the narrative that unfurls as pure discourse, emancipated but mad," and "narrative economy is reduced to zero as pages upon pages are filled, but next to nothing actually happens."[94] When we turn our attention from the plot(lessness) of the novel to the story of its production, however, another kind of narrative emerges: one constituted not by plot episodes of coherent plot structure, but rather by writing episodes, which Bernhard "sifted and sorted" in constructing the text. In this respect, Bernhard's notion of *Geschichtenzerstören*, which is reflected in and effected through the linguistic and structural aspects of his prose, is rooted in this concrete material practice.

Although junctures between page-episodes are rendered invisible in print, there is one remarkable moment in the first edition of *Correction* in which the visuality of the page-episode is actually reproduced typographically. At the single section break dividing the first section ("Die höllersche Dachkammer") from the second ("Sichten und Ordnen"), the final lines are compressed in now-familiar fashion at the bottom of the typescript page.[95] The printed pages of the first edition typically contain thirty-four lines of text, followed by an empty line and a line containing the page number. On the last page of the first section in the first edition, however, two additional lines of text are added in the space of these lines (yielding thirty-six text lines) before the new section begins on the following page. Rather than setting these lines alone on an otherwise blank page, or resetting the text entirely, the typesetter thus had adopted a strategy similar to Bernhard's, "squeezing" the last two lines onto the bottom of the page (figure 2.13). At this single break between the two sections, the visual structure of the page-episode, otherwise effaced, becomes re-presented in the typographical form of the printed page. What might otherwise appear as an innocuous "surface" feature of the printed text points to one of the most significant features of Bernhard's writing process, one that, as we have seen, crucially shapes his texts' form and contents.[96]

---

94. Frederick, *Unsettled Narratives*, 18, 101.

95. Thomas Bernhard, *Korrektur* (Frankfurt am Main: Suhrkamp, 1975), 192–93.

96. When *Correction* was reset for the subsequent 1988 and 2005 editions, this typographical irregularity was eliminated, the final words falling perfectly onto the final line in the text block.

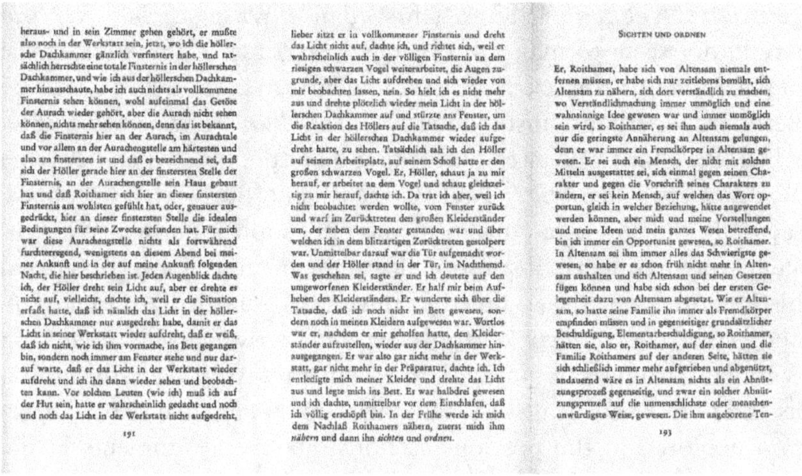

heraus- und in sein Zimmer gehen gehört, er mußte also noch in der Werkstatt sein, jetzt, wo ich die höllersche Dachkammer gänzlich verfinstert habe, und tatsächlich herrschte eine totale Finsternis in der höllerschen Dachkammer, und wie ich aus der höllerschen Dachkammer hinausschaute, habe ich auch nichts als vollkommene Finsternis sehen können, wohl aufeinmal das Getöse der Aurach wieder gehört, aber die Aurach nicht sehen können, nichts mehr sehen können, denn das ist bekannt, daß die Finsternis hier an der Aurach, im Aurachtale und vor allem an der Aurachengstelle am härtesten und also am finstersten ist und daß es bezeichnend sei, daß sich der Höller gerade hier an der finstersten Stelle der Finsternis, an der Aurachengstelle sein Haus gebaut hat und daß Roithamer sich hier an dieser finstersten Finsternis am wohlsten gefühlt hat, oder, genauer ausgedrückt, hier an dieser finstersten Stelle die idealen Bedingungen für seine Zwecke gefunden hat. Für mich war diese Aurachengstelle nichts als fortwährend furchterregend, wenigstens an diesem Abend bei meiner Ankunft und in der auf meine Ankunft folgenden Nacht, die hier beschrieben ist. Jeden Augenblick dachte ich, der Höller dreht sein Licht auf, aber er drehte es nicht auf, vielleicht, dachte ich, weil er die Situation erfaßt hatte, daß ich nämlich das Licht in der höllerschen Dachkammer nur ausgedreht habe, damit er das Licht in seiner Werkstatt wieder aufdreht, daß er weiß, daß ich nicht, wie ich ihm vormache, ins Bett gegangen bin, sondern noch immer am Fenster stehe und nur darauf warte, daß er das Licht in der Werkstatt wieder aufdreht und ich ihn dann wieder sehen und beobachten kann. Vor solchen Leuten (wie ich) muß ich auf der Hut sein, hatte er wahrscheinlich gedacht und noch und noch das Licht in der Werkstatt nicht aufgedreht,

191

lieber sitzt er in vollkommener Finsternis und dreht das Licht nicht auf, dachte ich, und richtet sich, weil er wahrscheinlich auch in der völligen Finsternis an dem riesigen schwarzen Vogel weiterarbeitet, die Augen zugrunde, aber das Licht aufdrehen und sich wieder von mir beobachten lassen, nein. So hielt ich es nicht mehr aus und drehte plötzlich wieder mein Licht in der höllerschen Dachkammer auf und stürzte ans Fenster, um die Reaktion des Höllers auf die Tatsache, daß ich das Licht in der höllerschen Dachkammer wieder aufgedreht hatte, zu sehen. Tatsächlich sah ich den Höller auf seinem Arbeitsplatz, auf seinem Schoß hatte er den großen schwarzen Vogel. Er, Höller, schaut ja zu mir herauf, er arbeitet an dem Vogel und schaut gleichzeitig zu mir herauf, dachte ich. Da trat ich aber, weil ich nicht beobachtet werden wollte, vom Fenster zurück und warf im Zurücktreten den großen Kleiderständer um, der neben dem Fenster gestanden war und über welchen ich in dem blitzartigen Zurücktreten gestolpert war. Unmittelbar darauf war die Tür aufgemacht worden und der Höller stand in der Tür, im Nachthemd. Was geschehen sei, sagte er und ich deutete auf den umgeworfenen Kleiderständer. Er half mir beim Aufheben des Kleiderständers. Er wunderte sich über die Tatsache, daß ich noch nicht im Bett gewesen, sondern noch in meinen Kleidern aufgewesen war. Wortlos war er, nachdem er mir geholfen hatte, den Kleiderständer aufzustellen, wieder aus der Dachkammer hinausgegangen. Er war also gar nicht mehr in der Werkstatt, gar nicht mehr in der Präparatur, dachte ich. Ich entledigte mich meiner Kleider und drehte das Licht aus und legte mich ins Bett. Es war halbdrei gewesen und ich dachte, unmittelbar vor dem Einschlafen, daß ich völlig erschöpft bin. In der Frühe werde ich mich dem Nachlaß Roithamers nähern, zuerst mich ihm *nähern* und dann ihn *sichten* und *ordnen*.

SICHTEN UND ORDNEN

Er, Roithamer, habe sich von Altensam niemals entfernen müssen, er habe sich nur zeitlebens bemüht, sich Altensam zu nähern, sich dort verständlich zu machen, wo Verständlichmachung immer unmöglich und eine wahnsinnige Idee gewesen war und immer unmöglich sein wird, so Roithamer, es sei ihm auch niemals auch nur die geringste Annäherung an Altensam gelungen, denn er war immer ein Fremdkörper in Altensam gewesen. Er sei auch ein Mensch, der nicht mit solchen Mitteln ausgestattet sei, sich einmal gegen seinen Charakter und gegen die Vorschrift seines Charakters zu ändern, er sei kein Mensch, auf welchen das Wort opportun, gleich in welcher Beziehung, hätte angewendet werden können, aber mich und meine Vorstellungen und meine Ideen und mein ganzes Wesen betreffend, bin ich immer ein Opportunist gewesen, so Roithamer. In Altensam sei ihm immer alles das Schwierigste gewesen, so habe er es schon früh nicht mehr in Altensam aushalten und sich Altensam und seinen Gesetzen fügen können und habe sich schon bei der ersten Gelegenheit dazu von Altensam abgesetzt. Wie er Altensam, so hatte seine Familie ihn immer als Fremdkörper empfinden müssen und in gegenseitiger grundsätzlicher Beschuldigung, Elementarbeschuldigung, so Roithamer, hätten sie, also er, Roithamer, auf der einen und die Familie Roithamers auf der anderen Seite, hätten sie sich schließlich immer mehr aufgerieben und abgenützt, andauernd wäre es in Altensam nichts als ein Abnützungsprozeß gegenseitig, und zwar ein solcher Abnützungsprozeß auf die unmenschlichste oder menschenunwürdigste Weise, gewesen. Die ihm angeborene Ten-

193

Figure 2.13. Thomas Bernhard, *Korrektur* (1975), 191–193. © Suhrkamp Verlag, Berlin.

Examining Bernhard's draft materials for *Correction* reveals resonances of Bernhard's process of writing that reverberate throughout the novel, a text that was very much about processes of representational content of the novel, which, in turn, is in large part about processes of textual composition and encounters with the materiality of writing. In this way, the published text and the process of its generation directly reflect upon one another. But examining Bernhard's process also has implications for the readings of texts that less directly analogize their own material production in their semantic content. Bernhard's material production practices were themselves also imbued with a key thematic dimension of his writing that he worked through in relation to his material production process: namely, a thematics of destruction.

Destruction

In this final section, I examine the material-semiotics of destruction in Bernhard's autobiographical novella *Wittgensteins Neffe* (*Witt-*

genstein's Nephew, 1982). At first glance *Wittgenstein's Nephew* would not seem to make an obvious case study of this topic, since destruction is thematized more prominently in many other works by Bernhard—perhaps most obviously *Auslöschung* (*Extinction*, 1986), which Bernhard was already working on at the time when he wrote *Wittgenstein's Nephew*.[97] Paul Wittgenstein (1907–79), a "nephew" (actually the son of a cousin) of the philosopher Ludwig Wittgenstein, was frequently institutionalized for mental illness, dissipated his inherited wealth, and died in poverty.[98] Subtitled *A Friendship*, *Wittgenstein's Nephew* portrays Bernhard's twelve-year friendship with Paul, from its origins and development to periods of turmoil to its end with Paul's death. The text picks up on key themes of *Correction* explored in the previous sections; at several moments in the text, for example, Bernhard describes Paul's struggle to work on a manuscript that he could never complete, that refused to be written. But *Wittgenstein's Nephew* itself has one of the most complex production histories of any work by Bernhard, particularly his late work. The work has been read as a "hymn to friendship" and "a memorial extending beyond death."[99] Yet the thematics of destruction are inscribed in Bernhard's textual depictions—of his relationship with Paul; of Paul's "destruction" by his family, his doctors and surgeons, and society at large; and of his physical decline and death—in ways that become all the more visible when viewed through the lens of the text's material production. Examining the unique complexities of the production of *Wittgenstein's Nephew* can thus, I suggest, also shed light on the way Bernhard thought about and worked through the thematics of destruction in his material process more generally.

---

97. Martin Huber and Manfred Mittermayer, *Bernhard Handbuch* (Stuttgart: Metzler, 2018), 120.

98. The title *Wittgensteins Neffe* is also an intertextual reference to Diderot's *Le Nevue de Rameau*. See Huber and Mittermayer, *Bernhard Handbuch*, 123.

99. Hans Höller and Manfred Mittermayer, commentary to Thomas Bernhard, *Erzählungen III* (W 13:352); Walter Wagner, "'Was ich im Grunde nicht entbehren kann', will ich existieren': Zum Begriff der Freundschaft bei Thomas Bernhard," *Thomas Bernhard Jahrbuch* (2003): 64.

Paper Portraits

Although titled *Wittgenstein's Nephew*, the text is not really about Paul Wittgenstein per se; there are passages in the text that have little or nothing to do with Paul whatsoever. As in the case of many Bernhardian narratives, what the work *is* "about" is difficult to grasp. Many of Bernhard's descriptions of Paul, of his life and behavior, of the nature and history of their friendship, are peculiarly evocative of certain formal, thematic, and process dimensions of Bernhard's writing, as explored in the previous sections. In *Wittgenstein's Nephew*, I argue, Bernhard's depiction of his friendship with Paul can be read as a figuration of Bernhard's own thinking about his writing on multiple levels: the origins of his works, his process of producing them, and his writerly project more broadly. Moreover, the representation of the development of his friendship with Paul—its *Entstehungsgeschichte*—is bound up, I will show, within the material *Entstehungsgeschichte* of the text itself.

Throughout the text, Bernhard asserts that Paul played an essential role in his life. Consider, for example, the following passage, in which Bernhard describes Paul as an indispensable conversation partner:

> Suddenly I longed for that person who had truly been the only male one with whom I was able to converse in a way that suited me [*auf die mir entsprechende Weise*], to have a subject and to develop it, no matter of what kind and be it the most difficult. How long had I been deprived of these conversations. . . . Only now, in the Hermann Pavilion, did I realize what I was missing, what I had been deprived of by my renewed illness and what, basically, I could not do without if I wished to exist. Of course I had friends, the very best of friends, but none whose prodigal inventiveness or whose sensibility could compare with Paul's, I thought, and from that moment onward I did everything to re-establish personal contact with my unfortunate spiritual partner as soon as possible. (WN 40–41)

For Bernhard, Paul is much more than a friend; because of his "inventiveness" and "sensibility," he is necessary for Bernhard's existence—specifically, for his *intellectual* existence. He describes Paul as an "intellectual partner" (*Geistespartner*) with whom he could broach a topic and "develop" it in conversation in a way that "corresponded" to Bernhard's own particular way of thinking (*auf die mir entsprechende Weise*). In another passage, Bernhard similarly describes Paul as the only one who could comprehend his mental "escapades": "a real friend again, one who understood even the craziest escapades of my, after all, rather complicated and therefore by no means straightforward, mind and who had the courage to get involved in the craziest escapades [*verrücktesten Eskapaden*] of my head [*meines Kopfes*]. . . . As soon as I even, in a manner of speaking, touched on a subject it began to develop in exactly the direction in which it was bound to develop in our heads [*in unseren Köpfen*]" (*WN* 24).[100] Bernhard describes Paul as the only person who allowed himself to be drawn into the "maddest escapades" of Bernhard's mind. But in the final sentence quoted above, "*my* head" shifts to "*our* heads": Paul becomes integrated into Bernhard's escapades as co-agent, their subjectivities intertwined. It has frequently been noted that Bernhard's portrait of Paul is in large part a *self-portrait*; that is, the representation of their relationship and interactions a bifurcated figuration of the internal dynamics of Bernhard's writing.[101] In describing the process by which, in conversation with Paul, topics were unfolded and developed, Bernhard all but names his method of writing in "episodes"—which we might alternatively think of as writerly "escapades"—introducing a thought or motif and "developing" it through linguistic and syntactic variations, repetitions, and manipulations. This process took place, not through conversations with another human, but instead through interactions with the typewriter and the page. Typing (*Tippen*), in fact, is indirectly invoked in his description of "touching on" a topic: "I had only to tap on a subject [*Wenn ich ein Thema auch nur antippte*]."

Such passages can thus be read as meditations on the extended agency of writing, which includes a multitude of actants (human, material, mediatic) and is premised on the deconstruction of mind-body dualism. The relationship between the mental and the physical is a

---

100. Translation modified.
101. Manfred Diersch, "Thomas Bernhards 'Wittgensteins Neffe': Selbstfindung im Spiegel des Anderen," in *"Sein und Schein—Traum und Wirklichkeit": Zur Poetik österreichischen Schriftsteller/innen im 20. Jahrhundert*, ed. Herbert Arlt and Manfred Diersch (Frankfurt am Main: Peter Lang, 1994), 145–52.

prominent theme in Bernhard's writing—one thinks of the relationship between walking and thinking in the novella *Walking*. In *Wittgenstein's Nephew*, Bernhard's portrayal of his relationship with Paul is enmeshed within such reflection: in the opening lines of the text, Bernhard is hospitalized in Pavilion Hermann, the pulmonary clinic of the Baumgartner Höhe hospital, while Paul is institutionalized in Pavilion Ludwig of the Steinhof mental institute. The mental patients (*Geisteskranken*) in the Pavilion Ludwig were segregated from the pulmonary patients (*Lungenkranken*) in Pavilion Hermann, separated by a mere 200 meters, but forbidden to move moving between the two areas—a spatial projection of the binary mind-body division. These two domains, however, are not hermetically sealed: the chain-link fence (*Gitter*) dividing them had become heavily rusted and filled with holes that patients could slip through (W 13:215).

Thus despite their categorical separation, there was actually a great deal of traffic (*Verkehr*) between the two areas. During one attempt to cross over and visit Paul, Bernhard pauses in exhaustion on a bench and observes the squirrels scurrying about, also unrestrained by the lattice border:

> From my seat I watched the squirrels which were scurrying up the trees and down the trees throughout the huge park, which seemed boundless from where I was sitting, and these squirrels seemed to have just one overriding passion; they snapped up the paper tissues which had been dropped by the chest patients and were lying everywhere on the ground and with them raced up into the trees. Everywhere they were scuttling about with those paper tissues in their mouths, from every direction into every direction, until all one could see in the dusk were the white patches, flashing hither and thither, of the paper tissues they were holding in their mouths. I sat there, enjoying this sight that, naturally enough, I accompanied by my thoughts which, as if by themselves, arose from these observations. It was June and the windows of the Pavilion were open, and in an actual counterpoint rhythm designed and eventually also composed by a genius [*in einem tatsächlich kontrapunktisch genial entworfenen und schließlich auch komponierten Rhythmus*] the patients were coughing out of the windows into the gathering dusk. (WN 10–11)

The rhythmic movement of the squirrels—scurrying back and forth, up and down, carrying in their mouths paper tissues that litter the yard, having been discarded by pulmonary patients—figures a common rhythmic structuring principle of Bernhard's writing. But in addition to this rhythmic movement, paper also plays a decisive role in this scene: all that remains visible are these white pieces of paper, flitting back and forth in a counterpoint rhythm in sync with the patients' coughing. This visual-auditory rhythm, Bernhard writes, incites thought, thought directly tied to these tissues that are already inscribed, in a sense, with the chest patients' phlegm.

This scene figures the interconnectedness of the physical and mental, a theme that pervades Bernhard's writing and is also crucial for understanding his writing process. Bernhard goes on to describe physical and mental illness as the very source of his art, deploying the terms *Verrücktheit* and *Lungenkrankheit* over and over again in a lengthy episode structured in rhythmic counterpoint, which is directly mirrored in the rhythmic movement of the squirrels and patients' coughing in the previous scene:

> Just as Paul's path time and again had to end, to be cut short, in a mental institution so my path time and again had to end, had to be cut short, in a chest institution. . . . Just as Paul had time and again been ultimately ruined by the psychiatrists and had nevertheless been eventually put on his feet again by his own energy, so I was time and again ruined by the chest specialists and put on my feet again by my own energy . . . The lunatics [*Verrückten*] decisively taught him how to live and exist, and I was taught by this, just as decisively, by the chest patients, as he was by lunacy [*Verrücktheit*] so I was by my chest disorder. (WN 21–22)

In this passage, syntactic parallelism figures a fundamental similarity between mental and physical illness, embodied in Paul and Bernhard: namely, a shared social and existential experience. As the episode progresses, the syntactic parallelism devolves into more rambling structures, within which the concepts of *Verrücktheit* and *Lungenkrankheit* are embedded, troubling the binary distinction between the mental and bodily as "sources" of Bernhard's art.

> But Paul was no more crazy than I am myself, because I am at least as crazy as Paul was. . . . Paul only had his madness and from that madness he existed; I, on top of my madness, have also had my chest disorder and I have exploited both, the madness as well as the chest condition: one day, from one moment to the next, I made *them* the *source of my*

existence ... so Paul safeguarded his madness throughout his life and maintained and utilized it and made it into his life's contents under all circumstances and with all his means, just as I have done with my chest disorder, as I have done with my madness, as eventually, out of this chest disorder and out of this madness, I have, as it were, done with my art [*wie ich schließlich aus dieser Lungenkrankheit und aus dieser Verrücktheit sozusagen meine Kunst*]. (WN 22–23)

Whereas previously Bernhard had been the *Lungenkranke* and Paul the *Verrückte*, Bernhard introduces the notion that he is not only physically ill but also *verrückt*, indeed more insane than Paul, and that he exploited both illnesses for his art and for his existence, making it into the very "contents of his life."

The positing of mental and physical illness as source and contents of Bernhard's art and existence speaks to a broad conception of the entanglement of the mental and the physical, which, as explored in previous sections, also conditioned his material process of writing. But there are also much more specific ways in which the story of Bernhard's friendship with Paul in *Wittgenstein's Nephew* parallels and reflects the story of the text's production. Bernhard narrates the "Anfang" (beginning) of the friendship in the Blumenstockgasse apartment of a mutual friend, Irina, and their time as patients on the Wilhelminenberg as a period of "Freundschaftsvertiefung." Bernhard describes the relationship as extremely strenuous, requiring continual work and renewal: "We soon after our first encounter in the Blumenstockgasse reached first a major and then of course the greatest, and finally the most extreme, degree of difficulty that in a friendship by which I had truly, all those years until his death, been permeated and guided, consciously or unconsciously, always elementally, as I now realize: permeated and guided by a friendship which we did not simply find and then possess but which, throughout that time, we had to work for most strenuously [*auf das mühevollste haben erarbeiten müssen*] ...." (WN 97). Paul and Bernhard had to "work hard for" their friendship, one meaning of the word *erarbeiten*. But *erarbeiten* also signifies the process of developing—that is, creating or working something out. Closely related is the term *bearbeiten*, meaning to edit or revise. The painstaking effort required to "work on" (*erarbeiten*) the friendship,

I suggest, is intertwined in the complex production history of the text, which underwent extensive editing (*Bearbeitung*). In the writing of the text, the *Entstehungsgeschichte* of the friendship thus becomes entangled within the *Entstehungsgeschichte* of the text itself.

Bernhard also explicitly thematizes the struggle to write *Wittgenstein's Nephew*, to create a textual image of Paul out of "notes" that he has accumulated over the years—a peculiar quasi-autobiographical conceit, considering that, as we have seen, note-taking per se was not a defining feature of Bernhard's process. Consider the following passage:

> But then this *life person* [*Lebensmensch*; that is, Hedwick Stavianicek] is not the center of these notes that I am jotting down about Paul, even though at the time when I was stationed on the Wilhelmeninberg, when I was isolated, shunted aside and written off, she played the main role in my life, in my existence; the center of these notes is my friend Paul, then stationed along me on the Wilhelminenberg, isolated, shunted aside and written off [*abgeschoben und abgeschrieben*], he whom I wish once more to emerge clearly from these notes [*noch einmal deutlich machen will*], these tattered memories [*Erinnerungsfetzen*], which at this moment may clarify to me [*verdeutlichen*], call into memory [*in Erinnerung rufen sollen*], not only the hopeless situation of my friend but also my own hopelessness at the time. (WN 20)[102]

Bernhard articulates the intention to call into memory (*in Erinnerung rufen*) a clear (*deutlich*) image of Paul with the help of material "Erinnerungsfetzen," literal "scraps" of memory, in the form of written "notes." This self-reflexive image both reveals and conceals: the text thematizes the act of textual memorialization, of attempting to capture life in language, to transform reality into text—an act mediated by the materiality of writing. But the linguistic representation of reality, for Bernhard, necessarily distorts. While gesturing to the material basis of this textual portrait of Paul, the self-reflexive gesture simultaneously obscures the "truth" of Bernhard's process. In *Wittgenstein's Nephew*—as in many of his representations of writers and writing practices—Bernhard incorporates distortion into the *representation* of the material act of writing it-

---

102. Translation modified.

self: the zone of contact where the material text and the world represented in it meet.

Though the facts of its genesis are partially obscured, the portrait of Paul that Bernhard constructs remains haunted by the materiality of writing in other ways. Certain details seem to directly register this condition: in the passage quoted above, for example, Bernhard describes Paul as "abgeschrieben," written off, and "abgeschoben," pushed aside to the margins: a figure marked by the materiality of writing, a figure of the page. Reflecting on a sense of enduring proximity even in Paul's death, Bernhard writes: "Of all those dead none is closer to me these days and at this moment than my friend Paul. I deliberately emphasize *my*, since these notes record on paper the picture that *I* have of my friend Paul Wittgenstein and none other" (*WN* 97). Bernhard's memorialization of Paul, then, is an emphatically paper portrait: an *Erinnerungsarbeit*, memory work, mediated by *Schreibarbeit*, writerly work. But while this is represented in the text in certain ways, the materiality of writing becomes incorporated into the textual representation in ways that become visible only when we examine the actual scene of writing.

Textual Operations

Textual representation and textual production are aligned from the very first sentence of *Wittgenstein's Nephew*, in which Bernhard references the writing and publication of his second novel *Verstörung* (*Gargoyles*, 1967): "In 1967 at the *Baumgartnerhöhe* one of those indefatigable religious sisters working in the Hermann Pavilion placed on my bed my just-published *Gargoyles*, which I had written the year before in Brussels in the rue de la Croix no. 60, but I lacked the strength to raise the book as I had only a few minutes previously come to from several hours of general anaesthetic, under which I had been put by those doctors who cut open my throat in order to be able to remove [*herausoperieren*] a fist-sized tumor from my thorax" (*WN* 1). Titled *Gargoyles* in English translation, *Verstörung*—which more literally translates as "disturbance"—shares with *Wittgenstein's Nephew* numerous themes and motifs, such as depictions of madness and the projection of internal states into external space. But this opening sentence creates more than an intertextual bridge: it directly aligns surgical operation and publication, *Herausoperieren* (literally, operating out) and *Herausgeben* (publication, more literally releasing or giving out). Like Bernhard's body, operated upon by doctors and nurses at the hospital, Bernhard's typescripts were operated on by copyists and editors at the publishing house. Just like the patient is unconscious during an operation, the author is "unconscious" for the final stages of book production, when final edits are implemented and the work is printed and bound. The tumor, a product of physical *Störung*, is directly aligned with the book—here *Verstörung*—a physical product of writing, which Bernhard does not have the strength to pick up. In this light, Fabjan's description of the exhausting physicality of Bernhard's writing process also strangely echoes the removal of a mass: "When he had written a novel, he was around a kilo lighter, downright exhausted. It was a kind of trance."[103]

Certain stages of revising and editing *Wittgenstein's Nephew* were literally akin to surgical procedures. In confronting messy passages of Bernhard's typescripts, copyists would typically transcribe a page in its entirety, inserting it into the text version behind the original page before the text was sent for typesetting. Bernhard's typescripts of *Wittgenstein's Nephew*, however, were sometimes physically dissected by copyists or editors. Difficult-to-read sections were cut out and sections of clean-copy text were transplanted, like diseased flesh excised and replaced with healthy tissue. In the following example, such editorial intervention—a material operation on the text in the publishing house—occurs precisely in a passage that actually thematizes publication. Paul Wittgenstein and Ludwig Wittgenstein were both philosophers, Bernhard writes, and both were "verrückt," but what differentiated them was the following: Ludwig was "Veröffentlicher," a publisher, whereas Paul was "Nichtveröffentlicher," a nonpublisher; "a man can also be a philosopher if he does not publish any of his own philosophizing, that is also if he does not write down or publish anything. Publication surely only makes manifest [*macht ja deutlich*] and produces a sensation [*Aufsehen*] by what has been made manifest" (*WN* 74). Here Bernhard defines publication as a

---

103. Fabjan and Kędzierski, "Jeder Tag," 90.

process of making manifest (*deutlich machen*), a process that is directly echoed in his stated intention for writing the text: to make Paul "clear" once again in memory, "noch einmal deutlich" (*WN* 20). Publication, Bernhard goes on to write, is a form of evidencing, of material instantiation. Because Paul did not publish, there is a lack of "recorded and printed, i.e. published, evidence [*aufgeschriebene und gedruckte und also veröffentlichte Beweise*]" for Paul's philosophy—that is, a lack of manuscripts and published texts—in contrast to Ludwig's, for which we have "such evidence . . . in our hands and our heads [*in der Hand und im Kopf*]" (*WN* 74). The characterization of publication as production of evidence, "Beweise," is also echoed in Bernhard's description of "proofs of friendship" in his relationship with Paul: "My relationship with Paul, which had its beginnings in our friend Irina's room on Blumenstockgasse, was naturally a difficult one, not a friendship without daily reconquest or renewal [*tagtägliche Wiedererringung und Erneuerung*], and in the course of time it proved most wearying [*die anstrengendste*]; it clung to its high and low points and to its *proofs of friendship* [*Freundschaftsbeweise*]" (*WN* 76). The emphasis on the importance of "Beweise," evidence or proof for Bernhard's relationship to Paul, together with the notion of writing and publication as a form of evidence, amplifies the importance of the "notes" from which Bernhard describes constructing his text. In the following passage, Bernhard describes his engagement with these notes, and what they ultimately "prove" (*beweisen*):

> I confined myself to seeking out, in my notes, those passages which related to Paul and to bringing him back to me from these notes which, as I now observe, go back, some of them, over twelve years, to bringing him back [*gegenwärtig zu machen*] as the one I wished to retain in my memory, *the living one not the dead one* [*den Lebendigen, nicht den Toten*]. But these notes . . . ultimately proved to be nothing other than a story of dying [*Sterbensgeschichte*]. I had met Paul, I now think, at the exact point from which onward he was quite obviously dying and, as these notes prove, I had followed [*verfolgt*] his dying for more than twelve years. (*WN* 118)

Spanning a period of twelve years, these notes are a form of textual evidence of Paul and of Bernhard's relationship with him; they are the material out of which he composes the text, part of its *Entstehungsgeschichte*. But these materials are at the same time documentary evidence of another story that they tell: a *Sterbensgeschichte*, the story of Paul's dying.

It is remarkable that Bernhard does not offer in the text any detail about the material status of these "notes." As we have seen, Bernhard's narration of his textual construction process in the work partially obscures its actual generation. Examining Bernhard's typescripts reveals the process that the text underwent in its production, involving techniques at times akin to surgical operation. Through the activity of transcribing and editing the work, the typescript was dissected through cut-and-paste operations. Designed to usher the work toward a finished, publishable state—to "heal" it by transforming it into a printed text—these operations left behind a desiccated textual body constructed of pieces produced on multiple machines, by multiple hands, and through multiple reproduction techniques (photocopy, transcription).[104] That is to say, acts of material textual destruction were inscribed into the production of the work.

A more comprehensive look at the material traces of Bernhard's production of *Wittgenstein's Nephew* highlights the extent to which this was the case. For many texts, particularly of his late work, Bernhard produced only a single text version, leaving a debris of draft pages and written sketches along the way (such as the "loose pages for *Correction*"). In writing *Wittgenstein's Nephew*, Bernhard produced not one but two complete versions, which testify to how intensively he worked on the text, his textual memorializa-

---

104. Additionally, several prominent sections were based on passages from another Bernhard manuscript, the posthumously published *Meine Preise* (Frankfurt am Main: Suhrkamp, 2009). Much of Bernhard's description of his experience at the Baumgartner Höhe hospital in the beginning of *Wittgensteins Neffe* is based on descriptions published as "Die Ehrengabe des Kulturkreises des Bundesverbandes der Deutschen Industrie," in Bernhard, *Meine Preise*, 20–31. The same is true for Bernhard's description of the ceremonies for the Grillparzer Prize (W 13:271–76) and the Österreichischer Staatspreis für Literatur in *Wittgensteins Neffe* (W 13:276–78); compare Bernhard, "Der Grillparzerpreis," in *Meine Preise*, 7–19; Bernhard, "Der Österreichische Staatspreis für Literatur," in *Meine Preise*, 66–85. In the accounts presented in *Meine Preise*, Paul Wittgenstein is not mentioned.

tion of Paul.[105] But unlike Handke, who would produce one version, edit it, and then transcribe it in producing a subsequent version, Bernhard worked directly from the partially photocopied, partially montaged version created at the publishing house, making further revisions by inserting sheets back into his typewriter or, when revisions were much more extensive, removing pages entirely and replacing them with new typescript pages.

In several cases Bernhard took up the knife himself, submitting already dissected pages to even further surgical operation. Consider page 47 from version 1 (figure 2.14), a photocopied, revised, and renumbered version of which reappears in the second draft (see figure 2.16). On these pages, Bernhard recalls meeting Paul at the climax of a personal crisis: "Who can tell how my development would have continued if I had not met Paul Wittgenstein at the very peak of that crisis" (*WN* 102). Soon thereafter, a new episode takes off in which Bernhard describes his routine travel between Vienna and Nathal:

> Thus I have made it a habit over the past few years to exchange Vienna for Nathal at least in a fortnightly rhythm [*Zweiwochenrhythmus*], and, vice versa, Nathal for Vienna; every fortnight [*alle vierzehn Tage*] I escape from Nathal to Vienna and, in consequence, in order to survive at all, have become a character driven hither and thither [*hin- und hergetriebener Charakter*] between Vienna and Nathal, one who can exist now only on the basis of this most determinedly imposed rhythm [*produzierten Rhythmus*]. I go to Nathal to calm down after Vienna, and in turn to Vienna to cure myself of Nathal. . . . During the final years of his life my friend had joined my toing-and-froing rhythm [*Hin- und Herreiserhythmus*] and had very often gone with me to Nathal and back again, or the other way around. When I arrive in Nathal, I ask myself what I am looking for in Nathal, when I arrive in Vienna, I ask myself what I am looking for in Vienna. (*W* 13:293–94)

---

105. Uwe Betz imagines the generation of the work to have been much less overwrought: "Thus *Wittgenstein's Nephew*, like the other works written in 1981 and 1982, gives the the impression of having poured out all at once [*wie aus einem Guss zu sein*]." Betz, "Wittgensteins Neffe," in *Bernhard Handbuch: Leben—Werk—Wirkung*, ed. Martin Huber and Manfred Mittermayer (Stuttgart: Metzler, 2018), 120. During this time Bernhard produced at a rapid pace, also writing *Ein Kind*, *Beton*, and *Auslöschung*, which together total over 1,250 printed pages (Betz, "Wittgensteins Neffe," 120).

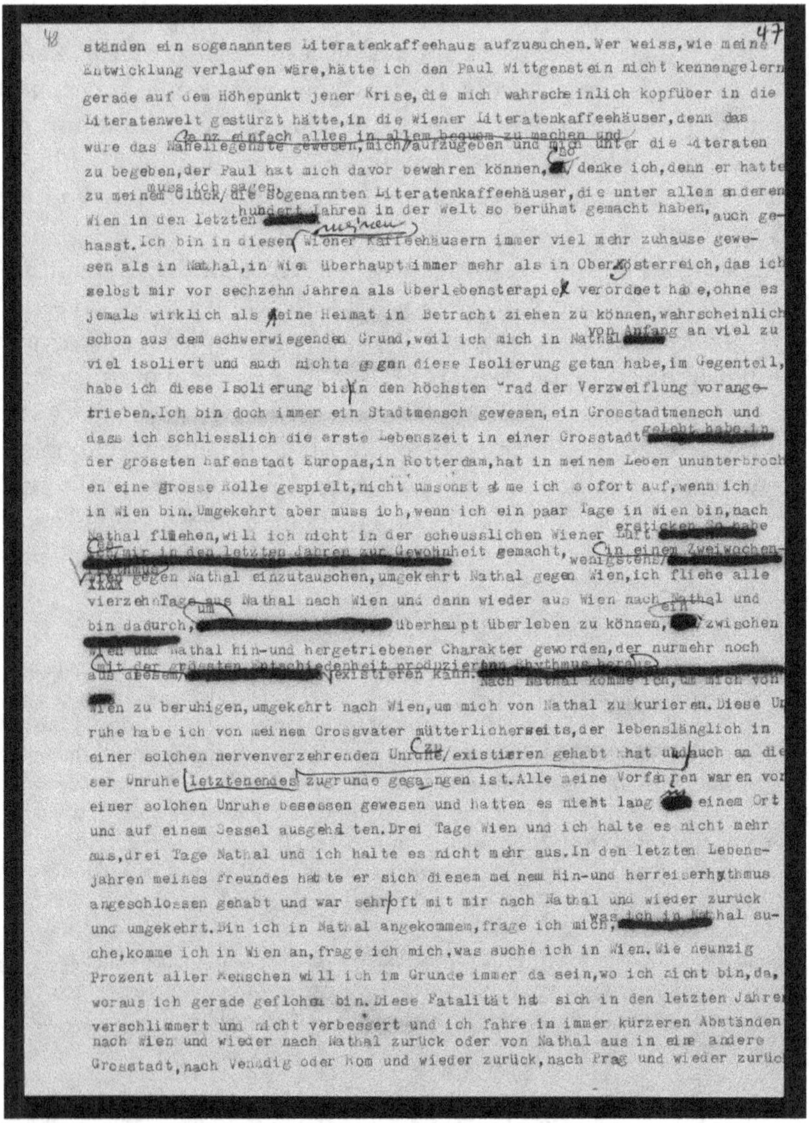

ständen ein sogenanntes Literatenkaffeehaus aufzusuchen. Wer weiss, wie meine Entwicklung verlaufen wäre, hätte ich den Paul Wittgenstein nicht kennengelernt gerade auf dem Höhepunkt jener Krise, die mich wahrscheinlich kopfüber in die Literatenwelt gestürzt hätte, in die Wiener Literatenkaffeehäuser, denn das wäre das Nahelegendste gewesen, mich aufzugeben und mich unter die Literaten zu begeben, der Paul hat mich davor bewahren können, denke ich, denn er hatte zu meinem Glück, die sogenannten Literatenkaffeehäuser, die unter allen anderen Wien in den letzten hundert Jahren in der Welt so berühmt gemacht haben, auch gehasst. Ich bin in diesen Wiener Kaffeehäusern immer viel mehr zuhause gewesen als in Nathal, in Wien überhaupt immer mehr als in Oberösterreich, das ich selbst mir vor sechzehn Jahren als Überlebenstherapie verordnet habe, ohne es jemals wirklich als meine Heimat in Betracht ziehen zu können, wahrscheinlich schon aus dem schwerwiegenden Grund, weil ich mich in Nathal von Anfang an viel zu viel isoliert und auch nichts gegen diese Isolierung getan habe, im Gegenteil, habe ich diese Isolierung bis an den höchsten Grad der Verzweiflung vorangetrieben. Ich bin doch immer ein Stadtmensch gewesen, ein Grossstadtmensch und dass ich schliesslich die erste Lebenszeit in einer Grossstadt gelebt habe, in der grössten Hafenstadt Europas, in Rotterdam, hat in meinem Leben ununterbrochen eine grosse Rolle gespielt, nicht umsonst atme ich sofort auf, wenn ich in Wien bin. Umgekehrt aber muss ich, wenn ich ein paar Tage in Wien bin, nach Nathal fliehen, will ich nicht in der scheusslichen Wiener Luft ersticken, ich habe mir in den letzten Jahren zur Gewohnheit gemacht, in einem Zweiwochenrhythmus, wenigstens, Wien gegen Nathal einzutauschen, umgekehrt Nathal gegen Wien, ich fliehe alle vierzehn Tage um aus Nathal nach Wien und dann wieder aus Wien nach Nathal und bin dadurch, ein überhaupt überleben zu können, zwischen Wien und Nathal hin-und hergetriebener Charakter geworden, der nunmehr noch mit der grössten Entschiedenheit produzierten Rhythmus herein existieren kann. Nach Nathal komme ich, um mich voll Wien zu beruhigen, umgekehrt nach Wien, um mich von Nathal zu kurieren. Diese Ruhe habe ich von meinem Grossvater mütterlicherseits, der lebenslänglich in einer solchen nervenverzehrenden Unruhe existiert gehabt hat und auch an dieser Unruhe letztenendes zugrunde gegangen ist. Alle meine Vorfahren waren von einer solchen Unruhe besessen gewesen und hatten es nicht lang an einem Ort und auf einem Sessel ausgehalten. Drei Tage Wien und ich halte es nicht mehr aus, drei Tage Nathal und ich halte es nicht mehr aus. In den letzten Lebensjahren meines Freundes hatte er sich diesem meinem Hin-und herreiserhythmus angeschlossen gehabt und war sehr oft mit mir nach Nathal und wieder zurück und umgekehrt. Bin ich in Nathal angekommen, frage ich mich, was ich in Nathal suche, komme ich in Wien an, frage ich mich, was suche ich in Wien. Wie neunzig Prozent aller Menschen will ich im Grunde immer da sein, wo ich nicht bin, da, woraus ich gerade geflohen bin. Diese Fatalität hat sich in den letzten Jahren verschlimmert und nicht verbessert und ich fahre in immer kürzeren Abständen nach Wien und wieder nach Nathal zurück oder von Nathal aus in eine andere Grossstadt, nach Venedig oder Rom und wieder zurück, nach Prag und wieder zurück

Figure 2.14. Thomas Bernhard, first version of *Wittgensteins Neffe*, ÖLA 563/W23/2, 47. Literaturarchiv der Österreichischen Nationalbibliothek, Vienna.

Descriptions of a "fortnightly rhythm [*Zweiwochenrhythmus*]" and "toing-and-froing rhythm [*Hin- und Herreiserhythmus*]" name the rhythmic structuring of Bernhard's travel, performed mimetically in the rhythmic structuring of the passage. In the first version, one observes traces of Bernhard's attempt to grasp this rhythmic structure conceptually, the terms "Zweiwochenrhythmus" and "produzierten Rhythmus" materializing through strike-through cancellation and interlinear addition. This section was subsequently excised by copyists and replaced with a clean-copy version (figure 2.15). In further revising, Bernhard made numerous interlinear additions at the top of the page, then crossed out those lines entirely and affixed a moveable paper flap with a revised version, in which he intensified his derision of Viennese literary society as "the most despicable of all worlds" and an "intellectual swamp" producing a "lethal effect [*tödliche Wirkung*]" (WN 102–3) (figure 2.16). Constructed of four individual text pieces, some photocopied and some original, produced on three different typewriters, this page—on which Bernhard narrates the "very peak of that crisis [*Höhepunkt jener Krise*]" (WN 109) in which he met Paul—is one of the most materially complex, overwrought pages of the entire manuscript.

In generating the second version, Bernhard also removed entire pages—twenty-nine in total from the original fifty-four-page typescript—and replaced them with extensively revised and/or expanded versions.[106] For example, in a multipage tirade, Bernhard rails against the "second-rate" actors who staged the premiere of his play *Hunting Party* (*Die Jagdgesellschaft*) at the Burgtheater in Vienna, conspiring together "against me and my play" such that they "squeezed the breath out [*den Geist ausgetrieben*]" of it (WN 115). Whereas many praised the performance, Paul was the only one who told him the truth: "He characterized the whole performance as a total misreading, as well as a total failure, and as a typical piece of Viennese cultural impertinence, as a showpiece of the Burgtheater's baseness vis-à-vis an author and his play. *You too have become a victim of the feeble-mindedness and the intrigues and the vile insidiousness in the Burgtheater*, he said" (WN 117). In the first version of

---

106. The second version of the text is sixty-one typescript pages in length.

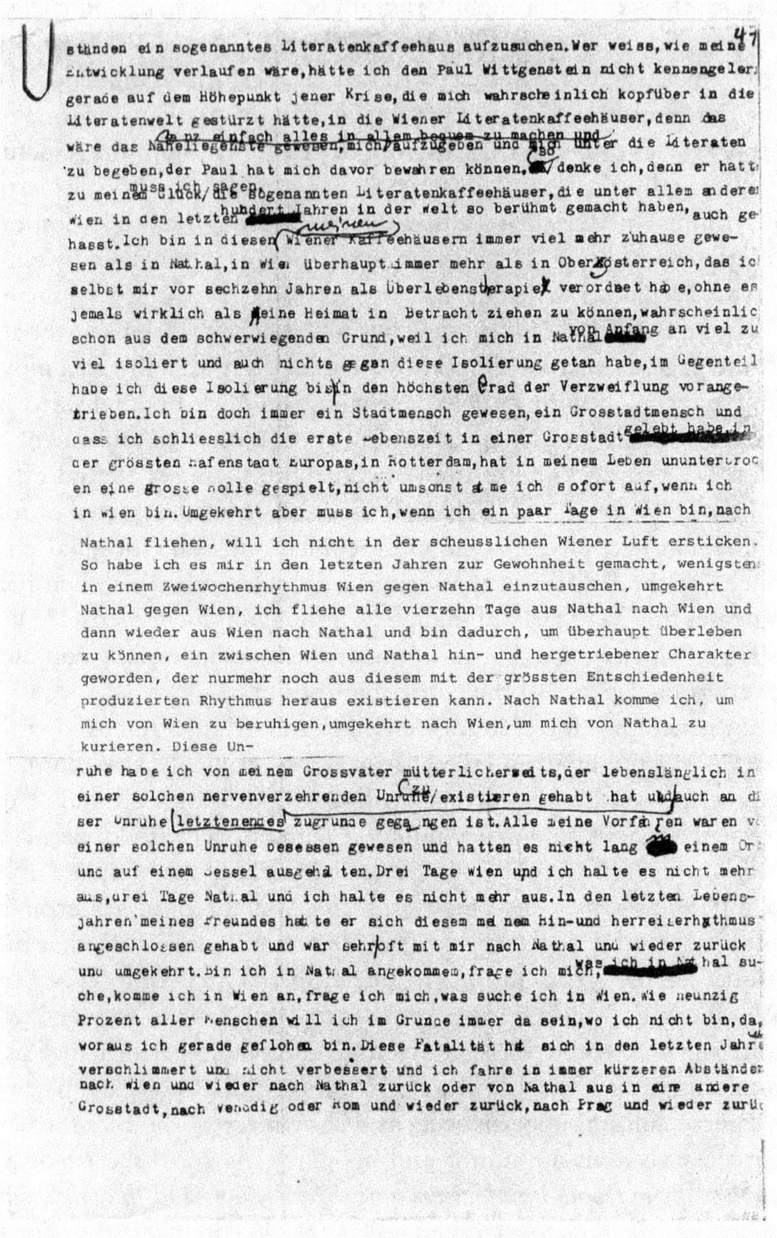

stünden ein sogenanntes Literatenkaffeehaus aufzusuchen. Wer weiss, wie meine
Entwicklung verlaufen wäre, hätte ich den Paul Wittgenstein nicht kennengelernt
gerade auf dem Höhepunkt jener Krise, die mich wahrscheinlich kopfüber in die
Literatenwelt gestürzt hätte, in die Wiener Literatenkaffeehäuser, denn das
wäre das Naheliegendste gewesen, mich aufzugeben und mich unter die Literaten
zu begeben, der Paul hat mich davor bewahren können. Ich denke ich, denn er hatte
zu meinem Unglück, die sogenannten Literatenkaffeehäuser, die unter allem anderen
Wien in den letzten hundert Jahren in der Welt so berühmt gemacht haben, auch gehasst. Ich bin in diesen Wiener Kaffeehäusern immer viel mehr zuhause gewesen als in Nathal, in Wien überhaupt immer mehr als in Oberösterreich, das ich
selbst mir vor sechzehn Jahren als Überlebenstherapie verordnet habe, ohne es
jemals wirklich als meine Heimat in Betracht ziehen zu können, wahrscheinlich
schon aus dem schwerwiegenden Grund, weil ich mich in Nathal von Anfang an viel zu
viel isoliert und auch nichts gegen diese Isolierung getan habe, im Gegenteil
habe ich diese Isolierung bis in den höchsten Grad der Verzweiflung vorangetrieben. Ich bin doch immer ein Stadtmensch gewesen, ein Grosstadtmensch und
dass ich schliesslich die erste Lebenszeit in einer Grosstadt gelebt habe, in
der grössten Hafenstadt Europas, in Rotterdam, hat in meinem Leben ununterbroch
en eine grosse Rolle gespielt, nicht umsonst atme ich sofort auf, wenn ich
in Wien bin. Umgekehrt aber muss ich, wenn ich ein paar Tage in Wien bin, nach

Nathal fliehen, will ich nicht in der scheusslichen Wiener Luft ersticken.
So habe ich es mir in den letzten Jahren zur Gewohnheit gemacht, wenigstens
in einem Zweiwochenrhythmus Wien gegen Nathal einzutauschen, umgekehrt
Nathal gegen Wien, ich fliehe alle vierzehn Tage aus Nathal nach Wien und
dann wieder aus Wien nach Nathal und bin dadurch, um überhaupt überleben
zu können, ein zwischen Wien und Nathal hin- und hergetriebener Charakter
geworden, der nurmehr noch aus diesem mit der grössten Entschiedenheit
produzierten Rhythmus heraus existieren kann. Nach Nathal komme ich, um
mich von Wien zu beruhigen, umgekehrt nach Wien, um mich von Nathal zu
kurieren. Diese Un-

ruhe habe ich von meinem Grossvater mütterlicherseits, der lebenslänglich in
einer solchen nervenverzehrenden Unruhe existieren gehabt hat und auch an di
ser Unruhe letztenendes zugrunde gegangen ist. Alle meine Vorfahren waren vo
einer solchen Unruhe besessen gewesen und hatten es nicht lang in einem Or
und auf einem Sessel ausgehalten. Drei Tage Wien und ich halte es nicht mehr
aus, drei Tage Nathal und ich halte es nicht mehr aus. In den letzten Lebensjahren meines Freundes hatte er sich diesem meinem hin- und herreiserhythmus
angeschlossen gehabt und war sehr oft mit mir nach Nathal und wieder zurück
und umgekehrt. Bin ich in Nathal angekommen, frage ich mich, was ich in Nathal suche, komme ich in Wien an, frage ich mich, was suche ich in Wien. Wie neunzig
Prozent aller Menschen will ich im Grunde immer da sein, wo ich nicht bin, da
woraus ich gerade geflohen bin. Diese Fatalität hat sich in den letzten Jahre
verschlimmert und nicht verbessert und ich fahre in immer kürzeren Abständen
nach Wien und wieder nach Nathal zurück oder von Nathal aus in eine andere
Grosstadt, nach Venedig oder Rom und wieder zurück, nach Prag und wieder zurü

Figure 2.15. Thomas Bernhard, photocopy with editorial interventions of the first version of *Wittgensteins Neffe*, 47. SU.2010.0002. Deutsches Literaturarchiv, Marbach.

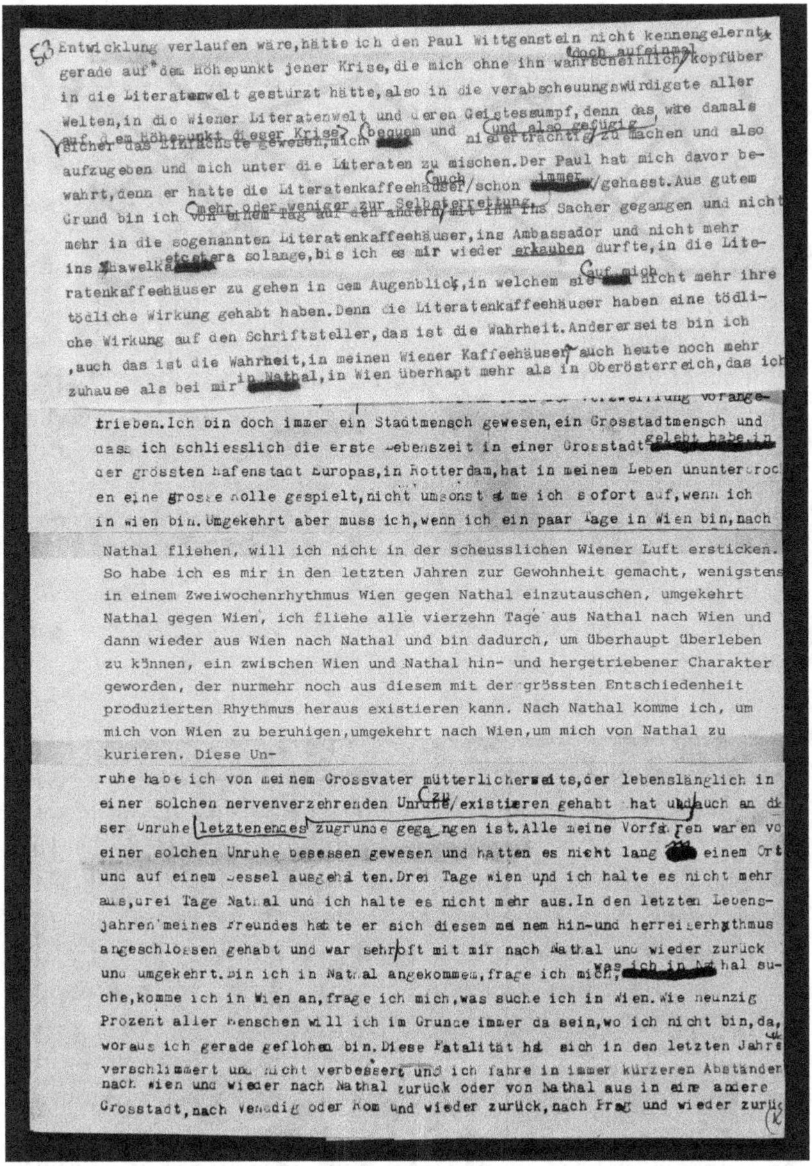

Entwicklung verlaufen wäre,hätte ich den Paul Wittgensteln nicht kennengelernt,
gerade auf dem Höhepunkt jener Krise,die mich ohne ihn wahrscheinlich kopfüber
in die Literatenwelt gestürzt hätte,also in die verabscheuungswürdigste aller
Welten,in die Wiener Literatenwelt und deren Geistessumpf,denn das, wie damals
welcher das literarische gewesen,mich niedertrachtig zu machen und also
aufzugeben und mich unter die Literaten zu mischen.Der Paul hat mich davor be-
wahrt,denn er hatte die Literatenkaffeehäuser/schon immer/gehasst.Aus gutem
Grund bin ich mehr oder weniger zur Selbsterhaltung ins Sacher gegangen und nicht
mehr in die sogenannten Literatenkaffeehäuser,ins Ambassador und nicht mehr
ins Hawelka etcetera solange,bis ich es mir wieder erkauben durfte,in die Literatenkaffeehäuser zu gehen in dem Augenblick,in welchem sie nicht mehr ihre
tödliche Wirkung gehabt haben.Denn die Literatenkaffeehäuser haben eine tödliche Wirkung auf den Schriftsteller,das ist die Wahrheit.Andererseits bin ich
,auch das ist die Wahrheit,in meinen Wiener Kaffeehäusern auch heute noch mehr
zuhause als bei mir in Nathal,in Wien überhapt mehr als in Oberösterreich,das ich

trieben.Ich bin doch immer ein Stadtmensch gewesen,ein Grosstadtmensch und
dass ich schliesslich die erste Lebenszeit in einer Grosstadt gelebt habe,in
der grössten hafenstadt Europas,in Rotterdam,hat in meinem Leben ununterbroc
en eine grosse nolle gespielt,nicht umsonst ame ich sofort auf,wenn ich
in Wien bin.Umgekehrt aber muss ich,wenn ich ein paar Tage in Wien bin,nach
Nathal fliehen, will ich nicht in der scheusslichen Wiener Luft ersticken.
So habe ich es mir in den letzten Jahren zur Gewohnheit gemacht, wenigstens
in einem Zweiwochenrhythmus Wien gegen Nathal einzutauschen, umgekehrt
Nathal gegen Wien, ich fliehe alle vierzehn Tage aus Nathal nach Wien und
dann wieder aus Wien nach Nathal und bin dadurch, um überhaupt überleben
zu können, ein zwischen Wien und Nathal hin- und hergetriebener Charakter
geworden, der nurmehr noch aus diesem mit der grössten Entschiedenheit
produzierten Rhythmus heraus existieren kann. Nach Nathal komme ich, um
mich von Wien zu beruhigen,umgekehrt nach Wien,um mich von Nathal zu
kurieren. Diese Un-
ruhe habe ich von meinem Grossvater mütterlicherseits,der lebenslänglich in
einer solchen nervenverzehrenden Unruhe/existieren gehabt hat und auch an di
ser Unruhe letztenendes zugrunde gegangen ist.Alle meine Vorfahren waren vo
einer solchen Unruhe besessen gewesen und hatten es nicht lang einem Ort
und auf einem sessel ausgehalten.Drei Tage Wien und ich halte es nicht mehr
aus,drei Tage Nathal und ich halte es nicht mehr aus.In den letzten Lebensjahren meines Freundes hatte er sich diesem meinem hin-und herreiserhythmus
angeschlossen gehabt und war sehroft mit mir nach Nathal und wieder zurück
und umgekehrt.Bin ich in Nathal angekommen,frage ich mich, was ich in Nathal suche,komme ich in Wien an,frage ich mich,was suche ich in Wien.Wie neunzig
Prozent aller menschen will ich im Grunde immer da sein,wo ich nicht bin,da
woraus ich gerade geflohen bin.Diese Fatalität hat sich in den letzten Jahre
verschlimmert und nicht verbessert und ich fahre in immer kürzeren Abständen
nach wien und wieder nach Nathal zurück oder von Nathal aus in eine andere
Grosstadt,nach Venedig oder Rom und wieder zurück,nach Prag und wieder zurüc

Figure 2.16. Thomas Bernhard, second version of
Wittgensteins Neffe, ÖLA 563/W23/3, 53. Literaturarchiv
der Österreichischen Nationalbibliothek, Vienna.

this episode, copyists excised a section and replaced with a piece of clean-copy text (figures 2.17 and 2.18). Bernhard ultimately abandoned this sheet entirely, producing the second version, replacing the cut-and-pasted page with a significantly revised and expanded version of the passage. Comparing the two, we see that the second version begins with the same words as the first version ("de gekommen, er redete nur noch in Satzfetzen") so that it will connect to the text on the preceding page, but that it soon departs from the text of the first version (figure 2.19). In this case, an intermediary stage of correcting, found in a bundle of loose discarded pages, is also extant: before retyping the page entirely, Bernhard began by editing the cut-and-pasted sheet from the first version with extensive interlinear additions (figure 2.20). He then abandoned this sheet and began retyping it on a new sheet, not simply transcribing the revised text but expanding the episode through yet further revisions and additions and amplifying the vehemence of his tirade (see figure 2.19). "Absolutely second-rate actors [*absolut zweitklassige Schauspieler*]" become "absolutely third-rate actors [*absolut drittklassige Schauspieler*]," prostitutes in a "theatrical brothel [*Theaterbordell*]." In version 1, the actors conspired "against the author and against the play [*gegen den Autor und gegen das Stück*]"; in version 2, Bernhard adds: "as if they wanted to say, *of course we are against this frightful, inferior, revolting play* [*so als wollten sie sagen wir sind* ja gegen dieses scheussliche, minderwertige, abstossende Stück]." Rather than acting as "midwives [*Geburtshelfer*]," Bernhard also adds, they aim to destroy his piece altogether. Bernhard ultimately flees, "not only from the demolition firm [*Vernichtungsanstalt*] of my play but from the demolition firm [*Vernichtungsanstalt*] of my entire mental capacity [*Geistesvermögens*]" (WN 116).

Bernhard's method of removing and replacing pages is another manifestation of his building-block system of composing. But in this stage, rather than starting with page-episodes to be arranged and rearranged, Bernhard would remove one or more sheets and fill in the gaps with revised versions. We see this method in action in one of the most famous episodes from *Wittgenstein's Nephew*—the search for the *Neue Zürcher Zeitung*. Here is an excerpt from the printed version:

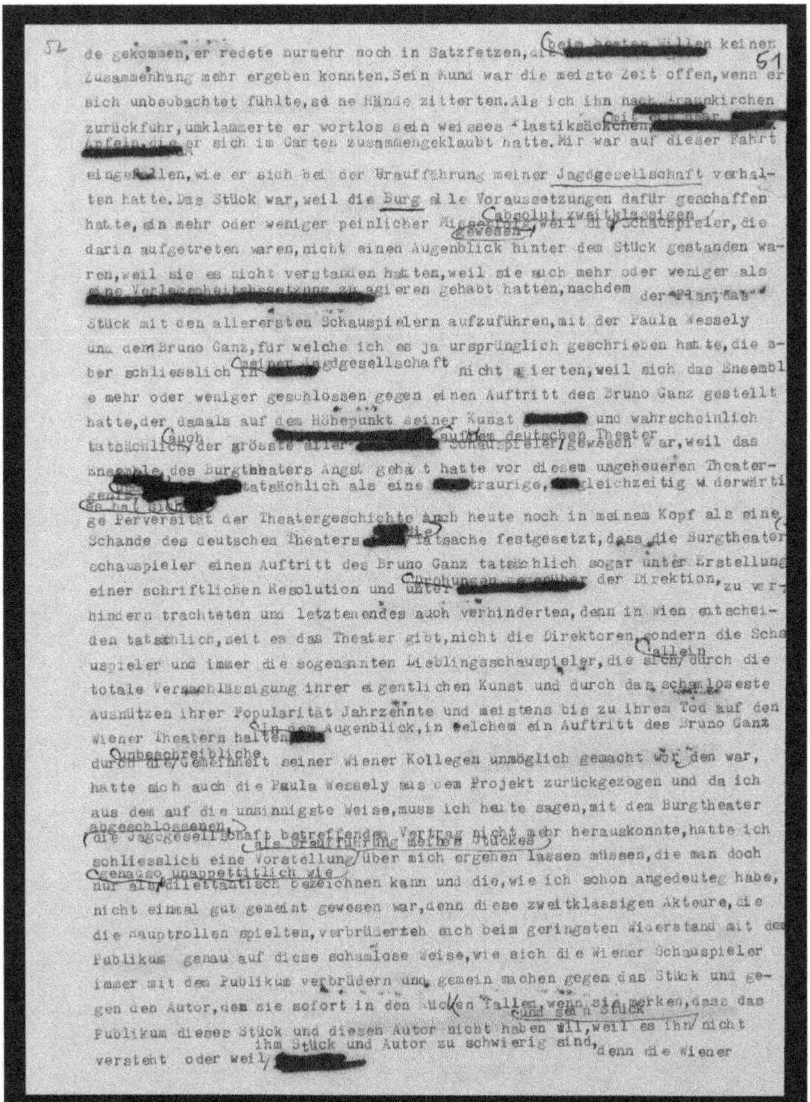

51

de gekommen, er redete nunmehr noch in Satzfetzen, die beim besten Willen keinen Zusammenhang mehr ergeben konnten. Sein Mund war die meiste Zeit offen, wenn er sich unbeobachtet fühlte, seine Hände zitterten. Als ich ihn nach Traunkirchen zurückfuhr, umklammerte er wortlos sein weisses Plastiksäckchen, in welchem Äpfeln, die er sich im Garten zusammengeklaubt hatte. Mir war auf dieser Fahrt eingefallen, wie er sich bei der Uraufführung meiner Jagdgesellschaft verhalten hatte. Das Stück war, weil die Burg alle Voraussetzungen dafür geschaffen hatte, ein mehr oder weniger peinlicher Misserfolg gewesen, weil die Schauspieler, die darin aufgetreten waren, nicht einen Augenblick hinter dem Stück gestanden waren, weil sie es nicht verstanden hatten, weil sie auch mehr oder weniger als eine Verlegenheitsbesetzung zu agieren gehabt hatten, nachdem der Plan, das Stück mit den allerersten Schauspielern aufzuführen, mit der Paula Wessely und dem Bruno Ganz, für welche ich es ja ursprünglich geschrieben hatte, die aber schliesslich in meiner Jagdgesellschaft nicht agierten, weil sich das Ensemble mehr oder weniger geschlossen gegen einen Auftritt des Bruno Ganz gestellt hatte, der damals auf dem Höhepunkt seiner Kunst und wahrscheinlich tatsächlich der grösste Schauspieler gewesen war, weil das Ensemble des Burgtheaters Angst gehabt hatte vor diesem ungeheueren Theatergenie, tatsächlich als eine traurige, zugleich zeitig widerwärtige Perversität der Theatergeschichte auch heute noch in meinem Kopf als eine Schande des deutschen Theaters Tatsache festgesetzt, dass die Burgtheaterschauspieler einen Auftritt des Bruno Ganz tatsächlich sogar unter Erstellung einer schriftlichen Resolution und Drohungen der Direktion, zu verhindern trachteten und letztenendes auch verhinderten, denn in Wien entscheiden tatsächlich, seit es das Theater gibt, nicht die Direktoren, sondern die Schauspieler und immer die sogenannten Lieblingsschauspieler, die sich durch die totale Vernachlässigung ihrer eigentlichen Kunst und durch das schamloseste Ausnützen ihrer Popularität Jahrzehnte und meistens bis zu ihrem Tod auf den Wiener Theatern halten. Augenblick, in welchem ein Auftritt des Bruno Ganz durch die Gemeinheit seiner Wiener Kollegen unmöglich gemacht worden war, hatte sich auch die Paula Wessely aus dem Projekt zurückgezogen und da ich aus dem auf die unsinnigste Weise, muss ich heute sagen, mit dem Burgtheater abgeschlossenen die Jagdgesellschaft betreffenden Vertrag nicht mehr herauskonnte, hatte ich schliesslich eine Vorstellung über mich ergehen lassen müssen, die man doch genauso unappetitlich wie nur als dilettantisch bezeichnen kann und die, wie ich schon angedeutet habe, nicht einmal gut gemeint gewesen war, denn diese zweitklassigen Akteure, die die Hauptrollen spielten, verbrüderten sich beim geringsten Widerstand mit dem Publikum genau auf diese schamlose Weise, wie sich die Wiener Schauspieler immer mit dem Publikum verbrüdern und gemein machen gegen das Stück und gegen den Autor, dem sie sofort in den Rücken fallen, wenn sie merken, dass das Publikum dieses Stück und diesen Autor nicht haben will, weil es ihm nicht ihm Stück und Autor zu schwierig sind, denn die Wiener versteht oder weil

Figure 2.17. Thomas Bernhard, first version of *Wittgensteins Neffe*, ÖLA 563/W23/2, 51. Literaturarchiv der Österreichischen Nationalbibliothek, Vienna.

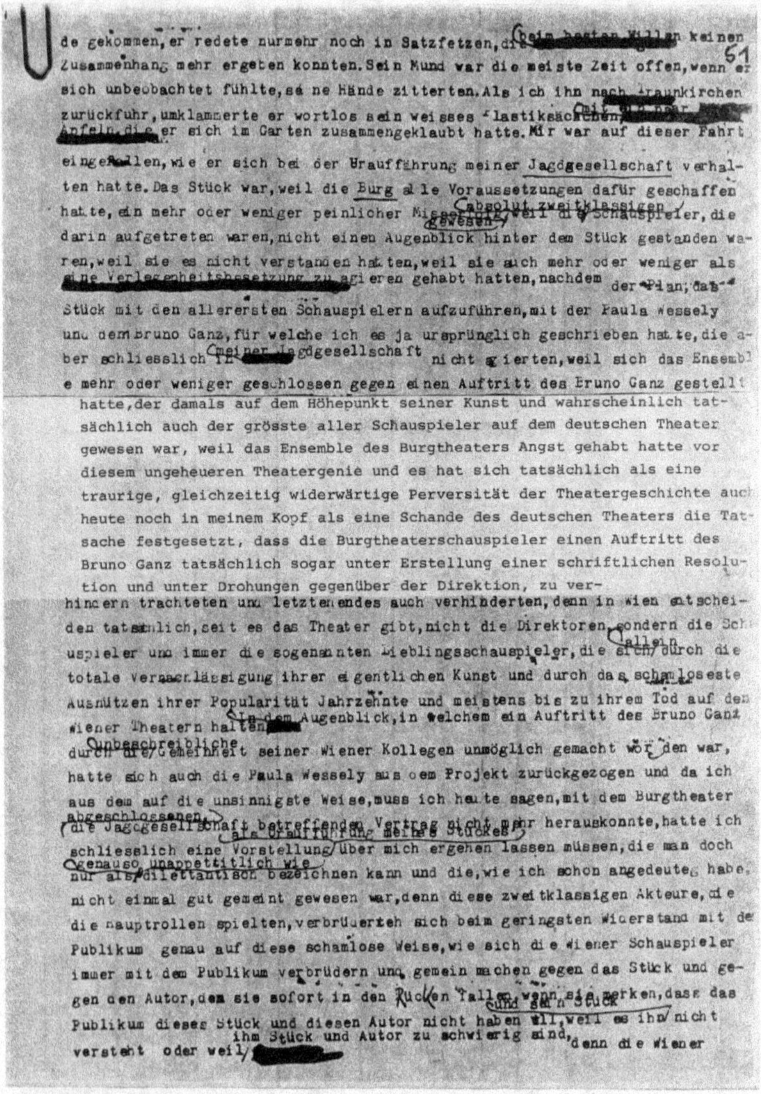

de gekommen,er redete nunmehr noch in Satzfetzen,die beim besten Willen keinen
Zusammenhang mehr ergeben konnten.Sein Mund war die meiste Zeit offen,wenn er
sich unbeobachtet fühlte,seine Hände zitterten.Als ich ihn nach Traunkirchen
zurückfuhr,umklammerte er wortlos sein weisses Plastiksäckchen, chien mit den
Äpfeln,die er sich im Garten zusammengeklaubt hatte.Mir war auf dieser Fahrt
eingefallen,wie er sich bei der Uraufführung meiner Jagdgesellschaft verhalten hatte.Das Stück war,weil die Burg alle Voraussetzungen dafür geschaffen
hatte,ein mehr oder weniger peinlicher Misserfolg,weil die Schauspieler, absolut zweitklassigen
gewesen, die
darin aufgetreten waren,nicht einen Augenblick hinter dem Stück gestanden waren,weil sie es nicht verstanden hatten,weil sie sich mehr oder weniger als
eine Verlegenheitsbesetzung zu agieren gehabt hatten,nachdem der Plan,das
Stück mit den allerersten Schauspielern aufzuführen,mit der Paula Wessely
und dem Bruno Ganz,für welche ich es ja ursprünglich geschrieben hatte,die aber schliesslich in meiner Jagdgesellschaft nicht agierten,weil sich das Ensembl
e mehr oder weniger geschlossen gegen einen Auftritt des Bruno Ganz gestellt
hatte,der damals auf dem Höhepunkt seiner Kunst und wahrscheinlich tatsächlich auch der grösste aller Schauspieler auf dem deutschen Theater
gewesen war, weil das Ensemble des Burgtheaters Angst gehabt hatte vor
diesem ungeheuren Theatergenie und es hat sich tatsächlich als eine
traurige, gleichzeitig widerwärtige Perversität der Theatergeschichte auch
heute noch in meinem Kopf als eine Schande des deutschen Theaters die Tatsache festgesetzt, dass die Burgtheaterschauspieler einen Auftritt des
Bruno Ganz tatsächlich sogar unter Erstellung einer schriftlichen Resolution und unter Drohungen gegenüber der Direktion, zu verhindern trachteten un letztendes auch verhinderten,denn in Wien entscheiden tatsächlich,seit es das Theater gibt,nicht die Direktoren,sondern die Sch
uspieler und immer die sogenannten Lieblingsschauspieler,die sich alle durch die
totale Vernachlässigung ihrer eigentlichen Kunst und durch das schamloseste
Ausnützen ihrer Popularität Jahrzehnte und meistens bis zu ihrem Tod auf den
Wiener Theatern halten.In dem Augenblick,in welchem ein Auftritt des Bruno Ganz
Unbeschreiblich durch die Gemeinheit seiner Wiener Kollegen unmöglich gemacht worden war,
hatte sich auch die Paula Wessely aus dem Projekt zurückgezogen und da ich
aus dem auf die unsinnigste Weise,muss ich heute sagen,mit dem Burgtheater
abgeschlossenen (die Jagdgesellschaft betreffenden Vertrag nicht mehr herauskonnte,hatte ich
schliesslich eine Vorstellung über mich ergehen lassen müssen,die man doch
genauso unappetitlich wie nur als dilettantisch bezeichnen kann und die,wie ich schon angedeutet habe,
nicht einmal gut gemeint gewesen war,denn diese zweitklassigen Akteure,die
die Hauptrollen spielten,verbrüderten sich beim geringsten Widerstand mit de
Publikum genau auf diese schamlose Weise,wie sich die Wiener Schauspieler
immer mit dem Publikum verbrüdern und gemein machen gegen das Stück und gegen den Autor,dem sie sofort in den Rücken fallen,wenn sie merken,dass das
Publikum dieses Stück und diesen Autor nicht haben will,weil es ihm nicht
ihm Stück und Autor zu schwierig sind,denn die Wiener
versteht oder weil

Figure 2.18. Thomas Bernhard, photocopy with editorial interventions of the first version of *Wittgensteins Neffe*, 51. SU.2010.0002. Deutsches Literaturarchiv, Marbach.

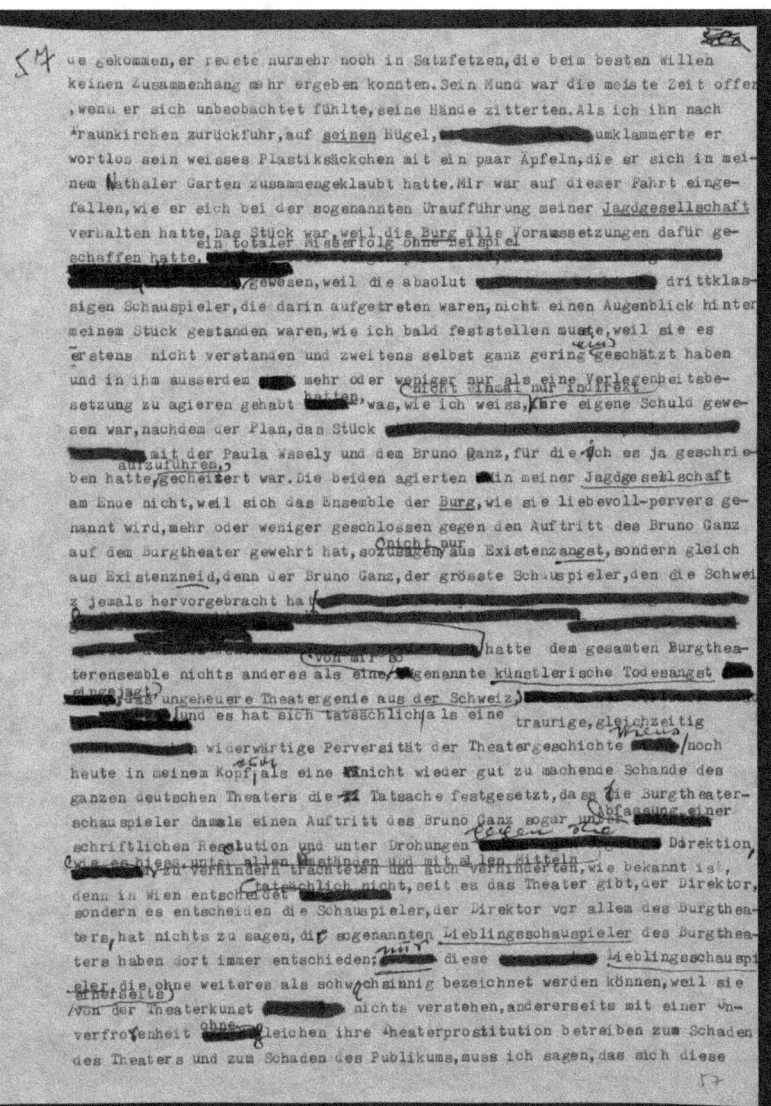

Figure 2.19. Thomas Bernhard, second version of *Wittgensteins Neffe*, ÖLA 563/W23/3, 57–58. Literaturarchiv der Österreichischen Nationalbibliothek, Vienna.

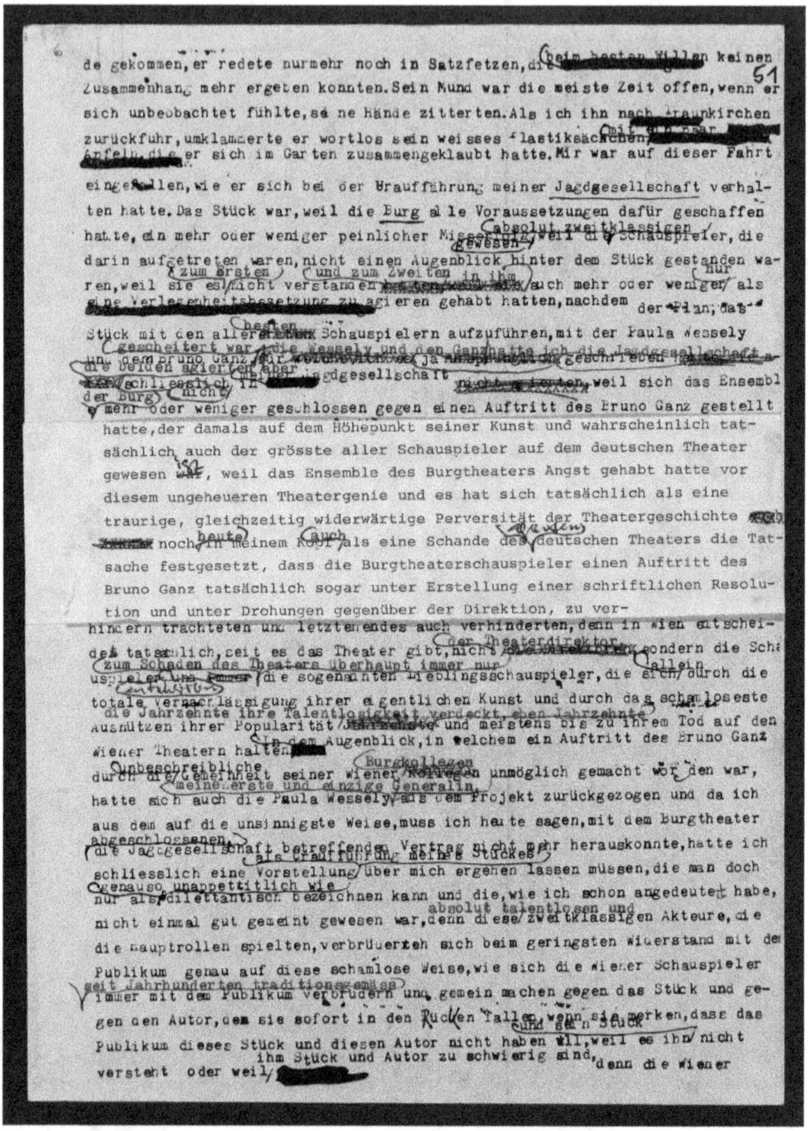

Figure 2.20. Thomas Bernhard, typescript fragment of *Wittgensteins Neffe*, ÖLA 563/W23/2a, [6]. Literaturarchiv der Österreichischen Nationalbibliothek, Vienna.

and since, as I believed, the *Neue Zürcher Zeitung* would only be available in Salzburg, which is eighty kilometers from here, I drove to Salzburg, that so-called *world-famous* festival city, in the car of a woman friend, along with her and Paul, in order to buy the *Neue Zürcher Zeitung* there. But I did not get the *Neue Zürcher Zeitung* in Salzburg. It therefore occurred to me to get the *Neue Zürcher Zeitung* in Bad Reichenhall and so we drove to Bad Reichenhall, to that *world-famous* spa. But I did not get the *Neue Zürcher Zeitung* in Bad Reichenhall either and so the three of us, more or less disappointed, drove back to Nathal. But when were some distance short of Nathal Paul suddenly suggested we should drive to Bad Hall, to that *world-famous* spa, because we were sure to get the *Neue Zürcher Zeitung*... there. But we did not get the *Neue Zürcher Zeitung* in Bad Hall either. (WN 62–63)

Just like Bernhard gradually covering the page with his typewriter, proceeding from one line to the next, occasionally halting to return for corrections, the three friends cover the entire region of Upper Austria by car, the endpoint of one route becoming the starting point of the next, occasionally returning to Nathal only to set out again. Ultimately, "totally exhausted," Bernhard and his travel companions are pushed "to the limits of our physical fettle [*an den Rand unserer physischen Möglichkeiten*]" (WN 63–64).

In the typescript versions of the text, Bernhard had removed the corresponding page from the first version and replaced it with the heavily revised version in figure 2.21. In approaching the bottom edge of page 33 in this second version, he decreased the line spacing, compressing the final lines (figure 2.21) so that they could connect seamlessly with the text of the following page, a renumbered photocopy from the first version. The description of the increasingly exhausting search for the newspaper corresponds to the material/visual compression of lines into the bottom edge of page 33; the final words of the page, inserted beneath the last full line, narrate the complete exhaustion induced by the journey: "So waren wir dann / völlig erschöpft" (So we were then totally exhausted).

Though perhaps based on actual experience, the textual representation of the quest for the *Neue Zürcher Zeitung* is obviously aestheticized and fictionalized, an escapade that takes place across the topography of the page. Throughout the text, Bernhard's semi-autobiographical portrayal of Paul and their friendship are highly

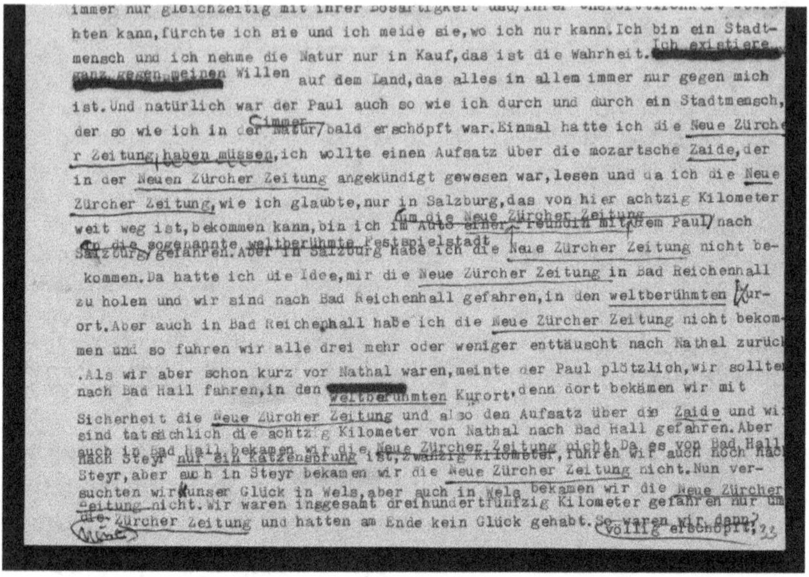

Figure 2.21. Thomas Bernhard, second version of *Wittgensteins Neffe*, ÖLA 563/W23/3, 33. Literaturarchiv der Österreichischen Nationalbibliothek, Vienna.

constructed images, representations that exist in language, on paper, bound up in the materiality of writing. Like the journey by car, proceeding from one town to the next with intermittent returns to Nathal until eventually covering a vast area, Bernhard covered his pages with the forward movement of writing, proceeding from one line to the next with intermittent returns for corrections. The goal of both quests, by car and by typewriter, is a text: the *Neue Zürcher Zeitung*, and a textual portrait of Paul. The travel route that was traversed, composed of numerous mini-routes, numerous beginnings and ends, reflects Bernhard's episodic method of textual construction, which informs—literally giving form to—the episodic narrative structure of this and other Bernhard texts. Just like the three companions traveled by car (a machine), Bernhard composed on a typewriter (a machine), rather than by hand; like the automobile, a mechanized carriage carrying passengers, the typewriter "carriage" holds the paper in place and moves it along during typing. In this passage, not only content and form, but also writing process, are entangled within one another: the zigzagging route of driving, the zigzagging movement of typing, the zigzagging rhythm of Bernhard's prose.[107]

There are a host of other passages in which the movements of writing and the space of the page are evoked in the semantic content of the text. Bernhard describes Paul's "habit, which often dragged me to the verge of insanity" of walking on the stone-slab pavement according to a "precisely prescribed [*vorgeschriebenen*] system, thus for instance after two flagstones [*Steinplatten*] stepping only on the third and then not at random or more or less without pattern placing his foot well in the middle of a flag [*Platte*] but with hairbreadth's precision at its nearer or its further edge accordingly" (*WN* 106–7). Like the gait of Karrer in *Walking*, Paul's unusual gait seems to figure specific features of typewriting: as Paul's legs strike the flagstone (*Steinplatte*), the typewriter arms strike the cylindrical platen, or *Platte* in German. Unlike handwriting, which can proceed more freely over the page, the movement of the typewriter arms is mechanically prescribed, operating according to a "precisely prescribed [*vorgeschriebenen*] system." Paul places his steps precisely in the lower or upper edges of the rectangular slabs; as we have seen, Bernhard's method of composing in page-episodes required

---

107. The physical exhaustion of the search for the *Neue Zürcher Zeitung* might be related to Bernhard's physically exhausting writerly process. The importance of writing process over finished product ("nur der *Prozeß* selbst interessiert ihn, nicht sein Ergebnis") is paralleled in Bernhard's description of being happiest while *unterwegs*, traveling by car: "Und die Wahrheit ist, daß ich nur *im Auto sitzend* zwischen dem einen Ort, den ich gerade verlassen habe und dem andern, auf den ich zufahre, *glücklich bin*, nur im Auto" (W 13:294). Bernhard wrote something similar in a letter to Unseld's secretary Burgel Zeeh during a period of intense productivity in which he composed *Wittgensteins Neffe*, *Beton*, and *Auslöschung*: "Die Arbeit macht immer auch das ganze übrige Glück." Martin Huber and Wendelin Schmidt-Dengler, commentary to Thomas Bernhard, *Beton* (W 5:144). Compare Robert Vellusig, who writes, "Wie die an Verrücktheit grenzende Gewohnheit, die Pflastersteine 'nach einem ganz genau vorgeschriebenen System zu betreten,' der Fortbewegung geometrische und symmetrische Züge verleiht, so verschwindet im Hinundher des Reisens das Ziel hinter der Qualität geordneter Bewegung." Vellusig, "Thomas Bernhard und 'Wittgensteins Neffe': Die Bewegung des Hinundher," *Modern Austrian Literature* 23, no. 3/4 (1990): 46.

a precise material-semantic navigation to successfully "place" the text on the page.

Other episodes evoke the speed and horizontal movement of typewriting. Toward the end of *Wittgenstein's Nephew*, Bernhard describes Paul's increasingly ghastly physical state. On what would be his final visit, Bernhard becomes so horrified by Paul's grotesque, death-imbued figure that he flees the apartment in a panic:

> I had suddenly been unable to bear him any longer, I kept thinking that I was no longer sitting there with a living person but with someone who had long been dead, and I had withdrawn from him.... I did not want to turn my head and I had descended the stairs as fast as I could and got out into the fresh air. I had run down Stallburggasse and then down Dorotheergasse and across the Stephansplatz to the Wollzeile, where at last I was able to take a few calmer steps. In what is called the Stadtpark I sat down on a seat and tried, by means of a breathing rhythm precisely dictated by my brain [*von meinem Kopf aus genau vorgeschriebenen Atemrhythmus*], to free myself from my condition. (WN 92–93)

On the typescript page, the process of inscription itself appears to be figured in the representation: as Bernhard runs breathlessly through the streets, "as fast as [he] could," the text flows across the page, proceeding uninterrupted from one line to the next. Only when Bernhard finally pauses to sit on a park bench to recover, "freeing" himself from the "vorgeschriebenen Atemrhythmus" (prescribed breathing rhythm) is the flow of typing halted by several immediate corrections (figure 2.22).

Here, sitting on this park bench, Bernhard recalls meeting Paul at the "peak of that crisis" (*WN* 102) and the continual, strenuous work required to maintain the friendship. It is here that he insists on the importance of capturing *his* image of Paul on paper: "I deliberately emphasize *my*, since these notes record on paper the picture that *I* have of my friend Paul Wittgenstein and none other" (*WN* 97). As we have explored, the portrait of Paul constructed in *Wittgenstein's Nephew* is a decidedly *textual* portrait, constructed on the page and through material processes that remain enmeshed within the text's form and content. The complex story of the text's production (*Entstehungsgeschichte*) is evoked in Bernhard's narration of the story of

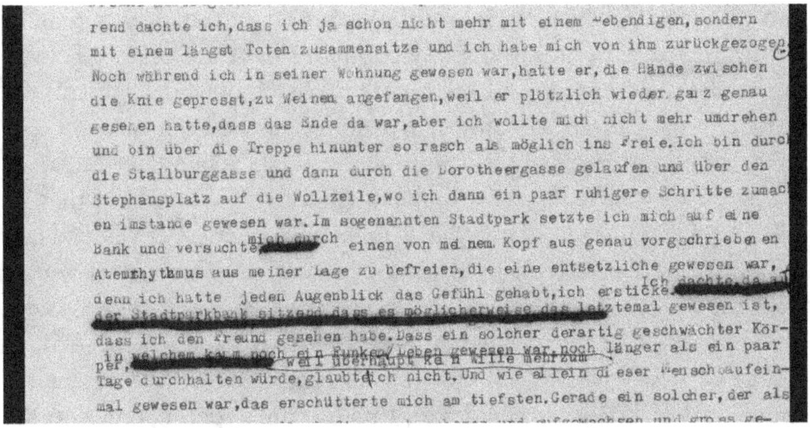

Figure 2.22. Thomas Bernhard, second version of *Wittgensteins Neffe*, ÖLA 563/W23/3, 42. Literaturarchiv der Österreichischen Nationalbibliothek, Vienna.

his friendship with Paul, its beginning followed by periods of deepening and extensive work (*Erarbeitung*) before ultimately culminating in Paul's death, which is narrated on the final page of the text. In the process of writing as narrated in the text—gathering of "notes" in order to make Paul "present": "*the living one not the dead one*" (*den Lebendigen, nicht den Toten*)—Bernhard ultimately realizes that the story of Paul Wittgenstein, which he is now attempting to capture in writing, is and always was a "story of dying" (*Sterbensgeschichte*) (*WN* 118). Bernhard writes that Paul is a figure always marked by death ("vom Tod gezeichnet") (*WN* 66), his death inscribed within him long before his actual death: "*his face* was already *marked* by death [der Tod war ihm doch schon *ins Gesicht geschrieben*]" (*WN* 58). Near the end of his life, Paul becomes a ghostly "shadow" of his former self, no longer familiar to Bernhard, a grotesque image before which he recoils in fear (*WN* 107). Bernhard is repulsed at the sight of Paul with bags of fruit and vegetables hanging from his emaciated arms, a pitiful, death-stricken figure no longer able to take in life force (*WN* 108–9). Bernhard is similarly disturbed by the disjuncture between Paul's decrepit body and the increasingly elegant clothing that covers it, which nonetheless reeks of the "the smell wretchedness and of death" (WN 110). In another example of the intertwining of textile and text, Bernhard directly compares the state of Paul's clothing to the disintegration of his speech: "His clothes, though still the same elegant clothes as before, now no longer had that man-of-the-world or at any rate respect-inspiring effect on the beholder but all of a sudden looked really worn out and shabby, like anything that he still dared to utter.... Moreover, no real conversation developed any longer, he talked only in fragments of sentences [*Satzfetzen*] which, with the best will in the world, no longer made sense [*keinen Zusammenhang mehr ergeben konnten*]. His mouth hung open for most of the time, whenever he thought himself unobserved, and his hands shook" (WN 110–11). The description of Paul's speech, deteriorated into "Satzfetzen," shreds or tatters of sentences, recalls the material state of the manuscript. Increasingly mutilated over the course of its production—not only at the hands of editors, but also in Bernhard's own hands—the most extensive cut-and-paste interventions occur precisely in these final pages of the manuscript.

These are the "notes," the memory tatters though which Bernhard present his "picture" of Paul Wittgenstein, "the living one not the dead one" (WN 118). The second, revised version of the text that Bernhard ultimately submitted to the publisher was apparently found to be in such disarray that it could not serve directly as the copy-text; instead it was deemed necessary to transcribe the text in its entirety, yielding a complete clean copy—bearing no material traces of Bernhard's hand—that typesetters could easily read.

Publishing House as Hospital

In considering these material reflections on Paul's death, I return to the beginning of the text, which opens in the hospital. Bernhard describes having just awakened from a surgery. Noting that Paul was in the Steinhof psychiatric institute at the same time, Bernhard's attention turns to Paul's psychiatrist, the famous Professor Salzer, whom he describes as a genius but also a murderer. In a tirade against medical institutions and practitioners, Bernhard writes, "The psychiatrist is the most incompetent of all medical practitioners and always closer to the rapist-killer than to his science ... and after I had had an occasion of observing the methods which they had practiced so unscrupulously for so many years upon my friend Paul I was afraid of them with a far more intense fear still. The psychiatrists are the real devils of our age. They ply their protected trade in the truest sense of the word ... in the most shameless manner" (*WN* 7). Rather than a scene of healing and regeneration, the hospital is a scene of destruction. But so is publication, for Bernhard. Surgical operation (the removal of Bernhard's tumor) and textual publication (the release of *Verstörung*)—*Herausoperieren* and *Herausgeben*—are aligned from the very first sentence. Thematized at various points throughout (for instance, Ludwig Wittgenstein as "publisher," Paul as "non-publisher"), a scene of publication is also indirectly but powerfully evoked at the end of the text: the performance of *Hunting Party*. But dramatic performance is also a kind of publication. After the performance, Bernhard decries the Burgtheater as "demolition firm [*Vernichtungsanstalt*] of my play" and "demolition firm [*Vernichtungsanstalt*] of my entire mental capacity [*Geistesvermögens*]" (*WN* 116), and the actors' betrayal of his piece as "shameless [*unverschämt*]" (*WN* 115)—the same adjective with which he condemns psychiatrists: the "most shameless [*unverschämteste*] manner" with which they practice their unscrupulous methods (*WN* 7).

In Bernhard's critiques of the hospital as "*todgeweihten* [doomed] Station" and the theater as "Vernichtungsanstalt," one hears echoes of Roithamer's critique of publication in *Correction*: "Was wir veröffentlichen, ist im Augenblick der Veröffentlichung vernichtet [whatever we publish is destroyed in the moment of its publication]" (*W* 4:302). In this light, what would it mean for Bernhard to publish a text about his friend? Bernhard articulates the aim to make "present" *his* image of Paul in writing: "I deliberately emphasize *my*." But is the image of Paul captured "in these notes," and in Bernhard's typescripts—an image marked by the materiality of writing—the same image that appears in the printed book? Or is this image necessarily destroyed, *vernichtet*, through the act of publication?

A host of other Bernhardian statements resonate in this context. In an interview edited and published as "The Publisher Publishes Everything" ("Der Verleger verlegt ja alles"), Bernhard stated that publishers "misplace" things—the German *verlegen* signifying both "to publish" and "to misplace": "He misplaces things and manuscripts that he accepts and then he cannot find them anymore. Either because he doesn't like them anymore, or because he is confused, they aren't there any longer. Misplaced. Forever. . . . And afterward everything is broken or unlocatable [*unauffindbar*]."[108] The published portrait of Paul, by extension, might be understood as a "broken" version of the image Bernhard constructed in his typescripts, "misplaced" by publishers, and "unlocatable" in print. In the same interview, Bernhard stated something similar about translation: "A translation is a different book. It has nothing to do with the original any more. It's the book of whoever translated it."[109] Publishing is itself a form of translation: namely, a translation from one materiality into another.[110] The "translation" of Paul into print, one might extrapolate, has nothing to do with the "original" image constructed in Bernhard's typescripts; no longer *Bernhard's* portrait, it is a product of the "destruction institute" (*Vernichtunganstalt*) of the publishing house.

Fundamentally, Bernhard's work is informed by a deep skepticism regarding the possibility of capturing truth in language, of transforming reality into writing—a position radically opposed to Handke's belief in realization as salvatory "transformation" of endangered things into art. In *Der Keller* (*The Cellar*), Bernhard articulates the impossibility of capturing truth in autobiographical writing as follows: "And to write about a period of one's life, no matter how remote or how recent, no matter how long or how short, means accumulating hundreds and thousands and millions of falsehoods and falsification. . . . We describe an object and believe that we have described it *truthfully* and *faithfully*, only to discover that it is not the truth."[111] In another interview Bernhard also reflected specifically on the impossibility of materially capturing reality on paper: "Even if you now have the urge or mania to write the truth one-hundred

---

108. Hofmann, *Aus Gesprächen*, 75.
109. Hofmann, *Aus Gesprächen*, 77.
110. Wilhelm G. Jacobs, "Materie—Materialität—Geist," *editio* 23 (2009): 20.
111. Thomas Bernhard, *Gathering Evidence*, trans. David McLintock (New York: Vintage, 2011), 160.

percent, you won't succeed, because you'd have to be able to slap [*klatschen*] reality onto paper, but that's not possible."¹¹²

Such notions would seem to undermine the task of capturing in writing an image of the "living" Paul. In *Wittgenstein's Nephew* itself, this aim is undercut by the realization that even in life, Paul was always marked by death: "written off," "pushed aside," extinguished by his family and by society. In this way, the *Sterbensgeschichte* (story of dying) that is Paul's life is also a *Vernichtungsgeschichte* (story of destruction). The publication of *Wittgenstein's Nephew* constitutes another manifestation of Paul's destruction, in which Bernhard, by his own definition, is complicit, even culpable. Just like Paul's family committed Paul to the *Vernichtungsanstalt* of the madhouse, Bernhard submitted Paul to the *Vernichtungsanstalt* of the publishing house, where he was subjected to the "scrupulously practiced methods" (WN 9) of editors and publishers. As we have seen, the text's material production was at once a process of material destruction, not only at editors' hands but also at Bernhard's. Bernhard describes a distinct sense of guilt surrounding his abandonment of Paul in his final days: "I did not dare address him. I preferred my guilty conscience to a meeting with him. I watched him and, suppressing my guilty conscience, I did not go over to him, I was suddenly afraid of him. We avoid those who bear the mark of death [*die vom Tod Gezeichneten*] and I too had yielded to that baseness. . . . I was thus watching him and, at the same time, felt ashamed. . . . I am not a good character. I am not, quite simply, a good person. . . . I feared the confrontation with death. Because *everything* about my friend was already death" (WN 108–9). Bernhard even confesses that he "exploited" Paul's death for his own purposes—"And I had profited from his dying, I had utilized [*ausgenützt*] it in every way I could" (WN 118)—artistic purposes perhaps, but of course also financial. In doing so, Bernhard drew Paul into the *Vernichtungsmechanismus* of his art, publishing a literary "memorial" to him that could only be, in the end, "Verfälschung" and "Vernichtung."

In the final lines of the text, Paul's death is brought into even more explicit relationship with textual destruction. Bernhard recalls

---

112. Hofmann, *Aus Gesprächen*, 21.

a statement Paul made, which also appears as the book's epithet: "*Two hundred friends will come to my funeral and you must make a speech at my graveside*" (WN 120). But Bernhard did not attend Paul's burial; instead, he was on the island of Crete, writing a play that he destroyed as soon as it was finished (WN 120). The final two sentences of *Wittgenstein's Nephew* read as follows: "He is buried, it is said, in Vienna's Central Cemetery. To this day I have not visited his grave" (WN 120). In place of the graveside eulogy stands the book *Wittgenstein's Nephew*, a kind of textual eulogy, with an audience far larger than the two hundred Paul imagined.

It has been suggested that Bernhard failed to attend Paul's burial not out of "heartlessness" but in order to preserve the living memory of Paul.[113] But can the printed text, a product of the *Vernichtungsanstalt* of publication, present anything but a "shadow" of the friend Bernhard knew, bearing little resemblance to his image of Paul as it exists in his typescript pages?[114] In the words of Walter Benjamin, "the work is the death mask of its conception."[115]

That Bernhard's publication of *Wittgenstein's Nephew* represents an act of destruction may initially strike one as unexpected. Paul was victim to the destructive forces of society and his family, against which Bernhard rails; Paul himself was not the target of Bernhardian annihilation. The underlying *Vernichtungsgedanke* in Bernhard's work has been described by David Price thus: "the forces of nature and society that impinge upon us function also within us, and Bernhard rightly points out that we must either tackle their combined monstrousness or succumb to them."[116] Bernhard's writing is a "countercampaign" of destructivity, a "metaphysics of annihilation"

---

113. Wagner, "'Was ich im Grunde nicht entbehren kann,'" 64.

114. Linguistically, the printed text was not exactly the text that Bernhard authored. Errors were introduced by editors in the final stages prior to printing. Bernhard made corrections to a copy of the first version, which were implemented in the third print run (1983). See Höller and Mittermayer, "Anmerkungen zur Textgestaltung," in *Erzählungen III*, 358, 370.

115. Walter Benjamin, "Einbahnstraße," in Walter Benjamin, *Gesammelte Schriften*, vol. 4.1, ed. Tillmann Rexroth (Frankfurt am Main: Suhrkamp, 1991), 107.

116. David W. Price, "Thoughts of Destruction and Annihilation in Thomas Bernhard," *Journal of English and Germanic Philology* 102, no. 2 (2003): 197.

not only expressed discursively but also "inscribed" linguistically and narratively into his texts.[117] As we have seen, the generativity of Bernhard's writing, which can overwhelm the reader, "destroying" attempts to make sense of the text, plays a crucial role in Bernhard's aesthetics of destruction. In both fictional and autobiographical works, Bernhard's language throws a wrench into the established machinery of signification, thwarting efforts to locate stable meaning or truth. In addition to overt condemnations of medical practitioners and theater actors in *Wittgenstein's Nephew*, Bernhard's highly aestheticized depictions of escapades with Paul explode any illusion of 'faithful' autobiographic writing.

There are less obvious ways in which destruction pervades *Wittgenstein's Nephew*, and these illuminate another dimension of Bernhard's *Vernichtungsgedanke*. This dimension can also be found elsewhere in Bernhard's work. Take, for example, Roithamer's conception of correction in *Correction*: "When I make corrections, I destroy [*zerstöre*], when I destroy, I annihilate [*vernichte*], so Roithamer.... Every correction is destruction, annihilation, so Roithamer" (C 266). But Roithamer's corrective destruction did not annihilate completely; at one point, the narrator finds a note in Roithamer's Nachlass declaring his intention to burn his manuscripts after destroying them through correction—an intention he did not ultimately realize (W 4:77). Rather, Roithamer's destructive correction left thousands of scrap pages in its wake, multiple versions of a study that was "zutode korrigiert [corrected to death]." Through this destruction, the narrator suggests, Roithamer did not entirely destroy his study, but instead transformed it into something new. A similar conception also appears in Bernhard's *Auslöschung* (*Extinction*): "to dismantle the old, in order to be able to annihilate [*auslöschen*] it in the end completely for the new. The old must be abandoned, destroyed [*vernichtet*], as difficult as this process is, in order to make possible the new, even if we cannot know what the new is, but that it must be, this we know, Gambetti, this I said to him, there is no going back" (W 9:166). At the core of these notions of destruction—the destruction of the old to enable something new

---

117. Price, "Thoughts of Destruction," 189, 193.

to emerge—is the logic of the strike-through. While canceling that which was written, the strike-through is materially additive, rendering that which was written fully illegible, or allowing it to remain legible to varying degrees.[118] In this sense the strike-through is a phenomenon of destruction and generation at once. But even when completely obscured, *that* something was written remains visible, present—materially if no longer semantically—in its absence. The strike-through, moreover, creates the possibility for something new: lexical replacement, structural reorganization, or textual expansion. In this sense, the strike-through is not purely destructive; rather, it is a mode of "productive negativity."[119]

For Derrida, all writing is "under erasure," *sous rature, durchgestrichen*. In "Plato's Pharmacy" he argues that death and writing are essentially connected: Thoth, the Egyptian god of writing, was also the god of death, and "death is always inscribed and prescribed with its [the living being's] structure."[120] Seen through this lens, Paul Wittgenstein appears in Bernhard's textual portrait—"vom Tod gezeichnet" (marked by death), his death inscribed with him during life (*WN* 66)—as a figure of writing itself.[121] To capture an image of the "living" Paul, to make him "present" in writing, is impossible from the outset. To write is to destroy—but not without a trace.

In Paul's final months, Bernhard witnesses Paul's effacement before his very eyes: a ghostlike shadow of his former self, clothed in

---

118. On the various forms of strike-throughs, see Grésillon, *Literarische Handschriften*, 89–94.

119. Hubert Thüring, "Streichen als Moment produktiver Negativität," in *Schreiben und Streichen: Zu einem Moment Produktiver Negativität*, ed. Lucas Marco Gisi, Hubert Thüring, and Irmgard M. Wirtz (Göttingen; Wallstein; Zurich: Chronos, 2011), 47–70.

120. Jacques Derrida, *Dissemination*, trans. Barbara Johnson (London: Athlone, 1981), 101.

121. Given Bernhard's repeated references to his "Bild" of Paul, one might also put him into dialogue with Roland Barthes, who describes photography in *Camera Lucida* as "this image which produces death while trying to conserve life." J. J. Long, "'Die Teufelskunst unserer Zeit?' Photographic Negotiations in Thomas Bernhard's Auslöschung," *Modern Austrian Literature* 35, no. 3/4 (2002): 90. Much has been written on the relationship between photography and death in *Extinction*, which Bernhard was working on during the year in which he wrote *Wittgenstein's Nephew*.

elegance that, like signifier divorced from signified, no longer corresponds to his pitiful physical state. "I had basically been nothing but a witness, over twelve years, of his dying, it seems to me" (*WN* 118). As a witness to the disintegration of Paul's body and speech as his death neared, Bernhard also witnessed the disintegration of his own typescripts—the material, linguistic body of his textual portrait—as its "completion" and publication neared. The process of constructing the text entailed repeated acts of material destruction, at both editors' hands and his own. What remained was a mutilated amalgam, a montage of texts from different machines and hands, interspersed or sliced and sutured together; a body that, through an ultimate act of striking out, was replaced with a cleaned-up, printed text bound neatly between covers, like Paul's embalmed body lying in an open coffin.

The process of publication, of translating the text from one materiality to another, would seem to entirely efface the scene of production. But in various ways, as we have seen, traces of the scene of writing remain. Hermeneutically, the memories of Paul presented in the published text, fixed in print, are marked by "Verfälschung" and "Vernichtung." In the process of writing, however, everything remains in motion: Hubert Thüring writes:

> Through the possibility that the text could be expanded or edited at any moment, perpetually and subject to whim, the process of writing is potentially endless.... In this way, a subject- and text-oriented space-time of indeterminate coordinates emerges: in each moment, the boundaries between subject and text [*Subjekt und Schrift*], inner and outer, beginning and end, self and other, imagination and perception, past and present, presence and absence can, in principle, shift, dissolve, or be drawn anew, more or less explicitly, more or less performatively, more or less self-consciously.[122]

When writing stops, the boundless potentiality of the text-in-process—in this case, the fluidity of Bernhard's memories of Paul in the process of writing *Wittgenstein's Nephew*—is extinguished. This is not to say that Bernhard's memory of Paul remained "alive"

---

122. Thüring, "Streichen," 56.

during the production process: as Derrida writes, living memory, *mnēmē*, is always already dependent on signs, always contaminated by *hypomnēsis*.[123] An *Erinnerungsarbeit* mediated by *Schreibarbeit*, Bernhard's textual memorial to Paul is thus doubly marked by absence.

But whereas Bernhard's writing—in *Wittgenstein's Nephew* and beyond—is infused by death and destructivity, the rhythmic, musical, bodily, intense, irritating, maddening language of Bernhard's prose is a language of presence.[124] And in the affective dimensions of Bernhard's prose, traces of the material scene of writing—and of the materially mediated *process* of remembering—can still be felt, spilling into the material scene of reading.

---

123. Derrida, *Dissemination*, 109.
124. Compare Hans Ulrich Gumbrecht, *Production of Presence: What Meaning Cannot Convey* (Stanford, CA: Stanford University Press, 2004), xiii.

3

RILKE'S EMBODIED FIGURATION

In the preceding chapters I have examined entanglements of textual process and textual product, and of writing and reading, across the whole arc of Handke's and Bernhard's textual production. The notions of material-semiotic entanglement I have put forth are both rooted both in these writers' works—Handke's descriptions of "Verschränkung" (entanglement) and "Ineinanderfügen" (interweaving); Bernhard's notion of a "whole" that is complete or bounded—and reflected in recent scholarship (for instance, Honold's notion of an "interplay . . . of topography and narration";[1] Buchholz's mobilization of the figure of "undergrowth"). My aim, and the proposition I put forth to literary studies, is to cultivate a kind of "new seeing," widening the scope of literary analysis in order to gain a broader, more complex sense of the material-semiotic entanglements that

---

1. Alexander Honold, *Der Erd-Erzähler: Peter Handkes Prosa der Orte, Räume und Landschaften* (Stuttgart: Metzler, 2017), 206.

constitute and ripple through the literary artwork; in other words, a broader, more complex sense of this "whole."

The notion of a new mode of seeing I invoke is informed not only by Handke, but also, of course, by Rilke. While both writers were profoundly influenced by the work of Paul Cézanne, what they learned to see, and the process of implementing this "new seeing" in their writing, differs in several key respects. Through Cézanne, Handke came to see a fundamental interconnectedness of things in ways that could be described as Spinozist and neo-Romantic but also specifically postmodernist—an intertextuality of all things. The Rilkean conceptions of *sehen lernen* and a *neues Sehen* are distinctly modernist: notions of *seeing through* the façades of reality, encounters—particularly in *The Notebooks of Malte Laurids Brigge*—with things unknown and ominous, at once corporeal and ghostly, lying beneath the surface.[2] In this book, however, my juxtaposition of Handke and Bernhard with Rilke is not only a literary historical one (postmodernism/modernism); it is also methodological. In the case of Handke and Bernhard, we have a relative wealth of archival material through which to examine the entanglement of material production within the formal, stylistic, thematic, affective dimensions of their works across the interconnected scenes of writing, editing, publishing, and reading. There are much scarcer material traces, by contrast, of Rilke's material production of *The Notebooks*. In this chapter I ask a broader question: Can we consider the entanglements of material process and textual product in cases where documentary evidence thereof is scarce, not available, or no longer extant?

Underlying my investigation of textual entanglements are two fundamental questions: To what degree is literature a material art form? What is the relationship between textual materiality and textual representation (signification, thematics, meaning)? These questions have frequently been articulated around distinctions between the *text* and the *work*. Grounded in the poststructuralist conceptions of the intertextuality of language, Roland Barthes argued that the

---

2. Rainer Maria Rilke, *The Notebooks of Malte Laurids Brigge*, trans. Robert Vilain (Oxford: Oxford University Press, 2016).

text is "held in language," whereas the "work" can be "held in the hand."[26] Roger Chartier, echoing Peter Shillingsburg and Jerome McGann before him, has characterized a divide in contemporary literary studies between frameworks focusing on "the immateriality of works" and "materiality of texts."[3] In tracing the emergence of posthermeneutic approaches out of the centuries-long domination of the hermeneutic paradigm, Hans Ulrich Gumbrecht speaks of an "oscillation" between "presence effects" (the material, affective dimensions of texts and readerly experience) and "meaning effects."[4] Yet no matter how infinitesimal the distance, this "oscillation" nonetheless implies a dualistic separation of presence effects and meanings, which similarly structures the categorical/conceptual distinctions between text and work.

In confronting the question of the relationship between materiality and signification, I turn from the late to the early twentieth century, to a text often considered the first modernist novel in German: Rainer Maria Rilke's *The Notebooks of Malte Laurids Brigge* (1910).[5] This work, Rilke's first and only experiment with the genre of the novel, is a manuscript fiction composed of seventy-one "Aufzeichnungen"—written sketches or journal-like entries penned by Malte, a twenty-eight-year-old Danish aspiring poet who has rejected his family's aristocratic position and ventured to Paris. Bombarded by sensory impressions against which he has no protection, and confronted at every corner by disease, death, and decay, Malte's picture of self and world become radically fractured.[6] He begins a

---

3. Peter Schillingsburg, *Resisting Texts* (Ann Arbor: University of Michigan Press, 1997), 3–4; Jerome McGann, *The Textual Condition* (Princeton, NJ: Princeton University Press, 1991), 7; Roger Chartier, *Inscription and Erasure*, trans. Arthur Goldhammer (Philadelphia: University of Pennsylvania Press, 2007), ix.

4. Hans Ulrich Gumbrecht, *Production of Presence: What Meaning Cannot Convey* (Stanford, CA: Stanford University Press, 2004), xv, 1–20.

5. Torsten Hoffmann, *Rainer Maria Rilke* (Baden-Baden: Tectum, 2021), 14, 115.

6. On Malte's lack of a "Reizschutz," see Andreas Huyssen, "Urban Experience and the Modernist Dream of a New Language," in *A New History of German Literature*, ed. David E. Wellbery, Judith Ryan, and Hans Ulrich Gumbrecht (Cambridge, MA: Harvard University Press, 2004), 679; Andreas Huyssen, "The Notebooks of Malte Laurids Brigge," in *The Cambridge Companion to Rilke*, ed. Karen Leeder and Robert Vilain (Cambridge: Cambridge University Press, 2010), 76–77;

process of "learning to see" (*sehen lernen*), an attempt to make the shock experiences productive in developing an ability to perceive in a fundamentally new way.[7] The process of learning to see is crucially bound up in a process of learning to write: "I have done something to combat my fear. I have sat writing all night long" (*MLB* 10). Malte's writing represents attempts to metabolize the experiences that befall him, to find a language and a mode of narration through which to grasp what he is learning to see.

Highly self-reflexive, *The Notebooks* is also semi-autobiographical.[8] The crises of perception and writing that Malte undergoes reflect Rilke's own experiences in Paris—in fact, numerous entries are based on passages from his own letters—and many of Malte's narrated childhood memories reflect details of Rilke's own.[9] This work was Rilke's only experiment with writing a longer prose work, and he had extraordinary difficulty finishing it; when he did complete it, he entered into a deep crisis of writing, doubting whether he would ever be able to publish again. In his correspondence Rilke described the enormous physical and mental toll that writing *The Notebooks* took; he felt that he barely "survived" it and viewed the work at times as a failure.[10] This crisis can be rooted, in part, I will argue, in Rilke's

---

Eric L. Santner, *The Royal Remains: The People's Two Bodies and the Endgames of Sovereignty* (Chicago: University of Chicago Press, 2011), 199.

7. Hoffmann, *Rainer Maria Rilke*, 117.

8. See Lorna Martens, "Autobiographical Narrative and the Use of Metaphor: Rilke's Techniques in *Die Aufzeichnungen des Malte Laurids Brigge*," *Studies in 20th and 21st Century Literature* 9, no. 2 (1985): 229–49; Linda Haverty Rugg, "A Self at Large in the Hall of Mirrors: Rilke's *Malte Laurids Brigge* as Autobiographical Act," *Seminar: A Journal of Germanic Studies* 29, no. 1 (1993): 43–54.

9. On Rilke's integration of letters, see Ernst Fedor Hoffmann, "Zum dichterischen Verfahren in Rilkes 'Aufzeichnungen des Malte Laurids Brigge,'" in *Materialien zu Rainer Maria Rilke: Die Aufzeichnungen des Malte Laurids Brigge*, ed. Hartmut Engelhardt (Frankfurt am Main: Suhrkamp, 1974), 214ff. See also Brigitte von Witzleben, *Untersuchungen zu Rainer Maria Rilkes "Aufzeichnungen des Malte Laurids Brigge": Studien zu den Quellen und zur Textüberlieferung* (Vaasa: Universität Vaasa, Institut für Deutsche Sprache und Literatur, 1996), 22–24.

10. Rilke to Lou Andreas-Salomé, December 28, 1911, in Rainer Maria Rilke and Lou Andreas-Salomé, *Briefwechsel*, ed. Ernst Pfeiffer (Zurich: Max Niehans, 1952), 245–51.

material struggle to compose his "Prosabuch" (prose book)—a struggle that also becomes incorporated into the work's thematics.

Relatively little is known about Rilke's material process of writing *The Notebooks*. In letters he mentions preparatory notes, an "older sizable manuscript" (likely an incomplete version), and small notebooks that contained a later version.[11] The typescript and page proofs, which in his letters Rilke described correcting, are also lost.[12] The largest and virtually only extant fragment of the work's genesis is the so-called Bernese Notebook (*Berner Taschenbuch*). Corresponding roughly to the second half of the novel, it is one of (likely) two notebooks that together contained the penultimate version.[13] In the Bernese Notebook one finds visible signs of Rilke's struggle: pages displaying extensive strike-throughs, some crossed out entirely; chunks of text written and rewritten, canceled, and sometimes returned to the text; annotations representing attempts to order and reorder passages on the limited space of the page; as well as additional entries—the most substantial of which are two versions of an "original ending" (*ursprünglicher Schluss*) comprising some twenty notebook pages—that were abandoned in the first published version.[14] In contrast to extant manuscripts of Rilke's poetry, which are largely fair copies in Rilke's famously beautiful handwriting, the Bernese Notebook is one of Rilke's very few extant working manuscripts; it reveals a picture of Rilke as *Papierarbeiter* (paper worker) whose creative process took place on the page,

---

11. Rainer Maria Rilke, *Die Aufzeichnungen des Malte Laurids Brigge*, ed. Manfred Engel (Stuttgart: Reclam, 1997), 320–22; Thomas Richter, "Editorischer Bericht," in *Die Aufzeichnungen des Malte Laurids Brigge: Das Manuskript des "Berner Taschenbuchs"—Textgenetische Edition*, ed. Thomas Richter and Franziska Kolp (Göttingen: Wallstein, 2012), 226–28.

12. "The other was probably lost when Rilke's possessions in Paris were confiscated and auctioned at the beginning of the First World War; the typescript "is believed to have been destroyed during the Second World War." Robert Vilain, introduction to *The Notebooks* (*MLB* xlvi–xlvii).

13. Richter, "Editorischer Bericht," 226.

14. Ernst Zinn describes these *Aufzeichnungen* as such in Rainer Maria Rilke, *Sämtliche Werke*, vol. 6, *Malte Laurids Brigge: Prosa 1906–1926*, ed. Ernst Zinn (Frankfurt: Insel, 1966), 948.

through the activity of writing and striking through. In attempting to complete the text, Rilke became so physically and mentally exhausted that he was incapable of producing a final clean copy, but recognized that the "theilweise schlechten Handschrift des Manuscriptvorraths" (at times poor-quality handwriting of the manuscript template) would make it impossible for a copyist to transcribe.[15] Ultimately, Rilke's publisher, Anton Kippenberg, invited Rilke to Leipzig, where he dictated the text orally to Kippenberg's secretary.

A text largely about fragmentation and ruin, the surviving manuscript of *The Notebooks* is itself a fragment, a ruin. For the second half of the novel, we can look "behind the scenes" of the printed text to examine how the materiality and visuality of Rilke's manuscript production become figured in the text. This experience, in turn, gives us a different view of the first half, which is equally haunted by its manuscript past, as if by a phantom limb. On the one hand, using the fragment to grasp the influence of Rilke's material process on the work enables us to sense this influence even where the material record is lacking. In this way, my investigation of *The Notebooks* serves as a provocation: To what degree we can apply the methodological lenses developed in the first two chapters, given that the material production of Rilke's work is only *partially* traceable? On the other hand, working with the manuscript fragment exposes the fact that all material records are incomplete, and no matter how intact or "whole" the record of a work's genesis may seem, we always have but fragments of material-creative processes that can never be fully known or reconstructed.

In describing the relationship between Rilke's material writing process and the published versions of *The Notebooks*, I take up the concept of *figuration*, a concept that is useful for understanding how the traces of Rilke's process remain enmeshed within the text—especially when material documentation thereof is absent—but that has also been used to discuss other aspects of Rilke's poetics. But what was the materiality of Rilkean figuration? In this chapter I

---

15. Rilke to Anton Kippenberg, October 20, 1909, in Rilke, *Briefwechsel mit Anton Kippenberg, 1906–1926*, ed. Ingeborg Schnack and Renate Scharffenberg, vol. 1 (Frankfurt am Main: Insel, 1955), 177.

explore both Rilke's material process of generating the text of the Bernese Notebook and how the materiality and visuality of Rilke's manuscript production became figured in *The Notebooks*: in explicit representations of material texts and scenes of writing and reading; in highly affective images of bodily and material excess that strangely evoke paper and ink; in the *genre* of manuscript fiction, an autobiographical concession of the work's manuscript origins.[16]

In art historical discourse, the term "figure" commonly refers to the human form. In rhetoric, figures of speech are nonliteral uses of language employed to produce specific effects. Poststructural definitions of the figure associate it with a disruption or loss of referentiality, rather than a fixity of meaning. Jean-François Lyotard, for example, defines the figural as the interruption of signification by the sensory dimensions of language, which thus makes language irreducible to pure signification.[17] The sensory is also a crucial dimension for Gilles Deleuze, whose definition of "the Figure" is derived in part from Cézanne: "Cézanne gave a simple name to this way of the Figure: sensation. The Figure is the sensible form related to a sensation: it acts immediately upon the nervous system, which is of the flesh, whereas abstract form is addressed to the head through the intermediary of the brain."[18] For Deleuze, "figuration" is associated with the hermeneutic: signification, referentiality, representation. "Figure," by contrast, is associated with the non-hermeneutic: sensation, affect, presence.[19]

Figure also has specific meanings in Rilkean poetics. In Rilke's middle period it was associated with sculpture and the autonomous

---

16. In several unusual moments, the text explicitly references an earlier manuscript version: six passages are bracketed in parentheses and annotated with the footnote "im Manuskript an den Rand geschrieben" (*KA* 3:531, 587, 592, 603, 617, 629).

17. Jean-François Lyotard, *Discourse, Figure*, trans. Antony Hudek and Mary Lydon (Minneapolis: University of Minnesota Press, 2011), 3, 7.

18. Gilles Deleuze, *Francis Bacon: The Logic of Sensation*, trans. Daniel W. Smith (Minneapolis: University of Minnesota Press, 2002), 31.

19. "Whereas 'figuration' refers to a form that is related to an object it is supposed to represent, the 'Figure' is the form that is connected to a sensation, and that conveys the violence of this sensation directly to the nervous system." Daniel W. Smith, "Deleuze and Bacon: Three Conceptual Trajectories in *The Logic of Sensation*," in Deleuze, *Francis Bacon*, xiii.

"art-thing" (*Kunst-Ding*).[20] The term became particularly prominent in Rilke's late work, where it has received the most scholarly attention. Paul de Man suggests that, unlike traditional metaphor, Rilkean Figure does not function to elucidate meaning, but instead represents liberation of the signifier from the "referential constraints of meaning."[21] Beda Allemann defines Rilkean Figure through the metaphor of constellation, a space of gathering, spanning, and connecting disparate elements through which *Dasein* is revealed; in turn, Figure is synonymous with poetry itself.[22] More recently, Hannah Eldridge has underscored that the figural, for Rilke, is constituted by relationality (*Bezug*): the figure organizes and holds together an interplay between abstract and concrete, the cognitive and the sensory, the conceptual and the perceptual.[23] Rilkean figurality, Eldridge writes, is a "project of revivifying language"—namely, the "capacity of language to evoke sensory presence or visual intensity"; through figuration, "the reader or hearer [is] pulled into the workings of mind, language, and world upon each other."[24]

All of these definitions of the Figure/figuration can be brought to bear on *The Notebooks*. Rilke's project of writing *The Notebooks* was essentially, I argue, a project of figuration. The figuration at work in *The Notebooks* bears clear relation to the figural program that Rilke developed in the *New Poems*: in his so-called *Dinggedichte* (thing poems) or *Figuren-Gedichte* (character poems), Rilke attempted to grasp things in their "dingliche Wirklichkeit" (objective reality) and, through a mode of "sachliches Sagen" (objective saying),

---

20. Manfred Engel, "Rilke als Autor der literarischen Moderne," in *Rilke Handbuch: Leben—Werk—Wirkung*, ed. Manfred Engel (Stuttgart: Metzler, 2013), 521.
21. Paul de Man, *Allegories of Reading* (New Haven, CT: Yale University Press, 1979), 47.
22. Beda Allemann, *Zeit und Figur beim Späten Rilke* (Pfullingen: Neske, 1961), 7, 33, 114–15, 235.
23. Hannah Vandegrift Eldridge, "Rilke's *Sonnets to Orpheus*: Figurality as Aspect-Seeing," in *Anschauung und Anschaulichkeit: Visualisierung im Wahrnehmen, Lesen und Denken*, ed. Hans Adler and Sabine Gross (Paderborn: Wilhelm Fink, 2016), 75–76.
24. Eldridge, "Rilke's *Sonnets*," 89.

transform them into lyrical "Kunst-Dinge" (art things).²⁵ In examining the figural in Rilke's poetry, scholars have focused primarily on imagery and metaphor, as well as oral/aural devices (rhyme, alliteration, assonance, and so forth). Yet Rilke was also keenly attuned to the visible, material dimensions of written language in generating meaning.²⁶ He was actively involved in the design of his books, from layout and typeface to paper and binding. In a letter to Kippenberg, Rilke described his initial encounter with the printed version of *The Notebooks* as follows: "The postal package has been here for two days; now, the 'Aufzeichnung des Malte Laurids Brigge' really do exist. I often have the book in my hand; I have looked at it, felt it, opened it to many passages, finally read it entirely. . . . I am thinking in particular of the green paperback; the bound edition is wonderful in its own way; but the other one, you will understand, is closer to me: it *is* the book, for me."²⁷ But Rilke also had a particularly vexed relationship with the medium of print.²⁸ He frequently produced handwritten copies of published poems, "translating" them from print back into manuscripts, which he gave away as gifts—a "performative expression of unease [*eines Unbehagens*] about the print medium."²⁹ Another expression of the attention Rilke gave to the

---

25. Engel, "Rilke als Autor," 521. This conception was influenced significantly by Rilke's encounters with Rodin and Cézanne, including Cézanne's method of realization. An extraordinary amount has been written on this topic, as well as on the relationship between Handke's and Rilke's receptions of Cézanne's realization; see, for the most comprehensive account, Martina Kurz, *Bild-Verdichtungen: Cézannes Realisation als poetisches Prinzip bei Rilke und Handke* (Göttingen: Vandenhoeck und Ruprecht, 2003). On Rilke's *sachliches Sagen* as "corporeal process of signification," see Anette Schwarz, "The Colors of Prose: Rilke's Program of 'Sachliches Sagen,'" *Germanic Review* 71, no. 3 (1996): 195–210.
26. On Rilke's "material poetics," compare Davide Giuriato, "Paper and Poetics," *Configurations* 18, no. 3 (2010): 211–29.
27. Rilke to Anton Kippenberg, June 9, 1910, in *Briefwechsel mit Anton Kippenberg*, 215–16.
28. Compare also Irmgard M. Wirtz, "'Schrift—Transkription—Typographie: Zur gemäßigt mimetischen Faksimile-Edition von Rilkes *Malte*-Fragment,'" *editio* 26 (2012): 145–46.
29. Wolfram Groddeck, "'und wollte wieder: lies. // Da las er: so, daß sich der Engel bog': Philologische Überlegungen zur kommentierten Ausgabe von Rilkes Werken," *Text: Kritische Beiträge* 5 (1999): 205.

material embodiment of his texts can be seen in his "calligraphic particularity and precision" in these fair-copy manuscripts.[30] This contrasts markedly, however, with the appearance of the Bernese Notebook, one of few extant working manuscripts by Rilke that displays the material messiness of his creative process.

For Rilke, who was primarily a poet, the task of composing a lengthier prose work was an undertaking fundamentally different from composing poetry, and it was plagued by struggle and crisis. Elements of Rilke's figural poetics of the *New Poems*—which Rilke published during the years he was working on his prose book—are at play in *The Notebooks*, but Rilke's project of figuration takes on different contours. In this sense, poststructuralist associations of the figural with the sensory are particularly useful. Filling *The Notebooks* are highly affective descriptions of bodiliness, abjection, and decay; Malte encounters an "excess" or "surplus" of fleshiness, of materiality that cannot be incorporated into the symbolic order, that lurks "on the edge of discourse."[31] In Lyotardian terms, Malte encounters the "inherent thickness" of the world that "is not to be read, but rather seen," and which "fall[s] into oblivion in the process of signification."[32] In Deleuzean terms, Figure encroaches into figuration, the non-hermeneutic into the hermeneutic, at times threatening to demolish signification altogether. In *The Notebooks*, and in its production, we witness a struggle with this underlying question: How could the overwhelming, world-shattering sensory experiences of the Parisian metropolis, and the new mode of seeing they engendered, be captured and represented in language, in written text, such that they could be adequately conveyed to the reader, that readers might experience these sensations themselves? It is just not just a question of representing materiality/material experience in language, but also of how linguistic/textual representation can produce material experience/bodily affect.

Rilke's project of figuration in *The Notebooks* is thus, more specifically, a project of embodied figuration.[33] It aimed at the

---

30. Wirtz, "'Schrift,'" 145.
31. Santner, *Royal Remains*, 199; Lyotard, *Discourse*, 7.
32. Lyotard, *Discourse*, 3.
33. Eldridge in fact roots the development of Rilke's later figural poetics in *The Notebooks*: "Rilke's career-long interest in the visual arts, his concern over

transgression of the boundaries between materiality and representation, the merging or fusion of, in Deleuze's terms, figuration (signification, the hermeneutic) with the Figure (the non-hermeneutic, sensation, affective, presence). Such a state is explicitly described/theorized in *The Notebooks*: "The age of the other interpretation will dawn and there shall not be left one word upon another, and every meaning will dissolve like clouds and descend like rain" (*MLB* 31). In this new order, meaning will dissolve into pure materiality, yielding what Walter Benjamin describes as "pure language": emancipated from and transcending the boundaries between signifier and signified.[34]

What connects the material/sensory phenomena/experiences represented *in* the text and the language *of* the text (and in turn, the reader's experience) is the materiality of writing. As we know, the process of writing was physically and mentally exhausting for Rilke and led to a deep crisis of writing. In the Bernese Notebook, we find traces of this process, indexing Rilke's material struggle to formulate and piece passages together in the text. Rilke generated this manuscript through the bodily activity of writing, but at the same time the material body of the manuscript also interacted in the production of the work. As I will explore, the materiality of this manuscript remains inscribed or enmeshed within the figurative dimensions of *The Notebooks*. In this respect, the most paradigmatic are representations of wounded, fragmented, indeed disfigured bodies that Malte encounters in Paris. Like sensations that bombard Malte, against which he has no protection, Rilke's figural language produces affective, bodily responses in the reader during the act of reading. In and through Rilke's figural language, bodies and bodiliness represented *in* the text, the body *of* the text, the body of the writer, and the body of the reader are drawn into relation: incorporated, entangled.

---

what kind of medium for artistic work is afforded by language, and his complaints in letters and in the novel *Die Aufzeichnungen des Malte Laurids Brigge* that modern subjects abdicate the greater part of their experience of living in the world and with others come to a head in the cycle's [Sonette an Orpheus] blending of seeing and thinking in poetically formed figures" ("Rilke's *Sonnets*," 89).

34. Walter Benjamin, "The Task of the Translator," in *Illuminations*, ed. Hannah Arendt, trans. Harry Zohn (New York: Schocken, 2007), 80.

I have divided this chapter into three sections, which are organized around three key concepts from *The Notebooks*: *Erzählen* (narrating), *Streichen* (striking), and *Sehen* (seeing). In the first section, "Narrating," I examine passages from the second half of the text—Malte's account of Count Brahe's storytelling, and his retelling of the death of the "false Tsar" Grischa Otrepow—in relation to their manuscript version in the Bernese Notebook, in order to develop an account of how the manuscript/materiality of writing became figured in the novel. The next section, "Striking," probes excessive images of fragmented, wounded bodies as figurations of the material, visual state of the manuscript; it also considers how the texture of reality in *The Notebooks*—fluid, fragmentary, in flux—figures the unfixity and open-endedness of the text-in-process. The third section examines Malte's "new seeing" in its media-historical context—specifically, discourse around the X-ray—to show how the text prompts us to "see" the manuscript "through" its printed surface.

Narrating

In the fourth entry, Malte describes his process of "learning to see": "I'm learning how to see [*Ich lerne sehen*]. I don't know what the reason is, but everything enters into me more deeply and no longer stops at the point where it used to come to an end. I have an inner self that I knew nothing about. Now everything goes into it. I don't know what happens there" (*MLB* 4). Malte's sensorium is bombarded by an onslaught of experiences that decimate the seemingly stable boundary protecting self from world, exposing previously unknown interior depths. From the beginning, Malte's experience of seeing is connected to writing—or rather, the seeming impossibility of writing. The entry continues: "I wrote a letter today, and as I was writing it, it struck me that I have only been here for three weeks. Three weeks somewhere else, in the country, say, could pass as quickly as a day; here they feel like years. I don't want to write any more letters either. Why should I tell someone that I am changing? If I change I'm no longer the person I was, and if I'm something different from what I used to be, I plainly don't have any friends. And I can't possibly write to strangers, people who don't know me" (*MLB* 31). Malte's crisis of seeing amounts to an epistemological crisis: because he himself is in flux, no one "knows" him anymore. Communication (letter writing) seems no longer possible. As this crisis intensifies, Malte questions whether humans have actually ever seen, thought, or communicated anything of real substance: "Is it possible ... that we have not yet seen, recognized, or said anything real or important? Is it possible that there have been millennia in which to look, cogitate, and make a record, and that we have allowed these millennia to pass by like the lunch-break at school when you eat your sandwich and an apple? Yes, it's possible" (*MLB* 13–14). In the face of this possibility, Malte does to the only thing he can think of doing: he writes. "But if all of this is possible, even if it has only the faintest glimmer of possibility, then something must be done, for heaven's sake! The first person to come along who has had this disquieting thought must begin to do something about what's been neglected; even if it's only one person, and by no means the one most suited to the task: there simply isn't anyone else to do it. This young, inconsequential foreigner, Brigge, will have to sit down, five storeys up, and write, day and night: yes, he'll have to write, that's what will have to happen" (*MLB* 15). Malte's project of learning to see is thus deeply entangled in a project of learning to write—that is to say, a project of figuration. *What* to write, and *how* to write, remain unclear. All that Malte knows is *that* he must write: day and night, aimlessly, out of the ruins of a reality that is crumbling around him, a hermeneutic order under erasure.

"That they narrated, really narrated"

"That they narrated, really narrated [*Dass man erzählte, wirklich erzählte*], that must have been before my time" (*MLB* 85).[35] Malte laments the disappearance of a mode of oral narration embodied in the figure of Count Brahe, Malte's maternal grandfather. Malte orients himself toward this lost mode of storytelling in searching for a mode of writing that can capture his experience of learning to see. But Malte did not encounter the Count's storytelling directly;

---

35. Translation modified.

rather, he learned of it from his aunt Abelone, Brahe's daughter, who did not possess his storytelling ability: "I never heard anyone tell a story. When Abelone used to talk to me about when Maman was young, it was very clear that she didn't have the art of story-telling. Old Count Brahe is said to have had it. I want to put down here [*aufschreiben*] what she knew about it" (*MLB* 85).

Abelone not only witnessed Brahe's storytelling but also served as his scribe. A bifurcated scene of dictating and transcribing, this "scene of writing" is decidedly fractured, the hand and the voice, *technē* and *logos*, split between the two figures. Culminating in an image of stigmatization, the scene of Brahe's and Abelone's writing evokes a host of media technologies and modes of inscription and transmission: oral narration and handwriting, but also typewriting and print. These media-historical reflections, however, are conditioned by Rilke's material writing process as it unfolded in the space of the Bernese Notebook. Reading the passage through this bifocal lens—in its print and manuscript incarnations—enables us to see how Rilke's project of figuration is crucially embedded in the material dimensions of textual production and reception in ways that remain perceptible in the published form.

From the start, Abelone's process of transcribing the Count's speech is riddled with difficulties:

> Count Brahe's dictation took its course for a few days. But then Abelone found herself unable to spell [*schreiben*] 'Eckernförde.' It was a proper noun, and she had never heard it before. The Count, who in truth had for quite a while been seeking a pretext to give up the business of writing [*das Schreiben aufzugeben*], which was too slow for his reminiscences [*Erinnerungen*], feigned reluctance.
>
> 'She can't spell it [*Sie kann es nicht schreiben*]' he said sharply, 'and other people won't be able to read it. And will they even *see* what I'm saying here?' he went on angrily, not taking his eyes off Abelone.
>
> 'Will they see him, this Saint-Germain?' he shouted at her. 'Have we said Saint-Germain? Cross it out. Write: the Marquis de Belmare.'
>
> Abelone crossed out and wrote. But the Count continued so quickly that she couldn't keep up. (*MLB* 87)

In Abelone's attempt to transcribe Brahe's stories, some things are lost in translation. When a word is unfamiliar or Abelone cannot spell it—the name of the town "Eckernförde," a proper noun, for instance—she cannot produce the corresponding visual, written form. Sometimes the pace of Brahe's speaking exceeds Abelone's ability to record it; here, the Count commands Abelone to strike through the name "Saint-Germain" and replace it with "Marquis de Belmare," but the time required make the material correction prevents her from keeping up with the train of his speech. These breakdowns are far from trivial. Brahe's storytelling is defined by an ability to speak into immediate, phenomenological presence the places and people he narrates; in other words, to make present the absent, overcoming the boundary between signifier and signified. At the heart of the matter is whether the same can be achieved in writing.

Calling into question the ability of writing to make present—"And will they even *see* what I'm saying here [*was ich da sage*]?"—the passage seems ripe for a Derridean critique. But the text, I suggest, already deconstructs itself. For Brahe himself is also a writer: strewn with papers covered in notes, Brahe's desk appears to Abelone "like a plain with books and piles of papers [*Schriftstößen*] as villages" (*MLB* 86). As dictation to be transcribed, Brahe's oration is also pervaded by the logic of writing. Brahe "dictates" in both sense: he speaks aloud a text to be written down, but also commands Abelone's hand: "'Have we said Saint-Germain? Cross it out. Write: the Marquis de Belmare.'"

In describing the scene, Malte focuses on the corporeal dimensions of Brahe's storytelling, the energetic movements of his body through space in the act of narrating: "Sometimes he would leap up and speak into the candles, making them flicker. Or when whole sentences had to be struck through yet again, he would pace vigorously to and fro, his silk eau-de-Nil nightgown billowing.... He was maniacally pacing up and down" (*MLB* 86, 88). Brahe's physical movement produces visual traces: the flickering candlelight registers the materiality of the breath, and his pacing back and forth sends scattered papers flying. The Count's speaking is also accompanied by gesticulation: "Trembling, the Count stood up and made a gesture as if putting something into the room, which remained. At that moment he became aware of Abelone. 'Can you see him?' he barked at her. And suddenly he grabbed the single silver candlestick

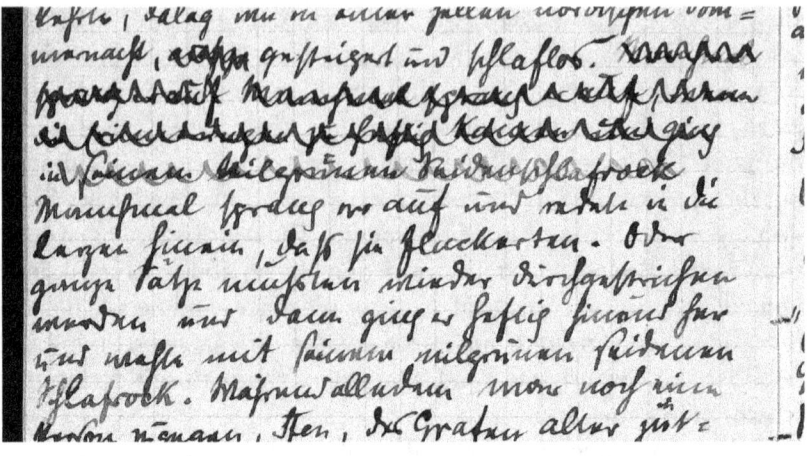

Figure 3.1. Rainer Maria Rilke, *Die Aufzeichnungen des Malte Laurids Brigge*, 2. Teil, 32. SLA-RMR-Ms_D_2. Schweizerisches Literaturarchiv, Bern.

and thrust it before her face, dazzling her. Abelone remembered that she had seen him" (*MLB* 88–89). Brahe's ability to make things present in his storytelling seems to originate not only in his speech, but also in his bodily movement: like the stroke of a writer's hand, which leaves a physical trace on the page, Brahe, with a manual gesture, had "put" something into the room "which remained."

A figure of storytelling, Brahe simultaneously appears as an embodiment of manu-script, his movements and visual mark-making evoking the logic of writing and striking. In the Bernese Notebook, certain descriptions of the Count directly mirror the activity of the pen across the page (figure 3.1).

> ... ~~Sometimes~~
> ~~he jumped up Sometimes he jumped up, whenever~~
> ~~the memories came too intensely and paced~~
> ~~in his nile-green silk dressing gown~~
> Sometimes he jumped up and spoke into the
> candles so that they flickered. Or
> whole sentences had to be crossed
> through again and then he went intensely back and forth

and billowed with his Nile-green silk
dressing gown

> ... ~~Manchmal~~
> ~~sprang er auf Manchmal sprang er auf, wenn~~
> ~~die Erinnerugen zu heftig kamen und ging~~
> ~~in seinem~~ ^N~~nilgrünen Seidenschlafrock~~
> Manchmal sprang er auf und redete in die
> Kerzen hinein, daß sie flackerten. Oder
> ganze Sätze mußten wieder durchgestrichen
> werden und dann ging er heftig hinund her
> und wehte mit seinem nilgrünen seidenen
> Schlafrock (*BT* 32)

Here, the narration of striking through is directly preceded in the manuscript by several attempts to compose a sentence, each abandoned and crossed out. In other words, the narration of cancellation directly corresponds to the material act of cancellation. Additionally, the accumulation of deictic prepositions—Brahe jumps *up*, speaks *into* the candles, lines are struck *through*, he paces *back and forth*—captures the unrestrained movement of the pen: unlike typing, handwriting can proceed in any direction, forward or backward, up and down the space of the page.

There are other correspondences between the space of representation and the space of the manuscript. In the printed version, Brahe had long wanted to quit dictating because the writing process was "too slow for his memories [*zu langsam war für seine Erinnerungen*]." This clause replaced an original one: "which only hindered him in his reminiscences [*das ihn nur in seinen Erinnerungen hemmte*]" (figure 3.2). But when Rilke returned to revise the line, he was met with a physical "hinderance" (*Hemmung*)—a lack of space on the page, which he navigated by writing the line vertically in the margin. Description of a *temporal* tension between the pace of remembering and writing corresponds to a *spatial* tension in the manuscript between the "shape" of the text and the space of the page.

Rilke's composition of this entry involved not simply the interaction of writer and manuscript notebook. In material he had gathered to incorporate into the novel, Rilke drew from a variety of

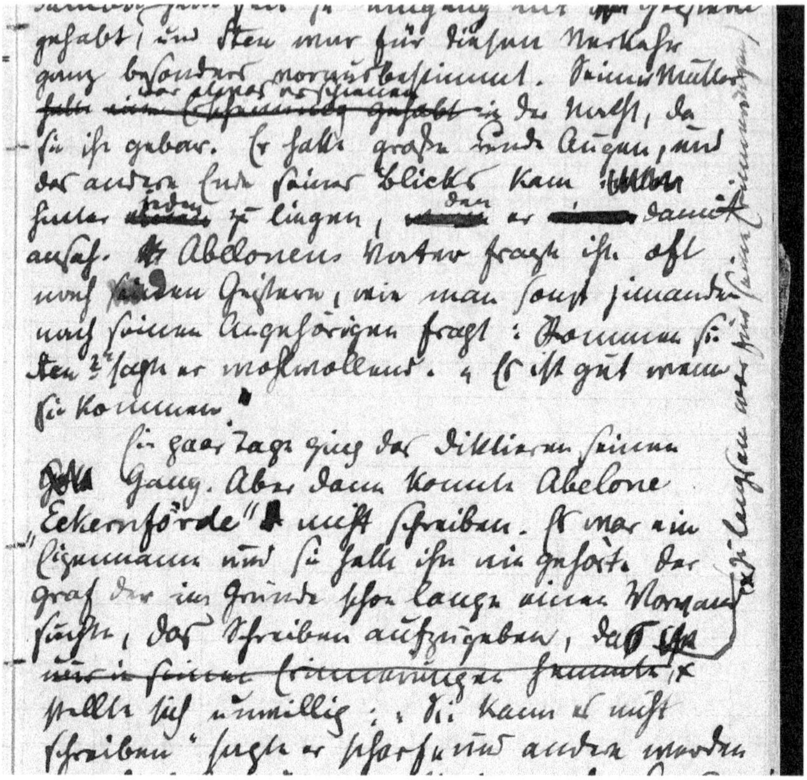

Figure 3.2. Rainer Maria Rilke, *Die Aufzeichnungen des Malte Laurids Brigge*, 2. Teil, 33. SLA-RMR-Ms_D_2. Schweizerisches Literaturarchiv, Bern.

other texts—his own letters, as well as an encyclopedia and other historical sources. This dimension of Rilke's process finds expression in the textual representation as well. For Brahe's tales of the Count of Saint-Germain, aka Marquis von Belmare, Rilke's primary source was Ersch and Gruber's *General Encyclopedia of Sciences and Arts (Allgemeine Encyklopädie der Wissenschaften und Künste)*.[36] Rumored to have practiced alchemy and to have communicated

---

36. B. Röse, "Germain (Saint-)," in *Allgemeine Encyklopädie der Wissenschaften und Künste in alphabetischer Folge*, ed. J. S. Ersch and J. G. Gruber (Leipzig: Gleditsch, 1818–1889), 1.61: 167.

with the dead, Saint-Germain (1712?–84) assumed various pseudonyms throughout his extensive travels, one of which was Belmare. As Brahe describes, Belmare possessed a similar ability to speak as well as *see* things into phenomenological presence: "But I took note of his eyes.... What those eyes could see didn't need to be there [*hätte nichts dasein müssen*], it was already within them. You've heard of Venice? Good. I tell you, those eyes—they'd have seen and brought Venice here [*Venedig hereingesehen*], right into this room, here as surely [*daß es da gewesen wäre*] as this desk is here" (*MLB* 87). Belmare's storytelling could also materialize absent smells: "I sat in the corner once and listened to him talking [*erzählte*] to my father about Persia, and sometimes I think my hands still smell of it" (*MLB* 87). The stories that Belmare told, Brahe goes onto describe, cannot be adequately captured in any books:

> 'Books have nothing in them [*Die Bücher sind leer*],' shouted the Count, with a furious gesture toward the walls, 'blood, that's what matters, blood's what you need to be able to read [*da muß man drin lesen können*]. This fellow Belmare, he had marvellous stories [*wunderliche Geschichten*] in his blood, and incredible illustrations; he could open [*aufschlagen*] the book of his blood wherever he wanted and there was always a depiction of something; there wasn't a blank page in there [*keine Seite in seinem Blut war überschlagen worden*]. And when he shut himself away betweentimes and browsed by himself [*allein drin blätterte*], he'd come to the bits about making gold from lead, and about precious stones, and about colours.' (*MLB* 87–88)

Any "books" that may have contained Belmare's stories are "empty" (*leer*), their contents meaningless. The power of Belmare's narration to make things present is rooted in his body: his eyes, his voice, the blood that circulates through him. Peculiarly, however, Belmare's body and blood are figured in bookish terms: like in an illustrated book or illuminated manuscript, the "marvellous stories" (*wunderliche Geschichten*) and "incredible illustrations" (*merkwürdige Abbildungen*) contained in Belmare's blood are composed of "pages" (*Seiten*) that could be "leafed" through (*blätterte*). The opening of a book is figured as the opening of the body, creating a wound (*Wund*) from which wondrous (*wunderliche*) stories flow.

Rilke revised this passage dramatically in the Bernese Notebook. A first version, spanning three pages and crossed out entirely with sweeping, crisscrossing lines (*BT* 34–36), was followed by a second version, significantly reworked and expanded by nearly two pages of text (*BT* 36–40).

In the first version, Rilke wrote,

> . . . Nothing is in the books"
> the count cried with a furious ges=
> ture toward the walls, "one has it
> or one doesn't have it. Now, and he had it"
> . . .
>
> . . . In den Büchern ist nichts"
> schrie der Graf mit einer wüthenden Ge=
> bärde nach den Wänden hin, "man hat es
> oder man hat es nicht. Nun, und er hatte es." (*BT* 35)

In revising, Rilke replaced the formulation "Nothing is in the books" (*In den Büchern ist nichts*) with "the books are empty" (*Die Bücher sind leer*) and the clarification "one has it / or one doesn't have it" (*man hat es / oder man hat es nicht*) with the description of "reading" Belmare's blood (*BT* 36–37). Rilke also adds further description of Belmare and his stories—nearly a page and a half worth—before the text resumes where it had broken off in the first version: "Already for a while the elder one wasn't addressing Abelone anymore, whom he had forgotten [*Seit einer Weile schon redete der Alte nichtmehr / auf Abelone ein, die er vergessen hatte*]" (*BT* 36, 38). In this revision, the narration of "opening" Belmare's blood to reveal "wondrous stories" *in* the text corresponds to the "opening" *of* the text and additional description of these stories.

The image of opening and reading evokes Rilke's process of gathering source material for the text, including consulting *books*—the Ersch-Gruber encyclopedia in this case.[37] Although from the manuscript alone we cannot determine when and how exactly Rilke consulted the encyclopedia, the nature of Rilke's revision to the

---

37. Röse, "Germain (Saint-)," 167.

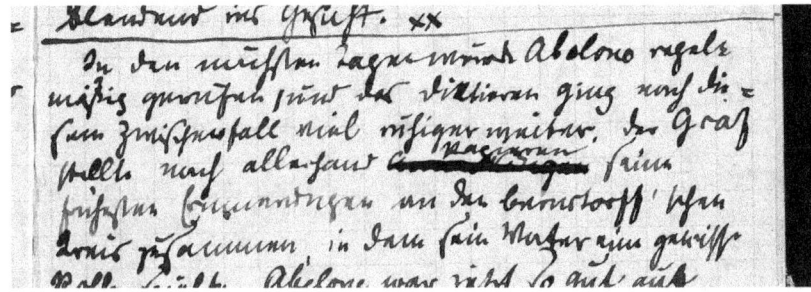

Figure 3.3. Rainer Maria Rilke, *Die Aufzeichnungen des Malte Laurids Brigge*, 2. Teil, 39. SLA-RMR-Ms_D_2. Schweizerisches Literaturarchiv, Bern.

passage—namely, an extensive addition consisting of numerous historical details—suggests that Rilke may have returned to the encyclopedia while drafting the passage, "opened" (*aufschlagen*) to the entry on Saint-Germain, and gathered the numerous stories recorded there to incorporate into the text. A similar process of textual gathering is represented in the text: "The count pieced together his earliest memories of the Bernstoff Circle from all kinds of papers [*Der Graf stellte nach allerhand Papieren seine frühesten Erinnerungen an den Bernstorff'schen Kreis zusammen*]"[38] (*BT* 39; figure 3.3). The gathering of notes underscores the *textual* basis of Brahe's storytelling: the memory is aided by written notes—in other words, *Aufzeichnungen* (records).

The mode of storytelling embodied by Brahe and Belmare is defined by its capacity to make things present: in their presence, their speech renders its contents visually, materially perceptible to the listener. But while questioning the ability of written text to similarly make present, the figuration of these scenes of oration is strangely haunted by the materiality of writing. This reflection comes to a head in the final passage of this entry, in which Abelone "receives"

---

38. In the *Berner Taschenbuch*, this description was added in the second version of the passage, *after* Rilke "opened" the text to insert additional material. In the manuscript, "Anmerkungen" is canceled and replaced by "Papieren," which emphasizes their material instantiation (*BT* 39).

the stigmata—a unique kind of image that is at once iconic, indexical, and symbolic.

> 'Tomorrow we'll write about Julie Reventlow,' he said, savouring every word; 'she was a saint.'
> Abelone must have looked at him disbelievingly. . . .
> He took Abelone's hands and opened them out [*schlug sie auf*] like a book.
> 'She had the stigmata,' he said, 'here, and here.' And he tapped her two palms quickly but firmly with his cold finger [*Und er tippte mit seinem kalten Finger hart und kurz in ihre beiden Handflächen*].
> Abelone didn't know the word 'stigmata.' It'll become clear, she thought; she was genuinely impatient to hear about the saint that her father had known [*noch gesehen hatte*]. But she wasn't summoned again after that, not the next day and not thereafter either—.
> 'Your family often talked about Countess Reventlow after that,' Abelone concluded curtly when I asked her to tell me more. She looked tired; she maintained also that she had forgotten the greater part of it. 'But I can still sometimes feel those spots [*Stellen*] in my palms,' she smiled, and couldn't help but look almost inquisitorially into her empty hands. (*MLB* 89)

Brahe narrates the stigmatization of Julie Reventlow (1763–1816), a member the Bernstorff circle.[39] When Abelone does not know the expression "stigmata," Brahe does not explain the concept verbally, but instead communicates it as a sensory image: "Und er tippte mit dem kalten Finger hart und kurz in ihre beiden Handflächen." Brahe's fingers figure the nails of the Passion, the verb "tippen" (tap or type) evoking Thomas the Apostle's reference to the mark or print—*typos* in Greek, *figura* in Latin—of the nails in Christ's hands: "Except I shall see in his hands the print of the nails [τον τυπον των ηλων; *figuram clavorum*], and put my finger into the place of the nails, and thrust my hand into his side, I will not believe."[40] Simultaneously, Brahe's fingers figure those of God, which, as recounted in Saint

---

39. Gräfin Frederike Juliane Reventlow (1763–1816); see *KA* 3:972–73.

40. John 20:25, *The Bible: Authorized King James Version*, ed. Robert P. Carroll and Stephen Prickett (Oxford: Oxford University Press, 2008), Oxford Scholarly Editions Online, https://www.oxfordscholarlyeditions.com/display/10.1093/actrade/9780199535941.book.1/actrade-9780199535941-div3-1210.

Bonaventure's *Legenda Maior*, transformed Saint Francis into an image of Christ by inscribing the nail marks into Francis's flesh:[41] a scene of trans-figuration through type (*typos*)-writing.

Inscribed with the marks of the stigmata, Abelone, transcriber of Brahe's speech, is herself transformed into a transcript: an *Abbild* (image) of an *Urbild* (archetype), an *Abschrift* (copy) of an *Urschrift* (original). The signifiers inscribed into her body are not symbolic, but instead indexical; the referent is not represented hermeneutically, but instead is physically reincarnated. It persists as a sense memory.[42] As a transcript, Abelone is manu-script and type-script at once. At the same time, her hands are figured as a book: Brahe "opened them out [*schlug sie auf*] like a book." The use of the verb *aufschlagen*—Rilke changed it from "öffnen" (to open), which he used in the earlier version of the passage—again recalls the *Aufschlagen* of Belmare's body to reveal stories in his blood.

The scene of Brahe's and Abelone's writing, culminating in the image of stigmatization, thus evokes a host of media technologies and modes of inscription and reception: oral narration, handwriting, typing, and print. Though Abelone presumably writes by hand, as the activity of crossing out would suggest, the relationship of Abelone and Brahe figures that of (female) typist and (male) dictator, an increasingly common configuration in the era of the typewriter.[43] But it also *prefigures* Rilke's dictation of the "prose book" to Kippenberg's secretary. In the final image, Abelone becomes like a textual surface, inscribed upon by the Count, the emblem of oral storytelling, who simultaneously appears as a typist. In transcribing, Abelone is also a recipient of the Count's narration, assuming the role of a reader. In this way, the scene of Abelone's "stigmatization" evokes

---

41. Bonaventure, "The Major Legend of Saint Francis," in *Francis of Assisi: Early Documents*, ed. J. A. Armstrong, Wayne Hellmann, and William J. Short (New York: New City Press, 1999), 13:634.

42. Compare Bernhard Teuber, "Sichtbare Wundmale und unsichtbare Durchbohrung: Die leibhafte Nachfolge Christi als Paradigma des anhermeneutischen Schreibens," in *Stigmata: Poetiken der Körperinschrift*, ed. Bettine Menke and Barbara Vinken (Munich: Fink, 2004), 155–79.

43. Friedrich Kittler, *Gramophone, Film, Typewriter*, trans. Geoffrey Winthrop-Young and Michael Wutz (Stanford, CA: Stanford University Press, 1999), 183–98.

the Deleuzian/Lyotardian concept of Figure: a form conveyed directly to the senses, non-hermeneutically. As a complex mesh of media-technological figurations, which simultaneously evokes the various mediatic processes at work in the generation of *The Notebooks*, this scene exemplifies the Rilkean notion of Figure as it is more typically understood (for instance, by Beda Allemann): a gathering of elements into an image that does not resolve into a clear, neat metaphor, instead opening a space for the play of signification.

But what happens when we metaphorically "open" the surface of the text and allow for its material production to come into play? We begin to sense the degree to which Malte's process of learning to write is entangled within Rilke's material struggles to write. As I explore in more depth in the following sections, the figuration of Rilke's manuscript production in the text operates not only in the semantic/representational dimensions, but also in the affective, corporeal dimensions of reading, "piercing" the reader over and over. Thus, whereas the constellation has been seen as Rilkean "figure of figurality" more generally,[44] the stigmata—at once a material trace and a symbol, generated through a process of transfiguration—is the figure of Rilke's embodied figuration par excellence.

"Please, a narrator, a narrator"

Though much time has passed since Abelone experienced Count Brahe's storytelling for herself, she still sometimes "feels" the marks of the Count's fingers in her palms. In another key passage of the novel, Malte reports somethings similar: lingering *impressions* from a story he encountered as a child—not one told to him orally, but one he *read* in a book. In attempting to retell this story, Malte's crisis of narration reaches a climax.

It was not only the story that impressed so powerfully upon Malte, but also the scene of reading, the material book itself in which he encountered it. The fifty-fourth entry begins: "Last night I thought again of the little green book that as a boy I must once have had in my possession" (*MLB* 107). Before Malte even gets to the story—

---

44. Eldridge, "Rilke's *Sonnets*," 75.

namely, the death of the "false Tsar" Grischa Otrepow—Malte describes in lengthy detail the significance of book's material form, which was a crucial part of the experience:

> It was permeated by connections, down to the very core, even to look at from its exterior. The green of the binding meant something, and you could see at once that its interior would be just the way it actually was. As if by arrangement, first the smooth, brilliant white watered endpaper, then the title-page, which was regarded as mysterious. There might have been pictures inside, or so it looked; but there weren't any, and it was almost against your will that you found yourself obliged to admit that even this was just as it should be. It made amends somehow to find the slim ribbon [*Leseband*] marking a particular place, which, fragile and a little askew, poignantly confident of still being pink, had been lying between the very same pages since heaven knows when. Perhaps it had never been used and the bookbinder had tucked it in there, quickly and efficiently, without looking properly where it went. But it's quite possible that it wasn't there by chance. It could be that someone had stopped reading just there, never to begin again; that fate knocked on his door at that moment to give him something to do so that he ended up far away from any books, which after all are not life. It wasn't possible to tell whether more of the book had been read. It might also be quite simply that the book was to be opened at this point [*diese Stelle aufzuschlagen*] time and again. (*MLB* 107–8)

Before Malte arrives at the stories the book contains, he describes the material scene of reading. The book was "permeated with connections [*voller Bezug*]," Malte writes; even from the outside, its visual, material form seemed meaningful. Malte describes a harmonious correspondence between the exterior and interior of the book—the green binding somehow anticipating the smooth, white endpapers and the title page[45]—and notes that, though its form would suggest an illustrated book, the lack of illustrations is simultaneously strangely fitting. The fragile, faded bookmark incites Malte to imagine the book's journey through the hands of its makers and readers. Perhaps it was never read, the bookmark remaining where the binder randomly placed it between two pages. Or perhaps the bookmark

---

45. The binding of the first edition of *The Notebooks* was also green, and Rilke, like Malte, seems to have attached particular significance to this green binding. See Rilke to Kippenberg, June 9, 1910, in *Briefwechsel mit Anton Kippenberg*, 216.

indexed another reader's activity, marking the cessation of reading, or a passage of particular significance to which its previous owner would open (*aufschlagen*) again and again.

Malte's recollection of this experience begins with the body of the book, its material form, its physical handling by makers and readers, just like Malte's narration of Grischa's death begins with Grischa's body—more specifically, his corpse—which impressed upon Malte most profoundly: "Heaven knows whether it made any impression on me at the time. But now, after so many years, I remember [*entsinne ich mich*] the description of how the corpse of the false Tsar was tossed into the crowd and lay there for three days, torn to ribbons [*zerfetzt*] and peppered with stab-wounds [*zerstochen*], a mask on his face. There is obviously no prospect of ever having that little book in my hands again. But that section [*Stelle*] must have been remarkable" (*MLB* 108). Here Malte describes the act of remembering itself in bodily terms: in contrast to the more common term for remembering, *sich erinnern*, the verb *sich entsinnen* contains the root *Sinn*, which like the English "sense" denotes both phenomenological sensory perception and meaning. What Malte remembers most vividly was the desecrated body of the "false Tsar." Just like certain details of her "stigmatization" lingered in Abelone's memory, the description of Grischa's corpse, lying exposed for three days, leaves a deep impression (*Eindruck*) on Malte. Just like the stigmata is transformed into a *partial* image of Christ, pierced only in specific spots—"But I can still sometimes feel those spots [*Stellen*]," Abelone reports (*MLB* 89)—only specific points in the story pierced Malte: "that section [*Stelle*] must have been remarkable."

Malte's memory of this story is bound up in his memory of its material instantiation, "the little green book." But this book, the text underlying Malte's rendition of the story, no longer remains. Emphasizing the bodily encounter with the handheld object, Malte writes: "There is obviously no prospect of ever having that little book in my hands again [*daß mir das kleine Buch je wieder in die Hände kommt*]." There is, in fact, another text that lies behind *Rilke's* narration of this story—not a "little green book" but instead, again, the Ersch and Gruber encyclopedia. Malte's written retelling of the story, filtered through his fragmented memory, is difficult to follow, indeed incoherent.[46] Comparing this encyclopedia text with Malte's retelling of the story highlights key features of Malte's narration.

In the entry "Dmitri, Dimitrij (Demetrier), die falschen" from the Ersch-Gruber encyclopedia, one can learn the following story. After the death of Ivan IV, the Terrible (1530–84), numerous imposters assumed the identity of his heir, Dmitriy Ivanovich—who had died mysteriously in 1591, at the age of nine—and attempted to claim the throne. The first of these was "the adventurer Jakob Otrepiew," who had taken the name "Griska (Gregor)" when he entered a monastic order at the age of fourteen.[47] For protection and political gain, Dimitry's mother, Marie Nagoi, claimed that Grischa was her son; he was subsequently crowned tsar and reigned for nearly a year (1605–6). Grischa married the Polish noblewoman Marina Mniszech, who became tsarina; once Grischa's false identity was revealed, Marina accepted a second "pseudo-Dimitri" as her husband. Prince Vasily Shuisky, who had originally investigated the real Dimitry's death, conspired against Grischa and led a mob to storm the castle. Grischa attempted to escape by jumping out of the window, and broke his leg. The *streltsy* (guard units), however, still recognized Grischa as the real tsar and continued to defended him. When Marie Nagoi finally revealed Grischa's true identity, he was

---

46. See Judith Ryan, "'Hypothetisches Erzählen': Zur Funktion von Phantasie und Einbildung in Rilkes 'Malte Laurids Brigge,'" in Engelhardt, *Materialien zu Rainer Maria Rilke*, 265. Confusion, Rilke later described, was in fact a desired effect: in a 1925 letter to Polish translator Witold Hulewicz, Rilke specified that the numerous unclear references should *not* be elucidated for the reader: "Im 'Malte' kann nicht davon die Rede sein, die vielfältigen Evokationen zu präzisieren und zu verselbstständigen. Der Leser kommuniziere nicht mit ihrer geschichtlichen oder imaginären Realität, sondern durch sie, mit Maltes Erlebnis.... Die Verbindung beruht in dem Umstande, daß die gerade Heraufbeschworenen dieselbe Schwingungszahl der Lebensintensität aufweisen, die eben in Maltes Wesen vibrieren.... Darum könnte es nur beirrlich werden, die nur angedeuteten Figuren namentlicher herauszustellen". Rilke to Witold Hulewicz, November 10, 1925, in Rilke, *Briefe in zwei Bänden*, vol. 2: *1919–1926*, ed. Horst Nalewski (Frankfurt am Main: Insel, 1991), 372–74.

47. J. C. Petri, "Dmitri, Dimitrij (Demetrier), die falschen," in *Allgemeine Encyklopädie der Wissenschaften und Künste*, pt. 26: Dir-Dominium Mundi, Erste Sektion A–G, 209.

executed by shooting and his mutilated body displayed in the marketplace for three days before being burned.[48]

Malte's retelling of the story is quite different. Malte name-drops without introducing the characters, leaves out crucial plot details, and offers no historical frame of reference. The comparison to Rilke's actual source text shows that, like for the other historical figures and events Malte narrates in his entries, Rilke's retelling of Grischa's death is not an attempt to accurately represent the factual details of the historical record, but instead an attempt to capture that which *affected* him most profoundly from the story as he encountered it—itself a figuration of historical events, as *Urtext*—in the little green book.

After identifying the story to be retold (Grischa's death) and the detail that struck him most vividly (the description of the corpse), Malte's narration proceeds as follows:

> I would also like to look up [*nachzulesen*] what happened during his encounter with his mother. He may have felt extremely secure, since he had her come to Moscow; I'm even convinced that at that point he believed so strongly in himself that he believed he was actually sending for his mother. And this Marie Nagaia [Naogi], who came from her miserable convent in a few days' journey, stood to gain everything if she went along with him. Perhaps his insecurity in fact began just at the point when she recognized him. I am not disinclined to believe that the power of his transformation may have resided in the fact of no longer being anybody's son.
>
> †(That, after all, is the power wielded by all young people who have left home).
>
> The people that wished him for themselves, without imagining any particular individual, only added to the freedom and boundlessness of the possibilities open to him [*machte ihn nur noch freier und unbegrenzter in seinen Möglichkeiten*]. But the declaration by his mother, even though it was a deliberate deception, yet had the capacity to diminish him; it lifted him out of the fullness of his invention; it restricted him to being a weary imitator; it reduced him to the level of the one person that he was not; it made him into an imposter. And now this Marina Mniszech came along, undoing him in a gentler fashion, denying him in her own way, as it later transpired, by believing not in him but in everyone. I can't of course guarantee how far all of this featured in that story. This, though, seems like something that ought to have been told.
>
> † Written in the margin of the manuscript. (*MLB 108*)

---

48. Petri, "Dmitri," 209–11.

Unable to return to the little green book, Malte's recollection of the facts spills into speculation about the character's internal experience ("He may have felt extremely secure," "I'm even convinced that . . . ," and so on). Malte ponders over things he cannot remember and wishes he could look up ("I would have also liked to look up"), over details that may not have been but "ought to have been told [*wäre zu erzählen gewesen*]." Filtered through his present experience, Malte's retelling is highly interpretative: like Malte, who deserted his family heritage to travel to Paris, Grischa shed his former identity to assume a new one, a liberating act that opened limitless possibilities to be anything. The people's belief in him bolstered this sense of boundlessness; it was diminished, in turn, by the identity-confirming and identity-denying acts of Marie Nagoi and Marina Mniszech.

In attempting to narrate the final, critical moments of Grischa's life, Malte confronts the limits of his narratorial ability. The fact that he can no longer consult the little green book is not the challenge: instead, it is the seeming impossibility of grasping and figuring in writing everything that happens in the final moments of Grischa's life, and all that he experiences in that instant. Confronted with his own limits, Malte conceives of a hypothetical narrator who could accomplish the task:

> One could conceive of a modern storyteller [*Es wäre jetzt ein Erzähler denkbar*], one who took great care [*Sorgfalt*] with last moments [*Augenblicke*]. . . . A good deal happens during them: how he leaped over to the window just as he was waking from the deepest sleep and out of the window into the courtyard between the guards. He can't get up on his own; they have to help him. His foot is probably broken. Supported by two of the men, he feels that they believe in him. He looks round: the others believe in him, too. They almost pity him, these enormous streltsy, things must have changed a good deal: they knew Ivan Grosnii in all his substantive reality, and they believe in him. He might have wished to disabuse them, but if he'd opened his mouth he would simply have screamed. The pain in his foot is excruciating, and at this moment he thinks so little of himself that all he knows is pain. And then there is no time. (*MLB* 109)

So much happens in these final moments, Malte indicates, that it seems impossible to grasp it all. He strings together events in list-like fashion, attempting to imagine what Grischa and the others must have felt. Hypothetical projection, marked by modal adverbs and the subjunctive mood (for instance, "His foot is probably broken.... He might have wished to disabuse them"), gives way to the present tense indicative mood. The narration continues with syntactically short clauses generating a palpable sense of immediacy and suspense: "It will soon be over. But then his guards close ranks. They won't hand him over. And a miracle occurs. The faith of these old men spreads amongst the others, suddenly no one wants to step forward. Shuisky, standing right in front of him, calls in desperation up to a window. He doesn't look round. He knows who is standing there; he knows that silence will fall, silence abruptly and without transition. Now the voice will come that he knows from before; the high, phoney voice overtaxing itself. And then he hears the Tsaritsa Mother repudiating him" (*MLB* 109).[49] Malte's struggle to render these moments culminates in a desperate plea for a narrator who could somehow accomplish the task:

> Until now the story has had its own momentum, but now, please, a narrator, a narrator [*Erzähler*]: for out of the few lines that remain there must proceed a force that will transcend any possible dissent. Whether it is said or not, we must swear that between voice and pistol-shot, infinitely compressed [*unendlich zusammengedrängt*], there was within him still sufficient will and power to be everything [*Wille und Macht, alles zu sein*]. Otherwise we won't understand how brilliantly consistent it is of them to pierce his nightgown and stab away at him to see if they'll strike the hardness of a real person. And that in death, for three whole days, he still wore the mask that he had almost relinquished. (MLB 190–110)

The difficulty Malte experiences is twofold. So much happens in the final moments (*Augenblicke,* literally glances or blinks of the eye) of Grischa's life, "infinitely compressed," that it seems impossible to capture it all. But what is compressed into these moments is not simply a series of events; rather, it is Grischa's own infinitude, a "will and power to be everything." To adequately capture this would require figuring it in such a way that could generate an enormous amount of "force," strong enough to defy all resistance. Malte

---

49. Compare Petri, "Dmitri," 210–11.

appears to apply a great deal of "care" in attempting to narrate this moment (*Augenblick*), unfolding temporally in language, onto the space of the page. But this is where the attempt fails, for it simultaneously betrays the unique spatiotemporality of the instant, unraveling its infinitely tight weave.

Malte's crisis of narration as represented in *The Notebooks* parallels Rilke's own struggle to construct this passage in the Bernese Notebook. Beginning with the phrase "But also beyond this [*Aber auch abgesehen davon*]" (*BT* 87), Rilke's writing proceeds with little interruption, until he writes, "Until this moment the story tells itself [*Bis hierher geht die Sache von selbst*]" (*BT* 88; figure 3.4). A horizontal line divides the page. Rilke then drafted a first version of Malte's plea for a narrator, which displays numerous strikethroughs and is canceled entirely with a large X; the text reads as follows:

> Until this moment the story tells itself // X But now: a narrator, please, a^whole narrator, a poet almost: because from these lines, which are still^where possible possible_remain are, must a pure current emanate, which convinces. One must swear on it, without it actually dass man es eigentlich being stated a power pour out, which which allows_knows no contradiction . . .
>
> Bis hierher geht die Sache von selbst // X Aber nun: Ein Erzähler, bitte, einen^ganzen Erzähler, ein Dichter beihnah: Denn von den paar Zeilen, die jetzt noch^womöglich _bleiben möglich sind, muss reiner Strom ausgehen, der überzeugt. Man muss darauf schwören, ohne dass man es eigentlich gesagt bekommt Gewalt ausgehen, die keinen Widerspruch zulässt_kennt (*BT* 88)

The distress that Malte experiences is reflected iconically in the visual appearance and the materiality of the manuscript page itself. Here, Malte pleads not simply for a narrator, but for "a whole narrator" [*einen ganzen Erzähler*]—a narrator who could overcome the

in Wunder geschieht. Der Glaube die der alten Männer flaut sich fort. Auf einmal will niemand mehr vor. ~~Er läuft~~ ~~vor ihm~~ ~~weist~~ noch einem Fenster hinauf. Er sieht sich nicht um; er muß nur dort sein. Er begreift daß er still wird, ganz ohne Übergang still. Jetzt wird ihm Drinnen kommen, die er vor damals zur Kunst; diese sehr falsche Klemme, die sich überanstrengt. Und ~~da~~ sieht er die Zaim nicht, die ihr nachläuft. ~~Wie jeder geht sie dach von selbst über ihn:~~ ~~ein Schäffer, bitte, einen Schäfler, einen~~ ~~ein Lämmel. Denn von der ganzen Villen,~~ ~~die jetzt noch möglich sind, muß bleiben~~ ~~einer aufgehen, der überzeugt. Man muß~~ ~~darauf schwören, oder daß was er eigentlich~~ ~~gehabt hat, einen Gewalt aufgehen, die~~ ~~keinen Widerspruch zuläßt.~~ Gleichviel ob man ab gesagt bekommt; ~~aber~~ man muß darauf schwören, daß zwischen dieser Absage und dem Pistolenschuß in der ~~einer~~ halben Sekunde, unendlich zusammen- gepreßt, wieder Willen und ~~Begierde~~ Glanz in ihm war, alles zu sein. Die verlaß man nicht wie glänzend konsequent es ist, daß sie sein Neuekleid durchbohrt ~~und~~ in ihm herumstecken, ob sie auf der ~~Haare~~ einer Feder stehen würden. Und daß

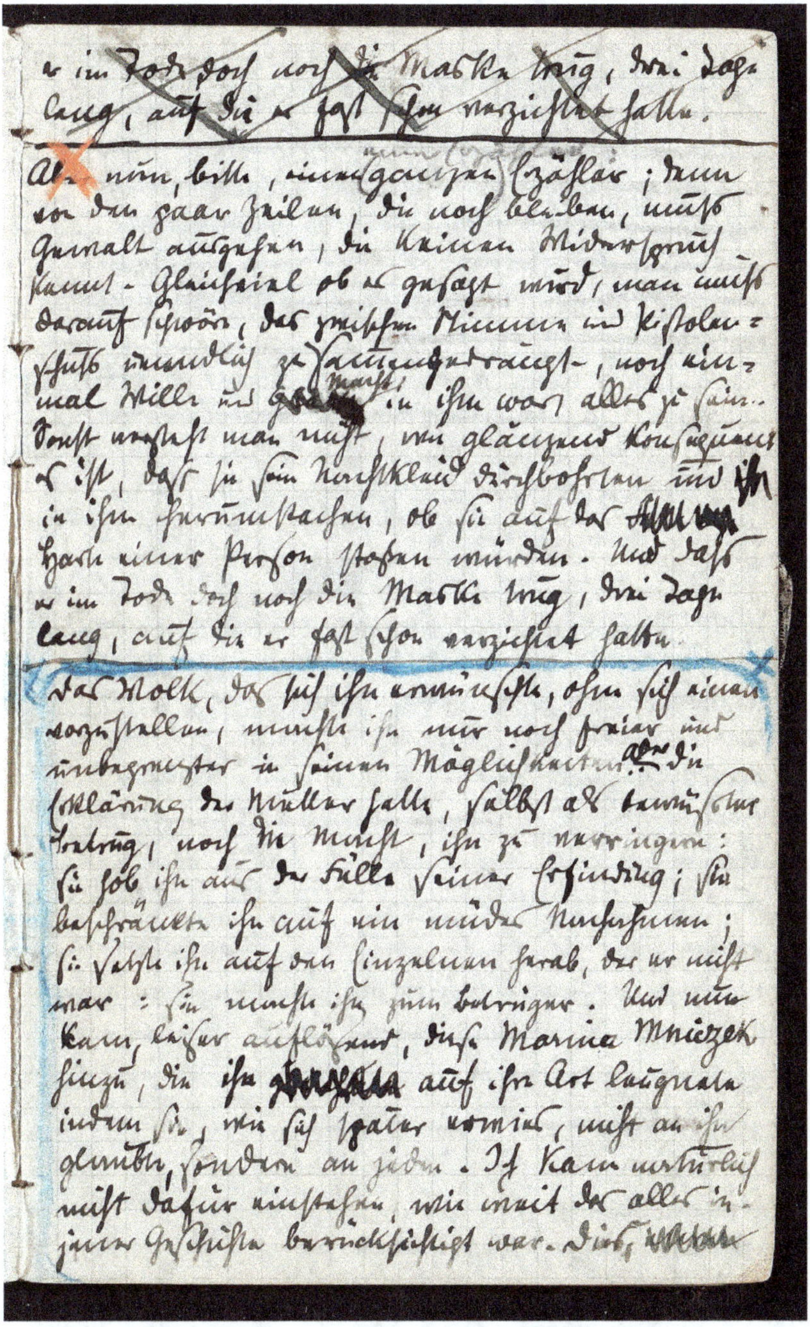

er im Tode doch noch die Maske trug, drei Tage
lang, auf die er fast schon verzichtet hatte.

Aber nun, bitte, einen ganzen Erzähler; denn
von den paar Zeilen, die noch bleiben, muß
Gewalt ausgehen, die keinen Widerspruch
kennt. Gleichviel ob es gesagt wird, man muß
darauf schwören, daß zwischen Stimme und Pistolenschuß unendlich zusammengedrängt, noch ein-
mal Wille und [illegible] Macht in ihm war alles zu sein.
Sonst versteht man nicht, wie glänzend konsequent
es ist, daß sie sein Nachtkleid durchbohrten und [illegible]
in ihm herumstachen, ob sie auf das [illegible]
Harte einer Person stoßen würden. Und daß
er im Tode doch noch die Maske trug, drei Tage
lang, auf die er fast schon verzichtet hatte.

Das Volk, das sich ihn wünschte, ohne sich einen
vorzustellen, machte ihn nur noch freier und
unbegrenzter in seinen Möglichkeiten. Aber die
Erklärung der Mutter hatte, selbst als bewußter
Betrug, noch die Macht, ihn zu verringern:
sie hob ihn aus der Fülle seiner Erfindung; sie
beschränkte ihn auf ein müdes Nachahmen;
sie setzte ihn auf den Einzelnen herab, der er nicht
war: sie machte ihn zum Betrüger. Und nun
kam, leiser auflösend, diese Marina Mniczek
hinzu, die ihn [illegible] auf ihre Art leugnete
indem sie, wie sich später erwies, nicht an ihn
glaubte, sondern an jeden. Ich kann natürlich
nicht dafür einstehen, wie weit das alles in
jener Geschichte berücksichtigt war. Dies, [illegible]

Figure 3.4. Rainer Maria Rilke, *Die Aufzeichnungen des Malte Laurids Brigge*, 2. Teil, 88–89. SLA-RMR-Ms_D_2. Schweizerisches Literaturarchiv, Bern.

fragmentation of self and world and grasp the fullness of these moments, a narrator with the the powers of a poet, "a poet almost [*einen Dichter beinah*]." The verb *dichten* signifies not only the composition of poetry, but also the act of tightening or tying together. A narrator thus conceived would be able to compact everything that happens in those final half-seconds ("in den / ~~paar~~ halben Sekunden, unendlich zusammen= / gepresst") into the space of a mere few lines of text ("den paar Zeilen"). A "pure stream [*reiner Strom*]" must emanate from these lines, a stream that draws readers into its current, affecting them so powerfully as to "convince" (*überzeugen*) them, as if they were "witnesses" (*Zeugen*) themselves, of Grischa's boundlessness in this moment. The word *Strom* also conjures a liquid that could be "poured" into these few lines, completely filling the space around the words. Rilke then strikes through the text, replacing "pure stream emanate, which convinces" with "force emanate, which ~~allows~~ knows no opposition [*Gewalt ausgehen, der keinen Widerspruch ~~zulässt~~ kennt*]." That is, a force must emanate from these lines, so powerful as to defy any opposition or contradiction.

On the following page, Rilke composed a revised version of this passage (*BT* 89, fig. 3.4). The addition "almost a poet [*einen Dichter beinah*]" has disappeared, but the adjective "whole [*ganz*]" remains ("einen ganzen Erzähler"). In a later correction, Rilke bracketed "ganzen" and added "einen Erzälher," again interlinearly. The formulation "Gewalt ausgehen, der keinen Widerspruch kennt"—a force that knows no opposition—was likely modified during the dictation or the proofs stage, such that the printed formulation appears as follows: "Gewalt ausgehen über jeden Widerspruch hinaus," a force that *transcends* all opposition.

X But now, please, a (whole)[a] [narrator] narrator; because
from these couple lines, which are still here, must
a force emanate

einen Erzähler
X Aber nun, bitte, einen (ganzen) Erzähler; denn
von den paar Zeilen, die noch bleiben, muss
Gewalt ausgehen, die keinen Widerspruch (*BT* 89)

The mode of narration Malte envisions is characterized above all by its affectivity, a non-hermeneutic "force" or "pure stream." This ideal narration is echoed in Malte's premonition of "the age of the other interpretation" in the eighteenth entry, an alternative hermeneutic order in which meaning (*Sinn*) will dissolve into pure materiality, raining down like water: "there shall not be left one word upon another [*kein Wort auf dem anderen bleiben*], and every meaning will dissolve like clouds and descend like rain" (*MLB* 31). In this new era, words will no longer lie "upon" one another; evoking the visual arrangement of lines in a text, one atop the other, the image conjures more specifically the logic of writing in the manuscript, where words can be added in the interlinear space, above other words, or even written on top of one another: an act of cancellation by materially transforming one word into another.

Malte cannot yet reach this new hermeneutic order, however, because he is "broken": "Only one step more and my profound wretchedness would turn into bliss. But I cannot take this step . . . because I am broken [*zerbrochen*]" (*MLB* 31). Malte is not "einen ganzen Erzähler": all that he can produce are written sketches, *Aufzeichnungen*, broken fragments that do not form a whole. This too is reflected in the Bernese Notebook: frequently Rilke would draft and redraft sections of text, canceling previous versions. To be able to navigate through the ruins of canceled, discarded text, Rilke would mark the end of one paragraph and the beginning of the next with colored pencil, a form of textual trailblazing (figure 3.5). On pages 88–89 of the Bernese Notebook (figure 3.4), red Xs connect the end of one passage with the beginning of the next. A passage on page 89 is outlined in blue pencil, indicating that it should appear four pages earlier, at a spot marked with blue Xs.

This passage, in which Malte's crisis of narration reaches its climax, is one of the most heavily edited in the entire manuscript. Rilke's material struggle to compose the passage becomes entangled within Malte's represented struggle to narrate—and not only for this passage, but throughout the work. Like the "little green book" of Malte's childhood, intimately connected in Malte's memory to the story of Grischa's death, the manuscripts of *The Notebooks* continue to haunt the printed text. In fact, the manuscript on which

bruch ja minder in die Hände kommt. Aber
diese Stelle müsste nachträglich gewesen
sein. Ich fälle auch Luffs, wiegelegen, wie
die Begegnung mit der Mutter neulich.
so mochte sich sehr gequält gefühlt haben, da er sie nach
Moskau kommen ließ; ich bin sogar über-
zeugt, daß er zu jener Zeit so stark an sich
glaubte, daß er in der That seine Mutter zu
kennen meinte. Und diese Marie Nagoi,
die in schnellen Tagreisen aus ihrem dürftigen
Kloster kam, gewann ja auch alles, wenn sie
zustimmte. Aber vielleicht began Ob aber
seine Unsicherheit nicht gerade damit begann,
daß sie ihn anerkannte? Ich bin nicht abgeneigt
zu glauben, die Kraft seiner Neuanwendung fällt
darin bemerkt, keiner einander Sohn mehr
zu sein. Das ist schließlich die Kraft aller
jüngeren Leute, die fortgegangen sind.)

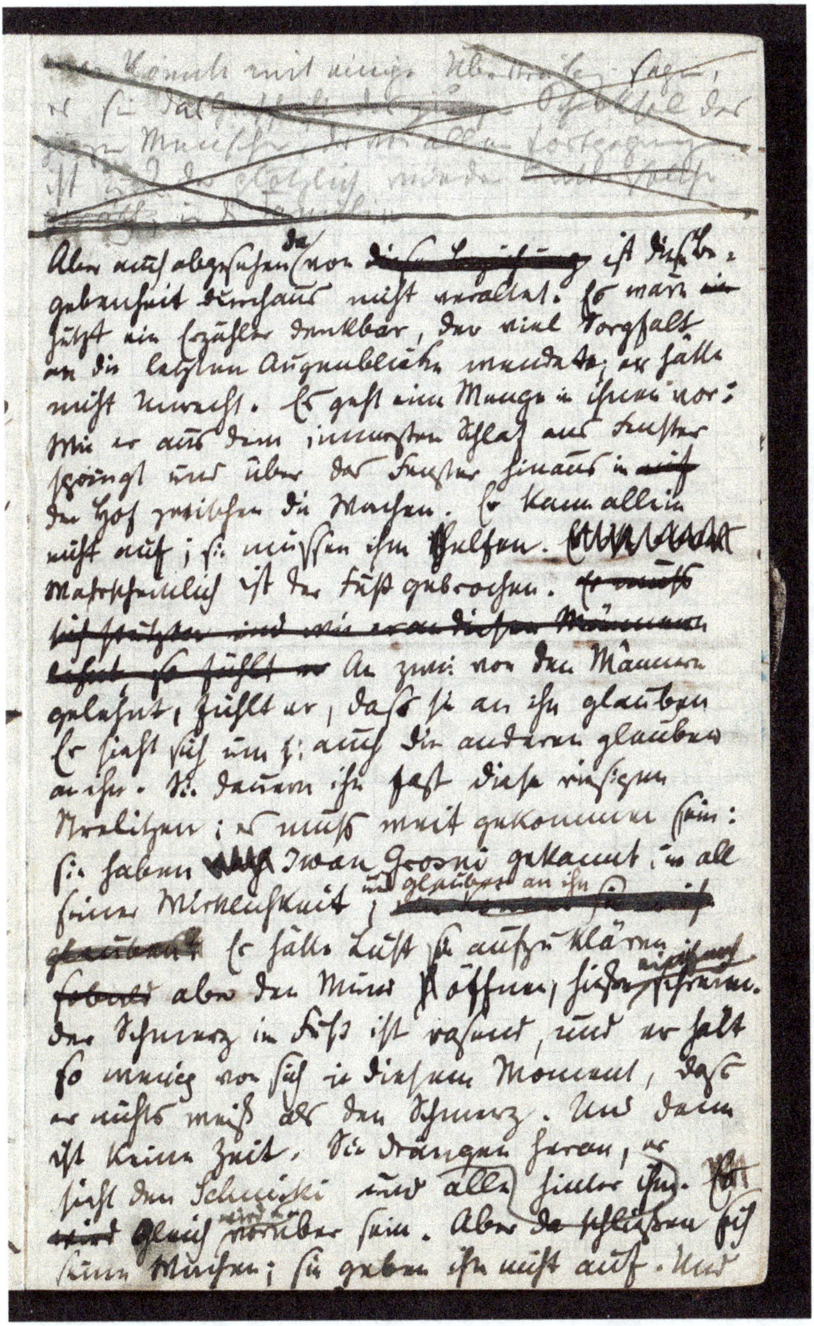

Figure 3.5. Rainer Maria Rilke, *Die Aufzeichnungen des Malte Laurids Brigge*, 2. Teil, 86–87. SLA-RMR-Ms_D_2. Schweizerisches Literaturarchiv, Bern.

the novel is based is *explicitly* referenced in several strange moments: six passages are bracketed in parentheses and annotated with the footnote "written in the margin of the manuscript [*im Manuskript an den Rand geschrieben*]."[50] One such passage appears in the retelling of Grischa's death; above the horizontal line marked with blue Xs on page 86, Rilke writes: "(That, after all, is the power wielded by all young people who have left home [*Das ist schließlich die Kraft aller jungen Leute, die fortgegangen sind*])" (figure 3.5). Puncturing the printed text, these sporadic references gesture to the activity of a fictional editor, to the printed text as an *Abschrift* of Malte's manuscript sketches. But these footnotes also gesture to the *real* manuscript underlying the printed form of Rilke's *The Notebooks*—its function, like stigmata, puncture marks through which the stigmatic's holiness becomes visible on their body, transformed into an *Abschrift* of an *Urschrift*.

The fact that the manuscript is referenced in the fifty-fourth entry is particularly striking because this section in fact thematizes the relationships between source text and "final" text: the little green book, Malte's fictional source text for *The Notebooks*, and the version he penned in his "manuscript," as referred to in the printed footnotes. In both cases, moreover, the materiality/mediality of these texts is foregrounded: Malte describes the little green book in detail; the footnote reference to the manuscript highlights the *printed* form of the text that derives from it. These texts can be brought into relationship—forming a kind of entangled constellation—with the *actual* texts that are the material record of the works' generation: the Ersch-Gruber encyclopedia, Rilke's primary source text for this entry; Rilke's manuscript of the novel, one part of which is the Bernese Notebook; and the actual printed edition of the novel, which was originally bound in green ("I am thinking in particular of the green paperback"), the same color as Malte's "little green book"; and *two* volumes: a material linkage to manuscript of the novel, contained in two notebooks.

But the explicit footnote annotations are not the only way in which the manuscript appears in the printed text, spilling into the

---

50. MLB 63, 108, 113, 122, 133, 143; KA 3:531, 587, 592, 603, 617, 629.

scene of reading. In the experience of reading, the reader is perpetually pierced by highly affective figures and figurations in the novel. As I will explore in more detail, the materiality and the visuality of the manuscript, incorporated into such figures, is thus not only represented semantically but also *felt,* inscribed into the reader's body in the act of reading. In this way the reader becomes transformed into an *Abschrift* of this *Urschrift,* a material presence that is rendered invisible but nonetheless haunts the printed text like a specter.

Striking

In the thirty-sixth entry, Malte describes a scene at his grandparents' dinner table: Upon discovering a few "blameless" wine stains on the spotless tablecloth, Margarete Brigge became outraged. Chamberlain Brigge was trying to calm her when "something completely unprecedented [*etwas nie Dagewesenes*] and wholly incomprehensible" caused her to "break off midsentence [*mitten im Satze stehen lassen*]" (MLB 71): the Chamberlain poured himself a glass of wine, yet once the red fluid reached the top of the vessel, he continued to pour, allowing the Dionysian liquid to overflow the boundaries of the glass container, spilling all over.

In the process of writing this episode, something also caused Rilke to break off midsentence: he had reached the end of his notebook. Writing did not end, however; it continued into another notebook—the one we now know as the Bernese Notebook—which in fact begins midsentence: "the cook couldn't just be dismissed in consequence [*man die Person daraufhin nicht entlassen könne*" (MLB 71; BT 3). This rupture falls in the middle of Malte's description of another of his grandmother's idiosyncrasies; namely, her refusal to allow illness in the house: "She could not bear anyone in the house to fall ill. Once, when the cook had injured herself and Grandmother saw her with her bandaged hand, she maintained she could smell antiseptic in the whole house and it was difficult to persuade her that the cook couldn't just be dismissed in consequence. She didn't want to be reminded of being ill" (MLB 71). The textual divide between the notebooks falls in the middle of the sentence describing the cook's wounded, bandaged hand. The final word in the previous notebook would have been the conjunction *daß* (that), conjoining the two notebooks like a dismembered body. The first line of the Bernese Notebook is a fragmentary clause, dependent on the first notebook (figure 3.6). Like wine stains on a tablecloth, or flecks of dried blood on skin, these words—ink stains on paper—persist on the edge of a textual wound that is invisibly bandaged in print.

Something else reminded Margarete Brigge of the presence of illness: the smell of iodoform. This odor is encountered at one other instance in *The Notebooks*, on the very first page. After describing what he *sees* ("I have seen: hospitals . . ."), Malte describes what he smells: "The street started to smell from every quarter. It smelled, as far as I could make out, of iodoform, of French fries, of fear" (*MLB* 3, translation modified). The first entry concludes with a child, its forehead disfigured by an "Ausschlag," a rash or eruption, inhaling the sickening air: "And what else? A child left sitting in a pram: it was fat, greenish, and had a distinct rash [*Ausschlag*] on its forehead, which was obviously healing and didn't hurt. The child was asleep, its mouth open, breathing in iodoform, chips, fear" (*MLB* 3).

The Notebooks is filled with representations of diseased, wounded, ruptured bodies. But the opening of the text, the opening (*aufschlagen*) of the book, also constitutes a wound. The opening sentence—"So, this is where people come to live. It seems to me, though, that it's dying that happens here"—represents a rupture of not only Malte's expectations of the metropolis, but also post-Enlightenment narratives of progress and civilization: Paris is a scene, not of life and vitality, but instead of disease and death. This rupture is generated by a *performative* act of cancellation: the prevailing view of life in the modern metropolis ("So, this is where people come to live") is effectively canceled, struck through. Malte thus writes out of the ruins, the debris of a world under erasure. The striking of the old creates an opening for something new to emerge.

Among the most striking of Malte's impressions of Paris are the highly affective depictions of bodies and bodiliness. Representations of fragmented and wounded bodies *in* the text, however, are enmeshed within, symptomatic of, the body *of* the text in the process of its production. Though bandaged and cleaned up in print, there remain scars, wounds that become reopened, allowing the materiality of the manuscript to erupt through the surface of the printed text and spill into the scene of reading.

The Throwaways

Images of infection, decay, and fragmented, wounded bodies pervade Malte's descriptions of Paris, his childhood memories, and his retellings of historical narratives. Most commonly, the fragmentation of the body in *The Notebooks* has been approached from a psychoanalytic framework as symbolizing the fragmentation of the self, an unsuccessful separation of self from world in the mirror phase of ego development, and/or the fragmentary experience of the metropolis.[51] Not merely represented, the base materialism of the disfigured body is also evoked, through highly graphic descriptions that produce bodily, affective responses while reading.

The representational (depictions of bodies) and the affective (readerly responses) constitute two dimensions of Rilke's material poetics in *The Notebooks*. But these dimensions of corporeality are haunted by another: the materiality of the manuscript, the textual *corpus*, in the process of its production. Consider Malte's description of the "Fortgeworfenen," the outcasts, discarded ones, literally "throwaways"—figures of a new social order that Malte begins to perceive: "For it is clear to me that these are outcasts, not merely beggars; no, not beggars at all in fact, it's important to make distinctions. They are scraps, the parings [*Schalen*] of people who have been spat out by fate. Damp with the spittle of destiny, they stick to a wall, a lamp-post, an advertising column, or they trickle slowly

---

51. See especially Eric L. Santner, *On Creaturely Life* (Chicago: University of Chicago Press, 2006); Santner, *Royal Remains*; Andreas Huyssen, "Paris/Childhood: The Fragmented Body in Rilke's *Notebooks of Malte Laurids Brigge*," in *Modernity and the Text*, ed. Andreas Huyssen and David Bathrick (New York: Columbia University Press, 1989, 113–41). See also Linda Haverty Rugg, "A Self at Large in the Hall of Mirrors: Rilke's *Malte Laurids Brigge* as Autobiographical Act," *seminar* 29, no. 1 (1993): 43–54; Patricia Linden, *"Im Manuskript an den Rand geschrieben": Spiegelschrift und Marginalität in Rainer Maria Rilkes* Die Aufzeichnungen des Malte Laurids Brigge (Tübingen: Francke, 2005).

1953/G 10735

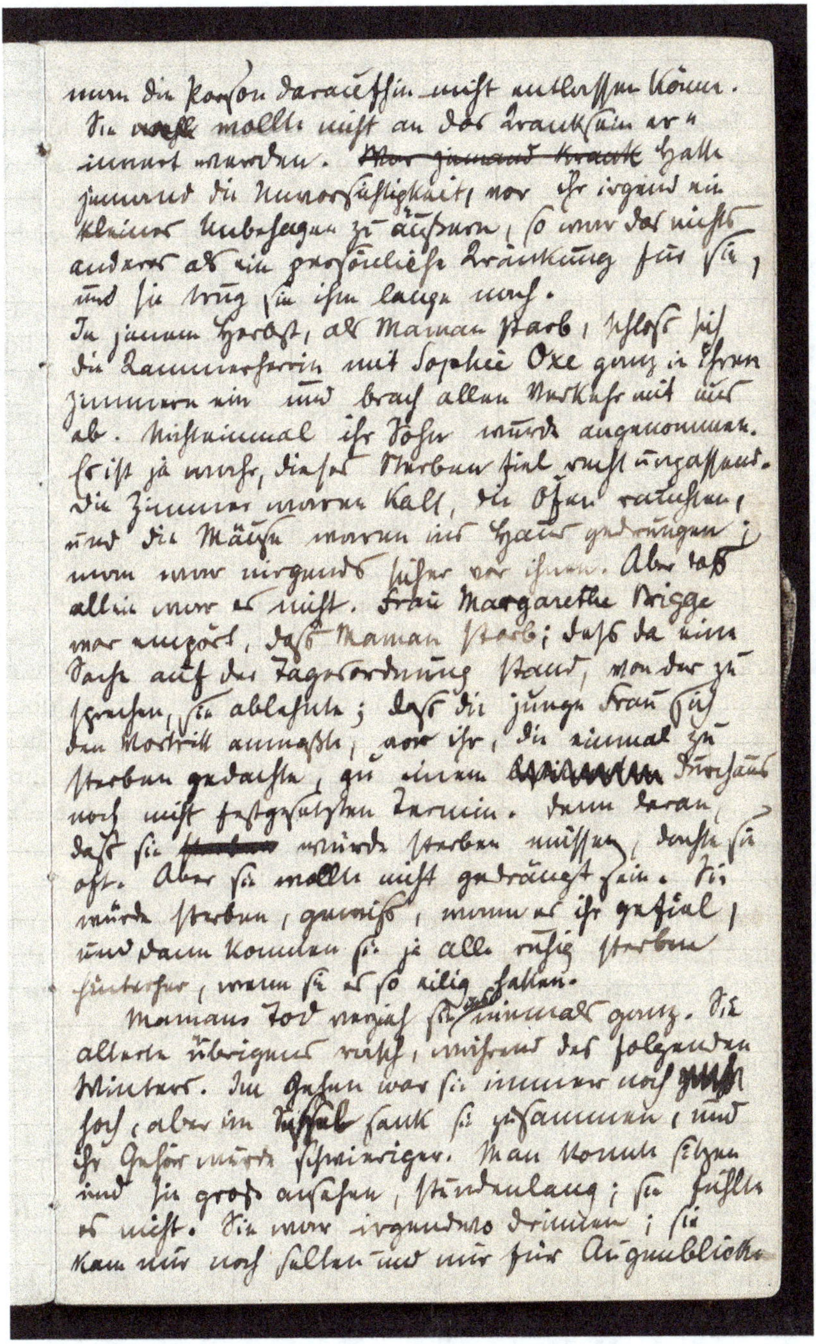

Figure 3.6. Rainer Maria Rilke, *Die Aufzeichnungen des Malte Laurids Brigge*, 2. Teil, 2–3. SLA-RMR-Ms_D_2. Schweizerisches Literaturarchiv, Bern.

down the alley leaving a dark, dirty trail behind them" (*MLB* 23–24). These abject figures occupy a liminal zone at the margins of society, on the edge of the symbolic order. They are described as trash (*Abfälle*), husks (*Schalen*) of humans whose substance has been emptied out. This image recalls Malte's depiction of faces in the fifth entry that can be put on and taken off, like masks that are "thin as paper [*dünn wie Papier*]" (*MLB* 5). The materiality of paper is evoked again in the description of the throwaways, who "stick" to the walls, lanterns, and advertising columns. The "glue" that holds them there, like paper advertisements on a surface, is the "spittle" of destiny personified. Ink is also evoked: like the pen running along lines of text and down the page, leaving behind a messy trace, "they trickle slowly down the alley leaving a dark, dirty trail behind them" (*KA* 3:481). The throwaways are explicitly associated with the implements of writing when a "little grey-haired woman" reaches out a pencil to Malte: "And how, back then, did that little grey-haired woman come to be standing next to me for a quarter of an hour in front of a shop window, showing me a long, ancient pencil pushing forth inexpressibly slowly from out of her filthy clasped hands? ... I felt it was a sign, a token that the outcasts would recognize [*ich fühlte, daß das ein Zeichen war, ein Zeichen für Eingeweihte, ein Zeichen, das die Fortgeworfenen kennen*]" (*MLB* 24).

The throwaways inhabiting the streets contrast with another group that Malte describes in the preceding passage: readers in the Bibliothèque nationale. "There are lots of people in the room, but I don't notice them. They are in the books. Sometimes they move amongst the pages like people asleep who turn over between two dreams. How good it is, though, to be amongst people reading!" (*MLB* 22). This scene of reading is defined by its media-material dimensions: rather than an encounter with language, Malte describes an encounter with books and pages, through which readers are transported, as in a dream.

This scene of reading, it appears, is one of privilege. Although he is now poor and destitute, as Malte describes himself, he is still able to pass as belonging to this milieu:

> But see what good fortune I have, I, perhaps the most paltry of all these readers, a foreigner: I have a poet. Even though I'm poor. Even though my suit, which I wear every day, is starting to wear thin in places [*gewisse Stellen zu bekommen*]. . . . My collar is clean, to be sure, my underwear, too, and I could go into any *pâtisserie* just as I am . . . and confidently reach out to one of the plates of cakes with my hand and take one. No one would notice anything remarkable about such an action, rebuke me, and ask me to leave, because it is after all a hand from the best circles, a hand washed four or five times every day. Yes indeed, there is no dirt under my fingernails, there is no ink on the third finger where I hold my pen, and my wrists in particular are immaculate. Poor people don't wash as far as the wrists—it's a well-known fact. So certain conclusions can be drawn from the cleanliness of the wrists. And are drawn. Drawn in shops. (*MLB* 23)

Malte can pass because of the cleanliness of his clothing and body, above all that of his hands, which allows him to navigate the public sphere freely without raising suspicion. In this description, textual processes are evoked: handwriting ("der Schreibfinger ist ohne Tinte") as well as reading and interpretation: "certain conclusions can be drawn from the cleanliness of the wrists." But Malte's cleanliness is a façade. In actuality, he does not belong to this world of confectionaries, shops, and fine clothes. It is the throwaways, cast out of the public realm and lurking on the margins, that are able to see through Malte's façade, to recognize *Sein* (being) beneath *Schein* (appearance):

> But there are nonetheless a few individuals [*Existenzen*], on the Boulevard Saint-Michel, for example, or the rue Racine, who can't be fooled and who don't give a fig for wrists. They look at me and know. They know that I am really one of them. . . . Who are these people? What do they want from me? Are they waiting for me? How do they recognize me? . . . What in the world did this old woman want from me, this person who . . . had crept out from a hole somewhere? Why did she always walk alongside me, watching me? As if she were trying to make me out with her watery eyes that looked as if some sick person had spat green phlegm at her bloodshot eyelids. (*MLB* 23–24)

In this entry, I suggest, the worlds of the readers and of the throwaways figure the spaces of the printed text and of the manuscript, respectively. Like the shops and patisseries, the library is a public space, its patrons defined by their cleanliness. Barely visible in the margins of society, crossed out from the symbolic order, the throwaways are figures of the manuscript page, embodying the material messiness of pencil and ink and paper.[52] By contrast with the manuscript page, the printed page is clean and tidy, sent out to circulate in the open. On the surface, as readers will primarily encounter him, Malte is a figure of the printed text. In actuality, Malte is a figure of another universe: that of the manuscript. Malte explicitly describes his "paper" existence: on another trip to the library, Malte is distracted by a "twitching" man moving spasmodically down the boulevard, writing, "yet there was something there again that picked me up like a piece of paper, crumpled me up, and threw me away [*fortwarf*]" (*MLB* 38).

"Limbs and members"

The passages discussed above appear in the first half of *The Notebooks*; no traces of their material generation are extant. But similarly abject figures and disfigured bodies are strewn throughout the Bernese Notebook. In the fifty-second entry, Malte describes certain "strange paintings" populated by errant objects and dismembered body parts: "How well I understand now the strange paintings [*wunderlichen Bilder*] in which things intended for limited and regular use loosen up and go at each other lasciviously and curiously, convulsing in the casual debauchery of dissipation [*zuckend in der ungefähren Unzucht der Zerstreuung*]. These cauldrons that go about boiling away, the pistons that get ideas, and the idle funnels that push their way into a hole for pleasure. And there are also limbs

---

52. Rilke's figuration of the *Fortgeworfenen* resonates with Almuth Grésillon's description of the in-between status of manuscripts: "Literarische Handschriften sind Zwitterwesen: weder direct Teil des Werks—bis in die jüngste Vergangenheit wurde nur dem Werk, nicht aber seinen Entstehungshandschriften die Ehre der Publikation zuteil—noch reiner Abfall." Grésillon, *Literarische Handschriften: Einführung in die "critique genetique*," trans. Frauke Rother and Wolfgang Günther (Bern: Peter Lang, 1999), 11. Malte's description of the *Fortgeworfenen* as "Abfall" also strangely recalls Handke's so-called Abfallblätter.

and members amongst them, thrown up by the jealous void, and faces that vomit warmly into them, and windy buttocks that offer them favours" (*MLB* 106). In these paintings (likely by Hieronymus Bosch and Pieter Breugel),[53] Malte observes a scene of disintegration: disorderly things breaking agentially out of their established roles, taking on a life of their own. Among them are scattered body parts, detached limbs, and detached orifices that are sites of bodily expulsion: mouths that vomit rather than speak, buttocks that blow gas like music. Malte describes a saint—likely from Bosch's *Triptych of the Temptation of St. Anthony* (1501)—who "writhes and convulses" at the sight of the monstrous scene: "And the Saint writhes and convulses, but in his eyes there was still a look that suggested he thought these things were possible: he has seen them. And his senses are already being precipitated [*und schon schlagen sich seine Sinne nieder*] in the clear solution of his soul. His prayer is already shedding its leaves [*entblättert sein Gebet*] and protruding from his mouth like a shrub that has died" (*MLB* 106). Assailed by a horrific, phantasmagoric vision of the late medieval world, Saint Anthony shares much in common with Malte, who is similarly overwhelmed by the horrors of the modern metropolis. For the first time, Malte grasps Bosch's project of figuration, a project captured succinctly Ernst Gombrich's analysis of Bosch's *Triptych*: "For the first and perhaps for the only time, an artist had succeeded in giving concrete and tangible shape to the fears that had haunted the minds of man in the Middle Ages. It was an achievement that was perhaps only possible at this very moment of time when the old ideas were still vigorous while the modern spirit has provided the artist with methods to represent what he saw."[54] In Bosch's painterly project, Malte finds a version of his own writerly project: an attempt to give "concrete and tangible shape" to the horrifying scenes that assail him, in the early twentieth-century metropolis, another period of transition in which "old ideas" about humankind and civilization were disintegrating. This notion is echoed in a

---

53. Robert Vilain, explanatory notes (*MLB* 177–78).
54. E. H. Gombrich, *The Story of Art* (Englewood Cliffs, NJ: Prentice-Hall, 1985 [1950]), 276.

letter from Rilke to Lou Andreas-Salomé from July 18, 1903—several passages of which were later incorporated into *The Notebooks*—in which Rilke described the horror and anxiety he experienced in Paris and his aesthetic goal of "making things out of fear [*Dinge machen aus Angst*]."[55]

The challenge—for Bosch and for Malte/Rilke—was one of figuration: an attempt to give concrete form to, but also manage or contain, the horrors and anxieties of modernity. In *The Notebooks*, Rilke narrates Malte's struggle to rise to this challenge. After the work's publication, Rilke suggested that Malte ultimately failed: in a letter to Lou Andreas-Salomé, he questioned whether Malte,

> who in part is made out of my experiences, goes under in it, in a sense to spare me the going under, or whether with these journals or whether I have really been thrown into the current that is tearing me away and driving me across. . . . After this book I have been left behind just like a survivor, helpless in my inmost soul, no longer to be used[.] The nearer I came to the end of writing it, the more strongly did I feel that it would be an indescribable division, a high watershed, as I kept telling myself; but now it turns out that all the water has flowed off toward the old side and I am going down into an aridity that will not change.[56]

Here Rilke describes Malte as a figure of his own experiences, but expresses doubt as to whether this project of figuration, with which he struggled so greatly, was ultimately successful: Did it enable him to *survive* the experiences that so traumatized him? Or was the attempt to write the novel also a cause or part of the crisis that befell him?

In the printed text, the material traces of Rilke's struggle to "make things out of fear"—in this case, to make his prose book—have largely been smoothed over. These traces remain visible, however, in the Bernese Notebook. A particularly vexed example is provided in the fifty-second entry, an intensively edited section of the manuscript—smoothed over in the transformation into print—in which Rilke makes various attempts to describe Bosch's fragmented,

---

55. Rilke to Lou Andreas-Salomé, July 18, 1903, in *Briefwechsel*, 64.
56. Rainer Maria Rilke, *Letters of Rainer Maria Rilke, 1906–1926*, trans. Jane Bannard Greene and M. D. Herter Norton (New York: W. W. Norton, 1972), 32–33.

discombobulated things. Bits and pieces are drafted and redrafted, sections formulated, canceled, and formulated again (figure 3.7). Consider the following bits written in pencil, which describe fragmented limbs and objects in the paintings:

> convulsing in the casual debauchery of dissipation / in which things of limited and regular use loosen up and go at each other lasciviously and curiously / ... And there are also limbs and members amongst them, thrown up by the jealous void, fa[ces]
>
> Zuckend in der ungefahren Unzucht der Zerstreuung
> darinnen dinge von beschränkten und regelmäßigen
> berufen sich ausspannen und sich lüstern und
> Neugierig aneinander versuchen.
> ...
> Und da sind auch schon, vom eifersüchtigen Nichts heraufgeworfen, Gliedmassen und Glieder unter ihnen und Ge   (BT 76–77)

Between these two fragments in the manuscript is an additional passage, containing both German and French; canceled with a diagonal stroke, it does not appear in the printed text. In this passage, Malte considers the nature of his writing to oscillate between something precious, a treasure to be guarded, and something precarious, strong yet fragile, like a spider's web or a snail's shell:

> (Sometimes it seems to me as if what I do is immensely precious and I wonder why I am not guarded over a little; but then I know again that my work is by and large very uncertain like a spider's web, or a snail's shell; they are often in the most inappropriate places, when morning comes and yet they hold up throughout the day and come unhurt into the next night. (Because I too am only weaving a spider web with a little moisture which hardens in the air, to lock up the few flies that our soul needs to live.))
>
> (Manchmal kommt es mir vor, als ob das
> was ich thue ungemein kostbar sei und ich
>
> wundere mich, dass man mich nicht ein wenig
> bewacht; aber dann weiß ich wieder, dass
> meine Arbeit im ganz großen unsicher⟨?⟩
> ist, wie ein Spinnengewebe, oder ein

wie sie es rings um sich ausgemacht sehen. Da machen sie den Versuch, sich ihren Auseinandersetzer zu unterziehen, sie wird ihm unlustig und unerfreulich, und die Leute sind gar nicht erstaunt, wenn sie sich sie auf einer Ausschweifung ertappen. Sie kennen sich so gut wie sie selbst. Sie ärgern sich, weil sie die Stärkeren sind, weil sie mehr Recht auf Abwechslung zu haben meinen, weil sie sich ungeneckt fühlen; aber sie lassen die doch gehen, wie sie sich selber gehen lassen. Wo aber einer ist, der sich zusammennimmt, ein einsamer eiUna, der so recht ernst auf sich besinnen wollte, Tag und Nacht, der fordert er geradezu den Widerspruch, den Hohn, den Hass der unterhalten Gemüther heraus, die in ihrem argen Gewissen nichts mehr ertragen können, was sich zusammenhält und noch seinen Sinnen strebt. Da verbinden sie sich, ihn zu stören, zu schrecken, zu beirren, und wissen, dass sie es können. Da fangen sie, sich einander zuzwinkernd, die Verführung an, die dann ins Ungemessene weiterwächst und alle Wesen und Gott selber hinreißt gegen den einen, der vielleicht übersteht: Die Heiligen.

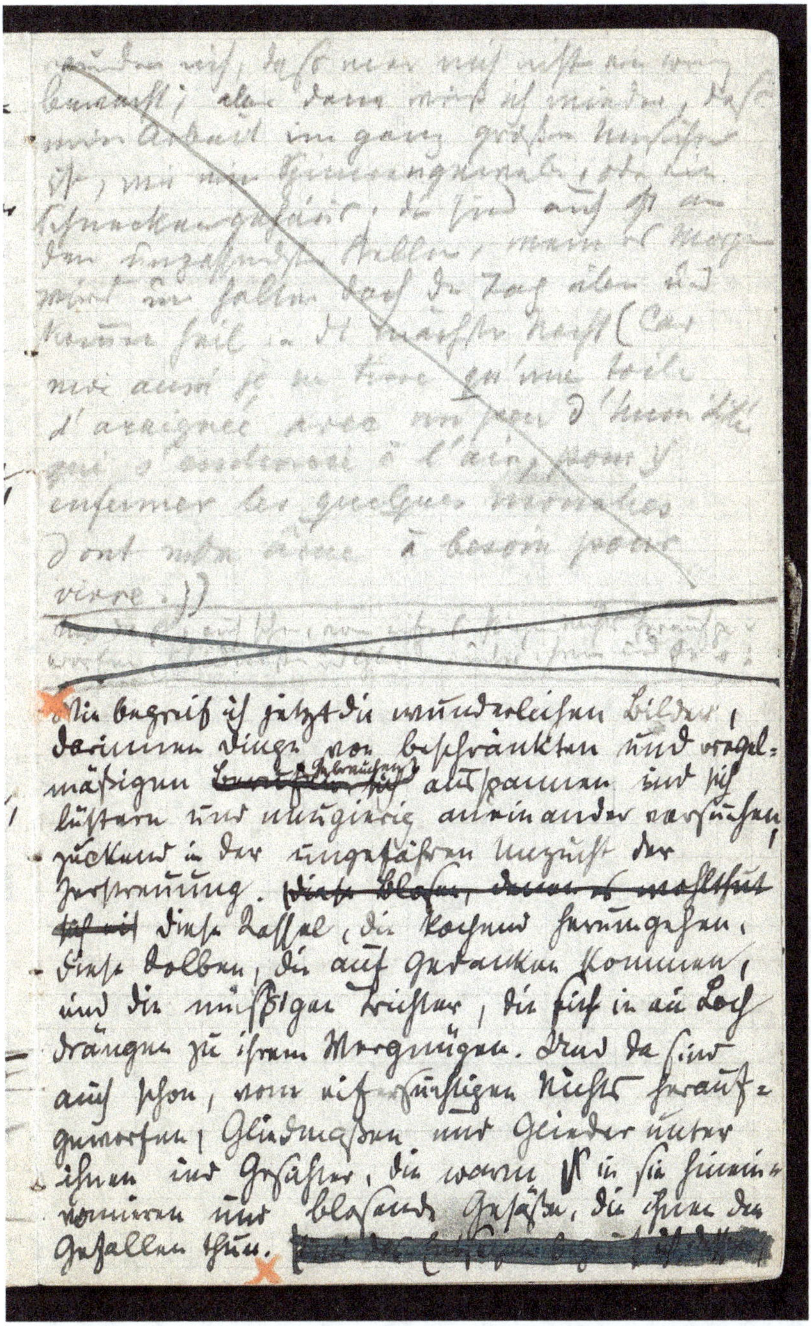

Figure 3.7. Rainer Maria Rilke, *Die Aufzeichnungen des Malte Laurids Brigge*, 2. Teil, 76–77. SLA-RMR-Ms_D_2. Schweizerisches Literaturarchiv, Bern.

> Schneckengehäus; die sind auch oft an
> den unpassendsten Stellen, wenn es morgen
> wird und⟨?⟩ halten doch den Tag über und
> komen heil in die nächste Nacht (Car
> moi aussi je ne tisse qu'une toile
> d'araignée avec un peu d'humidité
> qui s'endurci⟨?⟩ à l'air, pour y
> enfermer les quelques mouches
> dont notre âme à⟨sic⟩ besoin pour
> vivre.))   (BT 76–77)

On the following pages, between two draft versions of the description of Saint Anthony, is another passage that does not appear in *The Notebooks*: the poem "Prayer for the Lunatics and Convicts" ("Gebet für die Irren und Sträflinge")[57] (figure 3.8). Rilke's characterization of the lunatics and prisoners—"They, from whom being has quietly turned away its great face [*Ihr, von denen das Sein / leise sein großes Gesicht / wegwandte*]) (BT 78)—reminds of the throwaways, who exist on the margins, hovering between presence and absence. The context of the poem's placement in the manuscript associates it with the prayer "uttered" by Saint Anthony: "His prayer is already shedding its leaves [*entblättert sein Gebet*] and protruding from his mouth like a shrub that has died" (BT 80; figure 3.9). The third paragraph of the entries, in which Malte compares medieval saints to modern "solitaries" (*Einsamen*), similarly appears in pieces. An earlier version of the paragraph opening is doubly canceled:

> Who laughed before these pictures? Who said they are old pictures that are no longer valid? Since there are solitaries now, more than ever.
>
> ~~Wer hat gelacht vor diesen Bildern? Wer~~
> ~~hat gesagt, dass es alte Bilder sind, die nicht mehr~~
> ~~gelten? Da doch das Einsamsein gibt, mehr~~
> ~~als je.~~   (BT 80)

---

57. One of three poems that can be found interspersed throughout the Bernese Notebook, this poem was first published in 1911 in the *Insel-Almanach auf das Jahr 1912*.

A triptych, Bosch's *Temptation* consists of three hinged panels. When closed, the shutters display scenes from the Stations of the Cross; painted in grisaille, as typical for the time, these are relatively unremarkable. When opened, the viewer encounters the horrifying, phantasmagoric scene. The triptych structure is mirrored in the three-paragraph structure of the entry; the hinge-structure, moreover, also mirrors the structure of a book, its two covers attached by "hinges" to the spine. Like the closed alterpiece shutters, the book covers of the first edition of *The Notebooks* are unassuming. Upon opening the book, however, the readers (and period critics)[58] were confronted by a bizarre and unfamiliar scene: a nonlinear, confounding, genre-defying text constructed of disconnected, stylistically and thematically heterogeneous written entries, filled with unsettling, disconcerting images. Malte's description of the paintings, strewn with disorderly things and fragmentary bodies, recalls the appearance of the manuscript, sliced up into hunks and bits, fragmentary sections and canceled formulations that the writer at times struggled to incorporate; the material struggle of figuration itself, visible in the Bernese Notebook, remains enmeshed within the figurative, representational content of the text in ways that become apparent only when we examine the manuscript in which this struggle of figuration took place. This was *The Notebooks of Malte Laurids Brigge* as Rilke encountered it, that confronted him in increasingly tormented attempts to complete it.

Bandages

Examining *The Notebooks* in manuscript form illuminates how fluid the text was during the production process. This, in turn, enables us to see the printed text anew. We become increasingly aware of how powerfully the materiality and visuality of the manuscript are evoked in the published version and incorporated into its representational content.

With this in mind, I turn to one of the most extraordinary depictions of disfigured bodies in the novel. Waiting at the Salpêtrière

---

58. August Stahl, "Kommentar," *KA* 3:888–91.

Gebet für die Irren und Sträflinge.
Ihr, von denen das Sein
leise sein großes Gesicht
wegwandte: ein
vielleicht Seiender spricht
draußen in der Freiheit

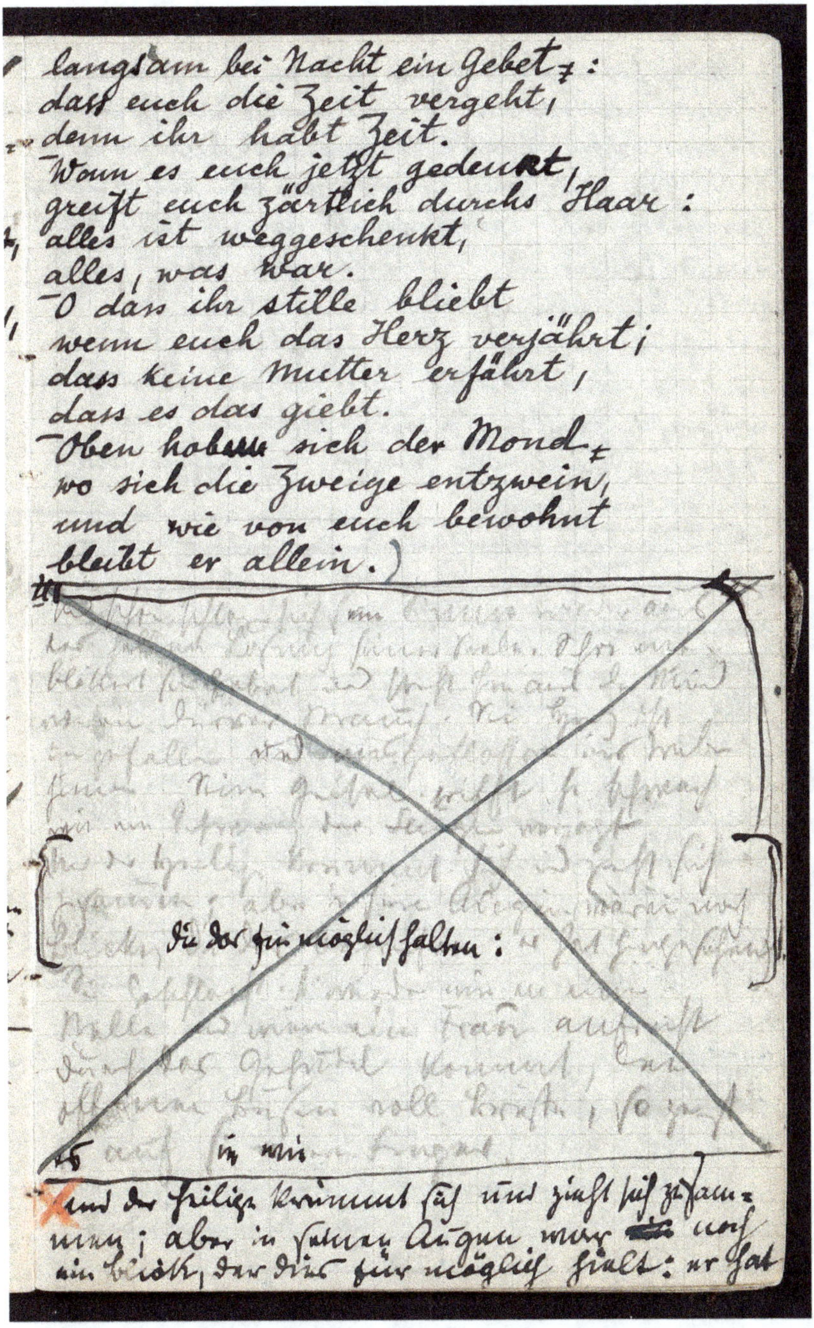

langsam bei Nacht ein Gebet:
dass euch die Zeit vergeht,
denn ihr habt Zeit.
Wenn es euch jetzt gedenkt,
greift euch zärtlich durchs Haar:
alles ist weggeschenkt,
alles, was war.
—O dass ihr stille bliebt
wenn euch das Herz veraltet;
dass keine Mutter erfährt,
dass es das giebt.
—Oben hebt sich der Mond,
wo sich die Zweige entzwein,
und wie von euch bewohnt
bleibt er allein.)

Die dies für möglich halten:

Und der Heilige kümmert sich und zieht sich zusammen; aber in seinen Augen war noch ein blick, der dies für möglich hält: er hat

Figure 3.8. Rainer Maria Rilke, *Die Aufzeichnungen des Malte Laurids Brigge*, 2. Teil, 78–79. SLA-RMR-Ms_D_2. Schweizerisches Literaturarchiv, Bern.

hinzusehen. Und schon schlagen sich seine Knien nieder auf der stillen Lösung seiner Seele. Schon entblättert sein Gebet und steht ihm aus dem Munde wie ein eingegangener Strauch. Sein Herz ist umgefallen und ausgeflossen ins Weite hinein. Seine Geißel trifft ihn schwach wie ein Schmerz, der sich geirrt hat. Seine Gesellschaft ist wieder nur an einer Stelle, und wenn ein Traum aufrecht durch das Gesiedel kommt, den obenan sitzen voll Brüsten, so zeigt es auf sie wie ein Finger.

~~Wer hat gelacht vor diesen Bildern? Wer hat gesagt, dass es alte Bilder sind, die nicht mehr gelten als das der Einsame gilt, wenn~~

~~Nichts~~ gab Zeiten, da ich diese Bilder für veraltet galt. Nicht als ob ich an ihnen zweifelte. Ich konnte mir denken, dass dies den Heiligen geschah, ~~den Heiligen~~, ~~Einzigen~~, die bald Gott aufzugehen wollten, um jeden Preis. Wir mutheten uns das nicht mehr zu. Wir ~~meinten~~ ahnen, dass er zu schwer ist für uns, dass wir ihn hinausschieben müssen, um langsam die lange Arbeit zu thun, die uns von ihm trennt. Nun aber weiß ich, dass diese Arbeit ~~~~ ~~~~ genau so bestritten ist wie das Heiligsein; dass dies da um jeden entsteht, der ~~mitten im~~ um ihretwillen einsam ist, wie es die Bibel um die einsamen Gottes in ihren Höhlen und leeren Herbergen, riecht.

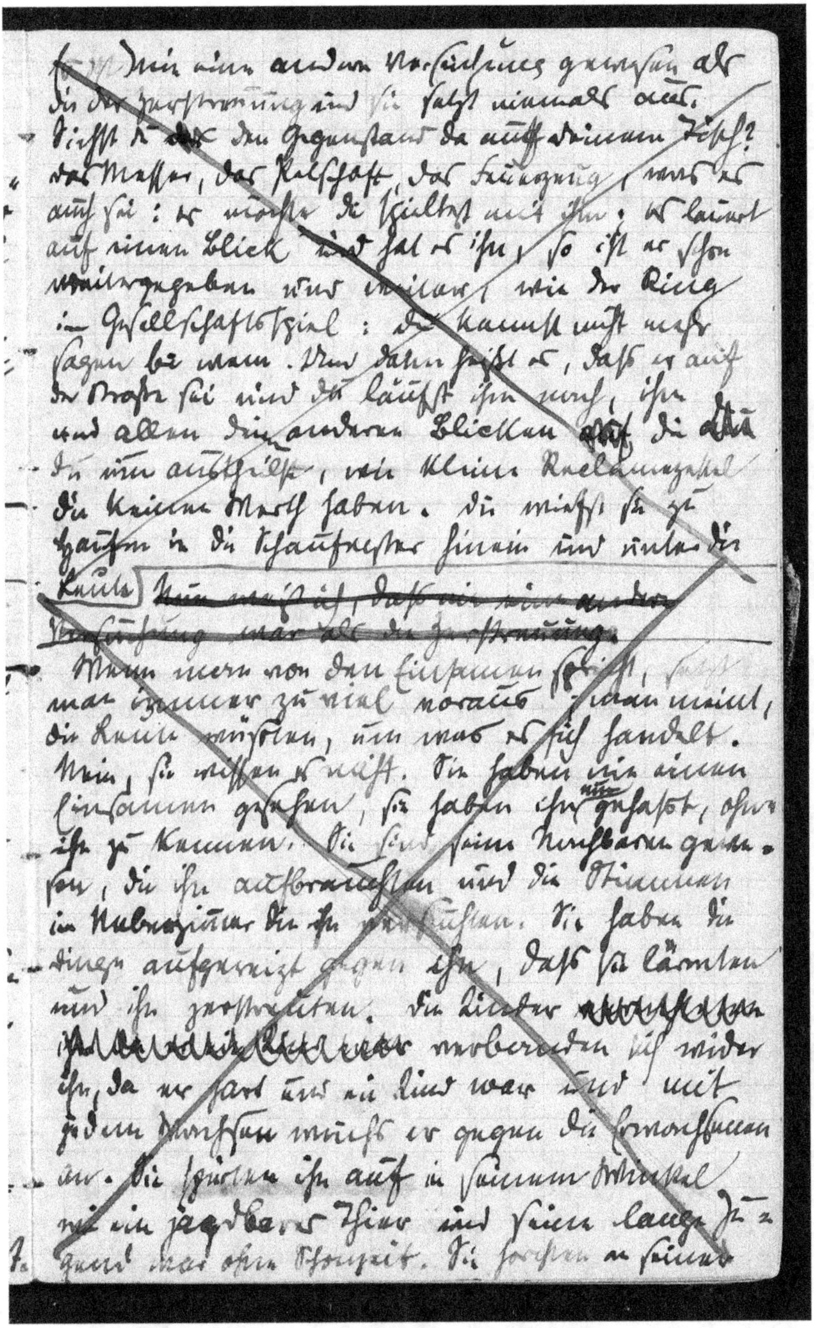

Figure 3.9. Rainer Maria Rilke, *Die Aufzeichnungen des Malte Laurids Brigge*, 2. Teil, 80–81. SLA-RMR-Ms_D_2. Schweizerisches Literaturarchiv, Bern.

hospital, where he is scheduled to receive electrotherapeutic treatment, Malte is surrounded by patients crammed together "in endless rows, shoulder to shoulder" (*MLB* 32). Descriptions of these patients fill line after line, page after page:

> One fat man with a red, swollen neck was bent forwards, staring at the floor, and from time to time he spat noisily at a stain that he appeared to think was a suitable target.... Not far from her they had put a girl with a smooth, round face and protruding, expressionless eyes; her mouth hung open so that you could see her slimy white gums, with teeth that were old and decayed.... it took a while for me to work out what was on my right. It was a huge, immobile mass, with a face and a large, heavy, motionless hand.... I observed all of this attentively, and it occurred to me that this must be the very seat that had been destined for me, since I now thought I had arrived at the point in my life where I would stay. (*MLB* 33–35)

What Malte encounters—bodies overflowing their boundaries, barely recognizable as human, not so much alive as undead—is described by Eric Santner as the *creaturely*, a concept developed in part from Rilke's conception of *die Kreatur* in the *Duino Elegies*.[59] But not only bodies are fragmented at the Salpêtrière: language itself also disintegrates. While waiting, Malte overhears a patient undergoing psychotherapeutic treatment:

> Suddenly, however, everything went silent, and into this silence came a supercilious, self-satisfied voice that I thought I knew: "*Riez!*" Pause. "*Riez. Mais riez, riez*" ... A machine started up with a judder, but at once fell silent again, words were exchanged, and then that same energetic voice arose and ordered: "*Dites-nous le mot: avant.*" Spelling it out: "*a—v—a—n—t*" ... Silence. "*On n'entend rien. Encore une fois: ...*" And then, while inside the warm, squishy babbling continued, then for the first time in many, many years it was there again. The thing that had caused the original deep terror when I was a child in bed with a fever: the Big Thing. (*MLB* 35–36)

In this scene—which has been the source of extensive theoretical discussion—language becomes reduced to material sound, a warm,

---

59. Santner, *On Creaturely Life*, 1–6.

squishy babbling. In *Discourse Networks, 1800/1900*, Friedrich Kittler describes this "discursive event," the "psychophysical decomposition of language" that Malte experiences, as the "secret code of an initiation": "Just like the word DADA, which occurs in a child's 'babbling phase' and reminds people 'of their honorably dirtied diapers and of the cry that is now supposed to delight the world,' the 'a-v-a-n-t' also leads to a short circuit between experiment and primal sound, psychophysics and children's language."[60] For Kittler, the disintegration of language within this landscape of material and bodily decomposition represents the "debris of a discourse network."[61] In this discourse network of 1800, Poetry belonged to the "Kingdom of God" in which an "Absolute Spirit" granted Poets the "the infinity of interpretation and the immortality of meaning."[62] In the discourse network of 1900—following the death of God, and of the Author—"there are no authors and works, but only writers and writings," and "messages become meaningless when there is no king at the origin and destination of discourses."[63] Out of this discourse network emerges *The Notebooks*, the text that for Kittler is the paradigmatic example.

In *The Royal Remains*, Santner suggests that Kittler misses something fundamental in his reading of the Salpêtrière scene, something that "cannot be accounted for by the discourse of even the most materialist media theory": namely, a "flare-up of the flesh."[64] Following from Ernst Kantornowicz's conception of the "King's Two Bodies," Santner argues that the transfer of power from the royal sovereign to the People generates an "excess of pressure" that constitutes the "'flesh' of the king's sublime body";[65] the effusive bodiliness in *The Notebooks*, then, is symptomatic of this historical-political shift from royal sovereignty to popular sovereignty in modern states. But Kittler's "most materialist media theory," I would

---

60. Friedrich Kittler, *Discourse Networks, 1800/1900*, trans. Michael Metteer (Stanford, CA: Stanford University Press, 1990), 318.
61. Kittler, *Discourse Networks*, 340.
62. Kittler, *Discourse Networks*, 335.
63. Kittler, *Discourse Networks*, 336, 338.
64. Santner, *Royal Remains*, 234.
65. Santner, *Royal Remains*, xxi.

counter, accounts for more than Santner suggests. Other "sovereign" entities of the discourse network of 1800—Man, the Author, Poetry—can be similarly understood to be constituted by a two-body structure: the Author as origin and authority of meaning, and the mere human body; the Poetic work, a coherent whole infused with the Author's voice, and the material text, composed of paper and ink and binding material. In turn, the death of the Author and of Poetry can similarly be thought to generate a residual "fleshiness." Once we recognize how textual materiality becomes enmeshed within Malte's figuration of wounded and perturbed bodies, we can also see the that "flare-up of the flesh" in *The Notebooks* is *also* imbricated within, a manifestation of, the disintegrated remains of the Author and of Poetry, the "debris" of the discourse network of 1800.

Malte's descriptions of wounded, bandaged bodies at the Salpêtrière resonate strongly with the visuality of the manuscript itself: "And there were many bandages. Bandages that covered the whole of people's heads, layer after layer, so that there was only an eye visible, which was no longer part of a person. Bandages that concealed, and bandages that showed what lay beneath. Bandages that had been opened and on which now lay, as if on a dirty bed, a hand that wasn't a hand any more, and a leg that had been bound up, sticking out from the row, big as a whole person" (*MLB* 33). Malte's descriptions of bandages—some of which completely cover, some of which show what lies beneath—resemble the strike-throughs in the manuscript: some completely cover the text, obscuring it entirely; others allow the writing to remain visible. Thomas Richter, editor of the facsimile edition of the Bernese Notebook, identifies at least three main kinds of cancellation in the manuscript:

—Individual words or sentences with a line.
    The text remains legible. . . .
—Obsolete paragraphs are diagonally crossed out once or twice (within this, one also can find older strike-throughs). . . . the earlier text remains—in varying quality—legible.
—Complete deletion.

... There are (at least) two different types: the wavy line, which ranges from the simple strike-through to the 'complete deletion,' which really fully deletes, makes illegible; and the complete deletion, which can be implemented with numerous strokes, either as concentrated wavy lines or hatching, a total darkening of the manuscript space.[66]

Richter questioned whether the "degree of deletion [*Grade des Gestrichenen*]" indicated the likelihood of a cancellation being reversed by Rilke in subsequent phases of the text's generation, and ultimately determined that it was not: "various degrees of deletion may be relevant for the individual reader of the manuscript alone, they were not so for the author's decision in 1910."[67]

Though insignificant in this respect, the *notions* of striking, deleting, erasing, and throwing away are extraordinarily significant in *The Notebooks*. The throwaways, cast off from society, literally discarded like trash, can be seen as figures of the canceled text in the manuscript: erased, yet still perceptible, hovering on the edge of the symbolic order. The wounded, bandaged bodies of the patients in the Salpêtrière mirror the appearance of the pages of the Bernese Notebook, cut up into at times barely legible sections that Rilke struggled to fit together.[68] Through the process of printing, the "wounds" of the manuscript appear to have healed—packaged in print, the text appears complete and whole. But invisible "scars" remain, I suggest, pointing to the material process of production that remains part of its constitution.

In addition to direct correlations between visual figures *in* the text and the visuality *of* the text, the logic of striking pervades the work more fundamentally. The opening sentence is a performative act of

---

66. Thomas Richter, "'diese amorphe Sache': Versuch einer Systematisierung der Streichungen in Rilkes Entwurfshandschrift zu den *Aufzeichnungen des Malte Laurids Brigge*," in *Schreiben und Streichen*, ed. Lucas Marco Gisi, Hubert Thüring, and Irmgard M. Wirtz (Göttingen: Wallstein; Zurich: Chronos, 2011), 190–91.

67. Richter, "diese amorphe Sache," 191–92.

68. On Rilke's "Montagetechnik," see *Die Aufzeichnungen des Malte Laurids Brigge*, ed. Engel, 348–50.

striking through: Malte cancels one view of Paris—"So, this is where people come to live"—and replaces it with another: "It seems to me, though, that it's dying that happens here." The surfaces of the once-familiar world are becoming effaced, yet what lies beneath, what Malte is *learning to see*, remains beyond reach, in a state of becoming. As Robert Vilain writes, "Via its own form, *Malte Laurids Brigge* manifests less confidence in the finished, polished, and lasting artistic monument than in an aesthetic of transience, ephemerality, and fragility."[69]

These formal and aesthetic textual effects, which would become paradigmatic of modernism and the discourse network of 1900, have a decidedly material, bodily dimension in *The Notebooks*. Indeed, the figural aesthetics of fragmentation, disintegration, and fluctuation directly reflect the material struggle of its making. The world of *The Notebooks* is a world of disintegrating boundaries: between subjectivity and objectivity, interior and exterior, past, present and future, reality and possibility, perception and imagination. In these respects, the nature of reality in *The Notebooks* is like that of an in-process text. Hubert Thüring's characterization of the strike-through as a procedure of "productive negativity," and of the manuscript as a space of the openness and fluctuation, is particularly apt:

> Through the possibility that the text could be expanded or edited at any moment, perpetually and subject to whim, the process of writing is potentially endless. . . . In this way, a subject- and text-oriented space-time of indeterminate coordinates emerges: in each moment, the boundaries between subject and text [*Subjekt und Schrift*], inner and outer, beginning and end, self and other, imagination and perception, past and present, presence and absence can, in principle, shift, dissolve, or be drawn anew, more or less explicitly, more or less performatively, more or less self-consciously.[70]

Malte's writing explores the spaces of fluctuation and transformation opened through the disintegration and collapse of existing

---

69. Vilain, introduction to *The Notebooks* (MLB xlv).
70. Hubert Thüring, "Streichen als Moment produktiver Negativität," in Gisi et al., *Schreiben und Streichen*, 56.

structures. Malte writes from the ruins of a reality that is under erasure, invalidated, in the process of being rewritten.

When one peels back the seemingly fixed, stable surface of the printed text to glimpse the manuscript lying beneath, one can discern how powerfully the materiality of writing is evoked by the figuration of *The Notebooks*. In addition to these more diffuse evocations of the materiality of writing, there is one figure in the novel that can be read as a figure of the manuscript itself: "the Big Thing."

The Big Thing

Malte's nightmarish experience in the Salpêtrière triggers the resurfacing of a childhood anxiety that, then and now, is too large for words:

> And then, while inside the warm, squishy babbling continued, then for the first time in many, many years it was there again . . . : the Big Thing. Yes, that's what I'd always called it when they were all standing round my bed, taking my pulse and asking what had frightened me: the Big Thing. . . . It was there now. Now it was growing out from within me like a tumour, like a second head, and it was a part of me, even though it couldn't possibly belong to me because it was so large. It was there, like a great big dead animal that had once, when it was alive, been my hand or my arm. And my blood flowed through me and through it, as if through one and the same body. And my heart had to struggle a good deal to drive the blood into the Big Thing: there was almost not enough blood there. And the blood only entered the Big Thing reluctantly and came back sickly and polluted. (*MLB* 36)

The return of the Big Thing is directly triggered by Malte's experience of the disintegration of language: the warm, squishy babbling of the patient undergoing psychoanalytic treatment. Like a tumor or second head, a carcass or dismembered limb, this anxiety is not a primarily mental phenomenon; rather, it is rooted in his body, an organic part of him while simultaneously foreign and external.

This passage has received multiple readings that highlight the bodiliness of the text's figuration. Santner, for example, interprets the resurfacing of the Big Thing as "the return of the *somatic sublime.*"[71] For Rochelle Tobias, "the unmistakable motif in this passage is that of pregnancy and birth. Malte gives birth to an entity connected to him by an umbilical cord that pumps ever more blood into it."[72] Kittler connects the Big Thing to language and writing: when Malte eventually flees the scene, he flees both the Salpêtrière and the "the Big Thing," rejecting psychotherapeutic treatment for writing—"I have done something to combat my fear. I have sat writing all night long" (*MLB* 10)—as a means of mitigating his anxiety.[73] "Writing therefore means: to put the exploded 'inner-world space,' the tumescent brain, down onto paper, rather than have the explosion or tumor treated by the appropriate scientific methods."[74]

I suggest that the Big Thing can also be read as a figure of the text itself, Rilke's "prose book." Pregnancy and birth, clearly alluded to in this passage, are also common metaphors for writing or textual genesis, and Rilke characterized the production of *The Notebooks* in these terms on numerous occasions.[75] In a letter to Marie von Thurn und Taxis, he wrote, "Not half an hour ago I dictated the final word from my manuscript; if I am not very much mistaken, a new book has arrived—finished, released from me, and established in its own reality."[76] In another letter, Rilke described Malte as his progeny: "Malte Laurids has ... developed into a figure, which completely detached from me, gained in existence and uniqueness, and which, as it became more distinct from me, interested me all the more strongly."[77] And in an earlier letter, Rilke directly evoked pregnancy and birth in outlining his publication plans, including those for *The Notebooks*: "One understands it for the most

---

71. Santner, *Royal Remains*, 234.
72. Rochelle Tobias, "Rilke's Landscape of the Heart: On *The Notebooks of Malte Laurids Brigge*," *Modernism/modernity* 24 (2014): 670.
73. Kittler, *Discourse Networks*, 318–19; *KA* 3:464.
74. Kittler, *Discourse Networks*, 319.
75. See, for example, Grésillon, *Literarische Handschriften*, 17.
76. Rilke to Marie Taxis, January 27, 1910, in Rainer Maria Rilke and Marie von Thurn und Taxis, *Briefwechsel*, vol. 1, ed. Ernst Zinn (Zurich: Max Niehans, 1951), 10. On Rilke's use of pregnancy metaphors, see also Vilain, introduction to *The Notebooks* (*MLB* xiii–xiv).
77. Rilke to Manon zu Solms-Laubach, April 11, 1910, in *Briefe in zwei Bänden*, vol. 1: *1896–1919*, ed. Horst Nalewski (Frankfurt am Main: Insel, 1991), 342.

impoverished woman who worries about finding a place to give birth, and does not expect that she will accomplish much more in her time here than a well-executed birth [*gut gearbeiteten Geburt*]. I want to have this birth behind me, which has filled me, and in this respect I am pleading for a delay, but one which will be justifiable, I hope, as soon as the child has arrived."[78] For Rilke the "pregnancy and birth" of *The Notebooks* were riddled with complications: He had expended an enormous amount of energy.[79] His health suffered in the final months of writing; he felt incapable of producing a clean, final copy of the manuscript, and ultimately delivered the work orally to Kippenberg's secretary.[80] In his description of the Big Thing, we hear something of Rilke's physical and emotional relationship to the work. Like the Big Thing, the manuscript grows out of the writer like a tumor, part of him but simultaneously a separate, foreign entity not entirely under his control. Covered in pen scratches and ink and disfigured pages, the manuscript appears at times like a mutilated body or carcass. Malte's descriptions of the Big Thing as a "second head" and severed "hand" evoke a scene of disconnected writing: a mind generating thoughts not entirely one's own, and a hand, the bodily instrument of writing, that operates independently. This figuration of the Big Thing resonates in particular with Malte's premonition of an "age of the other interpretation [*Zeit der anderen Auslegung*]": "I can write all this down and say it for a while yet. But there will come a day when my hand will be far away from me, and when I tell it to write it will write words that I do not intend" (*MLB* 31). Malte lingers in particular with the image of his blood pulsing through the body of the Big Thing, "as if through one and the same body." As for an exhausted writer, it

---

78. Rilke to Karl von der Heydt, February 21, 1907, in *Briefe in zwei Bänden*, 1:239–46, 245. Rilke was courting von der Heydt as a benefactor to help finance his stay in Paris. Kippenberg also described the production of *The Notebooks* in terms evocative of pregnancy and birth: see Kippenberg to Rilke, March 20 and May 19, 1910, in *Briefwechsel mit Anton Kippenberg*, 198, 210–11.

79. E.g., Rilke to Anton Kippenberg, January 2, 1909, in *Briefwechsel mit Anton Kippenberg*, 139–40.

80. E.g., Rilke to Anton Kippenberg, May 21 and October 20, 1909, in *Briefwechsel mit Anton Kippenberg*, 161–62, 177–78. In the October 20 letter, Rilke asks for the assistance of a copyist because his "Gesundheit ist immer noch halb" (177).

seems to Malte that there was "almost not enough blood there," his heart lacking strength to pump it into the foreign body. The manuscript is thus figured as a physical extension of the writer, composed of his own flesh and blood, interwoven within the tissue of the text to produce a second, only partially knowable, body.

The figures of bodiliness and materiality in *The Notebooks* are frequently haunted by another, "spectral" materiality: that of the manuscript. The materiality and visuality of the writing become incorporated into the work's (self-)referential structure. The referential, however, is but one dimension of the Figure/figural in *The Notebooks*. Recall Deleuze's definitions of Figure/figuration: "Whereas 'figuration' refers to a form that is related to an object it is supposed to represent, the 'Figure' is the form that is connected to a sensation, and that conveys the violence of this sensation directly to the nervous system."[81] Deleuze writes the following about the experience of viewing Cézanne's painting: "At one and the same time I become in the sensation and something happens through the sensation, one through the other, one in the other. And at the limit, it is the same body that, being both subject and object, gives and receives the sensation. As a spectator, I experience the sensation only by entering the painting, by reaching the unity of the sensing and the sensed."[82] In sensation the notional boundary between perceiving subject and perceived object—here, Cézanne's painting—is overcome. Something similar occurs in reading *The Notebooks*: Figure and figuration, affect and representation, the non-hermeneutic and the hermeneutic are in constant interplay. When pierced affectively—like Abelone receiving the stigmata—the reader also is transformed into an inscriptional surface, incorporated into the work, part of its structure. This, then, is the key idea of the Rilkean intersection of the body and the Figure: the bodily dynamics of the text (linguistic, semantic, affective) extend outward from it in all directions—back into its source text (the material manuscript) and forward to the reader—forming a kind of constellation that we can only see when the compositional dynamics of the work are in view.

---

81. Smith, "Deleuze and Bacon," viii.
82. Deleuze, *The Logic of Sensation*, 31.

Seeing

Malte's description of the Big Thing as a "big dead animal" recalls an earlier reference in the novel to Charles Baudelaire's poem "Une Charogne." Describing in vivid detail an encounter with a putrefying carcass, the poem epitomizes Baudelaire's so-called "aesthetics of ugliness." Alongside Rodin and Cézanne, Baudelaire exerted an enormous influence on Rilke, which manifests in *The Notebooks* both formally and thematically.[83] In a 1907 letter to his wife, Clara Rilke, Rilke describes the importance of the poem "Une Charogne" for the development of his poetics of "objective expression" (*sachliches Sagen*).

> You surely remember . . . from the *Notebooks of Malte Laurids* the passage that has to do with Baudelaire and with his poem: "The Carcass." I could not help thinking that without this poem the whole development toward objective expression, which we now think we recognize in Cézanne, could not have started. . . . Artistic observation had first to have prevailed upon itself far enough to see even in the horrible and apparently merely repulsive that which is and which, with everything else that is, is valid. The creator is no more allowed to discriminate than he is to turn away from anything that exists.[84]

Rilke's *sachliches Sagen,* a corporeal mode of figuration aimed at grasping things in their "objective reality [*dingliche Wirklichkeit*]," is rooted in a new mode of seeing.[85] In the letter, Rilke characterizes this new seeing as the ability to perceive the essential being *within* the horrible (*im Schrecklichen*), beneath the surfaces of appearances. In *The Notebooks*, Rilke quotes from this letter almost verbatim: "Do you remember Baudelaire's amazing poem 'Une Charogne'? I may

---

83. Huyssen writes, "Indeed, Rilke's text as a whole can be read through the Baudelairean veil as an attempt to write the city in a new way, to create a poetic prose adequate to the confusing and disorienting experience of the modern metropolis, an experience which required another, not yet known mode of poetic expression beyond verse, metre and rhyme, but also beyond fictional plot" (Huyssen, "The Notebooks," 75).

84. Rilke to Clara Rilke, October 19, 1907, in *Briefe in zwei Bänden*, 1:279–80; Bannard Greene and Norton, *Letters of Rainer Maria Rilke*, 314–15.

85. On the notion of Rilke's *sachliches Sagen* as "corporeal process of signification," see Schwarz, "The Colors of Prose."

understand it now, perhaps. Apart from the last stanza, he was right. What was he to do when he encountered that? It was his task to see in this horror, in what could apparently only be disgusting, the essence of its being that still obtains amongst all forms of being. Picking and choosing, or rejection, are not possible" (*MLB* 42). In this formulation, Malte describes a mode of perceiving the essential being that lies beneath the visible or perceptible manifestations of things.

One of the most significant themes of *The Notebooks*, the new mode of seeing that Malte is attempting to cultivate is specifically a mode of *seeing through* surface appearances. Throughout the text there are numerous paradigmatic moments in which this mode of seeing through surfaces is evoked—one thinks most obviously of Malte's encounters with faces and architectural façades—but the notion of *seeing through* also appears in less obvious places: for example, in Malte's conception of "intransitive love." These figurations, as I explore in this section, bear a striking resemblance to the early twentieth-century discourse around X-ray technology, a mediated mode of vision enabling humans to see through the surface of things.

The notion of "seeing through" also has methodological implications, I suggest, for considering the relationship between the printed text and the process of its production. As I have discussed, *The Notebooks* is a manuscript fiction, with several passages annotated "written in the margin of the manuscript [*im Manuskript an den Rand geschrieben*]." Based on the actual letter from Rilke to his wife, Clara, the twenty-second entry, in which Malte references Baudelaire's poem, is annotated with the footnote "a draft of a letter [*Ein Briefentwurf*]" (*MLB* 42)—another reference to a source text on which the printed text is based, thereby drawing attention to the constructedness of its printed incarnation. Turning Malte's "new seeing" onto the work itself allows us to "see" the materiality of the manuscript through the surface of the printed text—in ways that the work itself, I suggest, theorizes.

Seeing the Inside

In a series of moments in the text, Rilke enacts a process of learning to see through the surface of things. One paradigmatic trope is the "Gesicht," which in German signifies both "face" and sense of sight (*Gesichtssinn*). In the fifth entry, Malte explains his experience of learning to see by describing strange encounters with faces.

> Have I already said? I'm learning how to see. Yes, I'm starting. It's still not going well. But I want to make the most of my time.
>
> Surprising, for example, that I've never been properly aware of how many faces there are. There are many people, but even more faces, since everyone has several. There are people who wear a face for years, and of course it wears away, gets dirty, cracks in the creases, stretches like gloves you've worn whilst travelling . . . because they have several faces, what do they do with the others? They save them. Their children will wear them. But it sometimes happens that their dogs go out with them on.—But why not? A face is a face. (*MLB* 4)

Malte describes faces as something superficial, like masks that can be removed and exchanged, rather than something unique to an individual. The material condition of these faces—used, creased, brittle—reminds of worn-out gloves, but also of excessively handled paper. Malte makes this connection explicit when he describes the faces as "thin like paper," full of holes: "Other people change their faces over uncannily quickly. . . . They aren't used to looking after faces; their last wears through in a week, has holes in it, and in many places it's as thin as paper, and then gradually the base layer [*Unterlage*] starts to show through, the non-face [*das Nichtgesicht*]" (*MLB* 4–5). Reminding of the "thin spots" in the pants fabric in Bernhard's *Walking*, the thinness of these faces enables one to see through them, allowing the "base layer" or "non-face" beneath the surface to become visible.

In what follows, Malte describes another horrifying encounter with a face: "But the woman—the woman: she had completely collapsed into herself, forwards into her hands. . . . The woman was startled and lifted herself out of herself, too quickly, too fiercely, so that her face remained stuck in her hands. I could see it lying there, its shape hollow. It cost me an indescribable effort to go on looking at the hands and not to look at what had been ripped from them. I was terrified of seeing a face from the inside, but I was even more afraid of the naked, raw head with no face" (*MLB* 5). What Malte sees in this phantasmagoric vision, the faceless head and the "inner side" of the face, is terrifying. But it is also instructive, one of numerous entries in which Malte begins to discern dimensions behind or beneath that which he increasingly perceives as façade, mere surface. In the fourteenth entry, Malte questions whether everything humans have ever truly seen anything beneath the "surface" of life: "Is it possible that, despite inventions and progress, despite culture, religion, and philosophy, we have remained on the surface of life?" (*MLB* 14).

From the inner side of the face, Rilke moves to the inner side of architectural façades. In one of the most extraordinary passages of *The Notebooks*, Malte describes the exposed interior wall of an apartment building that was torn down in during the period of Georges-Eugene Hausmann's dramatic renovation of Paris.

> Houses? But to be precise, they were houses that were no longer there. Houses that had been torn down, from top to bottom. What was there were the other houses, the ones that had been next to them, tall adjoining houses. They were apparently at risk of falling down now that everything had been removed from alongside, since a whole scaffold of long tarred poles had been rammed into place at an angle from the rubble-strewn ground to the exposed wall. . . . You could see the inside of them. On each storey you could see the walls of rooms with wallpaper still sticking to them, and here and there places where the floors and ceilings had been fixed. Beside the walls of these rooms there was a dirty white space the whole length of the wall and along it crept, in unspeakably disgusting, squashily wormlike, almost digesting motions, the open, rust-flecked channel for the toilet plumbing. . . . The walls themselves were the most unforgettable part, however. The tenacious life of these rooms had refused to be stamped out. It was still there. . . . One could see in the paintwork that it had changed gradually, year on year, from blue into mildewed green, green into grey, and yellow into an old, stagnant, putrefying white. . . . It was in every tattered strip of paint, it was in the damp bubbles lifting the bottom edges of the wallpaper, it swayed in the tattered shreds, and the foul patches that had formed so long ago all exuded it. . . . There lay the midday meals and the illnesses and the exhalations and year-after-year's-worth of smoke and the sweat that oozes out from the armpits. . . . There lay the acridity of urine and the reek of burnt soot and grey steam from potatoes and the heavy, slick stench of rancid lard. The sweet, lingering smell of neglected nursing babies was there, and the anxious smell of children going to school, and the mugginess of the beds of older boys . . . and there was a good deal more there whose origins were unknown. I said,

didn't I, that all the walls had been pulled down apart from a final one—? Well, this is the wall I've been talking about all along. People will say that I'd been standing in front of it for ages, but I swear I started to run as soon as I recognized it. That's the really terrible thing, the fact that I recognized it. I recognize everything around here, and that's why it enters into me so easily: it is at home in me. (*MLB* 27–28)

In graphic detail, Malte describes the material traces of life that remain visible on the exposed interior walls. Initial descriptions more objective in nature soon give way to imaginative, hallucinatory vision. In certain details—the changing colors of the walls, for example—Malte can visualize transformations that occurred over time. Though the building has been torn down, "tenacious life" still clings to these walls, refusing to be "stamped out." Malte is able to *see* the life that transpired there over many years, "the midday meals and the illnesses and the exhalations." Lingering odors similarly conjure the presence of the former inhabitants, from smells directly indexing their origins ("the acridity of urine . . . the heavy, slick stench of rancid lard") to those more hallucinatory in nature ("The sweet, lingering smell of neglected nursing babies . . . the anxious smell of children"). Malte's vision of the apartment building wall is paradigmatic for his new mode of new seeing more generally, a seeing that penetrates through or rends asunder surfaces and façades to expose the invisible that lies beyond the visible, as well as the absent that still haunts the present.

"Spirits"

In his reading of this passage, Santner describes Malte as a "medium" in a double sense: his sensorium is like a photographic plate onto which is inscribed "not so much . . . what is there to behold," but rather "the traces of past lives and lost possibilities"; simultaneously, Malte's vision is akin to that of a clairvoyant medium, a "locus for communion with the dead." In turn, Santner characterizes "a peculiar sort of materialism at work here, one we might call 'spectral.'"[86] Whereas the inner side of the apartment building is "haunted" by

---

86. Santner, *On Creaturely Life*, 52.

lives once lived there, which remain spectrally present in material and visual traces, there are also scenes in *The Notebooks* in which ghosts actually appear. In the fifteenth entry, the ghost of Christine Brahe appears in a doorway leading to a "Zwischengeschoss"—a mezzanine, or literally an in-between floor—and passes through the dining hall before disappearing through the opposite wall (*MLB* 20). Brahe's valet Sten, an avid Swedenborg reader, is described as an especially capable medium, whom Brahe invites to summon spirits into his writing chamber: "'Will they come, Sten?' he would ask benevolently. 'It's good when they come'" (*MLB* 87).

The Brahe house at Urnekloster is haunted by ghosts, but there are other haunted houses in the text—or rather, houses that haunt. In the forty-second entry, Malte recalls a childhood visit to the Schulin family house, which had been partially destroyed by fire. The family continues to live in the house, confining themselves ("sich einschränkten") in the "two cramped wings [*Seitenflügeln*]" (*MLB* 80). Physically absent, the missing central part of the house continues to exert a palpable presence, particularly for Malte's mother, who can also see spirits. "'But there was a house there just now,' said Maman. . . . If Maman and I lived here, it would always be there. . . . Hardly had I joined her and sensed that she was trembling within than I knew that the house was only just at that moment starting to recede again" (*MLB* 81–83).[87]

Malte evokes the ghostly even more explicitly in other descriptions. "We're climbing around out here like ghosts," Malte's father exclaims as the guests stumble around in the darkness, climbing a staircase that now leads nowhere (*MLB* 81). Among other invisible, ghostly presences in the Schulin house are smells. Malte writes that the Schulins had become particularly paranoid about the possibility of future fires.

> 'Mama can smell something,' said Viera Schulin behind him, 'we all have to be quiet when that happens, she smells with her ears,' although she was herself standing there with raised eyebrows, alert and all nose.

---

87. Compare Rilke to Lou Andreas-Salomé, December 4, 1904, in *Briefwechsel*, 197–98.

> In this respect the Schulins had been somewhat peculiar since the fire. In their cramped, over-heated rooms a smell might develop at any moment, and when it did, it was investigated and everyone would give their opinion.... But suddenly ... I was overcome for the first time in my life by something akin to a fear of ghosts. I realized that all the clearly visible grown-ups who had just been talking and laughing were now walking around stooped over and occupied with something invisible, and that they acknowledged that there was something there that they couldn't see. And what frightened me was the fact that it was stronger than them all. (*MLB* 82–83)

Resembling ghost-hunters, the adults attempt to locate the invisible olfactory agents; Viera Schulin, "all nose" with a synesthetic ability to smell with her ears, appears like a psychic medium. The invisibly present is directly associated with the ghostly in Malte's recollection that he experienced something like a "fear of ghosts."

The manuscript is evoked as a ghostly presence in this scene. In describing the approach to the house, Malte writes, "The trees were standing as if they didn't know what to do in the fog.... Now and then it began to snow again silently, and now it was as if every last mark were being erased [*ausradiert*] and as if we were journeying into a blank page [*weißes Blatt*]" (*MLB* 80). In the falling snow, it appears to Malte as though they are driving into a "white page." This is notably not a blank page, a *leeres Blatt*; instead the trees, like lines of text, have been almost entirely "erased." The image of a landscape under erasure prefigures the liminal state of the Schulin house, while the "two cramped wings [*beiden engen Seitenflügeln*]" into which the Schulins confine themselves resemble covers of a book, the space between them haunted by the absent house. The guests in this scene appear as readers, analyzing and interpreting smells they perceive: "In their cramped, over-heated rooms a smell might develop at any moment, and when it did, it was investigated and everyone would give their opinion" (*MLB* 83).

Malte's vision of the "inner side" of faces and architectural façades shares something essential with the phenomenon of mediumistic seeing depicted in multiple entries: both are fundamentally *penetrative* in nature. The mode of seeing that Malte attempts to cultivate passes through boundaries between exterior and interior, visible and invisible, as well as between the present and the absent, the realm of the living and the realm of the dead. While Rilke's Rodin and Cézanne reception is an obvious influence, Malte's *neues Sehen* (new vision) and Rilke's *sachliches Sagen* (objective speech) are also marked profoundly, both by the media and by medical historical contexts—photography and ophthalmology, for instance—and *most* profoundly by the discourse around an imaging technology at the intersection of the two: the X-ray.[88]

"A larger, unusually thin hand"

In the twenty-ninth entry, Malte recalls a childhood experience that, both then and now, he cannot fully comprehend. While drawing (*zeichnen*), Malte crawls underneath the table to fetch a fallen crayon. Groping around in the semidarkness, Malte's hand appears strangely foreign to him; he is horrified when another hand emerges from the wall, groping toward him:

> I recognized in particular my own hand, with fingers outstretched, moving around under there all alone and exploring the bottom . . . it seemed to me as if it was capable of things that I had never taught it, groping around down there independently with movements that I had never seen it perform before. . . . But how on earth could I have been prepared for another hand suddenly to be coming out of the wall to meet it, a larger, unusually lean hand unlike any hand that I had ever seen before? It was searching in a similar way from the other side, and the two hands, fingers outstretched, were moving blindly towards each other. My curiosity was by no means exhausted, but suddenly it drained away leaving only horror in its place. I felt that one of the hands belonged to me and that it was becoming involved in something that could never be put right again. Summoning all the rights of ownership that I had over it, I stopped it moving and pulled it slowly back, flat against the floor, not letting the other hand out of my

---

88. See Stefanie Harris, "Exposures: Rilke, Photography, and the City," *New German Critique* 99, no. 33.3 (2006): 121–49; Andreas Huyssen, "Modernist Miniatures: Literary Snapshots of Urban Spaces," *PMLA* 22, no. 2 (2007): 27–42; Huyssen, "Paris/Childhood: The Fragmented Body in Rilke's *Notebooks of Malte Laurids Brigge*," in *Twilight Memories* (London: Routledge, 1995), 105–26; Santner, *Royal Remains*, 201, 219; Steffen Arndal, "Sehenlernen und Pseudoskopie: Zur visuellen Verarbeitung des Pariserlebnisses in R. M. Rilkes Die Aufzeichnungen des Malte Laurids Brigge," *Orbis Litterarum* 62, no. 3 (2007): 210–29.

sight as it carried on searching. I realized that it would not give up, but cannot say how I got back up again. (*MLB* 54–55)

The activity of Malte's hand has been interpreted as a figure of automatic writing, a figure simultaneously recalling Malte's vision of the "time of the other interpretation": "But there will come a day when my hand will be far away from me, and when I tell it to write it will write words that I do not intend" (*MLB* 31). Or the older, thinner hand, groping toward Malte's hand as it gropes for the crayon, might be seen as a mirror image spanning a temporal divide: Malte's adult hand reaches into his childhood past, attempting to grasp this event. Or the larger, older hand might even be interpreted as Rilke's, reaching autobiographically into his past as he writes Malte into existence.

The description of the large, thin, terrifying hand also recalls the first X-ray image produced by Wilhelm Conrad Röntgen—a sinister-looking image of his wife's hand.[89] When Röntgen presented his discovery of the X-ray in 1895 in Würzburg, news spread rapidly throughout Europe and beyond.[90] In 1896 alone, more than fifty books and pamphlets and thousands of papers were published on X-rays.[91] Yet these "invisible rays" also soon came to associated with clairvoyance and the unconscious; X-ray images were at times believed to be spirit photographs. Upon viewing the X-ray image of her hand, Anna Röntgen is purported to have declared, "I have seen my death." The notion that one could see one's own death, contained inside of them and newly visible through X-ray radiography, resonates with Malte's conception of one's "own death [*eigener Tod*]," which was "carried visibly" within a person: "Previously you

---

89. In the first paper he published on his discovery, Röntgen reports, "Hält man die Hand zwischen den Entladungsapparat und den Schirm, so sieht man die dunkleren Schatten der Handknochen in dem nur wenig dunklen Schattenbild der Hand." Röntgen, "Ueber eine neue Art von Strahlen: (Vorläufige Mittheilung)," *Sitzungs-Berichte der physikalisch-medicinischen Gesellschaft zu Würzburg* 9 (1895): 2.

90. Alexi Assmus, "Early History of X-Rays," *Beam Line* (Summer 1995): 10–24; Linda Simon, *Dark Light: Electricity and Anxiety from the Telegraph to the X-Ray* (Orlando, FL: Harcourt, 2004), 272–99.

91. Linda Dalrymple Henderson, "X-Rays and the Quest for Invisible Reality in the Art of Kupka, Duchamp, and the Cubists," *Art Journal* 47, no. 4 (1988): 323.

knew (or perhaps sensed) that you had your death *within* you, as the fruit contains its kernel.... With my grandfather, old Chamberlain Brigge, you could still tell that he carried a death within him" (*MLB* 7).

In the opening address at the 2005 meeting of the Deutsche Röntgen Gesellschaft, Ernst Peter Fischer described how the ability to see through the exterior surface of the body "suddenly showed the whole world in utter clarity, that the world is not as it appears to be."[92] Fischer, in fact, cited a passage from *The Notebooks* that we encountered earlier, in the context of Malte's *Neues Sehen*, and return to now through a new lens: "Is it possible ... that we have not yet seen, recognized, or said anything real or important? ... Is it possible that, despite inventions and progress, despite culture, religion, and philosophy, we have remained on the surface of life? Is it possible that even this surface, which might at least have been something, has been covered with an incredibly boring material so that it looks like the drawing-room furniture in the summer holidays?" (*MLB* 13–14). In this passage, the sheets covering the furniture resemble skin covering bones, like the paper-thin skin of the faces in the fifth entry. Like the X-ray, Malte's new seeing permeates or penetrates through the surfaces of reality. As the X-ray of her hand made Anna Röntgen's "death" visible to her, the first line of the novel might be seen as an X-ray image of Paris as a whole, penetrating through the lively surface ("So, this is where people come to live"), to reveal the death that lies beneath ("it seems to me, though, that its dying that happens here [*es stürbe sich hier*]" (*MLB* 3).

The discovery of the X-ray altered humans' relationship to the body and raised questions about the relationship between interiority and exteriority, the limits of human vision, and the nature of matter.[93] Röntgen's earliest report on his discovery spoke to the

---

92. "[Es] zeigte sich nämlich plötzlich in aller Deutlichkeit für das breite Publikum, daß die Welt nicht so ist, wie sie aussieht." Ernst Peter Fischer, "Der Durchblick des Jahrhunderts: Welt- und Menschenbilder seit den Tagen von Röntgen," Deutsche Röntgengesellschaft e. V., August 5, 2008, http://www.drg.de/fachinformationen/vortraege/99-roentgenkongress2005-rede.

93. Compare Fischer: "Es ist, wie bereits gesagt wurde—unser Weltbild wird zu einer Weltbildung, und dabei ergibt sich auch ein neues Menschenbild—eben

penetrability (*Durchlässigkeit*)—mentions of penetrability, permeability, or transmissibility appear thirty-two times in this first essay alone—of all bodies, despite their illusory appearance of solidity and stability: "One quickly discovers that all bodies are penetrable in the same way, but to very different degrees."[94] Such discoveries contributed to a more dynamic conceptualization of material reality, not as stable and fixed, but instead in perpetual flux and decay.[95] Investigation of the relationship between the visible and the invisible and the unconscious exploded in the fields of contemporary physics, medicine, philosophy, psychology, art, and literature.[96] Particularly notable among these were Charcot's experiments in X-raying hysterics at the Salpêtrière hospital.[97] Röntgen's investigation of the penetrability of all bodies elides the distinction between animate and inanimate; all substances and objects are composed of the same materiality, penetrable to varying degrees by the X-rays. As Fischer extrapolates in his speech at the Röntgen society, "We are no longer a (subjective) that confronts an (objective) world. We belong inextricably to the world."

Defined by notions of penetrability and associations with clairvoyance and death, the early twentieth-century discourse around X-ray imaging permeates *The Notebooks*.[98] It resonates not only

---

eine Menschenbildung. Wir sind nicht mehr nur Hervorbringungen (Schöpfungen) der Natur; die Natur ist auch unsere Schöpfung, unsere Bildung" (Fischer, "Der Durchblick"). For resonances with Rilkean materialism, compare Kaja Silverman, *Flesh of My Flesh* (Stanford, CA: Stanford University Press, 2009), 28, 64–65.

94. "Man findet bald, dass alle Körper für dasselbe durchlässig sind, aber in sehr verschiedenem Grade" (Röntgen, "Ueber eine neue Art von Strahlen," 1).

95. Compare Henderson, "X-Rays," 327–28. Henderson also connects the discoveries of the X-ray and radioactivity to Henri Bergson's dynamic conception of reality and his philosophy of becoming.

96. Henderson, "X-Rays," 323. The X-ray is represented explicitly in Thomas Mann's *Der Zauberberg*; see José van Dijck, "X-Ray Vision in Thomas Mann's *The Magic Mountain*," in *The Transparent Body: A Cultural Analysis of Medical Imaging* (Seattle: University of Washington Press, 2005), 83–99; and Henderson, "X-Rays," 325.

97. Henderson, "X-Rays," 326. On Charcot and photography, see Georges Didi-Hubermann, *Invention of Hysteria: Charcot and the Photographic Iconography of the Salpêtrière*, trans. Alisa Hartz (Cambridge, MA: MIT Press, 2003).

98. Compare Regina Karl: "In a certain sense, Malte can be considered the Röntgen of narrative prose, and his *Aufzeichnungen* the literary equivalent of Rönt-

with Malte's descriptions of seeing through surfaces, but also with less-visual thematics. One striking example is Malte's conception of "intransitive love," which he defines in terms of penetrating "Strahlen" (rays) in a way that evokes the German terms for X-rays: *X-Strahlen* or *Röntgenstrahlen*.[99] Malte describes numerous "great lovers" (such as Sappho, Gaspara Stampa, Bettina von Arnim) who embodied an ideal of love that does not possess but instead transcends its object—passing through like X-rays—and is not dependent on being loved in return.[100] A similar conception figures in Malte's version of the parable of the prodigal son as "the legend of one who didn't want to be loved" (*MLB* 144). In Malte's retelling, the prodigal son undertakes a process of learning to love God: "I can see more than him, I can see his very existence, which at that time began the long love towards God, the silent, goal-less work" (*MLB* 147). This God is not the Christian God, but instead a figure for the boundless and infinite, a "direction of love [*Richtung der Liebe*]" (*MLB* 143).[101] The "love towards God," in turn, is a transcendent love that surpasses any object. Rilke again employs language evocative of X-rays when he writes of the prodigal son, "Slowly he has learned to shine the rays [*Strahlen*] of his emotion

---

gen's images. This is because, firstly, *The Notebooks* show a keen sensitivity for the discourse at play regarding x-rays." Regina Karl, "Manipulations: The Hand as Symbol and Symptom in the Arts and Literature after 1900" (PhD diss., Yale University, 2019), 135. See also the references to Rilke in Charlotte Kurbjuhn, "Vom physiognomischen Fragment zur Röntgenatlas: Invasive Visualität, bildgebende Verfahren und Subjektkonstituierung bei Thomas Mann, M. Blecher, Thomas Kling und Durs Grünbein," *KulturPoetik* 16, no. 2 (2016): 227–52.

99. Käte Hamburger compares Rilke's notion of intransitive love to the Spinozan concept of *amor dei intellectualis*, defining it as a "'strahlende und durchdringende Liebe' eine Instanz außerhalb jeder menschlichen Vergleichbarkeit." Hamburger, "Die Geschichte des verlorenen Sohnes bei Rilke," *Rice University Studies* 51 (1971): 62–63.

100. "Solche Liebe bedarf keiner Erwiderung, sie hat Lockruf und Antwort in sich" (*KA* 3:598). In this transcendence, there is freedom: as Käte Hamburger summarizes, "Geliebtsein aber bedeutet Beschränkung, Angewiesenheit, Passivität und Ausgesetztsein Zuständen, Kräften, Wollungen, die nicht die eigene Freiheit sind" (Hamburger, "Die Geschichte," 60). It is in this sense that, Malte writes, "Schlecht leben die Geliebten und in Gefahr. Ach, daß sie sich überstünden und Liebende würden. Um die Liebenden ist lauter Sicherheit" (*KA* 3:618).

101. See Hamburger, "Die Geschichte," 60; Tobias, "Rilke's Landscape," 678.

through [*durchscheinen*] the object of his love rather than consume it within them" (*MLB* 147). In a canceled formulation in the Bernese Notebook, Malte defines God as a "parallelism of our heart rays [*Parallelism unserer Herzstrahlen*]" (*BT* 153), a formulation echoed in the description of "parallel beams of their hearts [*parallelen Herzstrahlen*]" (*MLB* 143) of Mechthild, Theresa of Avila, and Rosa of Lima in the published text. The notion that the beloved object could be destroyed, literally consumed by love's rays, recalls dangerous side effects of X-ray imaging, such as hair loss, skin lesions and burns, that doctors began reporting soon after Röntgen's discovery.[102] In a passage footnoted "written in the margin of the manuscript," Malte describes the dangerous effects of love's rays as follows: "Being loved means to be consumed by fire. Loving is to shine brightly with inexhaustible oil. Being loved is dying [*vergehen*]; loving is lasting [*dauern*]" (*MLB* 143).

Malte's "learning to love" and "learning to see" are thus connected not only with respect to notions of permeability and penetrability, *Durchscheinen* and *Durchlässigkeit*, but also with respect to the dangerous physical side effects of X-rays. From the moment Malte arrives in Paris, everything "seems to go right through him, even to annihilate him."[103] In learning to see, Malte applies a kind of X-ray vision to the city, exposing the sickness and death beneath the surface. The wounds, rashes, growths, and eruptions so prevalent throughout *The Notebooks* are like side effects of such a mode of vision, whose destructive potential is not understood or mitigated.

"Une ébauche lente à venir"

In his first publication after his discovery, "Über eine neue Art von Strahlen," Röntgen describes submitting various objects to X-rays. One of the first things he imaged was book: "One quickly discovers that all bodies are penetrable [*durchlässig*] in the same way, but to very different degrees. A few examples are as follows. Paper is

---

102. Ruben Pauwels, "History of Dental Radiography: Evolution of 2D and 3D Imaging Modalities," *Medical Physics International Journal* 3 (2020): 241–42.
103. Huyssen, "The Notebooks," 76.

very penetrable: behind a bound book of ca. 1,000 pages, I still saw the fluorescent screen clearly; the darkness of the printing ink appears to exert no resistance."[104] Less than a year later, Röntgen submitted a painting to X-rays for the first time—more specifically, a Dürer painting from the Alte Pinakothek museum in Munich, where Rilke was a student and taking art history courses at the time.[105] The application of X-rays to a painting allows for underdrawings, so-called ghost paintings—traces of the production process or earlier versions hidden beneath layers of paint—to become visible.

Though published several decades before Röntgen's experiments, Baudelaire's poem "Une Charogne" contains an image that strikingly resembles this technical process. In the eighth stanza, the poet compares the decomposition of the carcass to a painting whose superficial layers fade away, revealing the underdrawing beneath.

> Its forms were blurred as in a dream, nothing but a *slowly shaping sketch forgotten on the canvas*, which the artist must perfect from memory alone.

> Les formes s'effaçaient et n'étaient plus qu'un rêve,
> *Une ébauche lente à venir*
> *Sur la toile oubliée*, et que l'artiste achève
> Seulement par le souvenir.[106]

The verb *effacer* derives from the twelfth-century Old French *esfacier*, meaning "to wipe out, destroy," literally "to remove the face."[107] As such, the figure also recalls Malte's experiences of de-/effacement in *The Notebooks*: faces like masks that are removed

---

104. Röntgen, "Ueber eine neue Art von Strahlen," 1–2.
105. Regarding the early history of the X-ray examination of paintings, see A. Burroughs, *Art Criticism from a Laboratory* (Boston: Little, Brown, 1938); K. Wehlte, "Aus der Praxis der maltechnischen Röntgenographie," *Technische Mitteilungen für Malerei* 48 (1932): 71–72.
106. Charles Baudelaire, "Carrion," in *The Complete Verse*, trans. Francis Scarfe (London: Anvil Press Poetry, 2012), 103; Charles Baudelaire, "Une Charogne," in *Les Fleurs du Mal*, ed. John E. Jackson (Paris: Le Livre de Poche Classique, 1999), 78 (emphasis added).
107. "efface (v.)," *Online Etymology Dictionary*, https://www.etymonline.com/search?q=effacer.

or ripped off, the apartment building whose façade has been torn down. The *ébauche*, the draft or underdrawing (*Unterzeichnung*), recalls the "non-face," the "raw head [*wunden Kopf*] with no face" (*MLB* 5), or the "inner side [*Innenseite*]" of the apartment building.

As Malte's vision increasingly penetrates through the visible exteriors of things, dis-covering the underdrawings of reality, a kind of ghost-painting—like an unfinished manuscript in which things are in flux, under erasure, in the process of becoming—becomes perceptible. The world he confronts is like a rotting carcass, the seemingly stable façades and surfaces fading away, making it possible "to see," in an at-times horrifying way, "the essence of its being that still obtains amongst all forms of being [*das Seiende zu sehen, das unter allem Seienden gilt*]" (*MLB* 42). This is the realm that the throwaways inhabit, just beyond surface of visible, to whom Malte increasingly feels he belongs. From this space Malte begins the process not only of learning to see but also learning to write.

But of course, manuscripts and other prepublication materials do not visibly appear through the literal X-raying of a printed book. In an oil painting, underdrawings and other phases of the work's production remain inscribed within the object itself, even if rendered invisible by accumulated layers of paint. The printed text, by contrast, is the result of a multistep translation of the work from one materiality into another.[108] Whereas the underdrawing of a painting remains materially present, invisible beneath the surface, the manuscript of the novel—the *Unterzeichnungen* of Rilke's *Aufzeichnungen*—remains spectrally present. As "Les formes s'effaçaient," I suggest, *The Notebooks* perpetually *effaces* its visible surface—namely, the material form of the printed book—to expose its manuscript origins. At times this occurs through oblique figurations of the materiality of writing: such as faces "thin as paper" through which "the base layer [*Unterlage*] . . . the non-face" becomes visible. The text's self-effacement of its printed form is also enacted, moreover, through explicit evocations of a manuscript on which it is based: the footnotes

---

108. Compare Wilhelm G. Jacobs, "Materie—Materialität—Geist," *editio* 23 (2009): 20.

indicating that certain passages are "written in the margin of the manuscript."

The Textual Inside

What I am describing as the self-effacement of the novel's printed form has been sensed by others. Consider again Robert Vilain's comment about the aesthetics of the work: "Via its own form, *Malte Laurids Brigge* manifests less confidence in the finished, polished, and lasting artistic monument than in an aesthetic of transience, ephemerality, and fragility."[109] In part this aesthetics can be grounded in the work's material production.[110] Nowhere in the novel are the materiality and visuality of the manuscript more powerfully evoked, I suggest in closing, than in Malte's description of the inner wall of the demolished apartment building. An emblem of the massive transformations brought about by Hausmannization, this scene can also be viewed as a figurative X-ray image of the work, exposing the 'inner side' of the printed text, the manuscript lying beneath its surface. The actual manuscript pages on which Rilke composed this passage are no longer extant. Though it could be illuminating to examine these now-absent pages, their very absence prompts us to *look* at the text differently. Once we have grasped how powerfully the materiality and visuality of writing is also evoked in the work's figurative dimensions, we become able to "see" how the manuscript haunts the work.

Consider, by way of an example, a two-page opening from the second version of the posthumously published "original ending" (figure 3.10). Displaying numerous strike-throughs, the page is one of the most heavily edited in the entire manuscript. As such, it can serve as a kind of snapshot of Rilke's material process, his various techniques of writing and revising visible at once: the division of sections

---

109. Vilain, introduction to *The Notebooks* (*MLB* xlv).

110. Friedrich Kittler similarly describes an in-process, draftlike quality of the work: in describing Malte's experience at the Salpêtrière, Kittler writes, "Rilke's renunciation of psychoanalysis makes clear that *The Notebooks of Malte Laurids Brigge* indeed *are* the written page of a life in uncorrected rough form" (*Discourse Networks*, 333).

by horizontal lines, the rearrangement of text chunks via colored-pencil annotations, and the various material modes of cancellation. The text covering these pages has been struck out entirely. Largely still legible, their semantic contents have been negated, but not destroyed. Horizontal lines spanning the width of the page divide rooms of text like stories of a building. Broad diagonal strokes form a crisscross of intersecting lines, like the "whole scaffold of long tarred poles [that] had been rammed into place at an angle from the rubble-strewn ground to the exposed wall." "Beside the walls of these rooms there was a dirty white space the whole length of the wall," like the gutter between facing pages. Like intestines or plumbing pipes, thick, coiling strike-throughs creep "in unspeakably disgusting, squashily wormlike, almost digesting motions" across the upper halves of both pages. The "tenacious life" contained on these pages, fluctuating between presence and absence, refuses to be "stamped out." It remains in the ink that, like the wallpaper, will fade and discolor over time, in the paper that will yellow, become brittle, and disintegrate. The phrases "damp bubbles lifting the bottom edges of the wallpaper" and the "the foul patches that had formed so long ago" recall pools of spilled ink that saturate the paper, or perhaps dried droplets of the writer's sweat. As Malte stares at the exposed wall, penetrating it with his gaze, it simultaneously penetrates into *him*, into the inner depths of his self, a reflection of his own disintegration. "I recognize everything around here, and that's why it enters into me so easily: it is at home in me" (*MLB* 27–28).

The relationship between Malte and the exposed "inner side" of the building represents that of Rilke with his own manuscript, littered with traces of the process that remain partially legible, not completely "stamped out." As the house enters into Malte, becoming part of his physical being, the boundary between writer and written dissolves; the written text enters into him, becoming part of his being. The *Schreibszene*, the scene of writing, that is described here—and this, perhaps, is especially the case for Rilke, who had such difficulty writing his "prose book"—becomes a scene of fundamental terror.

The intimate familiarity with his manuscripts that Rilke must have experienced contrasts with his experience of the printed version of

mit den einigen Rollschach ich den sein
stille dem Mark achtung. Und wie er selber
wenn man von seinem Unwohl erzählen, die
so groß geworden war, daß er so ganz still
beisammensitzen mußte, um einer Buch stellen
~~...~~
~~...~~
~~...~~
~~...~~
Ich bilde mir ein, es giebt ~~...~~ an
~~...~~
~~...~~
~~...~~ irgendwo in dem traurigen Park
einen Denkstein, den ich nicht gefunden habe,
einen Säule, auf der nicht steht, als das
Datum jenes Vormittags, an dem er still
~~...~~ aufsah und aufschrieb, wie der Duft
war in der Gras, wie enorm die Ahornblätter
geworden waren, und daß ein Biene die
gelben blumen besucht und nach der dreizehnten abflog mit ihrem Schlag
~~...~~ Ich bilde mir ein, es giebt irgendwo
in dem traurigen Park einen Denkstein, den
ich nicht gefunden habe, einen Säule, auf der nicht
steht als der Dreizehntag, sich noch einmal
von sich überwältigt, still aufsah und aufschrieb:
wie der Duft war und wie das Gras, wie
enorm die Ahornblätter geworden waren, und
daß ein Biene die gelben blumen besucht und
nach der dreizehnten abflog mit einem Sei-
trag. Er bestand doch eine Gewissheit, daß
er selbst war. Wenn seine vierzehn Gestalt
aufstanden in den indulischen Nachgeb-
~~...~~ wenn es nach und nach klar wurde
daß ~~...~~
~~...~~
Stundenruf

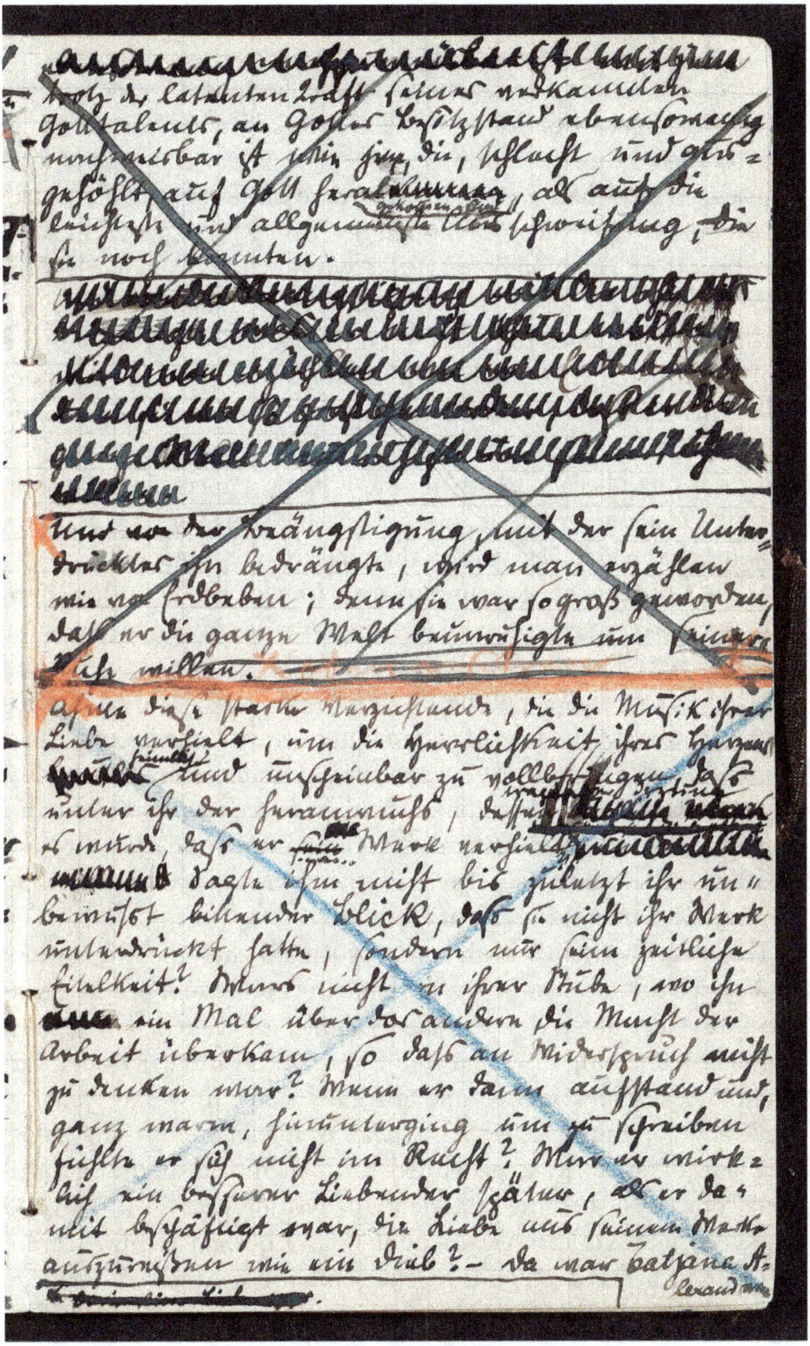

Figure 3.10. Rainer Maria Rilke, *Die Aufzeichnungen des Malte Laurids Brigge*, 2. Teil, 168–169. SLA-RMR-Ms_D_2. Schweizerisches Literaturarchiv, Bern.

the text. In a letter to Kippenberg, Rilke compared himself to the jester who served Charles the Bold (1433–77), whose death Malte also recalled from the "little green book." When the jester found Charles's body, it had been so disfigured, the face ripped off, that the jester could barely recognize him. In describing his experience of the page proofs of *The Notebooks*, Rilke wrote, "It was singularly difficult to go through this book [*durchzulesen*]. . . . I felt as sadly tickled as the fool of Charles the Bold when he sits and sees how they are verifying the coarse externals of his master's body."[111] Like the jester before his barely recognizable Lord, Rilke stood before his barely recognizable text. But whereas the duke had been de-faced, *The Notebooks* had been masked in print. Like the paper-thin, worn-out, masklike faces, however, the printed text contains "holes" (*MLB* 5), allowing that which lies beneath the surface to become visible.

Malte's process of "learning to see," I have argued in this chapter, is bound up in a process of learning to write. When we examine Rilke's material process, looking through the surface of the printed text, we can see how in numerous scenes, the materiality and visuality of writing, the body of the manuscript, become incorporated into the novel's figuration—and in turn, within the reader's bodily, affective experience of reading. Through Rilke's embodied figuration—an entangling of affect and representation, of materiality and meaning—the reader is perpetually *pierced*, the scene of writing surging forth into the scene of reading.

This phenomenon is at the crux of Rilke's embodied figuration: an attempt to represent in a way that can capture and produce sensory presence. But the particular dynamics of Rilke's writing also highlight something universal to all writing. If different media, different *Aufschreibesysteme*, fundamentally shape how and what we think and communicate—a basic tenet of media theory—and if the language of any text is generated through media-specific inscriptional practices, then the materiality of writing necessarily leaves a mark on the texts that we encounter in published form. At every moment in a text's generation, the semantic content of language

---

111. Rilke to Anton Kippenberg, March 25, 1910, in *Briefwechsel mit Anton Kippenberg*, 199–203, here 200.

inscribed on the page is inextricably interconnected in material processes of inscription. In turn, the materiality of writing remains entwined with the linguistic structure or seemingly immaterial semantic content of texts. This is what makes Rilke's project of embodied figuration such an illuminating case study within the broader context of this book: an investigation of ways in which the materiality of writing remains entangled within literary texts, their meanings, and their readings.

Epilogue

"The Whole" in the Digital Age

In 1975—the year Thomas Bernhard published *Correction*—the first volumes of D. E. Sattler's groundbreaking *Frankfurter Hölderlin Ausgabe (FHA)* were released. Unlike Friedrich Beißner's *Große Stuttgarter Ausgabe*, which presented edited reading texts of Hölderlin's poems separately from variants (that is, in separate volumes, so-called *Teilbände*), Sattler's historical-critical edition employed a new editorial principle.[1] Sattler explains in the introductory volume, "The edition model of the Frankfurter Ausgabe is oriented toward the draft character [*Entwurfscharakter*] of Hölderlin's late work. The conventional separation of reading text [*Lesetext*] from the critical apparatus is thus largely suspended. The text does not appear in isolation of that which preceded it, or 'cleansed' of its last revisions, but is instead presented in its processual context [*prozessualen*

---

1. Emery E. George, "The 'Frankfurter Hölderlin-Ausgabe,'" *Monatshefte* 70, no. 1 (1978): 58–67.

Zusammenhang]."² This approach to editing, which is now typical of German historical-critical editions—presenting all stages of a work together, rather than separating them and prioritizing the published version of a text (if available) over the *avant-texte*—is strangely figured in *Correction*. As I have discussed, the task of editing Roithamer's work becomes so overwhelming that the narrator decides to send all the versions of it together to a publisher: for "everything together is the *whole*." A similar conception, realized in the practice of presenting text and *avant-texte* together "in processual context," underlies contemporary German editorial theory. Nutt-Kofoth (citing Siegfried Scheibe) writes:

> The text of a work from the editorial perspective is constituted by the texts of *all* text versions that were produced by the author or per his instruction in the course of the process of generating a work. With this conception of the work, a working hypothesis has since undergirded edition philology that first and foremost negates the separation of a "finished" text from its production, its genesis, and instead clarifies that all text generated within the production of a work is *also part of the work*. Thus was achieved a turn away from the long-dominating perspective that only had the end product in view, the last stage of the text's development, and that saw all other texts belonging to the work as pre-text [*Vorstufe*] of this final product.³

A similar conception of the text as a "whole" has guided my approach to the work of Handke, Bernhard, and Rilke: one that does not prioritize "final product" over "earlier versions [*Vorstufe*]," but instead considers "all text versions" together, in the context of the whole process of textual production. However, it is not simply the case that earlier versions and draft materials of these writers' texts

---

2. D. E. Sattler, introduction to Friedrich Hölderlin, *Sämtliche Werke: Frankfurter Ausgabe—Historisch-kritische Ausgabe*, ed. D. E. Sattler, 20 vols. (Frankfurt am Main: Roter Stern, 1975–2008), 18.

3. Rüdiger Nutt-Kofoth, "Schreiben und Lesen: Für eine produktions- und rezeptionsorientierte Präsentation des Werktextes in der Edition," in *Text und Edition: Positionen und Perspektiven*, ed. Rüdiger Nutt-Kofoth (Berlin: Erich Schmidt, 2000), 169–170 (emphasis added); Siegfried Scheibe, "Zum editorischen Problem des Textes," in *Probleme neugermanistischer Edition*, ed. Norbert Ollers and Hartmut Steinecke, special issue, *Zeitschrift für deutsche Philologie* 101 (1982): 28.

are all equally part of "the work," alongside published versions; rather, the material *process* of textual production remains entangled *within* the published version of the text. The "whole" that has been my object of study in this book is not only the *process* of writing, not only textual *products* (published and prepublication), but instead the *project* of writing.

Today, the increasing proliferation of facsimile editions and digital projects presenting writers' manuscripts and other preproduction materials makes such an approach, such a *view* of literature, possible on a much broader scale than ever before, for scholars and students alike. During the time that I have been working on this book, editions and digital platforms for Handke, Bernhard, and Rilke have been completed or are in process. In 2015, work was completed on the massive digital platform Handke*online*, which includes overviews as well as detailed descriptions of Handke's notebooks from the years 1975–1990 and other archival materials relating to the writing and publishing of Handke's texts.[4] In 2024 a digital edition of twenty-one notebooks from 1976–1979—which overlaps the period of Handke's generation of *Die Lehre der Sainte-Victore*—was completed.[5] In 2021 the first historical-critical edition of any work by Bernhard—a digital edition of *Wittgenstein's Nephew*—went live, and second such edition, this time of *Heldenplatz* (1988), was completed in 2024.[6] And a printed facsimile edition of Rilke's *Berner Taschenbuch* has been available since 2012.[7]

The availability of such materials and resources has made possible the kind of research methodologies I have modeled in this book.

---

4. *Handkeonline*, ed. Klaust Kastberger, Katharina Pektor, and Christoph Kepplinger-Prinz, Österreichische Nationalbibliothek, handkeonline.onb.ac.at, 2011–15.

5. *Peter Handke Notizbücher: Digitale Edition*, ed. Ulrich von Bülow, Bernhard Fetz and Katharina Pektor, Deutsches Literaturarchiv Marbach and Österreichische Nationalbibliothek, https://edition.onb.ac.at/handke-notizbuecher/, 2024.

6. Thomas Bernhard, *Wittgensteins Neffe*, kommentierte ed., ed. Barbara Tumfart, Silvia Waltl, and Konstanze Fliedl, Austrian Corpora and Editions, Austrian Academy of Sciences, 2021, https://wn.ace.oeaw.ac.at/.

7. Rainer Maria Rilke, *Die Aufzeichnungen des Malte Laurids Brigge: Das Manuskript des "Berner Taschenbuchs"—Faksimile und textgenetische Edition*, ed. Thomas Richter and Franziska Kolp (Göttingen: Wallstein, 2012).

This puts these writers in a fortunate position relative to that of many authors. Not all authors have a Nachlass preserved in an archive. Writers may or may not save their notes and drafts, papers can be destroyed, or Nachlass materials may not have been institutionally collected and preserved to begin with. With a few notable exceptions, Nachlässe of women and people of color have received less attention than those of their white male counterparts, both scholarly and in the form of historical-critical editions and digital archives. As the field continues to widen and/or dismantle the traditional boundaries of the "canon," more attention is being given to historically underrepresented writers. This engagement is not only literary critical in nature—the writing processes of Ingeborg Bachmann and Fredericke Mayröcker, for example, have received significant scholarly attention—but is also increasingly taking the form of archival acquisitions, new institutions, and new projects and editions. To name just a few recent developments: the EOTO-Library of African Diaspora Literature was opened in Berlin in 2014; the Nachlass of May Ayim (1960–1996) was acquired by the Freie Universität Berlin in 2023; and since publication of the historical-critical edition of the work of Annette von Droste-Hülshoff (1797–1848), the Droste-Forschungstelle has developed and maintained the Droste-Portal, an exemplary digital platform for the study of Droste-Hülshoff's life, work, and scholarly reception.[8]

As further editorial and digital initiatives develop, however, it is important to recognize that there are limits to what can be done with digital facsimiles. Understanding process requires confronting the obduracy of the materials themselves. It is precisely these aspects of textual materiality that evade or resist digitization. The size of Handke's notebooks—small enough to slip in and out of a jacket pocket and thumb through easily, thereby facilitating the imaginative exercise of continual note-taking—is easily distorted in digital mediation, for example. Similarly defying conversion into facsimile are the material residues of plants and other objects pressed between Handke's notebook pages, traces of the places in and about which he took note; the facture of Bernhard's typescript pages, made of

---

8. Droste-Portal, https://www.droste-portal.lwl.org/de/.

paper so thin it could be easily punctured, bearing impressions of the force with which Bernhard pounded on the typewriter, yielding "schüttere Stellen" like that of Rustenschacher's threadbare fabric in *Gehen*; the fragility of Rilke's *Berner Taschenbuch*, its body having been perpetually scratched and segmented by the inky pen, which is figured in the bodies of the *Fortgeworfenen* (throwaways) and in visions of the "inner side" of torn-down structures. These features, not easily captured in digital scans, constitute the most direct traces of the ecosystems within which these writers' works emerged. These materials accompanied the writers on their journeys of textual production, as companions who also resisted their efforts at times, active participants in the complex agency of textual production. They are literally the stuff out of which their texts were made; and if materials do have agency, understanding this agency involves working with the materials themselves.

As they became available, the platforms and editions described above served as helpful tools complementing my archival research.[9] I could not have written this book, however, without examining the original documents themselves. Digital and print facsimile editions serve the aim of access, making it possible to examine archival materials without physically traveling to archives, and the aim of preservation of original material objects. This is enormously helpful—if the intent is primarily to access the linguistic text/content of manuscripts. But by and large, textual production is an extremely slow, protracted process; understanding it demands slow, close looking, painstakingly so at times. Working with original documents demands a slower pace of handling, owing in part to the documents' uniqueness and/or fragility, which facilitates a slower mode of looking. Similarly, the struggle to decipher illegible passages or unfamiliar hands necessitates *lingering* with textual materiality. Digital editions allow one to zoom in and "page through" materials much more rapidly, and reading is aided by transcriptions that ease or negate

---

9. Stefano Apostolo makes a compelling case for the possibilities of working with digital surrogates, in his introduction to *Thomas Bernhards unveröffentlichtes Romanprojekt Schwarzach St. Veit: Das Konvolut, die Fassungen und ihre Deutung* (Mattighofen: Korrektur, 2019), 34–37.

the challenge of deciphering "theilweise schlechte[] Handschrift," in Rilke's words.[10] Dwelling with a material page and viewing a digital surrogate will engender very different "scenes" of scholarship, thereby producing different analytical results.

Digital surrogates cannot replace archival work for another, more obvious reason: not everything is digitized. Some of the materials examined in this book are now available in digital or print editions, but the vast majority of materials pertaining to the publication of Handke's, Bernhard's, and Rilke's works are not accessible in such editions. On this front as well, there have been recent updates: after the initial acquisition of sixty-six Handke notebooks in 2007, the Deutsches Literaturarchiv acquired another 153 notebooks in 2017, together containing more than 33,000 pages—with more notebooks arriving periodically. Rilke's Nachlass, long locked away in family archive in Gernsbach, was acquired by the Deutsches Literaturarchiv in 2022. In the same year the Austrian National Library acquired Bernhard's Nachlass, which had been effectively inaccessible since the closing of the Thomas Bernhard Archive in Gmunden in 2015.

What this means is that, over time, both the amount of material available to be consulted, and the modes by which one can access it, perpetually shift and fluctuate. This raises the question: What exactly constitutes "the whole"? In the case of Handke and Bernhard, we have a relative wealth of materials that enable us to reconstruct a seemingly complete picture of their textual production processes. In the case of Rilke's *Aufzeichnungen*, the record is obviously partial, fragmented. But in fact, *all* records of the generation of literary works are partial, limited by what authors choose to keep, what they include in their Nachlass; in some cases, by what manages to escape destruction; and the circumstances by which they may or may not end up in publicly accessible archives. Paradoxically, "the whole" can never be complete; it is simply all that we have, never a totality.

---

10. Rilke to Anton Kippenberg, October 20, 1909, in *Briefwechsel mit Anton Kippenberg, 1906–1926*, ed. Ingeborg Schnack and Renate Scharffenberg, vol. 1 (Frankfurt am Main: Insel, 1955), 177.

The fact that we can never know the creative process in its entirety, then, requires that we be creative about what we can do with available material traces in attempts to understand and interpret it. Despite the limits of digitization, newer editions and resources are extraordinarily useful in opening up dimensions of material textual production to a broader public. But even as they become more accessible, the materials do not speak for themselves. Many scholars do not have a sense of what they can do with critical editions; they have no reason to cite them, for the outcome of their analytical work will be the same, regardless of which edition they cite. These resources have information that is largely and effectively untapped. By integrating and expanding on other efforts that have taken seriously the writing process, scenes of writing, the production process, and the materiality of texts, this book serves as a provocation for re-scrutinizing scholarly editions that have long been available, for scrutinizing new digital resources as they emerge, and for delving into archives for the unique insights they offer in the ongoing efforts of understanding "the whole" that is the literary artwork.

Index

Note: Page numbers in italics indicate figures.

The following abbreviations have been used: *The Notebooks of Malte Laurids Brigge* (Rilke): *The Notebooks*
The Lesson of Mont Sainte-Victoire (Handke): *The Lesson*
Paul Wittgenstein: Paul W.

affect: entangled materiality and, 167–68, 212, 213; entangled with representation, 276, 296; vs. fact, 35, 238, 239; figuration/bodiliness and, 217, 220, 221, 234, 248–49, 250–51, 276, 296; madness and, 20, 145–46, 157, 169–70; narration and, 233–34, 245; prosodic rhythm and, 45, 103, 145, 161, 164, 168, 173; rhythmicality and, 20, 122, 161, 164, 173, 210; the scene of writing and, 18, 20, 121, 167, 210, 212, 217; textual materiality and, 213; typography/punctuation and, 103, 106, 108, 144, 157

agency, material: assemblages and, 9, 11–13, 15–16, 44–45, 178; authorship and, 11, 12, 15, 16, 44; distributed, 11, 13, 15–16, 18, 178, 282–83; *Triptych of the Temptation of St. Anthony* (Bosch) and, 257; writing materials and, 12, 15–16, 44, 121, 124, 178, 302

Allemann, Beda, 218, 234
"Als ich 'Verstörung' von Thomas Bernhard las" (When I read *Gargoyles* by Thomas Bernhard, Handke), 120–21
Andreas-Salomé, Lou, 258
Apostolo, Stefano, 143n35, 302n9
Attridge, Derek, 122
authorship, 9, 10–15, 16, 44, 270
avant-texte, 3, 14, 125, 298–99

Badt, Kurt, 51–52, 53, 54, 85–86, 90
Barad, Karen, 13, 14, 16
Barthes, Roland, 44, 88, 208n121, 212–13
Baudelaire, Charles: "Une Charogne," 277–78, 290
Beißner, Friedrich, 298
Benjamin, Walter, 206, 221
Bennett, Jane, 13, 15, 41, 42, 44, 83n124
Bernese Notebook (*Berner Taschenbuch*, Rilke), 226, 228, 242–43, 246–47, 252–53, 260–61, 266–67, 294–95
  abject/disfigured bodies in, 21, 249–50, 256–57
  crisis of narration and, 241–45
  enmeshed with *The Notebooks* (Rilke): architecture and, 283, 293, 302; bodiliness and, 221, 250–51, 254, 255–56, 275, 276, 302; deletion/erasure and, 226–27, 245, 270–72, 283, 292–93; figuration and, 7, 21, 216–17, 221, 263, 296; the scene of reading and, 248–49, 250–51
  facsimile of, 300
  inserted text in, 230–31, 231n38
  material messiness and, 220, 245, 255, 275, 302
  pen reflected in text, 224, 226–27
  poor handwriting in, 216, 302–3
  reordering text in, 215, 245, 271, 293
  strike-throughs and, 215–16, 270–71, 289: reflected in the text, 270–72, 292–93; reflecting struggle, 215, 230, 241–44, 245–48, 258–59, 263; unused text in, 259–62
  See also *The Notebooks* (Rilke)
Bernhard, Thomas
  archival presence of, 6, 134, 212, 303
  destruction and: dissection of typescripts and, 184, 186, 187, 189, 192, 202, 205, 209; entangled with production, 124–25, 126–27, 207–8, 209; overarching the writing project, 122–23, 206–7; overtyped correction and, 136, 153; as "story destroyer," 20, 122, 125, 173–74 (see also *Correction* [Bernhard]: destruction in; *Wittgenstein's Nephew* [Bernhard]: destruction in)
  digital presence of, 300
  Drei Tage (*Three Days*, Radax) and, 125, 157
  Handke's reading of, 120–21
  madness and, 145–46, 153, 157, 158–59, 178 (see also *Correction* [Bernhard]: madness in)
  mechanical writing quality of, 166, 167, 168, 198–200
  musicality and, 122, 163–64, 165, 166–67, 168, 169, 171
  Nachlass of, 8, 127, 134–35, 137, 146n39
  rhythmicality and, 121: as affective, 20, 122, 161, 164, 173, 210; emerging from process, 124, 163, 167, 168; typing and, 124, 161, 173 (see also Bernhard, Thomas [writing process of]: rhythmicality and)
  self-reflexive writing and: Bernhard's Nachlass and, 8, 127, 137, 146n39; Bernhard's typescripts and, 150–51, 159; editing/reading of works and, 130, 144, 150; literary production/reception and, 21, 123–24, 127, 130–33, 153, 168–69, 171; Paul W. and, 182–83, 185

skepticism of truth, 204–5, 206, 207
textile and text intertwining and,
    152, 153, 202, 302
typography and, 127, 145, 157–59,
    174
Viennese literary society and, 189,
    192, 203, 207
Bernhard, Thomas (works): *Alte
    Meister*, 140–41; *Beton (Concrete)*, 1–2, 3, 187n105; *The
    Cellar (Der Keller)*, 204; *Cutting
    Timber (Holzfällen)*, 166–67, 170;
    Extinction (Auslöschung), 124,
    176, 207, 208n121; *Gargoyles
    (Verstörung)*, 120–21, 123n9, 145,
    159, 183–84, 203; *Hunting Party
    (Die Jagdgesellschaft)*, 189, 203;
    The Loser (Der Untergeher),
    130n19, 137; *Walking (Gehen)*,
    138, 150–52, *151*, *152*, 179, 199,
    279. See also *Correction*
    (Bernhard); *Wittgenstein's
    Nephew* (Bernhard)
Bernhard, Thomas (writing process of)
  Bernhard's comments on, 133,
      157–58, 165, 167
  building blocks and, 2, 154, 171,
      192
  correction and: across editions, 143,
      206n114; material addition and,
      137, 143, 189, 192; overtyped,
      135, 136, 150, 153, 187, 189,
      207–8
  creating editorial difficulty, 137, 143,
      144, 184, 186, 202
  dissection of typescripts and, 184,
      186, 187, 189, 192, 202, 205, 209
  filling the page space and, 134,
      153–57, 172, 197, 199–200
  the larger whole and, 125–26, 127,
      132, 136, 211, 299
  loose sheets and, 135–36, 154, 186,
      192
  madness and, 145–46, 151–52, 154
  mental/manual labor and, 169–71
  as music making, 162–64, 165,
      166–67

perceiving "fissures" in, 172–73
physicality and: as draining, 165,
    184, 185, 199n107; forceful
    intensity and, 134, 153, 162, 166,
    301–2; page-episodes and, 20–21,
    121, 133, 135, 171–76, 178,
    199–200; paper puncture and,
    153, 162, 166, 301–2; rhythmicality and, 164–65, 167–68;
    typewriter destruction and, 154,
    161–62
proofs stage and, 143
publication as translation and, 204
rearranging text within projects, 2,
    5, 171
repetition and, 136–37, 152
rhythmicality and, 158, 198–99:
    affecting reading, 167–68, 171,
    172, 173; as affective, 161, 173;
    bodily dimension of, 165, 167,
    169, 171, 187, 189, 200; as the
    "how" of his writing, 163,
    165–66, 170, 171–72; physicality
    and, 164–65, 167–68; repetition
    and, 20, 136–37, 166, 171,
    179–80, 187–89, 197
shaping his texts, 3, 7, 20–21,
    198
transferring text units between
    projects, 154, 171, 186n104
the typewriter and: conditioning the
    writing process, 2, 124, 155, 161,
    162–63, 171; as main instrument,
    133–34, 143, 151, 161, 165–66,
    178; mechanical text quality and,
    166, 198–200; noise and, 161,
    166, 167
typographic visibility, 158, 161, 172,
    174
Beton (Concrete, Bernhard), 1–2, 3,
    187n105
Betz, Uwe, 187n105
Bogost, Ian, 47, 53, 60
Bosch, Hieronymus: *Triptych of the
    Temptation of St. Anthony*,
    256–57, 258–59, 262–63
Buchholz, Paul, 131, 211

Campe, Rüdiger, 23, 43–44
Cézanne, Paul
  connecting Handke and Rilke, 4, 211, 219n25
  Gilles Deleuze and, 276
  figuration and, 217
  Handke and: Cézannean seeing and, 29–30, 46, 118–19; choreographic writing and, 34, 39–40, 118; narration and, 31, 35, 50, 72, 73–74 (see also *The Lesson* [Handke], Cézanne's process and)
  influence on Rilke, 4, 219n25, 277, 284
Cézanne, Paul (works): *Aix, Paysage rocheux*, 49, 64, 65; *Dans le parc du Château-Noir*, 49, 64–65; *La Carriére de Bibémus*, 32–34; *La Mer à l'Estaque*, 36–37; *Le Château Noir*, 37, 42; *Le grand pin*, 39–40, 113n176; *Le Pilon du Roi*, 56, 57; *Nature morte aux fruits*, 58, 59; *Pont de Maincy*, 64; *Rochers près des grottes au-dessus du Château-Noir*, 30–31, 49–50, 55–56, 63–64, 85; watercolors, 58, 76
Chartier, Roger, 213
correction: across editions, 143, 206n114; as destruction, 124, 126, 129–30, 132–33, 136, 207, 208; by hand, 69–70, 74–75, 136; overtyped, 135, 136, 150, 153, 187, 189, 207–8; pasted in/affixed, 72, 103, 137, 143, 189, 192. See also *Correction* (Bernhard): editing/correction in; *The Lesson* (Handke), versions; *Wittgenstein's Nephew* (Bernhard), versions
Correction (*Korrektur*, Bernhard), 127–50, *139, 142*, 152–57, *155, 156, 159*, 159–61, *161*, 175
  affective response to, 145–46, 157, 158–59, 161, 164, 167–69, 173–74
  destruction in, 149–50: the author's task and, 144, 169; creating a whole, 124–25, 128–29, 132–33; as creation, 129–30, 207; death and, 128, 129, 130; editing as, 124, 126, 129–30, 132–33, 136, 207
  editing/correction in: creating a whole, 132–33; as destruction, 124, 126, 129–30, 132–33, 136, 207; the narrator and, 130–31, 132–33, 144–45, 150, 152–53; self-reflexiveness and, 130, 144, 150
  intertextuality of, 153
  lack of paragraph and section breaks in, 127, 145, 157, 158–59, 174
  loose pages for, 134–35, 154–55, 186
  madness in: affectivity of text and, 145, 146–47, 151, 157, 158–59, 173–74; the narrator and, 131–32, 144–45, 146–47, 150, 152–53; Roithamer's project and, 126, 148–50, 152–53, 154–55
  repetition in, 127, 136–37, 144–45, 146–48, 152–53, 172, 173
  rhythmicality/musicality and, 127, 136–37, 167, 168, 169, 170, 173
  Roithamer's Nachlass in, 127–29: to be published as a whole, 132, 299; Bernhard's typescripts and, 159, 171; the Cone and, 127–28, 130, 147–48, 149; generative destruction and, 124, 207; as overwhelming/maddening, 137, 144–45, 146, 147–49, 150, 169
  as self-reflexive: Bernhard's Nachlass and, 8, 127, 137, 146n39; Bernhard's typescripts and Roithamer's Nachlass, 159, 171; editing/reading of works and, 130, 144, 150; literary production/reception and, 123–24, 130–33, 153, 168–69, 171
  typesetting of, 144, 145, 159
  verrückt as dis-ordered and, 146, 147, 151, 155, 158
  Wittgenstein's Nephew (Bernhard) connection, 176
  See also Bernhard, Thomas

dance/trembling/movement/vibration, 38–39; choreography and, 34, 39–40, 43, 45–46, 81, 111–12, 116, 118; danger and, 33, 37, 46–47, 65, 118; *The Grapes of Wrath* (Ford) and, 33, 37, 39, 40; *La Carriére de Bibémus* (Cézanne) and, 32–34, 38; *Le Château Noir* (Cézanne) and, 37; *Le grand pin* (Cézanne) and, 39–40; as part of realization, 38, 39–40; the *route Cézanne* and, 34, 38, 40–41, 43; the scene of reading and, 34, 40, 45–46, 81; the scene of writing and, 43–44, 45; Spinoza and, 41–42, 211. *See also* thing-picture-script-stroke-dance

Deleuze, Gilles, 42, 44, 217, 220, 221, 233–34, 276

De Man, Paul, 218

Derrida, Jacques, 208, 210, 225

destruction

Bernhard's writing project and, 122–23, 206–7: as "story destroyer," 20, 122, 125, 173–74

bodily: in Bernhard's works, 128, 144, 168–69, 203; in *The Notebooks* (Rilke), 236, 237–38, 240, 269, 275

dissection of typescripts and, 184, 186, 187, 189, 192, 202, 205, 209

editing/correction as, 124, 126, 129–30, 132–33, 136, 207, 208

entangled with production, 21, 122–23, 124–25, 126–27, 129–30, 207–8, 209

material-semiotics of, 175

overtyped correction and, 136, 153

publication as, 203–4, 205

theatrical production and, 192, 203

of typewriters, 154, 161–62

Paul W. and, 176, 185–86, 200, 201–3, 205–6, 208–9

See also *Correction* (Bernhard): destruction in

digitization, 300–304

Drei Tage (*Three Days*, Radax), 125, 157

editors, 78n121, 81, 270–71; challenges for, 135, 137, 144, 150, 184; clean copy for, 74, 135, 137, 184, 189; correspondence with, 3, 110, 199n107, 219, 295–96; fictional, 125, 130, 131, 150, 248 (see also *Correction* [Bernhard]: editing/correction in); interventions by, 184, 186–87, 189, 202, 205, 209; Anton Kippenberg, 216, 219, 233, 275, 296. *See also* typesetting: errors introduced in; Unseld, Siegfried

Eldridge, Hannah Vandergrift, 218, 220n33

entanglement: affect and, 167–68, 212, 213, 276, 296; definition of, 16–17; of destruction and production, 21, 122–23, 124–25, 126–27, 129–30, 207–8, 209; the interconnectedness of things and, 37, 50, 62, 113n176, 211; of materiality and meaning, 10, 14–15, 16–18, 21, 121–22, 145, 245, 248; materiality of authorship and, 12, 131; of material processes and text, 7, 17, 18, 77; material-semiotic, 17, 19, 153, 211–12; as a process, 50, 135–36; the reader and, 167–68, 212, 276, 296; of the scene of reading/writing, 121–22, 125–26, 168, 221, 248–49. *See also* Rilke, Rainer Maria (figuration and); thing-picture-script-stroke-dance; *individual works*

Ersch, Johann Samuel: *General Encyclopedia of Sciences and Arts* (with Johann Gruber), 228, 230–31, 236–38, 248

Extinction (*Auslöschung*, Bernhard), 124, 176, 207, 208n121

Eyckeler, Franz, 121, 159

Fabjan, Peter, 162, 165, 169, 184

Fellinger, Raimund, 78n121

figuration: affect and, 217, 220, 221, 234, 248–49, 250–51, 276, 296; definition, 217, 218; hermeneutics/Figure and, 217, 220, 221, 223, 233–34, 276. *See also* Rilke, Rainer Maria (figuration and); *The Notebooks* (Rilke): figuration and
Fischer, Ernst Peter, 286, 287
Fleckhaus, Willy, 109, 110
Fleischmann, Krista, 133, 134, 165
Ford, John: *The Grapes of Wrath*, 33, 37, 39, 40, 46, 49
Fragonard, Jean-Honoré, 55, 56
Frederick, Samuel, 123n9, 145, 173

Gargoyles (*Verstörung*, Bernhard), 120–21, 123n9, 145, 159, 183–84, 203
General Encyclopedia of Sciences and Arts (Ersch and Gruber), 228, 230–31, 236–37, 248
genetic criticism, 12–13, 14, 19, 24
Gombrich, Ernst, 257
Graf, Volker, 41n55
The Great Forest (Ruisdael), 91–92, 113n176
Grésillon, Almuth, 256n52
Gruber, Johann Gottfried: *General Encyclopedia of Sciences and Arts* (with Johann Ersch), 228, 230–31, 236–38, 248
Guattari, Félix, 42, 44
Gumbrecht, Hans Ulrich, 213

Hamburger, Käte, 288nn99–100
Handke, Peter: archival presence of, 6, 24n3, 69n112, 212, 303; Bernhard's work and, 4, 120–21; bibliographic materiality and, 109–11; crisis of writing of, 19–20, 24–25; digital presence of, 24n3, 26n9, 300, 301; journal volumes and facsimiles, 27–28; learning to see and, 4, 27, 32. *See also* Unseld, Siegfried
Handke, Peter (works): "Als ich 'Verstörung' von Thomas Bernhard las" (When I read *Gargoyles* by Thomas Bernhard), 120–21; *Slow Homecoming* (*Langsame Heimkehr*), 7–8, 25, 27, 70, 76n117, 110. *See also The Lesson* (Handke)
Handke, Peter (writing process of) as choreographic: guiding the reader, 45–46, 111–12; processing Cézanne's lesson and, 30, 34, 39–40, 118; strokes (*Striche*) and, 43, 81
Handke's comments on, 133
narration and, 50–51: guiding the reader, 92, 112, 116, 118; Handke's crisis of writing and, 24–25, 85, 90–91; parallel to Cézanne's process, 31, 34–35, 50, 72, 73–74
note-taking and: as Cézannean seeing, 29–30, 46, 118–19; as co-writing, 43; formulation and, 26, 65–69, 72; incorporating quotes from others, 31, 38, 90–91; integrating into text, 74, 82, 84, 92–97, 100, 106, 112–17; as media technology, 29, 30; notebook materiality and, 26–28, 133, 301; sketching and, 56–58, 96, 97, 110, 113nn174–75, 133; slowness and, 6, 19–20, 27, 29, 35–36, 46, 75, 112; typography and, 82, 84, 106 (see also *The Lesson* [Handke], Handke's notebooks and)
orthography and, 77–78, 80–81, 83, 106
as poetological, 7–8, 27, 30, 38–39, 43, 87, 89, 122–23
as slow and methodical, 5, 6–7, 35–36, 46, 75, 117–18
as strokelike/patchwork: combining notes and thoughts, 74, 92–93; as distilled unity, 88–89, 92, 109; embedding notes and, 69, 84, 88; em dashes and, 78, 80, 81–82, 106–7, 108; hyphens and, 78,

Index 311

80–81, 82–83, 106, 108; indexing process, 62–63, 83–84; intertextuality and, 45, 84, 88, 90–91, 112, 212; Domenika Kaesdorf and, 89, 90–91, 92, 106, 109, 118; material rearranging and, 72, 103, 109; paragraph, section, and chapter breaks, 69, 72, 78, 106, 108; the problem of connection/transition and, 89, 90, 109; the reader as witness to, 77, 83; rearranging text, 97, 99–103, 108–9; repeated observation and, 87–88, 92, 95–97; typography and, 83, 106, 108, 109, 111–12
  theory of writing and, 6, 20, 24, 30, 60, 91, 112, 118–19
  waste pages and, 72, 77, 135, 256n52
  See also *The Lesson* (Handke), versions
Heidegger, Martin, 26, 53–54, 60
Henderson, Linda Dalrymple, 287n95
Hennetmair, Karl, 161–62, 166
hermeneutics: dissolution of, 245, 275, 285; figuration/Figure and, 217, 220, 221, 223, 233–34, 276; post-hermeneutics and, 213; readerly methodology and, 23
Heuß, Marit, 30, 32n29
Heydt, Karl von der, 275n78
Hoesterey, Ingeborg, 83
Hofmann, Kurt, 134n25
Hohl, Ludwig, 31, 38–39
Hölderlin, Friedrich, 298
Honold, Alexander, 7, 41n55, 43, 211
Huber, Martin, 169
Hurlebusch, Klaus, 163n65
Huyssen, Andreas, 277n83

intertextuality: Thomas Bernhard and, 121, 153, 176n98, 183–84; extratextuality and, 9; Peter Handke and, 45, 84, 88, 90–91, 112, 212; materiality and, 12, 153; poststructuralism and, 10, 24, 212–13

Jeu de Paume, 31, 36, 55, 63
Jones, Calvin, 45

Kaesdorf, Domenika (D.), 89, 90–91, 92, 106, 109, 118
Kantornowicz, Ernst, 269
Karl, Regina, 287n98
Kędzierski, Marek, 162
Kippenberg, Anton, 216, 219, 233, 275, 296. *See also* Rilke, Rainer Maria
Kittler, Friedrich, 269–70, 274, 292n110
Köhnen, Ralph, 84, 85

labor, intellectual, 72, 169–71
labor, material, 72, 169–71, 215–16
The Lesson of Mont Sainte-Victoire (*Die Lehre der Sainte-Victoire*, Handke), 25–31, 57, 59–60, 66–67, 71, 74, 75, 79–80, 84–91, 94, 101, 102, 104–6, 107–8
  Buch/Buche/Blätter wordplay and, 97, 102, 117
  the geological gaze and, 7–8, 20, 82
  Grand Palais encounter and, 25–26, 32, 38, 51, 86
  "The Great Forest" (chapter) and, 87, 92–97, 108, 112–13
  The Great Forest (Ruisdael) and, 91–92, 113n176
  Handke's crisis/turn to nature and, 19–20, 24–25
  Handke's notebooks and: digital reproduction of, 300; direct use in published version, 32, 63–64, 84, 92–93, 96; heterogeneity of, 26–27, 69; in journal volumes, 27–28; notebook materiality, 26–28, 133, 301; patchwork derived from, 108–9, 115, 118–19; sketching and, 56–58, 110; small physical size of, 26–27, 69; use in developing process, 6, 27–30, 43, 65, 72, 83, 92, 116
Letters on Cézanne (*Briefe über Cézanne*, Rilke) and, 4

The Lesson of Mont Sainte-Victoire (*continued*)
"The Picture of Pictures" (chapter) and, 30–31, 35, 60, 64, 65–68, 70–72, 82, 108
printed *Striche* and, 54–61, 81–84
Rochers près des grottes au-dessus du Château-Noir (Cézanne) and, 30–31, 55–56, 63–64, 85
the *route Cézanne* and: first journey, 31–32, 36, 64; the Grand Palais exhibition and, 26; indexed in the book cover, 110; Morzg forest echoing, 115; second journey, 38, 52, 54, 55, 82, 89; as transformative process, 84–85; travel as dance and, 34, 40–41, 42–43
Slow Homecoming and, 7–8, 25, 110
Spinoza's *Ethics* and, 40–42, 44, 60, 91, 212
See also thing-picture-script-stroke-dance

The Lesson of Mont Sainte-Victoire (Handke), Cézanne's process and art historical scholarship and, 51–52, 53, 54, 85–86
brushwork and, 86: D.'s "coat of coats"/patchwork and, 87–88, 89, 90, 92; as material technique, 47, 51, 52–53, 54–56, 58, 61–63, 76; ontological connectedness and, 37, 61–62; picture-script and, 29, 73–74, 76; as *Striche*, 62–63, 65, 67, 73–74, 81, 82, 89, 108
capturing feeling and, 34–35
color and, 36–37, 42, 47, 50–53, 54, 58, 86, 119
comparison to other painters, 36, 48–49, 52, 53, 54, 55–56
edges and, 51, 54, 55, 58, 90
geology and, 7, 20, 82
The Grapes of Wrath (Ford) and, 33, 46–47, 49
Handke's sketching and, 20, 26, 56–58, 92, 96–97, 110, 113nn174–75

interconnectedness and, 47–51, 53–54, 60, 62, 64–65, 82, 88, 211
intermedial translation and, 28–29, 30, 46
La Carriére de Bibémus and, 32–34, 38
La Mer à l'Estaque analysis, 36–37
perspectival space and, 47, 51–53, 62, 65, 68, 83, 85
pictures behind pictures and, 32, 71
pictures of pictures and, 47, 48–49, 64, 68, 89, 90, 92
repeating motifs and, 28–29, 32
Rochers près des grottes au-dessus du Château-Noir and, 31, 49–50, 55–56, 63–64, 85
sensation of nearness and, 31, 33–34, 35, 37, 61–62, 63–64, 91
sense of urgency and, 46–47, 50–51
sensory perception and, 32, 36, 53
"shadow paths" and, 54, 58, 90
slowness and, 31, 36, 50, 56, 76, 112
See also thing-picture-script-stroke-dance

The Lesson of Mont Sainte-Victoire (Handke), Cézanne's process and dance/trembling/movement/vibration and, 38–39: choreography and, 34, 39–40, 43, 45–46, 81, 111–12, 116, 118; danger and, 33, 37, 46–47, 65, 118; *The Grapes of Wrath* (Ford) and, 33, 37, 39, 40; *La Carriére de Bibémus* (Cézanne) and, 32–34, 38; *Le Château Noir* (Cézanne) and, 37; *Le grand pin* (Cézanne) and, 39–40; as part of realization, 38, 39–40; the *route Cézanne* and, 34, 38, 40–41, 43; the scene of reading and, 34, 40, 45–46, 81; the scene of writing and, 43–44, 45; Spinoza and, 41–42, 211

The Lesson of Mont Sainte-Victoire (Handke), Cézanne's process and ("realization" and)
apotheosis of, 31
dance and, 38, 39, 43, 45

intermedial translation of, 43: as an effect, 35, 92; challenges of, 28–29, 46, 85, 87, 89–90; as theory of writing, 30, 61, 80–81, 109, 112–13, 117–18 (*see also* Handke, Peter [writing process of])
as ontography, 47, 48, 49, 53–54, 60
as parallel to nature, 25, 41, 42, 53, 65, 70, 72, 82, 86
as picture-writing, 53–54, 61–62, 64–65, 74, 76, 85–86, 114–15
revisiting motifs and, 28–29, 32, 46, 86–87
as sheltering/protecting, 47, 50–51, 68, 204
slowness of, 81, 117–18
thing-picture-script-stroke-dance and, 29, 80–81: early iterations, 70–71, 73, 77, 80; entanglement and, 34, 45, 50, 70–71, 82–83; as patchwork, 20, 63, 73–74, 108; slow understanding of, 25, 31–33, 71–72, 73, 108
as transformation/transubstantiation, 49, 50, 62, 65, 67, 68, 204
as undefined by Cézanne, 25, 91, 118
The Lesson of Mont Sainte-Victoire (Handke), versions
galley proofs, 6, 27, 77–81, 106, 117
version 1, 69–72, 92–97: Domenika Kaesdorf and, 89n140, 90; patchwork in, 92–93, 95–97, 103; revision of, 6, 65, 69–71, 74, 99–100, 117; typescript appearance, 69, 76, 106
version 2, 71n114, 72–76, 89n140, 106; 2a, 72–73, 74, 75, 99–100, 103, 117; 2b, 73; 2c, 73, 74–75, 77, 100–102, 117
version 3, 77, 81, 103, 106, 117
Louvre Museum, 36–37, 55–56
Lyotard, Jean-François, 217, 220, 233–34

madness: readerly affect and, 20, 145–46, 157, 169–70; as theme in Bernhard's writing, 145–46, 151–52, 153, 154, 157, 158–59, 178 (see also *Correction* [Bernhard]: madness in; *Wittgenstein's Nephew* [Bernhard]: madness in)
Marten, Catherine, 137n32, 158n58
materiality: artistic technique and, 47, 51, 52–53, 54–56, 58, 61–63, 76; correction as destruction and, 129, 208; distributed agency and, 13–14, 16; editorial evaluation of process and, 298–300, 304; enmeshed in bodies, 270, 279 (see also *The Notebooks* [Rilke]: bodiliness and); entangled with affect, 167–68, 212, 213; intertextuality and, 12, 153; of paper/writing in, 254, 255, 256, 279, 286; Rilke's fair-copy gifts and, 219–20; the scene of reading and, 45, 46, 158, 234–36; text appearance and, 76, 81, 83, 86, 106, 108, 116 (*see also* typography); textual interpretation and, 14, 18–19; textual representation and, 212, 213, 221. *See also* agency, material; entanglement of materiality and meaning; visuality; *individual works*
materiality, method/theory and, 11, 21, 300–301; distributed agency and, 11, 13, 15–16, 18, 178, 282–83; genetic criticism and, 12–13, 14, 19, 24
materiality of writing, 214–15, 221, 303; bibliographic, 109–11 (*see also* typescripts; typography); destruction and, 176, 203 (see also Bernhard, Thomas (writing process of): physicality and; digital access and, 300–304; editing and, 74, 82; encountered in published form, 296–97, 300; figuration and, 222, 224, 226–27, 231–32, 233, 273; notebook

materiality of writing (*continued*)
  materiality and, 26–28, 133, 301; publication as translation of, 17, 291; rearranging of text and, 103, 109; as zone of contact, 182–83, 198. *See also* scene of reading related to the scene of writing; typescripts; typewriters; *individual authors*
material processes: agential networks and, 11; entanglements of, 7, 211, 212, 271, 296–97, 300; as experimentation, 6, 9–10, 21, 24, 26, 30, 82, 118; fictional, 145. *See also individual authors' processes*
material-semiotics: complexity and, 15, 127, 173; of destruction, 175; entanglement and, 17, 19, 153, 211–12; the scenes of writing and reading, 121
McGann, Jerome, 23
McLuhan, Marshall, 163n65
media theory, 13, 161, 269–70, 296
methodology, 77, 150; digitization and, 22, 300–301; materiality and, 12–14, 18–19, 24, 278, 300–301; partial documentation and, 21–22, 212, 216
Metropolitan Museum of Art (the Met), 51, 53, 54
"Monologue" (Novalis), 123
Morton, Timothy, 13, 16–17, 40n53, 125
Morzg forest, 87, 92–97, 112, 113n176, 115–17. *See also The Lesson* (Handke)

Nachlässe
  Bernhard's, 6, 8, 134, 146n39, 303
  fictional: destruction and, 124, 132, 144, 168–69, 207; Höller's garret and, 128–29, 146; madness and, 144–45, 147–48, 150; self-reflexiveness and, 8, 127, 137, 146n39, 171
  literary criticism and, 11, 12, 301, 303

narration: Cézanne's process and, 31, 35, 50, 72, 73–74; entangled materiality and meaning and, 245, 248; guiding the reader, 92, 112, 116, 118; Handke's crisis of writing and, 24–25, 85, 90–91; oral, 223, 224, 233. *See also The Notebooks* (Rilke): narration and
National Gallery, London, 64, 71
new materialism, 11, 13, 44. *See also* Bennett, Jane
New Poems (Rilke), 218–19, 220
The Notebooks of Malte Laurids Brigge (*Die Aufzeichnungen des Malte Laurids Brigge*, Rilke)
  architecture in, 280–82, 283, 291, 292, 302
  the Big Thing in, 268, 273–76, 277
  bodiliness and: abjection, 21, 220, 253–54, 256–57; the Big Thing and, 268, 273–76, 277; bodily destruction and, 236, 237–38, 240, 269, 275; bodily disease and, 249–50, 255, 268, 273, 280–81; bodily fragmentation and, 256–57, 258–59, 263, 273; bodily injury and, 249–51, 270, 271, 289; bodily remembering and, 233, 236, 276; embedded in architecture, 280–81, 293; faces and, 279, 283, 286, 290–91, 296; Malte's own hand and, 284–85; the manuscript as parallel to, 221, 250–51, 275, 276; the physicality of narration and, 225, 229; the scene of reading and, 249, 251, 296; scent and, 250, 280–81, 282–83; stigmata and, 231–33, 234, 236, 276; "throw-aways" and, 251, 254, 255–56; two-body structures and, 269–70; "Une Charogne" (Baudelaire) and, 277–78
  book design and, 219–20, 235n45, 248
  dictated final version of, 216, 233, 244, 274, 275

dictation/transcription in, 224–25, 233–34
disintegration of language in, 268–69, 273
fact vs. affect in, 238, 239
figuration and: bodily affect and, 220–21, 276, 296, 297; Hieronymus Bosch and, 257; learning to see/write and, 223; material production/reception and, 222, 224, 226–27, 231–32, 233, 273; objective expression and, 218–19, 277, 284; questioning success of, 258; struggle and, 263, 275; "Une Charogne" (Baudelaire) and, 277
Figure and, 218, 221, 234, 276
fragmentation in, 216, 245, 256–57, 258–59, 263, 272, 273
ghosts in, 282–84
hermeneutics and, 223, 233, 234, 245, 275, 285
horror of modernity in, 257–58, 272–73
intransitive love in, 288–89
learning to see and: seeing beneath surfaces and, 272, 277–81, 286, 290–91, 293 (*see also* X-ray technology); the shock of experience and, 213–14, 220, 222–23, 289
learning to see and write together, 4, 9, 214, 223–24, 291, 296
learning to write and, 239–45, 274
the "little green book" in, 234–37, 238–39, 245, 248, 296
marginal notes in, 238, 248, 278, 289, 291–92
materiality of paper/writing in, 254, 255, 256, 279, 286
as modernist, 8–9, 21, 211, 213, 272
narration and: bodiliness and, 229–30, 232, 236; correspondence with materiality, 226–27; crisis of writing and, 234, 241–45; dictation and, 224, 225, 227, 233;

figuration/Figure and, 233–34, 238–39; as incoherent, 236–37; learning to see and, 214; as lost mode of storytelling, 223–25; plea for a narrator, 239, 240–41
poetics in, 244, 251, 255, 277
presence in, 225–26, 229, 231
printed text's gestures to the manuscript: Figure and, 276; through figuration, 217, 255–56, 296; through materiality of writing, 221, 227, 271–72, 291, 293; through parallels, 227; through the fictional manuscript, 248–49, 278, 291–92; as X-ray-like, 292–93
printed text smoothing over struggle, 258–59, 271, 296
proofs stage, 215, 244, 296
reception of, 263
record of production of, 5, 21, 212, 215, 216 (*see also* Bernese Notebook [Rilke])
Rilke's letters and, 214, 228, 258, 277–78
Salpêtrière hospital in, 263, 268–69, 270, 271, 273–74, 292n110
as semi-autobiographical, 214, 217, 274–76, 285, 293
struggle of producing, 216, 221, 234, 258, 263, 274–75, 296
textual sources for, 227–29, 230–31, 236–38
the "throwaways" and, 251, 254, 255–56, 262, 271, 291, 302
Triptych of the Temptation of St. Anthony (Bosch) and, 256–57, 258–59
"Une Charogne" (Baudelaire) and, 277–78, 290–91
writing crisis after completing, 214–15, 221, 258
X-ray technology and, 278, 285–89
See also Bernese Notebook (Rilke)
Novalis: "Monologue," 123
Novotny, Fritz, 85
Nutt-Kofoth, Rüdiger, 5n6, 299

316 Index

ontography, 30, 47, 48, 53–54, 60, 118
ontology, 13, 16, 37, 42, 45, 46, 47
orthography, 44–45, 77–78, 80–81, 83, 106, 143

Pektor, Katharina, 24n3, 26
phenomenology, 18, 163, 164, 225, 229, 236
photocopies, 69–70, 72–73, 103, 186, 197
picture-script, 29, 53–54, 65, 67, 82–83, 86, 113, 114–15
poetics: ambient, 17, 40n53; of destruction, 123, 124; figuration and, 216–17, 220; Figure and, 217–18; of image, 30; of madness, 145; material, 251; of objective expression, 277; of restoration, 123; of slowness, 19–20
poststructuralism, 10, 24, 88, 118, 212–13, 217, 220
Poussin, Nicolas, 52, 56
"Prayer for the Lunatics and Convicts" ("Gebet für die Irren und Sträflinge," Rilke), 262, 264–65
Price, David, 206

Radax, Ferry: *Drei Tage* (*Three Days*), 125, 157
rhythm: *Correction* (Bernhard) and, 127, 136–37, 167, 168, 169, 170, 173; readerly affect and, 45, 103, 145, 161, 164, 168, 173; typewriting and, 161, 172, 173, 174; *Wittgenstein's Nephew* (Bernhard) and, 179–81, 187, 189, 200. See also Bernhard, Thomas (writing process of): rhythmicality and
Richter, Thomas, 270–71
Rilke, Clara, 277, 278
Rilke, Rainer Maria
  archival presence of, 303
  book design and, 219–20, 235n45, 263
  Cézanne's influence on, 4, 219n25, 277, 284
  digital presence of, 300
  figuration and: art things (*Kunst-Dinge*) and, 217–18, 219; in the Bernese Notebook, 7, 21, 216–17, 221, 263, 296; Hieronymus Bosch and, 257; embedded in material production/reception, 222, 224, 226–27, 231–32, 233, 273; Figure and, 217, 218, 221, 276; learning to write and, 223; objective expression and, 218–19, 277, 284; producing bodily affect, 220–21, 276, 296, 297; questioning success of, 258; struggle and, 263, 275; "Une Charogne" (Baudelaire) and, 277
  Rodin's influence on, 219n25, 277, 284
  writing process of, 9, 215–16, 220, 221, 227, 230 (*see also* Bernese Notebook [Rilke]: creative process in)
  See also Kippenberg, Anton
Rilke, Rainer Maria (works): *Letters on Cézanne* (*Briefe über Cézanne*), 4; *New Poems*, 218–19, 220; "Prayer for the Lunatics and Convicts" ("Gebet für die Irren und Sträflinge"), 262, 264–65. *See also* Bernese Notebook (Rilke); *The Notebooks* (Rilke)
Rodin, Auguste, 219n25, 277, 284
Röntgen, Wilhelm Conrad, 285–87, 289–90
route Cézanne, 110, 115; Handke's first journey, 31–32, 36, 64; Handke's second journey, 38, 52, 54, 55, 82, 89; travel as dance and, 34, 38, 40–41, 43
Ruisdael, Jacob van: *The Great Forest*, 91–92, 113n176

Salpêtrière hospital, 263, 268–69, 270, 271, 273–74, 287, 292n110
Santner, Eric, 268, 269–70, 273–74, 281
Sattler, D. E., 298
scene of editing/publishing, 17–18
scene of reading: bodily dimension of, 45, 121, 166, 171, 235–36; as

choreographed, 34, 40, 45–46; components of, 17–18, 45, 46, 145–46, 234–35, 254; fictional, 128–29, 149, 254, 255–56; materiality of, 13, 20, 254

scene of reading related to the scene of writing: bodiliness and, 169, 171, 248–49; conception of the text and, 23; entanglement and, 17, 121–22, 125–26, 168, 248–49; materiality of writing and, 17–18, 161, 210, 250–51, 296; occupying the same space as the writer, 40n53; rhythmicality and, 167–68, 171, 172, 173; writing manifesting into reading, 14, 121–22, 125–26, 210, 296

scene of writing
as choreographed, 43–44, 45
components of, 18, 23–24
distributed agency and, 16, 44–45
fictional, 128–29, 149, 150, 168: vs. actual, 131, 149
fractured, 224
making creation and destruction visible, 127
materiality of, 161, 210, 293
as media-technical lens, 13, 14, 24
mediated directly, 133
as scene of making, 24, 25
the scene of note-taking and, 28
as scene of terror, 293
See also Bernhard, Thomas (writing process of): physicality and

Schapiro, Meyer, 109
Schiffleithner, Georg, 69n112
Schillingsburg, Peter L., 5n6
semiotics, 24, 148. *See also* material-semiotics
Slow Homecoming (*Langsame Heimkehr*, Handke), 7–8, 25, 27, 70, 76n117, 110
Smith, Daniel W., 217n19
Spinoza, Baruch: *Ethics*, 40–42, 44, 60, 91, 212, 288n99
Stingelin, Martin, 44

Suhrkamp Verlag, 6, 69n112, 78n121, 110, 150. *See also* Unseld, Siegfried

Theisen, Bianca, 159n60
thing-picture-script-stroke-dance, 29, 80–81; early iterations, 70–71, 73, 77, 80; entanglement and, 34, 45, 50, 70–71, 82–83; final typographical form of, 80–81; as patchwork, 20, 63, 73–74, 108; slow understanding of, 25, 31–33, 71–72, 73, 108. *See also* dance/trembling/movement/vibration; *The Lesson of Mont Sainte-Victoire* (Handke), Cézanne's process and ("realization" and)
Thüring, Hubert, 209, 272
Thurn und Taxis, Marie von, 274
Tobias, Rochelle, 274
Triptych of the Temptation of St. Anthony (Bosch), 256–57, 258–59, 262–63
typescripts: Bernhard's formatting of, 134, 136, 137, 157, 159, 172; dissection of, 184, 186, 187, 189, 192, 202, 205, 209; hand-corrected, 69–70, 74–75, 136; Handke's formatting of, 69–70, 72, 75–77; lost, 215; pasted/affixed correction and, 72, 103, 137, 143, 189, 192; vs. typeset, 77, 81
typesetting, 77–78, 117, 174; authorial instructions and, 78, 103; errors introduced in, 78–81, 159, 206n114; translating from typescript, 137, 144, 184, 202
typewriters
agency of, 121, 124
Bernhard's writing method and, 133–36: conditioned by the typewriter, 2, 124, 161, 162–63, 171; creating a mechanical text quality, 166, 198–200; destruction of typewriters, 154, 161–62; filling the page space and, 153–57, 171;

typewriters (*continued*)
forceful intensity and, 134, 153, 162, 166, 301–2; noise and, 161, 166, 167; page-episodes and, 20–21, 121, 133, 171–76, 178, 199–200; rhythmicality and, 161, 172, 173, 174; travel typewriters' faults and, 151, 162; typescript formatting and, 134, 136, 137, 157, 159, 172; typewriter as main instrument, 134, 143, 151, 161, 165–66, 178; typewriter destruction and, 154, 161–62
correction methods with, 136–37, 150
dictating the flow of writing, 75–76, 161, 162–63, 171
hyphens and, 81
material aesthetic of, 110–11
typography: Bernhard and, 2, 127, 143–44, 145, 157–59, 174; book design and, 110–11, 145, 158; em dashes, 78, 80, 81–82, 106–7, 108; Handke and, 80–81, 82, 83, 84, 106; hyphens, 78, 80, 81, 82–83, 106, 108; paragraph breaks, 78, 145; readerly affect and, 103, 106, 108, 144, 157; regularizing irregular typing, 151, 157, 172, 174
typography (*Schriftbild*): the choreographed scene of reading and, 46

"Une Charogne" (Baudelaire), 277–78, 290
Unseld, Siegfried, 6, 72, 74, 110, 199n107. *See also* Handke, Peter

Van Gogh, Vincent, 48, 53
Vilain, Robert, 272, 292
visuality: of Cézanne's realization, 82 (see also *The Lesson* [Handke], Cézanne's process and ["realization" and]); fictional, 148, 152; figured in the text, 216–17, 249, 263, 270, 276, 292, 296; of manuscript production, 7, 21, 216; recursive effect of, 121, 145, 150, 153; of the text, 111, 151, 174, 271–72

Walking (*Gehen*, Bernhard), *138*, 150–52, *151*, *152*, 179, 199, 279
Widrich, Hans, 72
Wittgenstein, Ludwig, 128n17, 176, 184, 185, 203
Wittgenstein's Nephew (*Wittgensteins Neffe*, Bernhard), 175–210, *188*, *190–91*, *193–96*, *198*, *200–201*; destruction in, 175–76, 186, 192, 203–4, 205–9, 210; intertextuality and, 176n98; madness and, 178, 179, 180–81, 184, 202–3, 205; mind-body division and, 179–81, 183; production history as complex, 176, 181–82, 184, 186–98, 202, 205; publication in, 184–86, 203–4, 205; rhythmicality and, 179–81, 187, 189, 200; versions, 187, 189, 192, 197, 202, 206n114; Paul W. emerging from his notes, 182, 185, 200–201, 202, 203, 204; Paul W.'s destruction/death and, 176, 185–86, 200, 201–3, 205–6, 208–9. *See also* Bernhard, Thomas (writing process of): physicality and; Bernhard, Thomas (writing process of): rhythmicality and
Wittgenstein's Nephew (Bernhard), as semi-autobiographical: Bernhard's writing project and, 177–78, 181–83, 185–86, 197–98, 200–201, 207; eulogizing Paul W., 175–76, 206, 209–10; Paul W. as self-portrait, 178, 182
writing, process of, 1–2; *Editionswissenschaft* and, 13, 14; material processes and the Text, 3, 5, 9–10, 11–12, 13–14, 18. *See also individual authors' processes*

X-ray technology, 278, 285–90

Zanetti, Sandro, 165n74

www.ingramcontent.com/pod-product-compliance
Lightning Source LLC
Chambersburg PA
CBHW070233240426
43673CB00044B/1777